MW01593364

GRANT ME TO FIND THE TASK

THE LIFE STORY OF CALEB WARNER

By Caleb Warner and A. Wendy Warner

Copyright © 2013 by Caleb Warner and A. Wendy Warner
All rights reserved.

ISBN: 1463638159
ISBN-13: 9781463638153

No part of this publication may be reproduced, distributed, or transmitted in any form
or by any means, including photocopying, recording, or other electronic or mechanical
methods, without the prior written permission of the publishers, except in the case of brief
quotations embodied in critical reviews and certain other noncommercial uses permitted
by copyright law. For permission requests, write to awendyw1@yahoo.com.
Ordering Information:
Available through Amazon.com.

Printed in the United States of America.

Grant me to find the task
For which my talents fit me
With steady strength to strive
That I may well acquit me;
And when my work is done
That something may remain
For men to use, that I
Shall not have lived in vain.

Cantata BWV 45/7 by J.S. Bach
"Oh Gott, du Frommer Gott" (second stanza)
English text as translated by Henry S. Drinker, Sr.

In memory of my wife,
Alice Sizer Warner
December 8, 1929 – May 19, 2006

To Alice, I give thanks beyond all others in my life. We were quite a pair as a married couple and as parents! With fundamentally different personalities, interests, and capabilities, our relationship was based on a set of shared hopes and expectations that brought us closely together and stayed with us throughout our married lives. For over half a century Alice loyally stood by my side. She was my good friend and loving wife. I miss her very much.

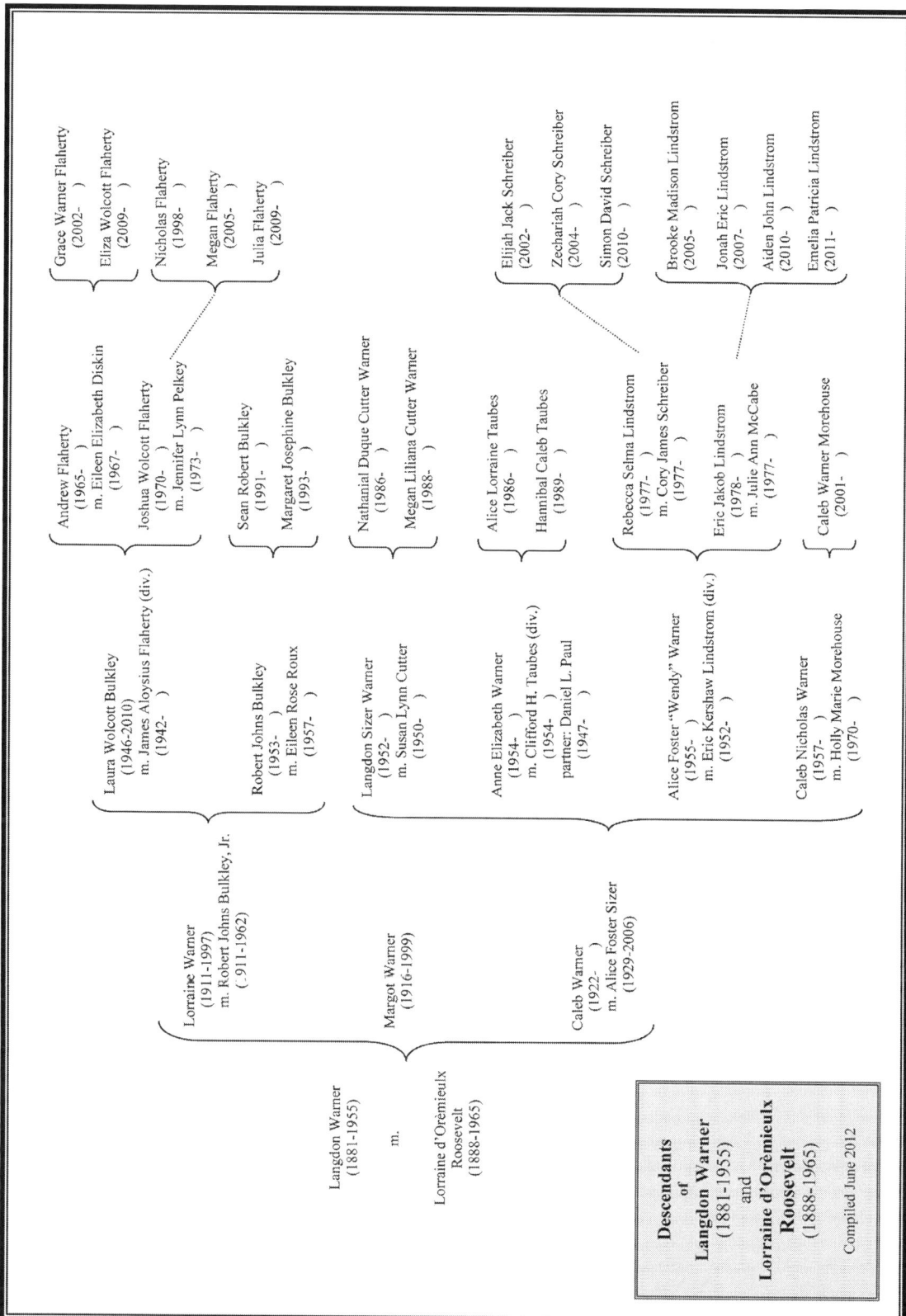

Descendants
of
Langdon Warner
(1881-1955)
and
**Lorraine d'Orémieulx
Roosevelt**
(1888-1965)

Compiled June 2012

Langdon Warner
(1881-1955)

m.

Lorraine d'Orémieulx
Roosevelt
(1888-1965)

Lorraine Warner
(1911-1997)
m. Robert Johns Bulkley
(.911-1962)

Margot Warner
(1916-1999)

Caleb Warner
(1922-   )
m. Alice Foster Sizer
(1929-2006)

Laura Wolcott Bulkley
(1946-2010)
m. James Aloysius Flaherty (div.)
(1942-   )

Robert Johns Bulkley
(1953-   )
m. Eileen Rose Roux
(1957-   )

Langdon Sizer Warner
(1952-   )
m. Susan Lynn Cutter
(1950-   )

Anne Elizabeth Warner
(1954-   )
m. Clifford H. Taubes (div.)
(1954-   )
partner: Daniel L. Paul
(1947-   )

Alice Foster "Wendy" Warner
(1955-   )
m. Eric Kershaw Lindstrom (div.)
(1952-   )

Caleb Nicholas Warner
(1957-   )
m. Holly Marie Morehouse
(1970-   )

Andrew Flaherty
(1965-   )
m. Eileen Elizabeth Diskin
(1967-   )

Joshua Wolcott Flaherty
(1970-   )
m. Jennifer Lynn Pelkey
(1973-   )

Sean Robert Bulkley
(1991-   )

Margaret Josephine Bulkley
(1993-   )

Nathanial Duque Cutter Warner
(1986-   )

Megan Liliana Cutter Warner
(1988-   )

Alice Lorraine Taubes
(1986-   )

Hannibal Caleb Taubes
(1989-   )

Rebecca Selma Lindstrom
(1977-   )
m. Cory James Schreiber
(1977-   )

Eric Jakob Lindstrom
(1978-   )
m. Julie Ann McCabe
(1977-   )

Caleb Warner Morehouse
(2001-   )

Grace Warner Flaherty
(2002-   )

Eliza Wolcott Flaherty
(2009-   )

Nicholas Flaherty
(1998-   )

Megan Flaherty
(2005-   )

Julia Flaherty
(2009-   )

Elijah Jack Schreiber
(2002-   )

Zechariah Cory Schreiber
(2004-   )

Simon David Schreiber
(2010-   )

Brooke Madison Lindstrom
(2005-   )

Jonah Eric Lindstrom
(2007-   )

Aiden John Lindstrom
(2010-   )

Emelia Patricia Lindstrom
(2011-   )

TABLE OF CONTENTS

My Swedish skerry cruiser, Baltic Maiden, sailing near Stockholm, (1947-48).

1

AS ALICE WOULD SAY...

September, 2007

Alice was gone, and I was in and out of it. There is a lot of that year that I cannot recall. I was 85 years old and I was ailing. At times I was delusional. Anne, our older daughter and a busy attorney, had taken on the responsibility of our care. I don't know how she did it.

Langdon and Nick, our two sons, in different states, called and visited me in Massachusetts when they could. Wendy, our younger daughter, living in Pennsylvania, had also been quite ill. She had been hit hard with a brain virus, and had been living through a long-term recovery herself until late in 2007 when she was well enough to live on her own. Knowing that Anne was giving her all and working a close-to-impossible schedule, Wendy decided to move to Massachusetts to help out.

Today, June 27, 2012

The rest is history, and this book is a direct result.

The writing of this book is a story in itself. Needless to say, my health improved, although I can feel the claws of Parkinson's tighten around me more every day. I am humbly grateful that my cognitive faculties have been somewhat slower to decline than they might have been. I'll admit to causing my share of a ruckus on occasion here in the continuing care facility in which I live because I am still sharp enough to care. I participate in daily living activities, and do what I can to help those around me.

As our health improved, and as Wendy and I got to know each other better, she began asking me to note down some of the stories I told others about my past. This is a common request made to people of my age, and, to be honest, I did not take it very seriously. She, however, started to bug me about it.

My reasons for NOT writing these stories made all the sense in the world to me. I am *not* a world-renowned Nobel Prize winner. I have *not* discovered or developed something monumental that has helped mankind or improved our planet. I am *not* "legendary" in any way, shape, or form. I felt no hesitation in telling my enthusiastic daughter that the written word carries with it a quality of import, and a sense of general value.

This argument was one that Wendy and I buffeted back and forth between us for several years. During that time, I lamely attempted to write several brief, unrelated stories about my life, in a basic hit-or-miss approach. Wendy, however, persisted.

Her argument: every person has a story to be told, and every generation has, at some point, a hunger to learn about the generations before it. Future generations, too, have no way of understanding what it was truly like for their forebears to live in their own centuries, in their own daily lives. For this reason alone, if a person of my age has the capability to leave a story to their future generations and illuminate one man's life in this century's significant era of change, then, perhaps, it is a responsibility to do so.

Wendy began to arrive at my assisted-living, dorm-sized room with her laptop, and took notes as I told her stories. She then left those notes for me to construct into more comprehensive pieces. It was in this way that I began writing in earnest. Before long, she and I physically laid the stories out on a table. We realized that we might have the basic structure to put together a memoir. I balked again. Wendy persisted again.

About two years ago, we realized we needed an editor, and only one person would fit the bill: Alice's cousin, Anne "Nancy" Morris. Nancy is not just a family member, she is a fast family friend. She had researched and written four previous books, two of which were family memoirs. Wendy and I were both impressed with her work. We were terribly concerned about asking for her help, however, as her husband Bob was not well. We celebrated when Nancy said she'd be delighted to come onboard. She has been a key member of our team ever since, and we will be forever grateful for her patience with us as inexperienced, bumbling, first-time authors.

So who wrote this book? The 89-year-old man with Parkinson's Disease, or the woman who has a history of a brain virus? The answer is that we did it together, with Nancy's very close involvement. I wrote the core of most chapters and Wendy wrote around my work. If we had any idea how many years it would take to write, and how hard the process would be, we might never have done it!

Together we set up a system. I wrote at home on my computer using the typing skills my wife insisted I learn almost 60 years ago. Then I visited Wendy to scan in photos or review chapters together. Her recliner saw a great deal of use for multiple shut-eye breaks during the day for vertigo/migraine-challenged Wendy, and I snoozed often, right in my desk chair. Many home-deliveries of Thai and Chinese food helped the process, and we should all buy stock in Dunkin' Donuts coffee. I'll admit that, along the way, we stopped writing, exasperated and exhausted, for months on end, an uncountable number of times.

As we worked, we asked Nancy to jump in time and again. She read what we had written, giving us sage editorial advice and sound encouragement. Wendy visited her in New Hampshire several times with manuscript in hand, and Nancy, in turn, visited us five times, staying in Wendy's two-room garret apartment, each time swearing that she would not leave until the book was finished. (Of course, the book was only finished once.) Nancy helped sort out abundant duplications and structural decisions, rewrote text, and made process suggestions. Her patience and helpfulness was unending. We are amateur, with the best of intentions: please note our mistakes are our own.

Rosie Segil came onboard near the end of the project. Hired when Wendy finally said she could do no more, Rosie arrived to find that the photos were in dire need of her expert help. Her excellent work has resulted in over 300 images that have added immeasurably to this book. She is a lovely person, skilled in her work, and a welcome addition to our team. We are delighted, now, that she has become a friend of the family.

The final copy of our manuscript was read by daughter Anne, and her partner Dan, in the hopes that they might uncover any inaccuracies included here due to my failing memory or to simple error. She, too, was willing and helpful, providing the critical last step as we wrapped up our book-writing process.

To our readers, we say this: memory is not perfect. This is a problem. My memory is fading and this book reflects my very best attempts to recollect my life accurately. To those of you who find blunders herein, we offer our apologies. If we have missed mentioning something or someone important to you, we ask for your forgiveness and forbearance. We welcome you to send your corrections on to Wendy at awendyw1@yahoo.com.

I would like to extend my appreciation to Rosie and Anne who took on the task of polishing at the end of our book-writing process, and to Nancy – our lifelong friend – we could not have done it without you!

But most of all to Wendy: Thank you. You have given me the truest of gifts.

With a great deal of patience, and many time-outs, we accomplished the writing of this book in four and a half years. We know, of course, it might well have taken a lot less time for someone *else* to write, but, as Alice would say, "Peace."

We did it.

Mother.

2

MY FAMILY

As a child, I lived in Cambridge, Massachusetts, the only son and last child of a Harvard curator of Oriental Art and a very musical mother My two sisters were quite a bit older, with interests different from my own. As we grew up, our household was often filled with our friends, family, and distinguished guests of our parents. Our house was built by ancestors of my father.

MOTHER

My mother's maiden name was Lorraine d'Orèmieulx Roosevelt. She was born in 1888, daughter of Laura d'Orèmieulx Roosevelt and Dr. James West Roosevelt (a first-cousin once-removed of U.S. President Theodore Roosevelt). My maternal grandfather, a physician and a specialist in the area of tuberculosis and other pulmonary illnesses, died quite unexpectedly of pneumonia at the age of 38. Mother was just 14 at the time.

My grandmother was very active as a resident of the mid-to-upper east side of New York City and Oyster Bay until her death in the late 1930s. I wish I knew more about my grandparents.

My mother was brought up in New York City and Oyster Bay, Long Island where she was

My mother as a school girl.

5

intimately involved with the very active Theodore Roosevelt clan. She was educated primarily by private tutors at home. In keeping with her family tradition, she was bilingual (French/English), skillful in several other Romance languages, and, later, even in Japanese and some Russian.

My mother's profession was music. She was an accomplished classical pianist, choir founder/conductor of the Bach Cantata Club, conductor of the Radcliffe College Choir, a music publisher, and school music teacher at Buckingham School in Cambridge, MA.

Her Bach Cantata Club chorus, which ran successfully for about 20 years with about 120 voices, was one of the first amateur choruses in the Boston area not connected to an academic institution, performing regularly with the Boston Symphony Orchestra (BSO) in the era of conductor Serge Koussevitsky. Mother prepared the Bach Cantata Club for the first BSO performance of Bach's Saint John Passion, conducted in Symphony Hall by Koussevitsky.

Her published works included a definitive collection of folk music brought to the Appalachian area of the U.S. from Scotland, which she put together with a close friend who had done the field research. She also was heavily involved in the so-called "Concord Series" of choral music books, primarily used in schools, published in the 1920s by G. Schirmer under the direction of Harvard's Archibald Davidson.

She had extensive contacts with European musicians and composers including Gustave Holst, Ralph Vaughan Williams, Nadia Boulanger, and Sir Steuart Wilson. She was involved in introducing into the U.S. such pioneering works as the Fauré Requiem and Honneger's King David.

My relationship with my mother was very close and exceedingly influential to me. She defended me when I sought to venture off in directions which were not traditional in our family. She assisted me as I sought to start early in orienting myself toward a journeyman-like existence. She certainly backed me later when the possibility came up of my venturing off to the University of Michigan instead of following family academic tradition. I always wanted to know how things worked and how to do things, rather than merely to become an observer, and she recognized this orientation. She was generally quite insistent on good behavior.

MOTHER'S IMMEDIATE FAMILY

Mother's brother, my Uncle Nicholas Roosevelt, was slightly younger than she was. Like my mother, he was brought up in the Theodore Roosevelt clan environment in the New York City and Oyster Bay area. He went to Harvard, and was an officer in the Army during World War I. As yet unmarried, he was appointed by the U.S. State Department to be *Chargé d'Affaires* in Hungary in the early 1930s. He issued a cry for help to my mother, who went over to assist with the functioning of the embassy as well as to apply her considerable linguistic capability to the difficult, non-Romance Hungarian language. After about four months, she returned home dejected, admitting that Hungarian was one language that she could not even begin to master. Later, Uncle Nick joined the editorial staff of the N.Y. Times and ran the paper's emerging classical music station (WQXR), as well as participating in the paper's editorial stance during World War II. Late in life, he married Tirzah Gates, the daughter of a prominent Californian family. They had no children. He then followed an active writing career in the conservation field as a resident of Big Sur in California, and was an associate of both the well-known photographer, Ansel Adams, and the pioneer conservationist, John Muir.

Mother's other younger brother, my Uncle Oliver, graduated from Harvard, married, moved to France, and had his first son, James West, there. We knew James only as "West". Uncle Oliver returned to Long Island to practice the profession of handling bond investments on Wall Street. He then remarried, having met Verdrey, a fascinating southern belle (familiarly known as Auntie Bee) who produced a son, Oliver Wolcott Roosevelt (called Wolcott within our family, but called Oliver by the rest of the world). Uncle Oliver died quite young in the early 1940s.

West Roosevelt became a senior purchasing agent for one of the large NYC retail firms. He attended Harvard College, graduating in 1939. While he was there, my parents welcomed him in our house, which became his home away from home. He died in 2007.

Wolcott Roosevelt graduated from Harvard in 1948. During his years at Harvard, he was heavily involved with a group concerned with the Baroque era of music; playing, conducting, research, and resurrection. Included in the group were researchers, instrumentalists, singers, and several conductors including Wolcott himself and Thomas Dunn. Several later became well-recognized in the field. They all were a bunch of characters. They insisted that I learn a lot about the use of the valveless trumpet of that era, and they encouraged me to play it, much to my chagrin at that

time. This kind of music was not a common thing to be playing then, so this gang did a lot to get interest going in Baroque era music in the local, regional, and even national community. We played at the Isabella Stewart Gardner Museum, Boston University, Sanders Theater, all kinds of churches, and lots of weddings. It was great fun, and certainly an education for a musician of my age and limited ability.

Wolcott married Ann Taylor, one of the five daughters of Charles Taylor, head of the Episcopal Theological School in Cambridge. Wolcott died in 2000 after a long and very successful career as a music critic for the Birmingham, Alabama newspaper. His widow has recently moved back to the Boston area to be near her daughter Carolyn who remains very active in Cambridge and Boston music circles.

FATHER

My father, Langdon Warner, was born in the Boston area in 1881 and was brought up in what later became our Cambridge house. He attended Noble and Greenough School, followed by Harvard, where he received an AB in 1903. Father's family had lived in

Father and his brother,
Roger Sherman Warner, Sr.

7

New England for many generations. One of the family's founders, Roger Sherman, was a signer of the Declaration of Independence and a general in George Washington's army. Men in the family traditionally practiced law.

My Warner grandfather was a partner in the Boston family law firm of Warner & Stackpole, and was a corporator of Radcliffe College in about 1901. The family summered on Gerrish Island, off Kittery, Maine. My father had one very close brother, a Boston lawyer named Roger Sherman Warner who, as an adult, summered in Ipswich, MA. Uncle Roger and his family have been very close to me throughout my lifetime, especially my first cousin, Sturgis Warner.

Immediately after graduating from Harvard, my father showed great interest in the art, history, and culture of the Orient. This led to a lifetime of exploration and archeological investigation into these little-understood aspects of Asia. He followed the Silk Road, crossed the Gobi Desert, explored much of China, and developed friends among the intellectuals of Japan, Korea, and Southeast Asia. This colorful and adventurous part of his life has led to some confusion about his possibly being an inspiration for some of the Indiana Jones legends that became hugely popular films in the 1980s and '90s.

My father referred to his Gobi Desert exploits as "kicking a Model T Ford across the deserts of China." He refused to drive at home for the rest of his life, leaving that important chore up to my long-suffering mother.

During WWI, Father became involved with Central European military units operating in the Orient. After the war, he settled into a career of museum curatorship in the field of Oriental Art with relationships with museums in Philadelphia, Cleveland, New York City, Honolulu, Boston, and Washington, D.C. In about 1920, he finally took up residence again in Cambridge, MA, at Harvard's Fogg Museum, as curator of Oriental Art and lecturer/instructor in the Harvard academic programs. My father did not speak Japanese fluently, and my mother's linguistic skills often proved helpful.

Before WWII, due to his intimacy with Japanese political and intellectual leaders, he was asked to author a position paper concerning U.S. and Japanese relations. The paper was in the hands of U.S. political leaders in Washington who were planning to deliver it to the Japanese ambassador. As the Japanese ambassador cooled his heels at the U.S. State Department awaiting the meeting, the meeting kept being delayed. This delay, it turned out, was because the attack on Pearl Harbor was just then taking place! The paper was never, in fact, delivered.

Throughout his adult life, my father was an ardent amateur arborist, matching my mother's all-consuming interest in gardening. He labored strenuously and very happily on the trees on our Essex, MA, summer house property and took great interest in the work of the neighboring orchard experts.

FATHER'S IMMEDIATE FAMILY

My Uncle Roger Warner took the place of my father in the many long summer periods when my father was away in the Orient and I was stashed away in our Essex summer house. The Roger Warners' Ipswich house was in the next town north of Essex, Massachusetts, several miles across mosquitoey marshes, or several hot bicycle miles over sweaty roads. I was with those Warners almost daily each summer up to age about 15 years. My aim was to get access to the marvelous workshop in their big barn, and also to act as a pair of functional legs for my polio-impacted but physically very active cousin and friend, Sturgis Warner.

Other members of the Uncle Roger Warner family were my cousins, Roger, Jr. and Rachel, plus their very special mother, Aunt Molly (Hooper) Warner. When I was a teenager, my relationship with my aunt was a significant influence on my life. She was concerned, understanding, and caring about what I was doing and thinking. She had high standards of behavior and taught me those standards in a non-judgmental, motherly way. She gave me much support.

Roger Jr. made a name for himself during WWII in developing military invasion techniques and hardware jointly with Britain's Lord Louis Mountbatten and American marine photographer Morris Rosenfeld. Among his developments was the infamous military invasion landing craft, the DUKW (now affectionately known as the "Duck" and still used as an amphibious tour boat). Although I do not know the details, he also was heavily involved in management of the production efforts of the Manhattan Project and was on chase planes behind the aircraft that dropped the two atomic bombs on Japan. He became the Director of Engineering of the U.S. Atomic Energy Commission.

My father's Uncle Harry Warner was a Boston lawyer who lived in nearby Lincoln, MA, and was quite close to my father. Closer still to me was Great Uncle Harry's older daughter, Peggy, who, just after she graduated from Radcliffe College in 1932, broke the "glass ceiling" of the U.S. Diplomatic Service by becoming the first woman to be a certified member of the Service. In the U.S. State Department's infinite wisdom, they posted Peggy to what they considered to be the safest overseas post – Switzerland – where she promptly married into the top echelon of the Swiss Diplomatic Service. Her husband, Jean Wagnière, was subsequently posted back to the U.S. as the Swiss Observer to the U.N. Later on, I spent an extraordinarily happy month with their family in Denmark, and two of their three sons camped out with us intermittently for almost eight years when they were Harvard graduate students. The eldest son, Georges, a PhD in chemical physics, became a leader of the faculty of the Swiss Technical Institute in Geneva. The next son, Daniel, a Harvard MBA, became a Vice President of W.R. Grace Co. in this country. The third son, Frederique, emigrated to Montreal and then moved to Toronto, becoming a nationally known newspaper correspondent on business and financial affairs in Canada. Continuing our family's relationship with Peggy's family, our daughter Anne has swapped houses with Peggy's granddaughter during extended visits, and we continue to welcome visits from various members of the family when they are in this country.

MY PARENTS' CAMBRIDGE HOUSE

My parents' house at 63 Garden St., Cambridge was built by my father's family in the mid-1800s, in an area of large houses and Harvard institutional facilities, across the street from the Harvard Observatory to the west, and the Grey Herbarium to the north, on a plot of land perhaps two city blocks square. This land later became the residence quadrangle and sports field for Radcliffe College, and is now completely overbuilt by dormitories of the Harvard University residence complex.

The house was a beautifully built wooden structure, quite simple in appearance, with no gingerbread work, and a substantial covered open porch on two sides. It was painted yellow, trimmed in white, with black stripes around the top course of its four brick-red chimneys. The main three-story body had a square footprint of approximately 60 feet on a side with a 46-foot long, 20-foot wide, two-story ell protruding from a back corner. The front face of the house was almost perpendicular to Garden Street. The driveway came in from Garden Street, across the front of the house, past the front steps, around to a parking circle in front of the garage in the rear ell, finally emptying out to the rear on Linnaean Street.

The entrance to the house off the driveway hosted a set of majestic steps, eight or ten feet wide. These led into a small enclosed mud-room-style entryway, and finally into a commodious front hall with a classical, but simple L-shaped stairway to the second and third floors. Continuing toward the rear of the house was the back hall, leading to the back door (on Linnaean St.). From the back hall, there was a narrow backstairs system going up to the second and third floors. Upon entering the front hall from the front driveway, to the left was a 26- by 24-foot living room with a coal/wood fireplace, and a similar adjacent music room with two grand pianos. A sliding wall enabled these two rooms to be joined, thus producing a small concert or function hall. To the right of the entrance hall was a 26-foot square dining room served by a pantry/refrigerator suite and a large eat-in-style kitchen with a commercial-style gas range.

The second story of the main house contained three large bedrooms, one large office (for my father), one small bedroom, two baths (no showers), and a small telephone/office/file room known affectionately as the "Parrot Room" (a room that apparently had housed parrots at one point).

The third floor contained a suite of three bedrooms and a bathroom. It was inhabited by our live-in cook and maid, as well as by occasional boarders.

Back on the first floor, in the ell beyond the kitchen, was a laundry. Down half a flight to ground level was a woodshed and finally a garage. Over the shed and garage was a storeroom. In the 1930s, the ell was converted into a silversmith's workshop to hold the activities of close friend Graham Carey's elegant silversmith activities.

Just prior to WWII, the ell was further converted to a separate apartment for my parents (with the separate address as 64 Linnaean Street) so the main house could be rented out. My parents lived in the apartment in the made-over ell for the final five years of my father's life. It had a large living/dining room, small kitchen, and three small bedrooms. The driveway for the main house was then cut off by the extended ell, and a stub driveway entering from Linnaean Street served as off-street parking for the two family cars.

Above: Mother (1906).

Right: My uncle, Roger Sherman Warner, Sr.

*Below: Uncle Nick Roosevelt and his wife, Tirzah, sailing
with a local charter-boat skipper.*

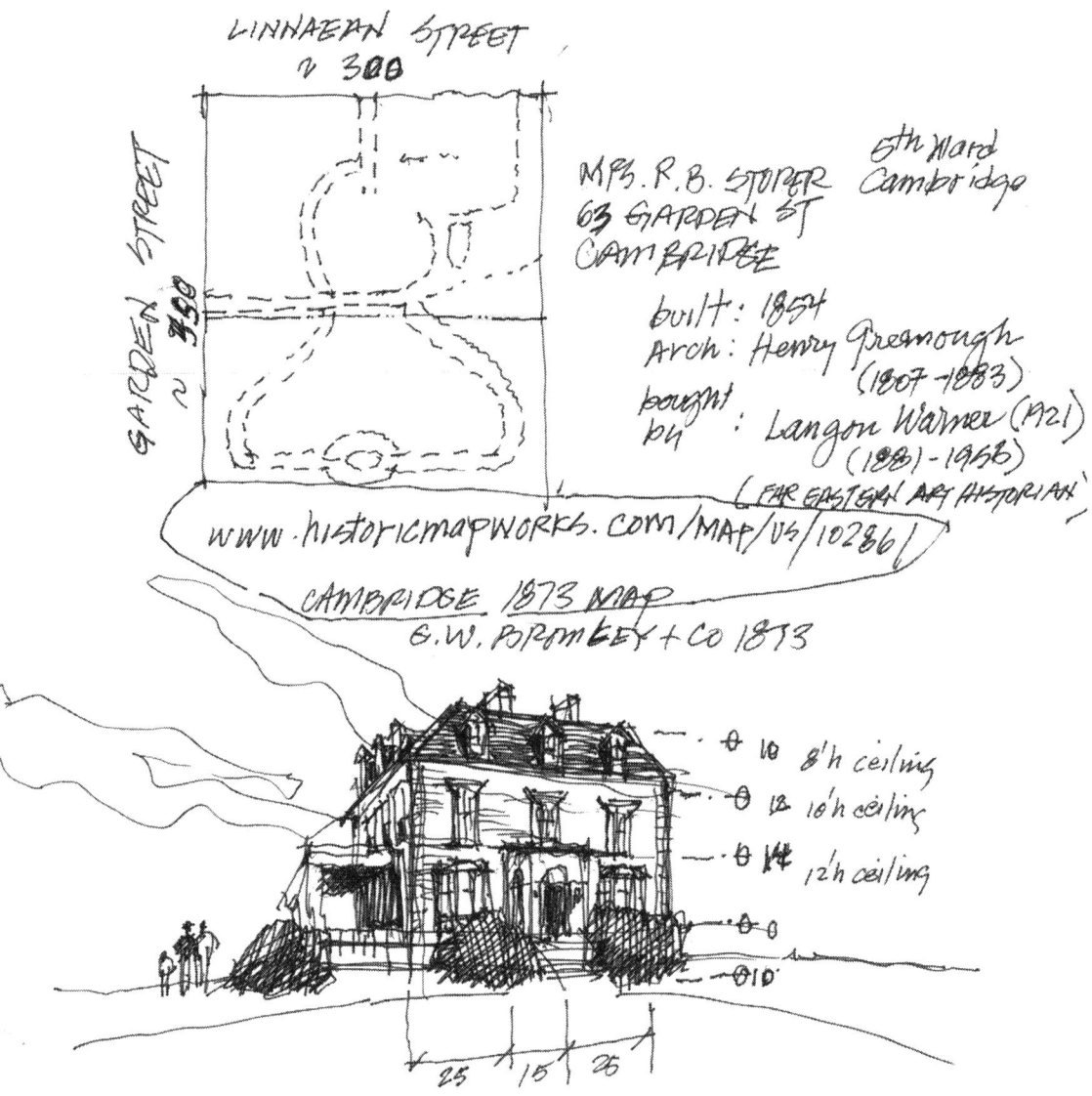

MRS. R.B. STORER

HISTORIC PHOTOS:
www.historic mapworks.com
/Buildings/index.php?state=
MA&city = Cambridge&id=15602

LINNAEAN STREET
~ 300

GARDEN STREET
~ 400

MRS. R.B. STORER   5th Ward
63 GARDEN ST   Cambridge
CAMBRIDGE

built: 1854
Arch: Henry Greenough
(1807-1883)
bought
by: Langdon Warner (A21)
(1881)-1955)
(FAR EASTERN ART HISTORIAN)

www.historicmapworks.com/MAP/US/10286/

CAMBRIDGE 1873 MAP
G.W. BROMLEY + CO 1873

10   8'h ceiling
12   10'h ceiling
14   12'h ceiling

25 15 25

My parents' house at 63 Garden St., Cambridge was located on the corner of what became Radcliffe's residence quadrangle and is now a Harvard University residence quadrangle. This rendering was done by Tim Martin, my friend and fellow resident at Carleton-Willard Village.

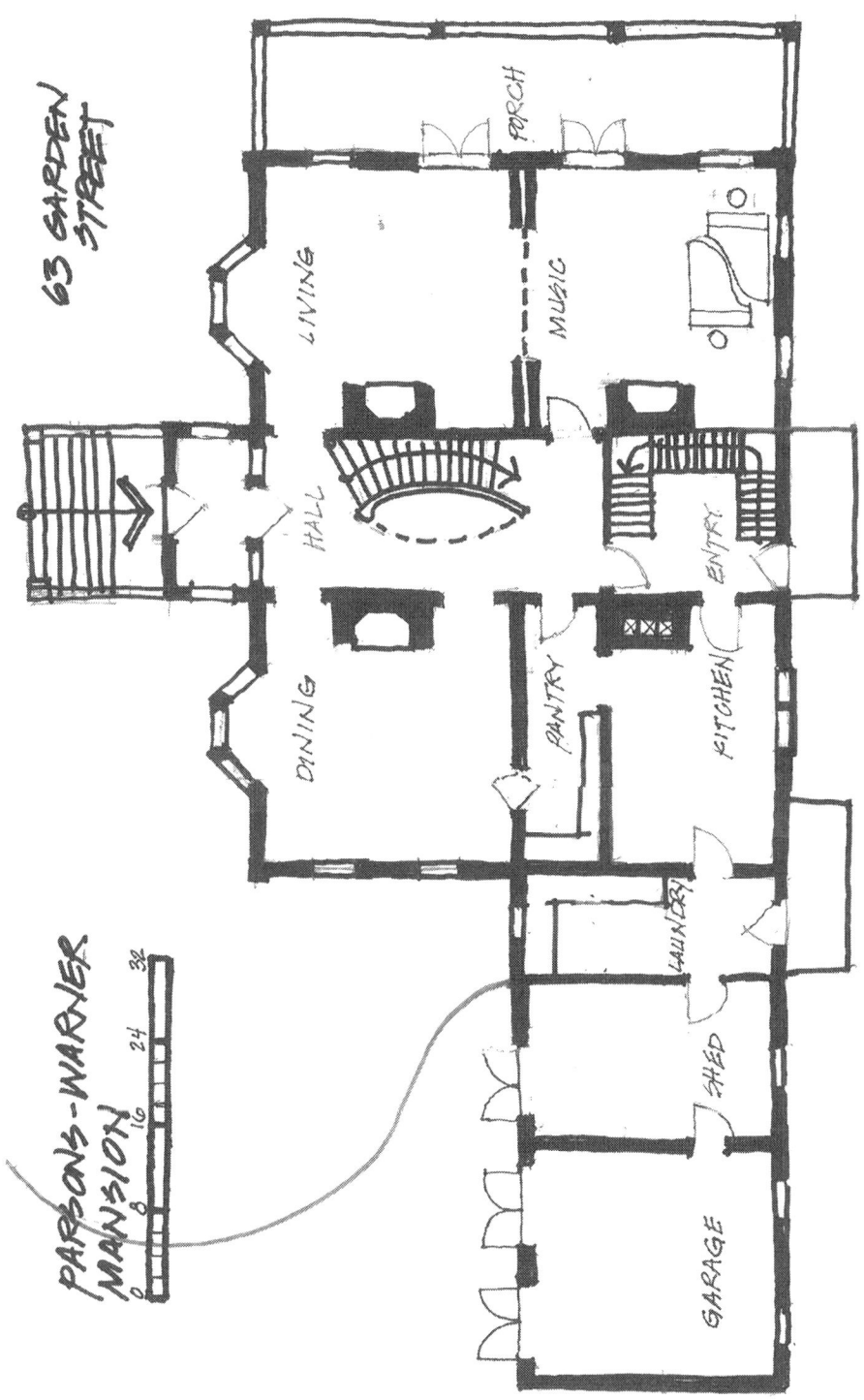

First floor. Rendering by Tim Martin.

The interior of the Garden Street house. Upper left: Fireplace in the main living room, with one of my mother's Japanese-style flower arrangements and Madame Liberty. Upper right: My father's study. Lower: Main living room, across from the above fireplace. Note the pocket doors are open on the right, leading to the music room, forming a concert hall space large enough to hold two grand pianos, musicians, and an audience.

Father and his father, Joseph Bangs Warner.

Mother and me in the Garden St. house.

3

EARLY CHILDHOOD

My Birth

I was born on September 12, 1922 at the Sloane Hospital for Women in New York City, the youngest child, with two older sisters. My parents chose to have me delivered in my mother's hometown as opposed to the Boston area where they were then living. They had previously had at least two difficulties with births elsewhere – a stillborn son and birth-delivery damage to my older sister Margot's arm. The combination of the familiar Sloane Hospital and the presence of my mother's family physician, Dr. Painter, in New York appeared to be a better situation. Amusingly enough, my birth certificate identifies my name only as "one male, Unitarian"! That moniker has caused me no end of complication, especially when trying to get paid in the Navy where a properly worded birth certificate is an essential part of the process.

Baby Caleb.

Earliest Years

As far as I know, my parents brought me right back to live in Cambridge just after I was born. Our household was well-suited to caring for young children. I do not have many detailed memories regarding this period other than the fact that everything seemed to be home-oriented. I remember my parents being very attentive to me.

Outside of several ear infections and bouts with the usual infant diseases, I believe that I was generally quite healthy. Our pediatrician, a close family friend, was the director of Children's Hospital in Boston. Unlike today's doctor/patient visits, he made house calls. I still remember, with horror, that he performed some rather nasty, but highly effective infected eardrum treatments on me at home, while I was in my parents' large four-poster bed. He used liquid ether anesthetic poured onto a gauze-covered mask that he held over my nose. He did this without assistance, relying on my good behavior and my mother's patience.

THE CAMBRIDGE HOUSEHOLD

I had a fundamental feeling of living in a secure, bustling household, surrounded by people providing important specialized services but also really participating in our family life. Two very important resident members of our household were our cook, Mrs. John Mahler, and our maid, Eileen O'Malley. Several non-residents were also significant contributors to our lifestyle. My parents made sure that I got to know each individual and respect them for their roles. This included a wonderful seamstress/washerwoman, Mrs. Frazier, and a very loyal and skilled janitor, Mr. Sullivan. The postman, the paper boy, the fish monger, the ice man, the milk man, the furnace tender, the grocery deliverer, the hair-care provider, the mobile knife-sharpener, the cop on the beat, the hurdy-gurdy player, the local firemen in the nearby fire house, were all made important for me. I owe a lot to all of them since they did much to help me grow up and I was genuinely fond of each of them. Although my mother served as primary care provider, the household staff acted also as an auxiliary set of parents with the encouragement of both Mother and Father.

Mrs. Mahler and me.

MRS. MAHLER

Mrs. John Mahler was my family's resident cook. My parents had the good fortune to hire this extraordinary person, and had the good sense to involve Mrs. Mahler in bringing me up. She was a first generation immigrant from Ireland, and I believe she fled from her country during one of the potato famines. She was a devout Catholic, and although I had been essentially pressed into Unitarianism, Mrs. Mahler often took me along to Catholic services where I came to understand and value the significance of that branch of Christianity.

I lived and slept very close to Mother's bedroom. She was generally quite attentive to me, in spite of a very demanding and full personal and professional life. She was much in charge of the household since my father was often overseas in Asia and extremely busy professionally at his job as curator at the Fogg Museum at Harvard.

In view of the fact that we had what amounted to a performance space on the first floor of our house, with the two large adjacent rooms opening into each other, there was a continual buzz of evening activities going on. My mother's own piano was a superb Steinway grand (about five and a half feet long). Additionally, a local professional concert pianist had provided Mother with a nine-foot concert grand piano which had been "retired" from the concert stage after having been condemned as "worn out" by piano technicians. (Incidentally, that piano was made by Chickering, probably in the era when my future wife Alice's grandfather, C.H.W. Foster, was running the company.) The presence of the two instruments rounded out the performance hall aspects of the two large rooms. My parents' activities were augmented by my older sisters who kept the house hopping with social activities. I was young enough to be a mere onlooker, but I was continuously amazed and impressed.

As my sisters gradually moved along, I inherited a full-sized room of my own that became a cross between a starter workshop and a functional toy maze. I had continual difficulty keeping within the required bounds of neatness, but my room was enjoyed jointly with my playmates and was a source of some wonderment on the part of my parents.

We had the great luxury of having a large front yard, perhaps 200 feet by 150 feet, completely screened from the busy street by a seven- or eight-foot high wooden, wall-like fence with a monstrous elm shade tree in the middle, making for an ideal protected play space for small children plus, of course, their very important pets, sand boxes, and the like. This yard not only provided a space for me to occupy myself safely and happily, but it attracted many of my preschool contemporaries.

One interesting feature of the house layout was a short hallway – essentially a landing in the rear stairway complex – leading to the bathroom used by us children. This important hallway contained a critical bookshelf specially built to hold a complete set of the iconic 11th edition of the Encyclopedia Britannica, bound in bathroom-proof style. I am truly sure that I read that wondrous collection from cover to cover over the 20 years that I lived there. That was my "bible" as I grew up, and I am afraid it made somewhat of a skeptic out of me regarding non-encyclopedic literature. Rightly or wrongly, I have since limited my reading to material dealing with usable information, rather than reading for enjoyment only.

Mother and Father (middle and right) with unknown fellow horseman in Asia.

With my father's professional orientation toward Asia, and my mother's toward Europe, my parents, either singly or together, were often away. I was taken care of for short periods by members of the household.

The lifestyle of our household was really quite remarkable. All meals were served at the large expandable table in the dining room. Everyone was required to come on time and stay to the end of each meal, and conversation was encouraged but directed toward addressing only "significant" subjects. Manners and behavior were carefully

19

scrutinized. Children were urged to bring guests. We all had definite bedtimes, wakeup hours and standards of room messiness/cleanliness.

The most notable feature of our meals took place on Friday and Saturday evenings when my parents often had guests who were distinguished and learned people. As children, we were sometimes excluded from formal meals, to our mixed emotions.

MY SISTERS

My sister Lorraine was born in 1911 when my parents were, I believe, living in Philadelphia. I know very little about her early years, except that she went to Shady Hill School shortly after the school was started, and possibly when it was in its original location.

By the time my memories of her begin, I was about five years old and, of course, she was already in her teens. After Shady Hill, she went to the Winsor School, a girls' school in Boston. She played tennis and lived a very active social life with her schoolmates, and participated in many community activities. They were often at our house. She was an enthusiastic summer camper at the Pinelands Camp in New Hampshire, and later became a happy counselor and swimming instructor. Lorraine was also a good figure skater and instilled in me my love of skating and being on the ice, starting while I was only a toddler. She was also a life-long choral singer, ultimately encouraging that interest for me as well.

Lorraine was fully involved in the social activities of the time in Greater Boston. She became a debutante, and her coming out party was at home, at 63 Garden Street, in the large double living room. She did not go to college, though many of her friends were local college students. I never knew the reasoning behind her not going, especially since she was an intellectually oriented person, and definitely quite bright.

My sister Margot was born in 1916, six years before me. The functioning of her right arm was severely nerve-damaged during delivery, making it limited in use throughout her life. Attempts my mother made at overcoming the limits, such devising as a special glove to allow Margot to operate the bow of a cello, were of questionable success.

Margot went first to the Shady Hill School where she seems to have been successful and happy, although I never really knew her well in that era. She also went on to the Winsor School, a typical step for Shady Hill girls. Margot was plucky in spirit. She did very well using only her good arm in athletics, especially field hockey in her teen years. Her social life was always blossoming.

My preschool years were well adjusted. I was healthy and happy, living in my family's two active households: the Cambridge house in the winters and the Essex house each summer.

Boy and boat.

Above: Sitting on a cannon on the Cambridge Common. Unseen is the sign that shows the location where my ancestor General Roger Sherman Warner released his troops to George Washington during the Revolutionary War.

Above, right: Checking the work of one of my silversmith ancestors, Caleb Warner, from whom I got my name.

Right: Ready for a swim.

Playing in the gardens. (Top right: Margot. Bottom left: Lorraine.)

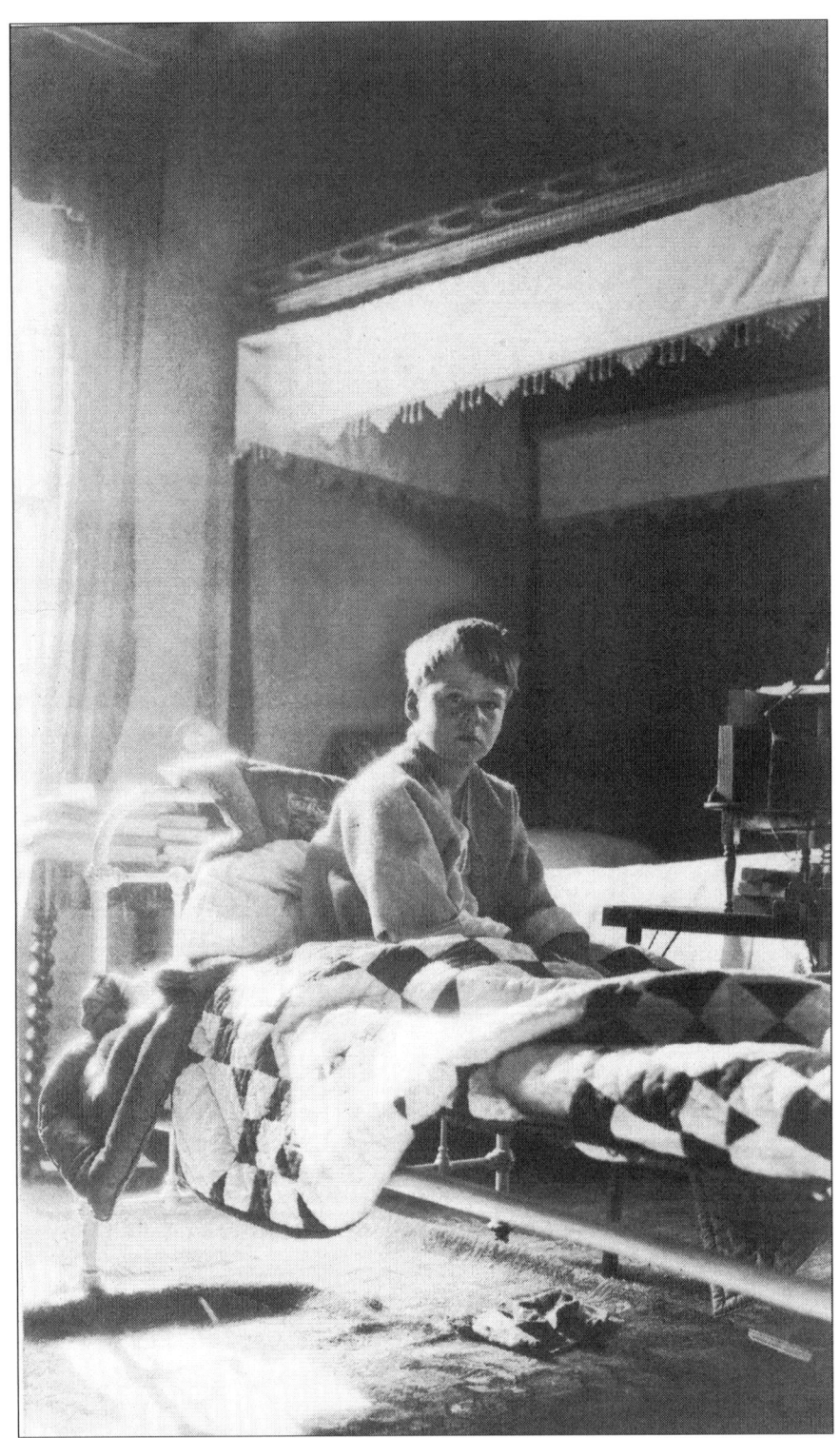

Playing with blocks while sick in bed.

4

GRADE SCHOOL YEARS

Our Household: Boarders and Guests

During my grade school and prep school years, there were "musical chairs" going on between me, my siblings, boarders, and guests. Our home's bedrooms never stood empty. Since Cambridge was such an attractive place for studying or participating in Boston's bustling activities, my parents offered to house a mixed parade of Cambridge-seeking people. Thus, we had a varied array of boarders among whom were cousins from away (like our Swiss Wagnière relatives), wannabe musicians, lovelorn offspring of friends, and even children of friends who were running away from home.

Additionally, we often had some fascinating guests for both brief and extended visits such as Nadia Boulanger and Sir Steuart Wilson, other iconic musical friends of my mother, and colleagues of my father, including several distinguished Asian scholars. Our home was often a wild and truly stimulating place.

Mother and me, shown sitting on the front lawn of the Essex house.

Shady Hill School

When I was young, tradition among Cambridge professionals and academics favored sending their children to private, not public, schools. Accordingly, I was sent to the Shady Hill School.

The school was founded in 1915 on the back porch of the Sachs estate called "Shady Hill" in Cambridge, almost next door to where Alice and

I lived many years later. It was coeducational from the beginning and an early example of the emerging "progressive education" movement, with the following characteristics: 1) encouragement of each individual's particular skills, and attention paid to individual's particular needs, 2) a highly diverse variety of subject matters, 3) very active athletics, 4) intense arts and crafts, 5) focus on sociological aspects of history and ethnic patterns.

An important aspect of Shady Hill was the Teacher Training Course, now called the "Apprentice Program". This offered hands-on training for young aspiring teachers, but not in the classical mode offered by the conventional "Normal Schools" or "Teachers Colleges". At Shady Hill, the candidate spent a full academic year apprenticed to a senior teacher.

This apprenticeship did not involve completing the requirements for formal teacher certification as required by various states, but generally readied the candidate for teaching in a private school. Those completing the year were generally snapped up by private schools, and even by savvy private industry personnel managers. These apprentices were often very important people in our lives at the school.

Class size was usually 15-20 students, one class to each grade, kindergarten through grade nine, preceded by a single year of pre-kindergarten or so-called "Beginners". The school had a total of approximately 200 students. There was some confusion about the apparent overlap with some high schools as there was a 9th grade at Shady Hill.

Each grade had a single home room teacher, with specialist teachers for math, science, Latin, music, shop, and art studio. Apprentices were assigned to each of these teachers. There were also several coaches for particular sports. The administrative force consisted of the principal, assistant principal, a financial specialist, a head of the library, and an office manager, backed up by a small team of janitors/maintenance people.

The current Shady Hill School plant was built starting about 1910 alongside the Charles River, almost next door to Mt. Auburn cemetery, the first "garden cemetery" designed by Frederick Law Olmstead, well-known for its beauty and environmental excellence. The school's buildings are situated on filled land about five feet above the flood plain. They are a collection of single-story, simple, unattached buildings, each housing two grade or classroom units. A single large building contains offices and an assembly hall. Extensive playing fields are almost at flood plain level of the Charles River.

The student body typically consisted of children of local academics, significant "captains of industry", distinguished professionals, socially prominent "old money" families, and the like. These families had one characteristic in common: they were universally in search of a meaningful education for their children. I am not really sure how the student body was selected nor am I sure about the nature or extent of the scholarship aid process.

During my years at Shady Hill, my playmates, associates, and friends were primarily those that I was with in school. We really seem to have stuck together. This group produced a lot of opportunity for being interestingly busy and occupied, and enabled us to take advantage of the wide and diverse offerings in the Cambridge/Boston area.

The depth and breadth of the education we received from Shady Hill School was exceptional. It laid a pretty remarkable basis for later education and set high standards of performance. The school's progressive approach involved a structure in which each grade was identified with an era in world development such as Greek, Roman, or New World Emergence. History, social development, and an understanding of ethnic issues were taught surrounding the core subject. Studies of Latin, French, English grammar and literature, world geography, physics, chemistry, mathematics, studio arts, music participation, social and political history were all required for everybody (and even a little Greek was offered, although I was not able to handle that!) Participation in competitive sports was required and close supervision was provided.

Fourth grade Greek "Olympic Games" (Jimmy Conant, Norm Jamieson, Caleb Warner, Bob Storer, and Tom Metcalf of the Class of 1937.)

The standards of education and preparation for continued study were such that subsequent application to demanding preparatory schools was generally successful.

Our Cambridge house was one and one-half miles from Shady Hill, and we were required to be at school for an 8:30 start. Beginning at about fourth grade, I walked to and from school daily until I was able to handle the trip on a bicycle. We were carefully checked into school each day. I lunched and snacked at school. Recess invariably involved running around, and sports were required each afternoon. Scheduled games often kept us at school as late as 4:30. Friday afternoons were reserved for academic makeup periods and special projects such as rehearsals or activities scheduled by our families. In my case, my mother required that I attend the Friday afternoon concerts of the Boston Symphony Orchestra. (My mother also launched me into music lessons, initially to play the violin. This was a disaster in the making. After hearing the first chair trumpet of the Boston Symphony Orchestra play "Pictures at an Exhibition," I rebelled, and took up the trumpet as an instrument, which I have played for the rest of my life.)

Biking was the way to get around in those days.

During my ten years at Shady Hill School I was generally much in awe and respectful of the teachers. I was also sometimes overwhelmed by the academic challenges.

LORRAINE IS MARRIED: PASS THE TEA

At age 21, Lorraine married Bob Bulkley while he was still in Harvard Law School. Bob was the son of the U.S. Democratic Senator from Ohio, living in Cleveland. The wedding took place in our home in the combined concert hall-style rooms. The guest list included friends, family, and both sets of parents' colleagues, from Harvard, Cleveland, Washington D.C., and the Orient. This, when I was only ten years old, wowed me. My job was to "pass the tea". The newlyweds then lived just down the street from our Cambridge house.

SUMMERS AT ESSEX

Before I was born, my parents purchased an extraordinary summer house from Mr. Burnham, one of the established merchants in Essex, MA, which was a center for antique dealers. The two-family house had been built in the 1620s on the riverfront of nearby Newburyport, one of a group of simple residences for waterfront workers. It had been carefully

Lorraine and Bob.

taken down and put in storage in Mr. Burnham's barn to preserve as an antique. The classic front hall, complete with a beautiful but simple staircase, had been sent to the Smithsonian Institution in Washington, D.C. as an example of typical early American houses.

The reconstruction of the house was assumed by my parents' friend and Ipswich neighbor, Arthur Shurcliff. He was a well-known landscape architect who had designed Colonial Williamsburg and Boston's Lower Charles River Basin. The house was reassembled on a six-acre hill in Essex overlooking the extensive Ipswich/Essex marshes, with a distant view of the rear of the dunes of Crane's Beach. The house attracted considerable admiration from antique lovers roaming the North Shore of Boston. Both house and grounds were dearly loved by my parents.

For me, at an early age, the Essex house was a challenge since it was remote from anything that I could consider as summer interests. At a young age I learned how to cross the two salt marshes on foot to reach the bustling summer activities of my Uncle Roger's house on Argilla Road in the bordering town of Ipswich.

STURGIS

Uncle Roger's son, my cousin Sturge, was about eight years older than I, and it wasn't until I was ten or twelve that I really got to know him well. My family joined that family for holidays. Christmas was at their house on Beacon Hill in Boston, Thanksgiving at our house in Cambridge, and July 4th and Memorial Day were celebrated in Essex/Ipswich. Easter was different each year, as I usually went wherever my mother was involved with music. But, although I knew Sturge as a child, it was not until I was in my early teens that I really began to be his friend and enjoy him. I didn't have an older brother figure to look up to, and Sturge filled that role.

My favorite picture of Sturgis, full of great spirit, pulled in a cart by the Ipswich gang of kids. Here, I am only about age two, held on someone's shoulders.

Once I could walk across the marshes to Uncle Roger's house on my own, I was there almost daily, visiting Sturge and his older brother Roger when he was at home. Roger, 12 years older than I, was already living the life of a busy adult. But he still found time for me, as did Aunt Molly and Uncle Roger. I always found much to do at that fascinating household, and spent as many summer days there as I could.

I was an eager younger "brother" and partner for Sturge. His disabilities, the result of polio when he was a young child, rarely caused his interest to wane in the areas of working in a shop and sailing, two areas of genuine appeal for me. Young as I was, I was able to provide some of the capabilities needed to supplement many of his daily physical challenges. I think his parents were quietly grateful to see us together.

Carpentry class at the Shurcliff's. Standing: Nancy Burrage, Sam Haydock, (unknown), Frances Tabor, John Sutherland. Kneeling: Cynthia Burrage, (unknown) Moseley, Elizabeth Osborn, me.

We took pleasure in our common interests. He taught me the basics in their well-stocked workshop in the barn. I learned metalworking, elementary electronics, and even how to handle pre-fiberglass-era materials under Sturge's patient tutelage.

Argilla Road was a jumping scene in other ways, a gold mine of activity, with sailing and swimming in the tidal creek, carpentry lessons at the Shurcliff woodworking shop next door, choral singing at the Galacar's house with my mother as conductor, community hymn singing on Sundays, tennis at several places, general camaraderie of people my own age, and the upbeat role of my Uncle Roger's family. Summers were a truly formative part of my grade school years.

During one summer in the early 1930s, both my parents were abroad, first together and then apart. The family of our Ear, Nose and Throat doctor, Dr. Robert Goodale, a Cambridge and Ipswich neighbor, kindly took me in as a boarder in their wonderful household on the Ipswich marsh. Mrs. Goodale was a very likeable overseer of the household. It was a happy time for me and a great relief not to have to travel each day over to Argilla Road from Essex. There were four Goodale children, the oldest being a year or two younger than I—Susan (now Sue Hay, who lives in my current-day continuing care community). There was one additional boarder, Nancy Clancy (more recently, Nancy Caskie). Nancy later became a nearby neighbor in Lincoln when we lived in Lexington.

A SUMMER ON LONG ISLAND

During another summer, in the mid-1930s, both my parents were abroad and I went to stay with the family of my uncle Oliver Roosevelt in their wonderful household in Lawrence, Long Island, NY. This was a grand summer, featuring lots of sailing and swimming in the excellent shallow bays of the southwestern shore of Long Island. My constant companions and first cousins, West and Wolcott, were both fun and a lot of support.

PARENTS' FRIENDS AND ASSOCIATES

My parents invited a constant parade of extraordinary guests to our dinner table. Many were of great celebrity. During these dinners, my parents encouraged my inclusion in their conversations, introducing me as a youth to some possibly interesting avenues that I could consider in my future choice of career.

The visitors included associates of my father at Harvard and other universities as well as representatives of the Asian cultures with which he had personal and professional relations. The list also included a highly regarded philosopher, several museum directors and art collectors, a pioneering etymologist, a renowned sculptor, a pioneer physicist, several distinguished Asian art scholars and the like. My mother's associates were primarily in the field of music, and included noted European composers, world-class music mentors, teachers, conductors and performing professionals.

Although I'm sure my parents hoped that these people would provide positive role models for me, I found, instead, that I was haunted by this amazing set of individuals. As the years went on, I really struggled with the idea that I would never, ever, be able to rise up to the professional levels that these people represented to me and to my parents. They set standards that were hard or impossible for me to meet in my life.

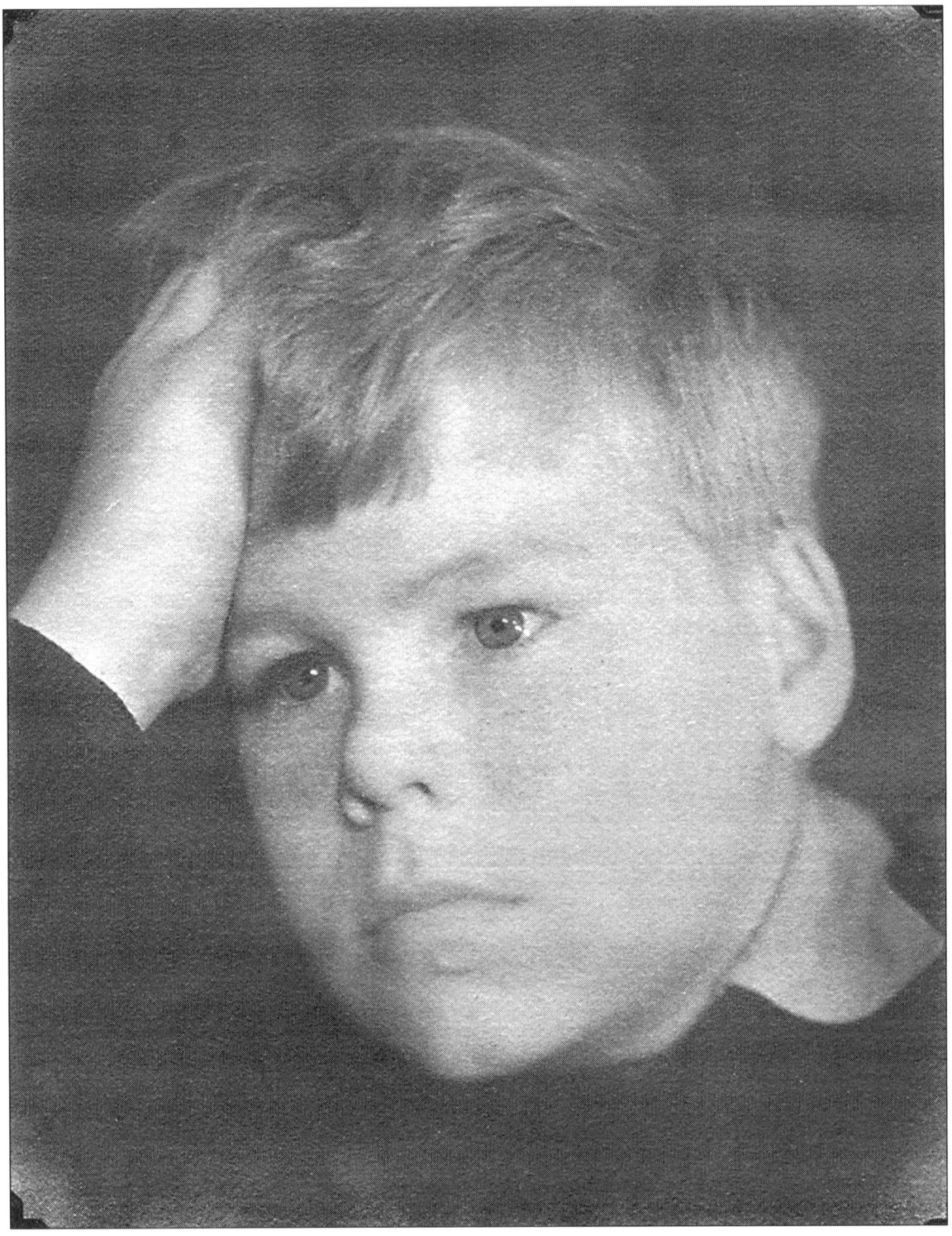

This portrait was taken by Ethel Mary Partridge, the wife of an art colleague of my father's, Ananda Kentish Coomaraswamy.

Above: Training Sir John Peel, my sister Margot's dog. Peel was present at all the Radcliffe field hockey games; he was named their official mascot. He spent his days at Radcliffe and his nights at home. He was "skunked" more than once, and returned to us by the Radcliffe girls reeking of perfume as well as skunk. He then had to be locked up for days, poor guy!

Right: Taken at the time of my working for Ben Olken at the Bicycle Exchange in Cambridge, my very first job.

The Essex summer house. Top left: Wood shed and carport. Center left: Entry to front walk off the driveway. Upper right: Approaching the house from the front walk. Bottom: Back of the house (originally used as the front of the house when it was built in Newburyport), which faces the rear of Crane Beach dunes. The small house on the right was used for guests, as well as for respite for both parents and children. My parents named it "Parents' Assistance" which was shortened by the children to "Parrot's Sister".

The Essex summer house, interior. Upper left: the walk-in fireplace with bread ovens. Upper right: One of my favorite Asian-style arrangements made by my mother, hanging from the living room rafters. Bottom: One of the three smaller fireplaces.

Sailing on the North Shore of Boston.
(For those who know my grandson Jakob, the resemblance is striking!)

5

PREP SCHOOL YEARS

SELECTION AND ENTRANCE PROCESS

I have never been certain of exactly what happened during the process of choosing and gaining entrance to Phillips Exeter Academy (PEA). I have no memory of taking any particular examinations, nor of visiting the place nor even considering any alternatives. Admittedly, going to a school like Exeter generally was "the thing to do" among the boys who went all the way through Shady Hill. (Exeter was still a boys-only school at that time.) In the eyes of many of my parents' associates, the two Phillips academies, Exeter and Andover, shared high marks educationally and in lifestyle, and appeared to be a logical continuation of the successful track initiated by Shady Hill. There were no family traditions involved about which private school to attend. All of a sudden I seemed to be headed to Exeter as a so-called Lower Middler boarding student (equivalent to 10th grade in other schools), facing three years of preparation for entering college.

The only picture remaining of my father and me together.

PHILLIPS EXETER'S STATUS AND MISSION

The moniker "preparatory" school certainly applies well to Exeter in that it was dedicated to serving as a stepping stone to a college education. In all written or spoken descriptions of Exeter the so-called "Harkness Plan" is still cited as a prominent feature of the school's approach to education. A "Harkness oval table" in every classroom is touted as an aid in encouraging frank and open two-way interchange between teacher and students. However, in my experience, I observed, perhaps cynically, that it was certainly not a *round* table which would encourage equal exchange, but of an oval shape that, to me, reflected the social/educational relationships I saw throughout the school. The student body contained an extraordinary percentage of high achievers, both intellectually and athletically. Exeter tradition encouraged competition within the student body and public recognition of achievement. "Hubris"–almost arrogance–was the order of the day among my classmates, not equality and mutual respect. Altogether, it was rough for me.

LIFE AT EXETER

The school placed me with an assigned roommate in a dormitory which housed students of my grade only. I lucked out in the first year with an unobtrusive but very cooperative roommate with whom I did not really have a lot in common. For the remaining two years, we were able to choose our roommates and dormitories. My choice of a roommate for those two years proved to be very fortuitous as Larry Erdman became probably my closest friend for the next 40 years.

Every weekday and weekend at Exeter was filled. Attendance was, of course, required at academic and certain school functions such as chapel services, and daily morning assemblies. Optional activities such as band, orchestra, chorus, plays, entertainment, dances, club meetings, sports watching and the like were encouraged and had to be shoehorned into the busy, required activity schedule.

Larry Erdman, my best friend for many decades.

THE ACADEMIC PROGRAM

Academics were profound and offered great breadth and depth. Classroom participation and homework were demanding and closely tracked by the teachers and dormitory monitors. The English courses were especially practical in that they included a very thorough drill in grammar and considerable practice in structured writing, skills which later became important in my professional career. Looking back at Latin, I realize now its role in developing an appreciation for and understanding of language in general. It was difficult for me at the time, however, and I often wondered why it was required.

Mathematics had already proven to be a real problem for me, and continued to plague me throughout my professional life. I obviously have some sort of mental block which impacts my handling of more advanced math, so I cannot with good conscience blame it on the school. I wish that my introduction to calculus had been more successful. In later professional life, I finally learned how to duck being dependent on it by surrounding myself with colleagues who could do it for me!

Physics was a genuine pleasure since it was taught with the orientation of learning how and why things work. I found it enlightening and genuinely inspiring. Chemistry, like math, was somewhat of a failure because it was presented more as the "way" things were, not "why" things were. Unfortunately, biology was, I think, an optional course and I did not take it. If I had the opportunity to do it again, I would make sure that I got a good foundation in that subject.

Overall, my academic record was far from outstanding. I think that I was about in the middle of my class. However, I was extremely impressed by the academics and the training that I received in how to study. By the time I graduated I was thoroughly ready to continue my education.

THE ATHLETIC PROGRAM

Every student was required to participate in athletics. A wide choice of sports was available beyond the established old standards of football, baseball, soccer, and basketball. The alternatives included squash, swimming, tennis, lacrosse, ice hockey, and even golf and rowing.

The classic two-level system of varsity and intramural competition was in place. Varsity sports held an elevated position and were highly revered by both faculty and student body. As I did not qualify for varsities, my social status was limited. However, I did participate seriously and happily at the intramural level in baseball, hockey, football, and a little bit in rowing.

MUSIC AT EXETER

At Exeter in 1937, participation in music was optional, but the opportunities were excellent. I took part in almost every aspect, although I think there was some sort of class-work in music history or music appreciation which I did not take.

At Exeter, I found the help I needed to address my apparent trumpet playing block . I obtained the good services of a brass and woodwind teacher hired by the school to give lessons in a variety of instruments. He was a skilled troubleshooter, a rather unusual type of teacher. He carefully analyzed my problems and pushed me into highly systemized drills that gave me a working level of proficiency. The school supported my trumpet playing by providing opportunities in their symphony orchestra, marching band, dance band and wind ensemble. The school further encouraged musical activity through its busy and well-structured church choir and men's chorus, both of which I enjoyed.

This was my first exposure to marching bands and dance bands. The experience set the stage for what became a very important part of my music activity throughout the rest of my life. The marching band was very active, and played at inter-school sports games. A serious orchestra, with about 40 players, rehearsed regularly and played four or five times a year with the chorus in concerts at or with nearby schools. This was conducted by another specialist who was available for stringed instrument lessons. With a mellophone, which I had never seen before, I was able to fill in for the orchestra's lack of a French horn player. The church choir of 10-12 voices sang at the Sunday church services. A much larger chorus of perhaps 40-50 voices toured to other schools and was very professionally conducted.

A student-organized dance band with four saxes, five brasses, and four rhythm instruments rehearsed weekly and played for dances at the nearby schools. The guys in this group, the Royal Exonians, became very close friends and we were generally enthusiastically egged on by the student body. My roommate, Larry Erdman, and I organized, played in, and generally ran the operation with wholehearted but quite removed backing by the faculty.

Music was a very happy and extraordinarily busy activity for me. The dance band and chorus activities made a significant contribution to my social life, as we joined perhaps five girls' schools scattered around New England each year to give concerts and participate in dances afterwards. In our daily lives, the Exeter musicians seemed to be drawn together through our common interests in music.

Music thus became a large part of my preparatory school life, and was an area in which I could attain some degree of achievement. By the time I finished Exeter, I was convinced that I wanted to continue to be musically involved, but music definitely should not be my primary life's work, especially <u>not</u> my profession. My understanding and capable remedial trumpet teacher got me ready to pursue playing the instrument seriously once I got to college.

EXETER'S OTHER EXTRA-CURRICULAR ACTIVITIES

Each weekday morning, all students were required to attend so-called "chapel" in a large assembly hall which could accommodate all 750 students. Attendance was taken, absences were duly noted, and a restriction put on students who were absent or late. Attendees participated in a very brief prayer and then heard announcements of general concern. Occasionally a distinguished guest briefly addressed the school body.

Sunday church services were obligatory and were conducted by fascinating, usually notable guests, some of whom were religiously oriented, all of whom had a message of considerable value. When formally religious, those conducting the services were mostly Christian, but other faiths were strongly represented. Students with other-than-Christian faiths were permitted to attend religious services closer to their beliefs if so requested by their parents, but everybody was required to attend an organized service somewhere.

Every Saturday night movies were provided in the large gymnasium. Perhaps three times a year, special formal dances were held in that gymnasium featuring up-and-coming big bands from New York (Glen Miller, Jimmy Lunceford, Bunny Berrigan, and the like). These were gold star social occasions in which students invited their girlfriends from home to stay at the local inn for the weekend. I think that I had a guest for only two of those dances. The rest of the time I had the great privilege of becoming a "go-fer" for the visiting bands, a situation that I really welcomed because I got to know some of the great musicians of the big band swing era.

Surprisingly to me, fraternities flourished at that time at Exeter, I suppose reflecting what was then going on in college communities. Each fraternity was identified as to its orientation or social ranking. I joined one, but found the structure quite bothersome. I did not fit in well.

EPIPHANY

By the time I was considering where to go to college and what to study there, I realized I was attracted to pursuing maritime activities. To enter that field, I needed to study naval architecture and marine engineering. With World War II breaking out in Europe, I also wanted to point myself toward service in the Navy. Four college-level institutions seemed to be the only candidates: M.I.T., Stevens Institute of Technology, Webb Institute of Naval Architecture, and the University of Michigan. I felt that I probably could not qualify for entrance to MIT or Stevens Institute (about which I knew little) based on my modest academic record at Exeter, nor was I qualified for the fully-tuition-subsidized Webb Institute.

By extreme luck, I met a University of Michigan Naval Architecture student while I was passing through Ann Arbor on a train heading for a summer on the West Coast. This was the summer of 1938, just before I started my senior year at Exeter. This student's useful information and enthusiasm for his studies at Michigan triggered my interest and efforts to go there.

GETTING READY FOR COLLEGE

An interesting, and perhaps quite telling incident happened just as I approached the end of my prep school era. A high-up in the administration of Exeter called me in to sign a letter. I was surprised and somewhat dismayed to find that the letter from the school was addressed to my father and stated that *in no way had the Exeter faculty advised me against going to Harvard.* This was done, I assume, in deference to the fact that my father was on the Harvard faculty.

By that time, I had pretty much made up my mind to go to University of Michigan to study naval architecture, a course not available at any Ivy League school. Furthermore, if I were not going to Michigan, I wanted to apply to Yale. I frankly thought that I might not be able to qualify for an Ivy League school or MIT anyway. If the truth is to be known now, Mr. Darcy Curwen, my favorite Exeter teacher, was also encouraging me to avoid the Ivy League schools (and for good reason–Michigan was a perfect fit for my wartime service career goals and was also a school I could reasonably get accepted into) even though that same teacher was infamously and publicly very vocal about the fact that he personally had a tremendous respect and liking for Harvard as a logical next step for many Exeter students.

When confronted with that unhappy letter, I asked what would happen if I refused to sign (or co-sign) the letter to my father. I believe that I was told (or perhaps it may have been implied) that I might have trouble graduating from Exeter if I did not sign. I frankly do not remember whether or not I finally signed, but I assuredly told my parents about the letter and registered my unhappiness all around. My parents' reactions are not printable here.

Looking back, I now appreciate that Exeter provided a true launching pad into college. Although my educational record was far from distinguished up to that point, I was fully primed and ready to go.

OUT AND ABOUT WITH STURGE AND ROGER

In the summers before I went to college, Sturge and I sailed together often, and he taught me the basics, both in and out of the water. It was my physical capability that enabled us to operate the boat, but it was Sturge who taught me the intricacies of sailing and the craft of caring for a boat as we stood side by side in the shop over a damaged hull. I learned a great deal.

Roger, Sturge, and I had frequent outings, some planned and some on the spur of the moment—sometimes in the dead of winter. We drove down to the Boston harbor waterfront, especially the fish pier, the Navy Yard, and the freighters loading/unloading docks as well as the shipbuilding yards. Either we would get the car close enough so Sturge could get out and walk, or we would just sit in the car to watch and talk.

"Now look at that winch," Sturge would say. We'd look at the winch and he'd tell me how it differed from winches used on other vessels for catching different kinds of fish. We'd look at other gear, at what was on each vessel, and what it did, what kind of fish the men were going after, and how both gear and boat differed from other fishing vessels. Then we'd turn and look across the street at where the fish was being processed and the catch auctioned. We talked about where the fish was going, how far it would go, and ultimately whose tables it was going to grace.

We toured the two Ford Motor Company plants in Boston and Somerville to see how the newly minted Ford V8-powered series of cars were assembled. We went to the Rope Walk in the Navy Yard in Charlestown—a brick building about 1300 feet long by about 40 feet wide, an arcane facility to make (or "lay") rope. I was continually enthralled. We also visited the Portsmouth Naval Shipyard, where submarines were, and still are, repaired. When in Portsmouth, we also checked in on the historic Warner house where our ancestors had lived. We went to the Essex Institute and the Derby Wharf in Salem. In Boston, we visited the South Boston dry dock, the only facility on this side of the Atlantic large enough to accommodate monstrous-sized ocean liners.

America's historic ship, the USS Constitution, was restored at the Charlestown Navy Yard when I was a young teen. Imagine the fun I had with my two older cousins as they brought me back to the site more than once to watch the restoration of the aged hull. Sturge explained the ship's history as well as its structure and repair process as we watched, checking on its progress.

All during this period, I was a young, energetic guy beginning to look around in the world. It was terrific. Sturge had exceedingly high standards and intellectual curiosity. He wanted to know the background of what was happening in the rest of the world. He was a persistent newspaper reader and he wanted to be engaged in what was going on. He answered my questions, and gave me much to think about. He helped me discover the wonders of sailing. He introduced me to working with my hands.

I look back now and see that these experiences developed in me the joy of working hard, to be challenged both by my hands and head together. In Sturge, the capacity of his abilities, character, and spirit were far more obvious to me than the severity of his "disabilities." As a young boy, I absorbed this from the start, learning from the gut what this kind of spirit was all about. He went as far as he could go, and every single time, I learned, it was truly far enough. Sturge and I found a lifelong respect and kinship.

SUMMER APPRENTICESHIPS IN THE BOAT BUILDING SHOP

Thanks to my fascination with the woodworking and metalworking opportunities I had found in Ipswich, by about the summer of 1936 I was ready to get serious about working around boats. I was welcomed into the shop of a local production builder of small wooden boats as an unpaid apprentice–a win-win deal both for the boat builder and me. I turned up at the shop every weekday at 8:00 a.m. and stayed until the end of the work day at 4:30. I started as a "go-fer" but soon graduated to being a true production hand, assisting the one real pro who nobody else could get along with but who really produced for the shop. Fellow workers found him difficult to work with, but he treated me really well as long as I worked hard. I ended up very happily apprenticing for two successive summers.

MY NEXT-TO-LAST SUMMER BEFORE COLLEGE

Before my senior year at Exeter, I spent a truly formative summer visiting the western U.S. My father had gone on leave from Harvard to take over setting up the Pacific Basin section of the World's Fair in San Francisco. The fair was to be held in the middle of San Francisco Bay, half way between Berkeley and San Francisco, on Treasure Island. My parents had moved to Berkeley. I later realized that it was an enormously savvy move on their part. I had resisted heartily when they sent for me to come out and took the trip reluctantly at first, and then enormously happily, as it proved to be a pivotal, life-changing excursion for me.

I was told to come out on the famous Santa Fe Line's streamlined diesel-electric train to drink in the sights on the way. I was to get off for a month's stay to help a sculptor-friend of my father's in the Santa Fe region do some work on his adobe house.

The adobe house turned out to be more than a little problematic. As was well-known to others, but not then known to me, an adobe structure is a parade of individually shaped walls with non-rectangular corners. My job was to try to fit door frames in so that the structure could become livable and privacy could be established between one room and the next. It was more than a struggle. I called to mind the cartoon on my Uncle Roger's workshop wall in Ipswich in which the main character, dressed in carpenter's garb, proudly shouts "Look! I did it! I actually hung a door!"

The second difficulty I had was with a *mule*. My host and hostess owned a classy, shiny, black adult mule. The mule was under contract to a prominent Hollywood studio which was on location on the banks of the nearby Rio Grande River, filming Kipling's "The Light That Failed". To this day, I am not sure what that darned mule's role was in the movie, but apparently it was important, and the beast looked elegant enough to be a winner in any Hollywood scene. My job was to deliver the beast to the movie set every morning at 8:00 AM and bring it back home at the end of the shooting day. Again, as everyone else seemed to know except me (I learned a lot on that trip!), a mule can kick sideways and definitely likes to do so when handled by a mule-ignorant person like me. That darned animal practiced the sidewise kick on me every time I came near it.

I was on more friendly terms with a family of beavers that attracted me almost every day up to a stream in the local mountains.

While I was in Santa Fe, Alfred Hitchcock was visiting a local art gallery, introducing his two early thrillers, "The Thirty-Nine Steps" and "The Lady Vanishes", which later became two of both Alice's and my favorite films.

In total, it was a fascinating visit.

From Santa Fe I continued on to Berkeley, from which I went by ferry every morning to the World's Fair on Treasure Island. Since my father was on the management team of the event, I was allowed a special pass that got me in to witness the daily rehearsals of the Benny Goodman Band for almost

LANGDON WARNER – 1938-9 – Taken at the Golden Gate San Francisco World's Fair

(Note that this is the first of many examples of Alice's distinctive handwriting, found throughout this book.)

a full month. I gradually weaseled my way into becoming a "go-fer" for the band, chasing after their coffee each day. Exposure to the inner workings of Goodman and his associates (especially Fletcher Henderson) was an eye-opener for me, an experience I will never forget. It was an introduction into the world of jazz, and a real-life education in music.

My summer continued as I traveled from San Francisco to Tuolumne Meadows in the Yosemite National Park. There I was privileged to go on two successive two-week burro trail trips on foot, organized by the Sierra Club. I became burro master for the second trip, which was led by a man whose name I unfortunately cannot remember. I do remember, however, that I learned that burros were just like cats; they do only what they want to do. But, unlike that darned mule in Santa Fe, mankind can master them.

The summer ended with a weeklong trip to a beautiful farm northeast of Portland, Oregon, in the foothills of the Sierras, where I finally ran into my first (and unfortunately my last) friendly member of the horse family–a lovely Percheron–one of the loveliest draught horses you'll see. They are enormous, and are among the strongest work horses in the world. This one was friendly, and a relief from the mule and the burros I had been handling. He decided he didn't want me to ride him, however, so he brushed me off with a low tree limb by trotting under it.

THE SHORE WAS BEYOND REACH

On the way back from the mountains, we visited Lake Tahoe. There I learned a valuable lesson, not just on how to survive a canoe capsizing in serious surf, but more importantly, about the perils of overconfidence and inadequate preparation.

When we arrived at the lake, the wind was blowing 40 or 50 knots. We were on the lee shore; in other words very strong, blustering winds were blowing toward us from the lake. My new friend was an MD, quite a knowledgeable outdoorsman, and had been the leader of my lengthy Sierra Club hike.

We wanted to get out for a good look around the lake, and without hesitation, we launched our canoe, paddling away from shore through the breaking waves. Quite suddenly, when we were pretty far out, a wave capsized us. Surprised, we found ourselves in cold, rough water near the upside-down canoe. It was instantly clear that we would be unable to swim to shore. Both paddles were also far beyond reach, and neither of us was wearing a life jacket. My friend and I grabbed onto the small boat. He told me not to try to right it, as it kept a good amount of air underneath; the canoe could be used for shelter, should we need it. He instructed us to get on opposite sides, mid-ship, and hold hands over the top of the submerged canoe, keeping us both afloat and together as we waited about two hours for the blustering wind to blow us close to shore. We were lucky to have started at a beach, so that we did not get blown into rocks. We would not have made it if the wind had been blowing the other direction.

FAMILY LIFE IN THIS PERIOD

While I was preparing to leave home and childhood, my sisters were entering the adult world. My brother-in-law, Bob Bulkley, had passed the Massachusetts Bar Exams. He and Lorraine moved to New York where he started work as a cub reporter in the City Room of the New York Herald Tribune. They lived in a tiny apartment on the fourth floor of a four-story "walk-up." It was on 93rd Street, the Upper East Side of Manhattan, overlooking the East River, right across from Gracie Mansion. Lorraine became very active with the famous Dalcroze Chorus and its music school. She also did a great deal of volunteer service.

I was very close to Lorraine and Bob in that New York period, and spent a lot of time with them while also visiting my mother's family in the city. Bob saw to it that I was welcomed at the Herald Tribune City Room almost daily, where I could pick up free tickets to the various events and shows in the vibrant city. I came to really know my way around New York, and to enjoy it thoroughly.

Margot's social life was very active. Although she never married, she was intensely pursued by several young men. Our parents encouraged her to follow a serious career in singing rather than going to college. Margot was sent to Europe and England for one or two years to study with some world-class musicians such as Sir Steuart Wilson, a member of the well-known singing group "The English Singers", and later director of Covent Garden. Margot also studied abroad with Nadia Boulanger, the internationally known music authority, teacher, and coach of prominent people of music such as Leonard Bernstein. Margot's career in music included solo singing very briefly but intensively, and thereafter directing choirs, teaching singing, and directing and organizing amateur performances of musicals. She based her activities out of her house in Boston and then Essex.

When visiting the U.S., Mme. Boulanger stayed at my parents' house several times during my teen years. Without first consulting me, Mother once offered me up as a personal assistant for the *Grande Dame de Musique*. I escorted Mme. Boulanger down to Harvard Yard daily to ensure that she got safely to the organ at Memorial Church to practice. It was assumed that I was learned enough in the arcane art of the organ to "pull stops" for her, providing the two extra hands needed to turn on and off the various pipe sections of the instrument as she played She also sent me into the organ loft first to find, then to pull out faulty pipes when she discovered they were misbehaving during her check of the instrument at the start of each practice session. All Mme. Boulanger's actions were in the spirit of a kind soul, and I grew musically, mechanically and spiritually from assisting her. In hindsight, I think these experiences got me started in what later turned out to be a fascination with the organ and all its idiosyncrasies.

Senior portrait at Exeter.

I traveled back and forth to the University of Michigan, Ann Arbor, by train.
It was a direct route, and an overnight trip.

6

COLLEGE ERA

TRAINS AND ALARM CLOCKS: ARRIVING AT COLLEGE

I traveled by train to the University of Michigan (U.M.) in Ann Arbor, arriving before 8:00 A.M. on an early September day in 1940. I taxied up from the station, struggling with a full gunny sack and several heavy suitcases containing what I needed to set up my dorm room. Upon reaching the uptown shopping area adjacent to the college campus, I made my first prophetic encounter with a U.M. student. The young man, with tousled hair and a strained look on this face, stopped me to find out if I knew where he could buy an alarm clock. Knowing nothing about the town, I glanced about and pointed him toward what appeared to be a rather busy drugstore. He shook his head, saying that he had already depleted the store's entire stock of alarm clocks. Apparently he had been forced to buy a new clock every day the week before after throwing one across the room each daybreak as it sounded its alarm for the very early morning tough placement exams. As I left him to his search, I had only one thought: I was in for it!

An Oriental Art specialist colleague of my father's, Professor James Plummer, put me up for several days while I explored the university and performed the usual orientation tasks. I was fortunate; this gentleman and his family would remain my "local family" throughout my college years.

As incoming students, we were given physical exams. We were further evaluated as we ran a half mile on the indoor track, and swam a number of laps in the pool. As a result, we were assigned to a required physical conditioning program for our freshman year which was tailored to our individual needs. I later learned that Michigan pioneered this physical evaluation of incoming college students and the National Institute of Health promoted the approach nationally.

Our speech and reading ability was also evaluated. Some students were sent on for further examination or remedial training. I was sent to have my speech tape recorded, and was surprised to learn that the recording would be stored in school archives as an example of one of the Eastern U.S. accents, and be used by the academic department, which was studying American regional speech patterns.

Course selection was straightforward since I had arrived with the clear goal of pursuing the Marine Engineering track. Courses for all incoming engineering students were mostly proscribed for the freshman year, regardless of what branch of engineering we were headed into.

I was also placed in an English evaluation program, so that the engineering faculty could assess my writing and language skills. Thanks to Exeter's strict training, I breezed through in a month, and was happy to learn that I was excused from further course work in English. Many of my less fortunate colleagues were hustled into a crash course in writing where they remained until cleared by the faculty. My French credits had also been transferred from Exeter, which allowed me to bypass foreign language study at the college level. All of this would later give me enough credit hours to get my degree in time and enter military service upon graduation.

I scheduled my courses with classes that started at 8:00 A.M. when I could. I figured that this might be useful in keeping a lighted fire under me. I quickly discovered that this was good idea since I had the advantage of attending classes that were not crowded. It proved mighty difficult later during wartime, however, when our beloved President Roosevelt enforced a compulsory double Daylight Savings Time to provide a longer workday and enhance wartime production. Since Ann Arbor is in the western end of our time zone, I found myself going to classes before the sun came up.

I was assigned to an advisor, a senior professor in the Metallurgical Engineering Department. During our first meeting, I asked him why a metallurgical man had been elected to advise me when my plan of study was in the Naval Architecture/Marine Engineering Department. His wonderful reply was something like, "My job is to see that *your* department is doing well by you. I would not take on a student in my own department."

All incoming freshmen were assigned rooms in dormitory quadrangles. I had requested that I be given a friend from Exeter as a roommate. The two of us shared a spartan, but entirely adequate single room unit in a three-floor dormitory building housing perhaps 75 male undergraduates.

Our quadrangle of dormitory buildings was a definite social unit (like the "Houses" at Harvard and the "Colleges" of Yale), each with a name to identify it but with no unity of the area of education represented. There was a fairly complete and strict code of behavior involving practical matters such as quiet hours, permissible visitors, and when to be in at night.

Each dormitory was overseen by a house mother who was very much in charge, always aware of what was going on, and surprisingly helpful. I found myself quite close to two of them. (One of them turned up in a similar position at Wellesley College after the war, and played a significant role building up my post-war dating life!)

Each dormitory had its own dining commons with sit-down meals. Waitstaff served the meals, except for the morning buffet breakfast. The food was remarkably good, somewhat favoring Midwest traditions.

ENGINEERING SCHOOL STUDIES

BASIC SCIENCES

The Physics and Chemistry Departments of the Liberal Arts and Sciences Division included some world-class faculty members. As engineering students, we were fortunate to have some of them as lecturers in basic science courses specifically oriented to the needs of engineers. These lecturers were limited to speaking in lecture-hall classes of several hundred students. The senior faculty members were supported by much smaller, discussion-style, parallel classes, taught by junior lecturers, many of whom were graduate students in various related fields. I found this a valuable approach that served my needs as a potential practicing engineer. The graduate school level lecturers proved to be particularly interesting.

Our mathematics instruction was also shared by faculty from both divisions of the university, but clearly directed toward the needs of engineering students. As I had experienced at Exeter, I again found myself challenged and not notably successful in this area of study, especially when taught by the senior faculty. The presence of junior, sympathetic graduate school lecturers thus helped me a great deal.

Later on, living somewhat dangerously, I took an optional course in differential equations given by the iconic provost of the University. This was mostly out of reverence for his support of the band programs I played in, rather than because I needed the particular mathematical skills addressed. In spite of my out-of-the-ordinary reasoning for taking the course, I emerged with a lot more admiration for the teacher. He was truly a symbol of what the university stood for.

ANALYTICAL STUDIES

These are the fundamental tools of engineering, and, as such, a critical part of a college-level engineering education. Strength of materials, structural design, and

A TRUE "COLLEGE JOE"

During orientation week, while still in my evaluation period at the school, I kept running into one fellow student, an incoming freshman about to study in the same course structure in the Naval Architecture/Marine Engineering Department that I, too, had planned. Amazingly, he was also one of the few incoming students from my hometown area. I was curious about him. He was clearly concentrating on how to "work" the college social scene.

He was short of cash, and sought any kind of job with the university. As a result, he arrived for school a week early to help the staff set up, organize and take photographs for student identification cards. His job was to sort out the letters and numbers used to spell out the name and college address of each student. His nefarious scheme was to take careful note of addresses of any attractive girls and record these with descriptive notes on the girls' appearance in his "little black book". This information was then available to the rest of us—for a price, of course—for the rest of the college year. Later on, I was fascinated to watch how successful this was in helping him meet college expenses while at the same time greasing the social wheels for him. He continued this practice at the start of each term throughout his years at the school. He was labeled the "facebook man" by his colleagues. This was long before the current Facebook rage appeared on the internet!

the understanding of engineering materials were addressed in courses widely required of almost all engineering students. In these courses, I found a real challenge; I did not easily understand them because of my inherent weakness in math, and the extensive memorization needed had also been historically difficult for me. I worked as best I could in all my coursework, and was able to produce grades that were better than I had expected.

Unfortunately, the critical course required in fluid dynamics and hydrodynamics presented a scheduling conflict. As a reward for my high academic record (I was both thrilled and relieved to be finally doing well at school!), I was excused from attending the classes, and I simply took the final exam. Later, when faced with the accelerated wartime schooling schedules, these credit hours further helped me to graduate on time for military service.

Naval Architecture and Marine Engineering (NA/MarE)

Of course, this is really why I came to Michigan. Until I arrived in Ann Arbor, I had not realized that these were two separate degrees, requiring slightly different course selections. I was not required to choose between them until my junior year since they had the same introductory course requirements. I chose the Marine Engineering option because I thought it would be of more use in the type of Navy duty that, by that time, I knew I was facing. Marine engineering study was essentially mechanical engineering with a few special areas of marine technology thrown in. The choice of closely following the broad mechanical engineering curriculum later proved to be definitely useful, not only for my stint in the Navy, but especially throughout my later civilian professional career which was not solely in the marine field.

Entering into the NA/MarE Department was something like joining a select club. As a group, we were set apart from many of the engineering students in other disciplines. I frankly suspect that our classmates in other curricula thought that our kind of engineering did not compare well with their own more popular engineering selections.

Unlike our colleagues, we studied for many hours in groups, making outsized study drawings of ship hulls that only we thought were beautifully shaped. The most fundamental aspect of dealing with the complex design of ships/boats, vessels, or other marine objects is to be able work with and understand the shapes that enable a vessel to become waterborne. We were suddenly thrown into the new, fascinating world of three-dimensional shapes, and introduced to the need to accurately describe and manipulate them. Drawings were done by hand, and the calculations done on paper—quite different from what is done today, as computer-aided design was yet to be invented. We learned how to draft, on a two-dimensional piece of paper, the extremely complicated three-dimensional curved shape of the body of a vessel.

We spent many hours, individually and in groups, hunched over the large 6 x 4-foot drafting tables in a monstrous room holding about 30 of them. The process was policed by an infinitely patient professor who watched over our shoulders, commenting helpfully on our every move. The drafting room remained open 24 hours a day to accommodate the needs of all 50-75 students in the department. Needless to say, that room and its attendant drafting process was an awesome institution for each of us, and the skill and long-suffering capability of the instructors seemed out of the ordinary. Producing a set of "lines" is well known in the trade as an ultimate challenge that represents an art, a science, and a display of very specialized engineering knowledge.

Next, we learned about vessel geometry and its effects on performance, vessel layout or functional design, and vessel structures. These steps were addressed in a series of increasingly comprehensive specialized courses, terminating in a senior thesis. Preparation of this thesis involved two-student teams, one from the naval architecture track and one from the marine engineering track, who then produced an integrated, complete preliminary design for a given vessel in enough detail that it could be turned over to a drafting crew to be made into a set of fabrication drawings.

Our coursework definitely prepared us well to begin work at a professional engineering level. With 20/20 hindsight, however, I feel that the business, managerial and operational aspects of the marine field were not addressed in meaningful detail, and would probably require more diversified education for a student pursuing a non-engineering marine career.

FACULTY ASSISTANTSHIPS

My principal professor in Mechanical Engineering had an extensive practice as a troubleshooter in the internal combustion engine industry. He brought to his students an understanding of what mechanical engineers could do to assist the manufacturing industry. He took some of us on as research assistants, where we did thorough literature searches in very specific, often arcane areas of mechanical engineering technology needed by him in his professional work. He rewarded us by giving us small incremental academic credits.

THE ENGINEERING HONOR SOCIETY

I became a candidate for Tau Beta Pi, the engineering honor society. My department head informed all 20 candidates to appear for an entrance exam the day before the swearing-in ceremony. We all turned up the next morning with great apprehension. Our dean was quite stern as he escorted our group into the examination room. He carefully explained that we had 1½ hours to complete the exam. The results would not be available until the next morning just before the ceremony. I sat down to a bluebook consisting of a set of test problems which, as far as I could see, were inherently impossible to solve in the time available. The exam had been quite skillfully written to reflect many of the classically difficult conundrums of engineering.

Well, of course it was all a sham. A masterful bit of hazing by our faculty! Furthermore, I was not clued in until the following day, so I'd had a long and sleepless night. I remain mystified as to how the sham was kept secret—things like that usually are leaked out between students!

NAVAL ROTC

BACKGROUND AND SELECTION

During the orientation period, just after arriving in Ann Arbor, I discovered that a Naval Reserve Officers Training Corps was about to get under way. There had been a well-regarded and successful Army ROTC there for years, but not an equivalent Navy group until the time that I arrived. I was immediately interested, so I applied. This was to become a very significant part of my college experience, and, of course, an important track to inevitable war service.

The Navy set a goal of 100 "Regular" cadets for the Corps. They also added 20 "Provisionals" that could fill out the ranks if and when any Regulars proved to be unsuccessful.

As applicants, we were given a thorough physical exam plus a thorough interview. I survived the application process and immediately went into conference with my advisor and NA/MarE faculty to see how the additional NROTC class work, study, and training activities could be shoehorned into my demanding engineering schedule. It was a relief to find out that the integration of the two programs had already been well addressed by the faculties involved, and enthusiasm for my entrance was voiced by all.

NAVY STATUS

When I started the NROTC program in September of 1940, it was 15 months before Pearl Harbor and the U.S. was not yet at war. As a result, we were not on active duty and were classed as Naval Reserve Cadets. Accordingly, we were not required to be in uniform except during marching training on Saturdays and on certain Navy "show" occasions such as parades, or military dances. We were allowed to pursue our normal lives as students pretty much as the non-cadet students were.

All this suddenly changed when I woke up early one Sunday morning and, listening the radio while getting ready for the day, heard that Pearl Harbor had been attacked. We had all known that U.S. involvement was imminent, but none of us could have imagined that it could come in that horrific form. Within hours, we were notified by telephone that we had been put on active duty.

From that point on, the Navy picked up all our living and college tuition expenses. We were required to be in uniform at all times. The Navy also kept a sharp eye on us to be sure that we were upholding our grades and good behavior.

As a Naval Reserve Officers' Training Corps Cadet.

Eventually, more and more military groups (such as many hundreds of Navy V-5 officer trainees and Army language trainees) were assigned to the University. In response, the Michigan NROTC group was spread out into various college dormitories and given duties as cadet officers over all incoming trainees, and even over officer candidates from other military services. My roommate and I were assigned to organize a Navy marching band to be available to nucleate the weekend marching maneuvers and miscellaneous parades. I, of course, landed the job of bugler, so I was first up in the morning and last to bed at night, as well as generally on call for various occasions throughout the day.

PROGRAM

The NROTC educational program consisted of one course titled "Naval Science" each semester. This gave me 1½ credits per semester, requiring about two class hours each week. There were also occasional special sessions in the evenings, some weekend maneuvers, and two summer cruises of two weeks each. The subject matter of the program was a classic mixture of the old and the new. Longstanding Navy traditions were drilled into us, as well as the latest developments in warfare technology.

NROTC SUMMER CRUISES

The two summer cruises introduced our cadet group to life on board ship. In peacetime, these cruises were unusually informative, often involving overseas experiences. In our case, because it was wartime, we were limited to cruises on the Great Lakes, out of Chicago.

There were two rather unusual aspects to our particular cruises. We were aboard a vessel with a notorious history and we were in the company of a most unusual naval vessel.

Our ship had been involved in a tragic accident many years previously, while she was serving as a ferry in the Chicago area. Apparently she was near the scene of some sort of event that attracted the attention of her passengers, who rushed to one side of the vessel, causing it to list (tip) to one side, throwing passengers into the water, causing many fatalities. I had been brought up with the maritime lore that, once a ship had had bad luck, it was classified as a "Jonah" and condemned to a further life of bad luck. Of course, this is unreasonable, but it kept haunting me throughout the cruises.

Our assignment during the cruises was to accompany a vessel that fascinated me. It was a steam-powered side-wheeler, built probably more than 50 years previously, but recently converted to an aircraft carrier used for training naval aircraft crews in the difficulties of operating off a modern naval carrier. It was an amazing combination of the old and the new.

The Navy in Washington had apparently put real focus on the advent of this program at Michigan by assigning a very senior four-striped Captain (soon to become an Admiral) to head it up, aided by a stellar collection of Naval Academy commissioned officers, plus a staff of very senior Non-Commissioned Officers (NCOs). I imagine that the emphasis the Navy put on this startup may have been generated by its long history of close relations with the NA/MarE department at the University.

SOCIAL AND COMMUNITY LIFE AT COLLEGE

GENERAL SOCIAL STRUCTURE

My social life revolved around my NROTC cadet friends, plus the student body of the NA/MarE Department. Some of these friendships turned into lifelong relationships. It had become clear when I entered college that, as freshmen, we were encouraged to make our own way both academically and socially, not necessarily directed by tradition, who we were, or where we were from. I found this refreshing after my prep school experience.

Fraternities were the exception, however. That fraternities even existed at Michigan turned out to be an unexpected problem for me. The fact that I had come from Exeter more or less "paired" with Jim Conant, my roommate, old Cambridge friend, and son of the then President of Harvard, proved to be a complication, not an inspiration. Apparently, those social-climbing fraternity recruiters were aggressively seeking Jim. It became quickly obvious that they thought they could reach him through recruiting me. They had it all wrong. In no way was I any influence over the strong-willed Jim. I had taken a careful look at fraternities, allowing myself to get into a quasi-test, pre-membership relationship with one of them. I soon realized the life-long, social ladder-climbing emphasis inherent in the fraternity, and I quickly backed away. Jim was wiser than I. He stayed out of the whole mess.

DATING

As I had not attended a coeducational high school, I came to Ann Arbor as a bit of a bumbling, unskilled guy in the area of dating. This was the first time in my life that I found myself so close to such a great group of young women, and I felt ill-equipped to deal with them. My first misadventure was to win a lottery (of all things), rigged up by students in the School of Engineering, in which the prize was a date with the sole female engineering student in our class. To my utter amazement, I won the lottery drawing, which proved to be a highly publicized event. Instead of being happy about it, however, I found myself very uncomfortable and had a really hard time dealing with it. Luckily, she was a decent sort, and took it all jovially. I never dated her a second time in the years we were in school together, although we certainly remained good friends. She became far too popular to be within my reach!

Luckily, the code among my gang of engineering students and NROTC cadets was to introduce the girls that they knew to those of us less socially-gifted colleagues. This helped a lot. I eventually ventured out on my own since the university was pretty well socially organized to promote dating.

While serving as part of the uniformed color guard at a swank NROTC dance, I spotted a very attractive, blond, second-generation Swedish student nurse from the heavily Scandinavian farming area of Nebraska. She appeared as the date of a cadet, a good friend of mine. Sometime after that night, I asked him to introduce us and got permission to take her out. That was the beginning of a wonderful friendship with her that lasted throughout the last three of my college years.

She and I often studied together at the library, especially when preparing for difficult exams. We attended church, sports, lectures, and movies together, and danced together almost every Saturday night at the Student Union where the university regularly maintained an open ballroom with a standing big dance band. She left her mark on me, and I owe her a lot. She fulfilled the role of a companion in a highly charged college social community where I felt my limitations.

Sadly, she was later lured away from me by an MD student. I received the news in a "Dear John" letter when I was overseas with the Navy, and hence defenseless. Later, I consciously sought to find someone like her by applying for an engineering fellowship after the war to Sweden. Ironically, it was during that fellowship in Sweden where I met my beloved American wife to be!

EXPOSURE TO RELIGION

The City of Ann Arbor harbored the Episcopal Cathedral, which was the diocesan headquarters of the Ann Arbor region. It had a superb all-male choir, in true Church of England tradition. I happily joined the choir for my freshman year. The director was George Faxon, a colleague of famed organist Virgil Fox and a friend of Leonard Bernstein from their Tanglewood summer school days. He was an inspiring choir director, a brilliant organist, and a kind personal voice teacher as I studied the gentle art of church choir singing. He later turned up in Boston as head of the Organ Department at the New England Conservatory of Music and the organist at Trinity Church where I was lucky enough to continue to see him occasionally.

I next vowed to broaden my exposure to include a variety of Christian denominations. My girlfriend had been brought up in a strict Lutheran tradition. She was thoroughly fed up with that church and all that it stood for, and agreed that exploring other denominations would be a good idea. We attended a service at a different church each week, not becoming formalized members of any of them. This, along with the Catholic service experiences given to me by our cook at home, set me up well when I later became an assistant to a Navy Chaplain while overseas, an experience that I later valued highly.

MUSICAL ACTIVITIES

Opportunities for participating in music were numerous, and I jumped in with both feet. I kept music as an extracurricular activity; I had already decided that music was not to become my professional future. As at Exeter, I chose not to take any courses in it, except for auditing one choral music course, as I wanted my academic efforts to concentrate on my engineering education.

I found myself highly satisfied by participating, playing, and performing rather than studying music. Music provided a supportive outlet for me as a student immersed in an intense, engineering, pre-active duty education.

A False Start: The Marching Band

Although I didn't know it before coming to Ann Arbor, the university had always been famous for its marching band. During introductory conversations with the engineering school faculty, I was encouraged to participate.

Shortly after my arrival, I went to the music building to audition for the band. As I approached, I was overwhelmed by what I heard coming through an open window. A cornet player inside was playing some of the virtuoso Clark solos, including "The Flight of the Bumblebee", at such a high speed and degree of proficiency that I thought, shocked, it was surely impossible for a person to play this well. Believing this would likely be the individual who was waiting to audition me, I panicked, turned around, and ran away, ending any possibility of playing in the band my freshman year!

Little did I know that Michigan was the music school to which our national military service bands (such as the U.S. Navy, Marine Corps, and Army Bands) sent their first chair players to get Masters degrees. I learned later that I had most likely overheard fellow student Ray Crisara, then first chair trumpet of the U.S. Navy Band, who had been sent to become a graduate student. Ray later became first chair in the Metropolitan Opera Orchestra.

University Chorus

During my freshman year, as I did not play for the marching band, I turned to the university's chorus, a safer musical arena for my first year in college. The chorus had 125-150 voices, and rehearsed and performed in the Hill Auditorium. We had the good fortune to have Thor Johnson as director just before he moved up to become conductor of a major U.S. orchestra. He was a masterful and sympathetic musician.

The chorus performed an annual series of Messiah concerts accompanied by the university's symphony orchestra just before Christmas, which was regularly sold out to Michiganders from all over the State. They also did two concerts with the Philadelphia Orchestra during the annual weeklong May Music Festival (one conducted by Eugene Ormandy, the other by Thor Johnson), plus two more local programs. One year, we sang Honegger's "King David" at the May Festival. It has always been one of my favorites.

Roger McAleer, my senior year roommate, turned out to be noteworthy in several unusual ways. When Maria Callas, the rather unusual coloratura opera diva, turned up several times to perform in the May Music Festival in Ann Arbor, he was the only student that could be found willing to provide "dog walking" services for her pet lion cub.

A Real Start: The Marching Band

At the beginning of my sophomore year, I drummed up my courage, scheduled a trumpet audition, and *went*. I then happily joined the marching band. I ended up as second or third chair in the trumpet and cornet section. This turned out to be an extraordinary experience.

John Philip Sousa was the "saint" of all march composers, according to Michigan's band director. In Sousa's memory, some of the unusual instruments used in Sousa's era were available for our use. Most interesting for me to play was the high E-flat cornet which Sousa had traditionally used as the sort of "leading violin" of the otherwise brass/woodwind band. It is almost never used in bands today since it is a veritable beast to tame. These instruments led me to specialize in Baroque high trumpet playing later in life.

While in Michigan's band, I also had a lot of fun playing the heraldic trumpets, complete with heavy banners hung on them. We took these instruments out only on special occasions for show purposes. I was lucky that they were only occasionally required because Ann Arbor's poorly maintained streets produced some lip-smashing and nose-bumping problems as I stumbled in and out of potholes while marching and playing. Streets like this were common during the low-infrastructure maintenance era surrounding WWII. I often found myself cursing those darned heraldic trumpets!

Early on in my sophomore year, during one fateful Michigan Marching Band rehearsal, the director ceremoniously halted us, and summoned me forward. He took my instrument, sniffed it somewhat dramatically in front of the 225 member band, and announced to all that my trumpet was dirty. I was summarily dismissed and told to return after the instrument had been cleaned. I felt like I crawled out of that rehearsal room on my hands and knees. I hastened over to the chemistry laboratory where I poured muriatic acid through the old trumpet, producing a smelly, thick, yellow stream out the mouthpiece. Rinsing it off, I put the trumpet to my lips, and found to my surprise, that it produced a wonderfully loud, broad and bright new sound.

I returned to the band rehearsal. Again I was summoned forward by the director. This time I was asked to demonstrate the instrument. When the beautiful new sound burst out of my trumpet, he responded with a grin. Before I knew it, I had been appointed to be the "point man", to precede the marching band out onto the playing field at each football game in that 85,700-seat stadium. Then I was

HELEN TRAUBEL

Helen Traubel was at the top of her career while I was in Ann Arbor. A star in the worldwide opera scene, she made headlines as the "mascot" of one of the major league baseball teams in nearby Ohio as well as establishing a record as a much sought-after cabaret singer in the better nightclubs in her home state. She seemed the epitome of how a Hollywood opera star might be portrayed. She was obviously a lively character. While in the chorus in my freshman year, I had the great pleasure of witnessing Traubel in action while participating in the May Music Festival with the Philadelphia Orchestra, conducted by Eugene Ormandy.

I will never forget her appearance at our dress rehearsal in the monstrous Hill Auditorium. She burst in through the rear door of the stage ceremoniously, swooping down through the chorus seated on the risers on the stage, kissing everybody as she progressed. She was sporting an enormous, wide-brimmed floppy hat. Arriving finally at the front of the stage alongside Ormandy, she grabbed the brim of her hat and frisbeed it off into the audience seats where it lifted itself up and flew for a good 50 feet. Next she turned around and literally lifted Ormandy off his feet into the air and kissed him. Through all of this, we hollered, cheered, and clapped. She then repeated the kissing attack on several of the much-embarrassed, pleased but blushing first-chair players. In the concert the next night, her musical skill and exuberance were contagious, and the audience loved her.

to play the bugle solo for the raising of the flag. Being point man was exhilarating, and it also proved to help tame my stage fright in the years thereafter.

REVELLI AND HIS BRAIN STAFF now turn to a complex arrangement for the Michigan-Indiana game. It shows the Axis on the left, Allies on the right and V for Victory in the center. They determine what moves each man has to make to arrive at the correct position, then instructions are written.

I am third from the left, with William Revelli, our band director, fourth from left, next to me. Detroit Free Press (November 14, 1943).

Happily, the marching band was held in high regard in the university, among faculty as well as students. The provost of the university himself was a great supporter, and took on the band as his personal pet. Against all odds, he had fought to give academic credit to students serving in the band. He even went so far as to convince the graduate-level Business School into giving academic credit to its students who worked out the individual marching directions. These students, with whom I also worked, designed and calculated the specific steps each band member took to create letter and other formations on the field during games. Again, this was the era before the availability of computers which finally today make the frustrating and time-consuming process relatively easy.

The provost also arranged for the Buick Division of General Motors to sponsor one trip each year for the whole band to support the football team in an away game. This process resulted in an especially noteworthy occasion in which the person arranging rail transport for the band to New York City scheduled the band to disembark their train underground at Grand Central Station right at the height of Friday afternoon commuter rush hour. Blocked by an impenetrable crowd of commuters, and worried about how many students he'd lose in simply getting 225 college students up the stairs, through the terminal and out the door, the band leader quickly pulled the band into formation at train side. He immediately called up that famous Michigan football fight song, "Hail to the Victors". The crowd enthusiastically parted, cheering and waving the playing band up, onwards, and out of the station. This incident received some surprising national publicity, due to a picture on the front cover of Time Magazine.

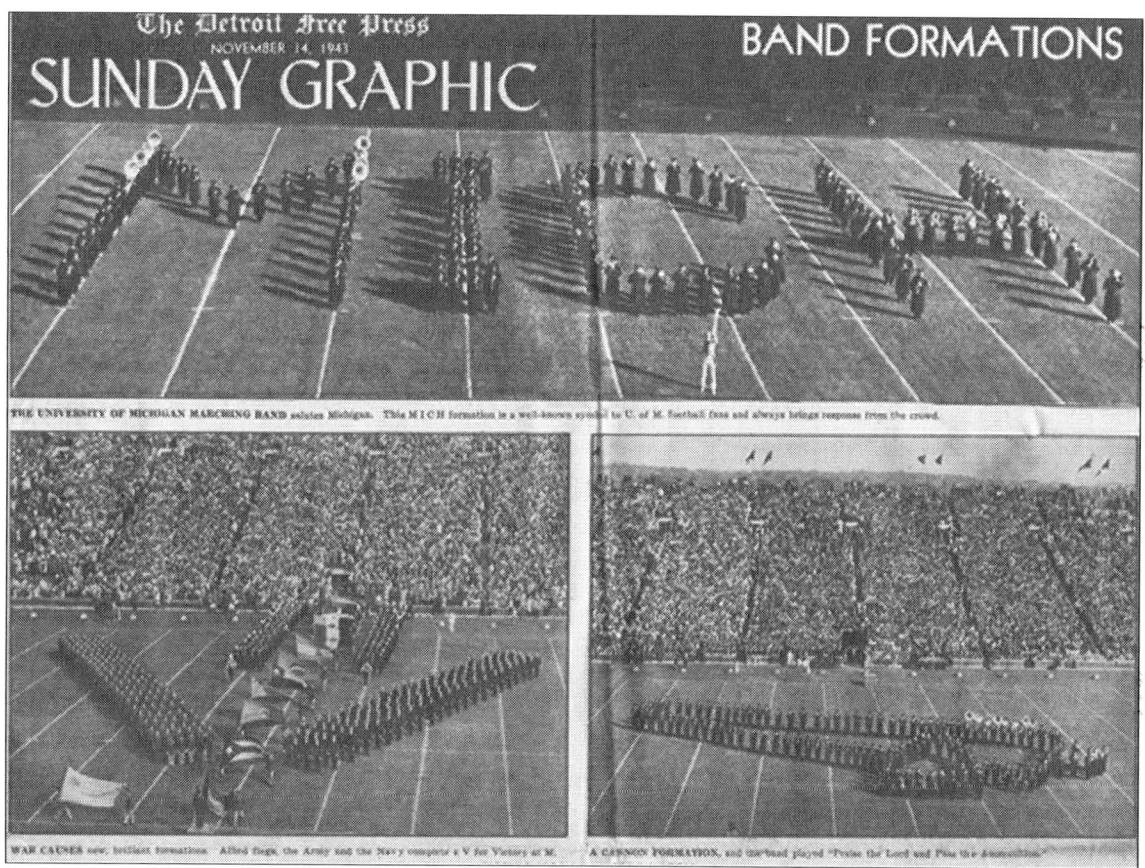

The University of Michigan Marching Band. Detroit Free Press (November 14, 1943).

During the two and a half years I played with the band, I had great fun. I took on more and more responsibility, composing, arranging and playing new so-called "fight fanfares" which had always been crowd pleasers. They were 10 to 20 seconds long, rousing tunes in which the crowd joined, clapping in time. They were played by a select choir of five to ten brass instruments after noteworthy happenings during games. This resulted in a battle between me and the band director who continually accused me of not honoring what I considered "time-worn" harmonization protocols. Of course I was bent on introducing modern big dance band sounds!

SYMPHONIC BAND

During the football off-seasons, I played second or third chair trumpet in the symphonic band, consisting of about 100 players. We did several concerts a year in the over 4000-seat Hill Auditorium. We had the good fortune to work under some of the great visiting band directors from other parts of the country, like Ferdie Grofé of "Grand Canyon Suite" fame and the conductor (whose name I don't recall) of the Eastman Wind Ensemble.

SUMMERTIME MUSIC TEACHERS SUPPORT THE BAND

The University of Michigan music school was flooded each summer with school teachers obtaining credits for advanced training or seeking recertification. The Music Department organized a standing band of 50-75 players for the teachers to use to improve conducting skills or to check out their new compositions. I welcomed the opportunity to participate during the two summers I was in summer school in Ann Arbor. The engineering faculty made it possible by providing me with some special scheduling breaks. The band met each weekday and was made up mostly of music majors. Music school students were even paid, although I was not so privileged since I was in the School of Engineering. To qualify, we were required to play a minimum of three different instruments so that there would be some flexibility in the instrumentation available. I played B-flat and E-flat trumpets, as well as baritone horn and the mellophone.

ADVENTURES AND MISADVENTURES IN HILL AUDITORIUM

I ended up with a few unusual, adventurous assignments in the Hill Auditorium. Once, I was asked to stand in the rear door of the stage, which had been cracked open enough for me to relay the conductor's arm signals to an offstage orchestra. More than once I was also assigned the nasty job of turning on the auditorium's heat early in the morning of rehearsals and concerts in order to bring those whopping big (up to 32 foot long) organ pipes up to playing temperature.

I was also asked to perform the questionable task of climbing up into the so-called "echo organ" high in the dome ceiling, to report down to the stage while Ferdie Grofé himself was conducting a rehearsal of his Grand Canyon Suite. The idea was to determine whether the soloists were standing properly in the focus spot of the acoustic shell. Amusingly, high up in the ceiling of the enormous auditorium, I found that I could even hear the metallic squeak of the poorly lubricated English horn key in its ever-familiar solo as composer Grofé himself was rehearsing on the stage.

I miserably flunked out of one job, however. I was asked to "pull stops" for the organist (i.e. manipulate the draw knobs on the monstrous, five-manual organ). This was terribly frustrating and too complicated for me. This organ was built by the Farrand & Votey Company in 1893 for the Columbian Exposition in Chicago and moved to University Hall at the University of Michigan in 1894.

Navy Band at Michigan

When all branches of the U.S. military started moving some of their officer training programs into the university, my roommate, who was a drummer, and I were singled out to form a Navy marching band to support the marching maneuvers for the swelling ranks each Saturday morning. We were able to field about 75 Navy trainees for a rather good group.

Navy Marching Band and University of Michigan band marching down the pothole-laden streets of Ann Arbor. Notice the Army uniform-clad guest participants.

Both my roommate and I continued as active members of the University's main marching band, but we were frankly sick and tired of the trend of college marching bands trying to march competitively faster and faster each year. To us, it looked more like silly dancing than marching. He came up with a brilliant solution. He went to a local museum and ferreted out a collection of Civil War marching band drum cadences that were so complicated that nobody could play them fast. That returned our band to a martial marching clip of 120 steps per minute.

Together, we instituted another innovation by excluding woodwind instruments, except piccolos, from our newly-formed Navy band so that we could replicate our favorite British marching band sound.

At one point, we got into difficulty when the Athletics Department of the university built a 12-foot high brick wall around the football practice field to keep opposing teams from spying on Michigan's new plays. The field and its wall were at one end of the playing field complex, right next to where we performed our military marching drills. The new wall, it turned out, acted as a sound reflector, echoing our marching band cadences back into the troops behind us with a slight delay in the beat. The troops at our rear were always inevitably out of step with the band.

The Navy hired a group of the Chicago Bears football team players as marching instructors. It turned out they were more than tough on our out-of-step marchers. The footballers clearly didn't understand why our comrades were consistently out of step. A fracas developed each Saturday until we were forced to change the locale of our marching drills.

We received an unexpected boost when one or our staff Naval officers quietly suggested that he could arrange transfers into our band from other Big Ten schools if we were shorthanded in any of our instrument sections. Frankly, we never dared to pursue that advantage. It was comforting to know, however, since we purposely overdid the number of trombones so we could have two rows of 'bones at the head of the band for show purposes. We also succeeded in having a full third rank of sousaphones. We never had to recruit additional players, as somehow they enthusiastically kept coming out of the woodwork voluntarily.

CHORAL LITERATURE SURVEY COURSE

The Music Department at Michigan had a course that fascinated me. It consisted of assembling a working choir to sight-read choral music starting way back at the Gregorian chant era and going the whole way up through to music of leading contemporary composers. This study choir met four days each week for one class period (50 minutes). Additionally, it assembled in the college radio station on Sunday mornings and performed a hymn service, sight-reading perhaps five to eight hymns with only a start-and-stop rehearsal and look in advance to assure that the order of the program and associated cues were fully understood. This was truly a confidence generator for the singers. The course was required for all the students in the music school except the vocal performing students whose voices were assumed to be too sensitive to survive the drill. Participants were given academic credit for their efforts after passing some stiff examinations.

> ### DEVELOPING MY "CHOPS"
>
> *As result of bugling in the early morning, playing in various marching band procedures, often followed by playing for evening dances, and ending with taps bugling duties near midnight, my marathon-like schedule did much to improve my "endurance chops" for trumpet playing. This became very useful later when participating in Baroque oratorios.*

I was welcomed by the music faculty, especially since I was not fussy about which range I sang in–countertenor, first tenor, baritone or bass. My Naval Architecture/Marine Engineering faculty gave me enthusiastic permission to audit the course. It was a wonderful experience, and provided me with a new group of friends. I only did it for one semester, but that was surely adequate to get the full benefits from the exercise.

MY VENTURE INTO THE DJ WORLD

As a result of my exposure to Benny Goodman during the summer between prep school and college, and also of my participation in playing dance band music at Exeter, I had collected an extensive library of big dance band recordings and assembled a good personal high fidelity public address sound system. I hired myself out as a disc jockey for the many small dances held at fraternities, sororities and residence halls. This gave me a healthy amount of pocket money. It also got me out into a broader social world than I was already awkwardly functioning in. It was particularly convenient because I could take my date along with me.

SPORTS

INTRAMURAL HOCKEY

I played on an intramural team representing my dormitory. This was pretty serious hockey, played at ungodly hours (like at 1:00 a.m.) because of the limited ice time available. Even though it was an intramural sport, it was played at a high enough skill level that I had a difficult time, although I definitely enjoyed the experience.

INTERCOLLEGIATE SAIL RACING

Michigan had already established a good record in this sport, having achieved top ranking among midwestern schools in the well-known international league named the Inter-Collegiate Yacht Racing Association (ICYRA). The prominence of Michigan in this sport was due to the fact that the NA/MarE courses had historically attracted serious sailing-oriented people from all over the world who were on their way to practicing marine professions.

A two-mile-long lake about six miles outside of Ann Arbor provided the venue. A student-run, student-financed, faculty-overseen sailing club had been organized which, in turn, spawned a team to represent the university. The sport was officially recognized and encouraged but not yet subsidized by the University. All costs, including travel away to regattas all over country, were met by student members. The activity attracted a particularly dedicated and unusually competent group of students and performed extraordinarily well, in spite of its "impoverished cousin" position with the school.

The sailing club really was the equivalent of a fraternity for me, and in some ways superior to a fraternity in my mind since it had a real *raison d'etre*. We traveled to about five away regattas each year, primarily on the East Coast. We were lucky to have three to five skippers who already were world-class regatta champions. That select group attained for us a good performance record in most inter-collegiate competitions. My job was primarily as crew to those experienced skippers plus a lot of maintenance on the boats and organizational work in support of the total effort.

Amusingly enough, in later years when Alice and I sought a place in the University where our paltry $50 annual alumni contribution could meaningfully go (other than into the depersonalized "general gift" program), we singled out the women's sailing team, with the result that we were bombarded with gratitude from the team, complete with thank you letters and gifts of monogrammed sweatshirts and other good things.

EDUCATIONAL RECORD

COURSE GRADE PERFORMANCE

Thanks to three important factors, I managed to end up with a percentile rating in the high 90s for my academic ranking in my Engineering School class. First, Exeter had obviously done an excellent job of preparing me for college, even though my grades there had not been good. Secondly, I was studying in a field that really interested me and which I really enjoyed; and last, the

University of Michigan provided me a welcoming, encouraging, and stimulating environment in which to pursue a college education. This ranking gave me a lot of privileges. I was pleased to learn that my Michigan academic standing was forwarded back to Exeter, where, need I remind you, I had *not* done very well academically.

COLLEGE ERA SUMMERS

INTERNSHIP AT BATH IRON WORKS (BIW)

I wanted to increase my understanding of practical aspects of ship/boat construction following a very informative, two-summer apprenticeship building wooden boats in Ipswich, MA. As I was just completing my first year of NA/MarE studies at Michigan, I felt that I was a likely candidate to obtain a meaningful internship in a real shipyard. The Bath Iron Works, in Bath, Maine seemed a likely target since it was very busy building sophisticated vessels, including Navy destroyers, in a location relatively close to home. I inquired, and learned that I would be more than welcome.

Accordingly, I hustled up to Maine and just tumbled into ideal living arrangements. I found an excellent place to bunk and a boarding house where I could get meals. My living space was within close walking distance of the shipyard and was owned by a widow in need of someone to help with house maintenance as her son had just married and moved away. She was a mother figure to me through both summers I was there, and she was most thankful for the help that I willingly provided.

The boarding house which provided my meals was just down the street, right next to the shipyard. It was classic, and right out of Hollywood's old "situation" movies. Approximately ten souls ate two meals a day there, and a box lunch for each noon meal at the yard was provided as needed. The lady who cooked for and ran this operation was an extraordinary individual in her mid-60s, tough as nails, resilient, and amazingly proficient at her job. The characters who consumed her meals were all hourly workers at the shipyard and were a fascinating potpourri of personalities. It was both an enjoyable and rewarding experience for me.

INTERNING AS A SHIPFITTER

My first summer, in 1941, was spent assigned to a shipfitting crew. "Shipfitting" was usually defined as outdoor work on the launching ramps, actually erecting the preformed metal shapes initially fabricated in the indoor shops to form the ship hulls.

In keeping with the long-established traditions of shipyard labor organization, a typical crew consisted of just under 10 men, experienced in their trade, who remained working together—a team under the direction of a single sub-foreman or crew chief. Historically the work was first broken up into single identifiable tasks by supervisors. Individual crews would then bid competitively against each other to obtain, in a sense, a "contract" to perform each well-defined task. My crew chief was somewhat secretive about this subject.

I was fortunate to have a crew chief who was an inspiration to work for. He was a member of the principal family from nearby Bailey's Island of local swordfishing fame. He knew his trade well, was extremely demanding, and surprisingly likable. Happily he was a good teacher as well, which is what I really needed.

I was given the questionable additional job of occasionally taking over the supervision of the starting line of the University of Maine football team that Bath Iron Works typically hired for the summer, ostensibly as the shipyard's donation to the broader community. These footballers' idea of a day's work was to put a heavy steel beam over their shoulders and run back and forth for the full length of the shipyard. I was supposed to redirect their energies into productive work towards building the ships. I am embarrassed to admit that I did not perform very well at that particular task!

INTERNING AS AN OUTSIDE ENGINEER

My second summer, 1942, proved to be a golden experience for any budding marine engineer. I was an "Outside Engineer," defined as a person working on the ships' machinery.

I was assigned to assist an old-timer who had an unbelievable job. He was responsible for the placement of the many brass identification labels on each one of the 1500 or so valves scattered throughout the full length and breadth of the ship. These labels identified the function of each valve of the ship's operating plant. We had to know with certainty exactly where every valve was, as well as exactly what it did.

The old-timer to whom I was apprenticed was probably the only person in the shipyard who knew the destroyer's machinery complex that well. He had two problems; firstly, he was a difficult old codger, and secondly, one hand and wrist had been badly mangled in a shipyard accident many years before. He needed support from a sympathetic assistant. Happily, he was basically kind, very understanding, and definitely profoundly knowledgeable. We also had an important characteristic in common as he, too, had been brought up working in the wooden boat yards.

I cannot think of a better assignment for an interning marine engineering student, since Navy destroyers have very sophisticated machinery systems and are incredibly complicated. In accomplishing this task, I got to know and understand the vessel's machinery suite very well.

DESTROYER TEST AND DELIVERY TRIPS OUT OF BATH

In peacetime, newly-launched destroyers from BIW were allowed a leisurely test and shake-down period in a nearby coastal bay in Maine. Because of the war-induced threat of submarines, we had to perform all of our shake-down operations within the confines of our river, which was closed off by antisubmarine nets. BIW was then responsible for delivering the ship to the Boston Naval Shipyard for finishing off with the installation of her classified military gear such as gun fire-control equipment. The ship was delivered without Navy personnel, with only civilian personnel as crew, from Bath to Boston through submarine-infested waters.

During my second summer at Bath Iron Works, I received a rather scary assignment. I am not sure how it came about, but BIW management knew that I was in NROTC training at the University of Michigan, and I had been trained on the type of main armament found on destroyers–the five-inch, 38-calibre guns. BIW assigned me to prepare the guns that they installed and to organize their manning during the delivery trip. There was no sophisticated fire control system aboard yet since that was militarily classified and awaited installation once the ship reached the Boston Navy Yard. So I was responsible for putting the guns into a "manual control mode". I could only do that by bore-sighting on the most applicable target on the river's shoreline. This is more or less like preparing an astronomical telescope to find a star in the star-crowded night sky. I then had to pick and train a gun crew. My candidates for assistance were local farmers and fishermen accustomed to hunting, Maine-style, with shotguns. Our newly built ship was exactly like that, without its eventual fire-control gear. Here I had a lot of faith in our crew.

The Navy then arranged to safeguard these delivery trips by assigning an anti-submarine vessel to convoy us and stationing a blimp close above us for the trip. Everything went safely, thank goodness.

INTERNING AS A DECKHAND ON A FISHING TRAWLER

One week before college started at the end of my second summer at the Bath Iron Works, my college roommate, Bill Maccoun, and I arranged to go out to the deep-sea fishing banks from Portland, ME. We wanted to experience the offshore life of the typical fishermen and better understand the role of their special type of vessel. This proved to be a challenging experience.

We made a deal with the owner of the O'Hara fleet of deep-sea trawlers in Portland to take us on as unpaid deck hands for one week. The vessel was a conventional bottom-fishing, side trawler of wooden construction, about 90 feet long. It was built probably in the early 1930s in Maine. It was crewed by a skipper plus about four hands. I was given the spare bunk in the skipper's quarters. (It was so cold I ended up sleeping with my mattress on top of me, as I had not brought the correct clothes.)

We ran for four to six hours eastward out of Casco Bay to an area known for availability of redfish. I believe that the exact location was not divulged to us, probably to protect the secretive knowledge that experienced boat skippers keep to themselves about where best to fish. The trawl net, complete with its classic "doors" that hold the leading mouth open to scoop up the bottom-feeding ground fish, was immediately put over the side. After two to three hours, the skipper would judge that it was time to haul back the trawl which then was left dangling over the deck from the boom of the trawl derrick array.

Being the junior hands aboard, Bill and I were immediately dispatched to go underneath the swaying trawl net so as to untie the latch string and dump it. Usually, the first things that would fall out and often challenged our toes were the rocks and heavy detritus that had been inadvertently scooped up. Next came up to a half ton of slimy redfish intermixed with that infamous mixture of so-called "by-catch" fish, some of which are marketable and many of which are not. Once the fish were on deck we helped in sorting the haul. The marketable fish were then thrown, along with ice as needed, down through a hatch into the wet-well below.

We fished around the clock, relieved by intermittent half hour catnaps when we had completed sorting each trawl and the next trawl was on the sea bottom. The life was extremely challenging, especially since I suffered from severe seasickness, a curse which continued with me until the happy advent of the transdermal scopolamine patch years later.

After about three days of round-the-clock fishing, misfortune struck. One of the professional crew started having epileptic seizures. Upon consulting the Coast Guard medical team by radio, it was deemed more practical for our boat to return to shore than for them to attempt a hazardous helicopter rescue or to cause a delay by dispatching one of their small rescue boats out to us.

This short offshore commercial fishing session was a useful experience for Bill and me as we both were venturing into the complexities of naval architecture and marine engineering, fields in which commercial offshore fishing was an important component. This was also very useful to me later, in dealing with small Naval vessels in the service.

GRADUATION

I reached enough credits to graduate by the end of the first semester of 1944. A Navy commission and call to duty awaited me. With my girlfriend in tow, I took a train to Detroit, my first time in 3½ years, to have my uniforms selected and fitted. To my surprise, this was somewhat of an unexpected ceremony to go through, a special punctuation point, and a time which I will not easily forget.

Graduation ceremonies were held during the first week of February. The academic graduation was held in Hill Auditorium, followed immediately by the Naval commissioning ceremony in the smaller but more elegant auditorium connected to the graduate schools. I do not recall the details of the academic graduation, but it was a pretty staid event in view of the prevailing wartime conditions. My sister Margot, then a full-time performer, was the only family member able to be with me at the time. I am very grateful to her for her caring interest.

The commissioning ceremony was, interestingly enough, much more of a show than graduation. A distinguished, three-star admiral, the Director of the Navy's Bureau of Ships ("BuShips"), held forth with an impressive speech on the importance of education in developing a successful, technically qualified officer corps in the areas of national security served by BuShips.

With sheepskin in hand and an ensign's commission stripe on each uniform sleeve, I was more than ready to get under way.

My sister Margot Warner as a performer, in one of her publicity photographs.

IN RETROSPECT

After the questionable episode of the letter from Exeter to my parents limiting the Exeter faculty's "liability" for my not applying to Harvard, my family had been somewhat shaky about my decision to go to Ann Arbor. My mother, on the surface, was strongly supportive, and I believe that my father was at least sensibly quiet about the situation. While I now realize that I may have forfeited some of the advantages of continuing on in the Ivy League groove, Michigan really fit my needs at the time. It certainly helped advance me along maritime lines while the NROTC program set me up to enter a truly productive wartime duty assignment on an expedited basis. I found it to be an enormously satisfying and happy experience.

My family and I corresponded regularly while I was at college, and I think that my parents were quite happy with what they witnessed in my letters, and we truly and effectively communicated during that time. In the end, both parents and family ended up very supportive as I studied and ultimately graduated from the University of Michigan.

Like everyone, however, my parents were unfortunately limited as to how much they could travel during the war period, so that I did not have the privilege of a visit from them while I was at Michigan. My sister Margot did visit several times, bless her soul, and turned up for the annual May Festival musical week when Eugene Ormandy and the Philadelphia Orchestra were in town, and she got into the spirit of things very well. My cousin, Roger Warner, Jr., terribly busy with all that was going on at the Manhattan Project and with his development of invasion craft, also kindly made time to stop in Ann Arbor as he came through by train when going back and forth between East and West Coasts. He was enormously supportive. (By the time the war had ended, Roger became Director of Engineering in the Atomic Energy Commission as the USA sought peaceful uses of nuclear energy.)

The diversity of courses that I had completed was of course somewhat limited, due to how much time I had to complete my college training under the pressure to hurry into wartime service. It would have been a luxury to branch out into such fields as the natural sciences, social sciences, history, or liberal arts. I feel that I was educated, trained and experienced enough to start practicing marine engineering at a rather high level upon graduation, and was able to perform my subsequent repairship services effectively in the Navy. Michigan had certainly done well in preparing me to go into such work.

The cost of getting me through college was a true bargain by today's standards. The tuition for an out-of-state student at the time was, I believe, about $2,500 a year, while living expenses and college-related costs were perhaps an additional

ROGER S. WARNER JR. of Ipswich, director of engineering of the Atomic Energy Commission.

My cousin Roger.

$200-$300 per month. Furthermore, the Navy assumed virtually all my expenses starting from Pearl Harbor onward, so my parents really only had to support about one-third of my education. As this book is written, the cost at University of Michigan is for one year is $50,352, including room and board, for-out-of-state residents.

Michigan proved to be a very satisfying choice for me. I learned a great deal about my chosen field, and a great deal about myself. I was ready to get on with the rest of my life, and I was ready to go on active duty.

The Navy Marching Band playing in Hill Auditorium.

The NROTC Marching Band at University of Michigan.

In the shipboard machine shop, looking at the plans of equipment to be repaired. I am on the right, with several of the good men who, although they were assigned to work <u>for</u> me, they worked very much <u>with</u> me.

7

NAVY SERVICE

CHANGING MY ORDERS

Immediately after obtaining my commission as an Ensign at the University of Michigan during the last week in February 1944, I received orders to report to Destroyer Training School to qualify for engineering and deck officer duties. Almost all of my fellow cadets received similar orders, although I was one of the few who was offered joint deck/engineering qualification in view of my degree in Marine Engineering plus my NROTC training.

I was eager to obtain duty in a slot which could benefit from both my professional training and my shipyard experience, rather than be channeled into routine duty on destroyers. Thanks to my brother-in-law, Bob Bulkley, who was then a lieutenant in public relations for the Navy, I was able to schedule an appointment with a very senior officer in the Navy Bureau of Ships who interviewed me in considerable detail. He ended by literally asking me, "Are your bags packed yet? Can you leave immediately to go overseas?" I replied that I was eager to go and needed only a few days to finish getting ready. I was immediately booked to leave in a week, headed for active duty aboard a repair ship stationed in Scotland, perhaps the first of my NROTC classmates to go overseas.

A repair ship was a mobile facility that could fix a myriad of troubles or damage to vessels at sea or in port. To have been given this kind of duty seemed exactly what I had been preparing for. It looked like a perfect fit.

A SOBERING REALIZATION

I now realize that this change of assignment from Destroyer School to immediate duty on a repair ship may well have been a lifesaver for me. In my repair ship duty in the European Theatre I was significantly luckier than many of my NROTC cadet mates. Many lost their lives in the last few months of the war in the Pacific, primarily in the gruesome days of the suicide bombings of destroyers by the Japanese off Guadalcanal.

ENTER A SIZER

It was on my visit to Washington seeking new orders that I first met a bright young woman named Hilda Sizer. Hilda was dating my good friend and cousin Sturgis, and working in the War Department. They married less than a year later. Little did I know that Hilda, some day, would be my sister-in-law!

ACROSS TO THE EUROPEAN THEATER

Brother-in-law Bob saw me off on the S.S. Isle de France, leaving from Bayonne, NJ in the first week of March 1944. This ship, built in the early 1930s in France, had a distinguished record in the highly competitive trans-Atlantic passenger trade, and had recently been converted to a troop ship. By this time the S.S. Normandy was *hors de combat,* lying on her side as a fire-ravaged wreck inside a superliner slip on the west side of Manhattan. The S.S. Isle de France had the reputation of being about the best of the superliner fleet in terms of sea-kindliness to those aboard her due to her easy motion in a seaway, but was admittedly somewhat slower than the competing liners, performing a normal crossing from New York to Southampton in perhaps six days, versus four or five days for the leaders. She ranked behind the RMS Queen Mary, S.S. Bremen, and RMS Queen Elizabeth, the topflight luxury liners at that time. In total, however, we had the luck to draw a pretty fine vessel in which to make the trip.

Sturgis Warner, my cousin, who was like an older brother to me.

Many of us aboard had understandable fear, however, because our ship (like the other superliners) was making Atlantic crossings without the protection of naval ship escort in the era of intense German submarine activity in the North Atlantic. The rationale was that the superliners were fast enough to outrun the German submarines and their attendant torpedoes, and that escort flotillas would have slowed us down, thereby increasing our exposure to attack. I personally was never at ease about that particular strategic thinking, having been thoroughly brainwashed on the value of escorted transit. Happily, during the crossing our ship's crew observed a true awareness of the submarine threat by following an aggressive zigzag course. However, we welcomed the additional occasional presence of antisubmarine aircraft patrols overhead as we drew near the U.K.

Our faith in our security was somewhat challenged by continual Abandon Ship drills throughout the trip. These drills consisted of crowding all the troops on deck with their waistband inflatable life vests at the ready, not yet inflated. Invariably some clumsy individual would accidentally trigger his CO_2 inflation cartridges and bulge out suddenly at the waist. Since we were all standing shoulder-to-shoulder, of course, we got jostled like dominoes struggling to stay upright, a comical sight.

The Isle de France in normal peacetime had a passenger capacity of something over 1,500 people (versus 2,000 for the leading superliners). My guess is that we were loaded to 200-300% or so of that capacity with troops and their personal fighting gear. The manifest also included members of the top echelons of General Patton's U.S. Army troops. Officers rated housing in the upper deck cabins, while enlisted personnel were housed below in overcrowded conditions.

I was berthed in a cabin with 12-15 other officers where only two to four passengers would have been accommodated in peacetime. We were in bunks that were two to four high. The bunk over me was occupied by a fascinating army officer, General Patton's K-9 chief. He owned the kennel in the Midwest from which Lassie, of movie fame, had come. The original Lassie was the runt of her litter, and as such was essentially unsalable, so he made a bet with a neighboring kennel owner that she could be trained to be useful in the movies.

ARRIVAL IN SCOTLAND

At the end of our trans-Atlantic run, our troopship anchored near the mouth of the Firth of Clyde, off Greenock/Gourock, about 25 miles toward the open sea from Glasgow. The Firth widens out at this point so that it could well accommodate the large fleet of converted liners, cargo and naval vessels carrying troops and materiel for the oncoming invasion of continental Europe. The resulting fleet was an extraordinary, continually changing array of well over 100 major ships–the cream of the crop of the ocean fleets of the world. I was awed.

Unceremoniously I found myself taken ashore among a contingent of Patton's headquarters personnel. I was dispatched to Portpatrick, Galloway, Great Britain, to take the ferry across the North Channel of the Irish Sea to Belfast, Northern Ireland. Before I had a chance to look around Belfast, I learned that I should have stayed back at Greenock; my ship, the USS Melville, was there. I turned around and back I went to Scotland.

The trip between Scotland and Ireland and back again was an eye opener for me. That was the first time I had been on maneuvers, Army-style. We had to carry every bit of our own awkward baggage, not very effectively belted to our bodies, marching Army-style, everywhere we went. That was a bit of a chore for a Navy person like me, but even more for the poor civilian consultants who were burdened with trunks full of Patton's bureaucratic papers. One poor guy near me had old-fashioned steamer trunks full of engineering drawings from Lockheed to update the P-38 aircraft engaged in the war. Needless to say, most of my energies were spent helping him carry his trunks as well as my own gear. Finally, back in Greenock, I got aboard my ship, which was tied up at the town dock.

THE USS MELVILLE

My ship was the USS Melville (AD-2), nominally a Destroyer Tender, and one of the oldest ships still in commission in the U.S. Navy. Built in Camden, N.J. and commissioned in December 1915, it was the first ship in our Navy powered by geared steam turbines. The Melville was 417 feet long, with a 55-foot beam and a 20-foot draft. She displaced about 7,265 tons. Although built specifically to take care of destroyer-type vessels (hence the class AD, or "Auxiliary, Destroyer"), she had been used as a general repair ship during most of her later life and had a superlative record of achievement. In 1944, the ship was in remarkably good condition as only a repair ship, which can more or less "heal itself", could be. She held a complement of about 50 officers and about 350 enlisted personnel.

The USS Melville, one of the oldest active ships in the Navy during World War II.

I was brought aboard as the #3 officer in the Repair Department. Above me, at #1, was the Chief Repair Officer, a Lieutenant Commander with long civilian experience in the land-bound construction industry. Next, as #2, came a very senior Chief Warrant Officer (a "Mustang" or up-through-the-ranks warrant officer) who grew up solely in U.S. Navy repair duty. My top boss and I were both Naval Reserve officers while the Warrant Officer was, as expected, "regular Navy". I was the only one aboard who had formal marine engineering education and specific shipyard/boatyard experience.

The facilities aboard the Melville were widely capable, as one would expect, to meet the diverse requirements for repair of ships in remote locations. We had a completely equipped machine shop, woodworking and pattern making shop, nonferrous/ferrous foundry, instrument repair shop, electrical/electronic shop, sheet metal working shop, welding/brazing facility, optical repair shop, blacksmith shop, diving gear center, and more. It was also the home base for an outside (offsite) machinist crew. The boatswain's department (for rigging, hauling, lifting, etc.) was similarly extensive and diverse in capability. There was a complete medical and surgical facility aboard. Miscellaneous services such as payroll, chaplain, catering, personnel handling, and radio/telegraph/postal messaging were also available. To man this eclectic collection of services obviously required a diverse crew of specialists.

Quite frankly, the deck officer and mundane ship operating men were somewhat of a problem. (You didn't hear this from me!) The Navy had, not unexpectedly, decided that these slots on a noncombatant ship such as ours might safely be filled with some under-performing personnel in view of the fact that the ship was not going to engage in any shooting war. On the other hand, the repair personnel were, to a man, a really capable group.

PERSONNEL OF THE USS MELVILLE

Our captain was a Naval Academy graduate, probably in a class of the mid-1920s. Presumably this was going to be his last command.

There were many situations that developed aboard the USS Melville that resembled some of the famous Hollywood post-WWII farces about Navy shipboard life. During postwar reunions among the Melville gang, we often wondered whether the infamous later movie titled "Mr. Roberts" was based on the happenings aboard our ship. We actually had our version of Captain Queeg. Our skipper had his "sacred treasure", like Queeg's potted plant, which, in the movie, was methodically and repeatedly stolen from inside Queeg's cabin and ceremoniously thrown overboard, much to the skipper's extreme annoyance. Our skipper's "treasure" was a cast bronze statue of a pet animal. Luckily for us, we had the unusual shipboard ability to redo the casting in our foundry each time the statue was heaved over the side, each replacement costing us a lot of unnecessary work, time, expense and considerable annoyance for our hard-pressed repair crew.

Our initial executive officer (#2 in the "pecking order" aboard ship) was a Naval Reserve Officer, who, sadly, had not yet found help for his alcohol habit. When we eventually got to Weymouth, on the south coast of England, he concentrated almost full time on organizing and running the shoreside naval officers' club, an infamous drinking institution. He was replaced, in routine naval officers' rotation manner, by a very mature, sensitive and caring Reserve Officer who then skillfully guided us through the many ups and downs of shipboard life.

As the newest and youngest officer aboard the Melville, I was given a Cat o' Nine Tails, a mock ceremony for the most junior officer aboard.

The warrant officers were a most unusual group, not found on many ships of that era. In view of the level of professional competence needed to perform ship repair operations, the Navy assigned a group of warrant officers who specialized not only in repair, but so-called "deck" skills (rigging, salvaging – the skills of the boatswain) plus paymaster and Supply Corps services.

There were approximately 20 junior commissioned officers (Ensigns, Lieutenants Junior grade, and full Lieutenants, with an occasional Lt. Commander) aboard. These were typically officers designated USNR (for Naval Reserve), otherwise known as "90-day wonders" since most of them had been through no more than a 90-day training course to qualify for commission as an officer.

As I did not go to the Naval Academy, I was not automatically considered "Regular Navy", the term that describes those who plan a lifelong career with the Navy. However, with my college NROTC training, my Marine Engineering degree, and my commission directly out of college, I was considered by others to be "close to Regular Navy."

The non-commissioned officers (NCOs) were universally Regular Navy (i.e., career Navy) personnel with long histories in repair work. They turned out to be the most critical and useful people aboard. They taught me a lot and I am everlastingly indebted to them for their cooperation and patience with me, and their general "it can be done" attitude.

The 150 or so enlisted personnel who manned the repair and specialized service departments were also a rather extraordinary group. They were more skilled, more mature, more knowledgeable and typically older than I had seen in the bulk of the Navy when I was in NROTC training and at the Bath Irons Works. These men were mostly Reserve Navy enlistees, recruited from relevant civilian jobs such as railroad repair, journeyman machinist, and toolmaker. The remaining 75 or so ship's operating crew members were generally representative of what could be found elsewhere in the Navy. (By chance, we also ended up with some pretty good musicians with whom I sang and played in a dance band!)

I shared a cabin with a rather extraordinary person, the Assistant Chief Repair Officer, i.e., the #2 officer in the Ship Repair Department–obviously, the most significant department of this ship. He had probably 20 years service in the U.S. Navy and had achieved the relatively unusual rank of Chief Warrant Officer, the highest noncommissioned level in the Navy. He was a very difficult, enormously hardworking, profoundly experienced, and intensely "old Navy loyal" man. I worked hard to get to know him, to show respect to him, and to serve him as my boss. He returned my efforts by thoroughly backing me up through some rather difficult times.

The next cabin housed the senior surgeon, a very fine, sensitive and capable doctor, with the rank of full Commander in the Naval Reserve, perhaps 20 years older than I, who had only recently volunteered into active Navy service. It was unusual that, in spite of our differing backgrounds, ages and professions, we found much in common.

Probably the officer that I was closest to initially was the navigator, later to become Executive Officer (i.e., the next officer below the ship's captain). He was perhaps 10-15 years older than I, and a stalwart professional from the Boston world of finance. He was a true friend and an excellent handler of the people around and under him.

As expected in any military unit, there was a definite social structure based on rank and, using the British term, "rating". This was reflected in the location of living quarters and leisure spaces, as well as the makeup of eating groups, or "messes". The Captain lived in his own suite and often had his meals delivered there while meeting with or entertaining his immediate commissioned officer aides. The commissioned and warrant officers ate together in the so-called "officers mess", and were served by waiters, while the top NCO's (consisting of very senior chief petty officers) had their own messes. Enlisted personnel ate, cafeteria-style, in areas also serving as their leisure spaces.

I am sad to say that the U.S. Navy (at least on board the "Old Navy" style USS Melville), was far from integrated. Men of color were limited to serving meals and cleaning officer areas. There had never been any female members of the ship's company. Happily, much has changed since that time.

Because of their common goal and close-knit working conditions, the ship repair contingent came much closer to fraternizing among themselves than with the rest of the crew.

MY ROLE ON THE SHIP

My assigned role as #3 in the repair function also included a number of routine ship operation duties, such as assistant operating engineer when underway, daily watch standing, and taking turns at crew supervision.

Those in the commissioned officer corps of the ship were required to stand "watch officer in charge" duties on a rotating basis around the clock. Even though I had continual specialized ship repair responsibilities, I was required to take my turn at watch standing, which meant being just outside the deck cabins in a small hut on the main deck, armed with a 45-calibre hand gun and a boatswain's whistle, adjacent to a public address microphone, a telephone, and a log book. All this was located at the head of a stair-like boarding ladder that hung over the side of the ship, with the boarding stage at the bottom at water level. The watch-stander's tasks were to identify, greet, and dismiss all persons coming aboard or leaving the ship, to make general announcements to the crew, to monitor generally what was going on around the harbor, and to log certain key activities throughout the day. Since I did not drink at all at the time and hence had no continual need to go ashore to the officers' club, and since my repair duties required me to be available at any time, day or night, I was often sought out to fill in watch-standing aboard ship, substituting for other officers who went ashore.

Beyond my assigned duty as #3 repair officer, I sought (or in reality created) several additional voluntary roles such as assistant to the chaplain, surgical operating room assistant, band director, truck driver for special shoreside activities, bugler, and maintenance man for our own ship's repair needs.

BLACK MARK ON MY RECORD

Although I have never confirmed my actual record since leaving active Navy duty, I think that it must show one black mark on it, and that came from a very serious misdeed on my part. While serving as an operating room "go-fer" for my close friend, our Chief Surgeon, I was simultaneously acting as assistant to our Chaplain. In juggling these two concurrent roles, I made a grave error.

We had a young enlisted man on the operating table who had been seriously wounded in an accident aboard a small Navy vessel in our harbor. While performing gunnery practice using a 3" or 5" gun, the sailor had opened the breach of the gun too soon after it had been fired and was attempting to reload the gun with a fresh charge before it could cool down. The charge prematurely went off, tearing into his lower body. It was quite clear that he was likely to die. We were all hustling under the direction of the surgeon to try to save him.

His skipper, who had been only nominally overseeing the reloading, and accordingly was partly responsible for the accident, was anxiously watching our work in the operating room through a window in the door. Like a fool, I was too busy to remember to perform my chaplain duties of calling in a priest to perform last rites on our Catholic patient before the poor man died.

The victim's skipper reported my error and pushed to have my ship's skipper put me on official report. My skipper roundly scolded me. The event was then publicized to the ship's crew as an example of unbecoming performance on my part. This probably sits on my record somewhere deep in the bowels of Navy records. As far as I know, this black mark is the only one that I attained in my 5½ years of active Navy service. I will long remember the young man we tried to save that day and I regret that I did not give him the opportunity to receive his last rites, as I am sure he would have wished.

SHIP REPAIR ACTIVITIES WHILE IN SCOTLAND

Since the Firth of Clyde was the terminus of the trans-Atlantic run of American vessels servicing the European Theatre of Operations (ETO), and we were the only U.S. repair facility north of the Mediterranean, we were very busy patching up the wear and tear of the hard-pressed convoy vessels after they arrived from the stormy winter of the North Atlantic. Although the Firth of Clyde is a

The USS Melville, left, and two LSTs. The LSTs were the workhorses of the anticipated invasion of Europe, and were the ships we most often repaired. Ships came to us in all manner of disrepair and damage. Sometimes we had as many as seven tied up alongside of us. In order to get men and equipment to the farthest ship, we had to cross from ship to ship, an awkward affair as we carried our heavy gear and materials.

world-class shipbuilding area, we luckily were not called on to repair major war-induced damages on ships. We did a lot of what might be called "garage mechanic style" work on a variety of interesting vessels, both Navy and non-Navy, because we were situated at a major destination for ships of the world. We also helped local British ship engineering experts with repair problems peculiar to American vessels or shipboard equipment under their jurisdiction with which they were not particularly familiar.

Advent of the LST

Starting just before 1940, the U.S. Navy, in anticipation of the fast-emerging, beach-landing type of warfare, developed a novel type of ship: the Landing Ship Tank, familiarly known as the LST. The initial strategy was that the LSTs would be "one way carriers," serving to get men and materiel only to the warfare scene, with little significant duty thereafter. The basic design of the vessel, developed by the British, featured ease of rapid mass construction by almost any shoreside facility, even those not necessarily skilled in the art of shipbuilding. The more the newborn LSTs were used, however, the more the U.S. Navy realized how valuable this kind of vessel was as we faced the rapidly increasing need to transport men by sea to and from remote locations and to invade via beach landings.

To meet the initial requirements of easy manufacture and limited life expectancy, many compromises in design were made. One, in particular, drew us on the USS Melville into the fray. The propellers initially specified were to be made of cast iron, not the preferred bronze, reflecting the U.S. wartime shortage of copper (a major component of marine quality bronze). Marine engineers had long since determined that bronze was absolutely necessary as a metal for propellers. When used in salt water, the less expensive cast iron results in a self-destructing propeller due to pitting caused by cavitation (or vacuum-induced bubbles) on the blades of the propeller.

At the request of the Navy, the USS Melville and our Mediterranean-based counterpart (the only other US repair ship in the European Theatre of Operations) jointly developed a specialty for dealing with the flood of LSTs arriving from the U.S. with faulty propellers. We set up a production line process for changing over propellers *in situ* without the need to haul the vessels out ashore, since shoreside facilities were often not available or too busy. We brought the LST alongside our repair ship and lowered a platform from our ship into the water at the stern of the LST so that repair personnel could get at the propellers to swap off the cast iron propellers for new bronze ones. This was, at best, a tricky process because our designated outside machinists had to don full, old-fashioned, "hard-hat" diving gear (a ball-shaped, fully enclosed helmet as opposed to current open-face scuba gear) to work from the platform in surface wave-induced surging water. My job was to oversee this process which meant that I had to be on that platform in full hard-hat gear myself. We swapped propellers on perhaps fifty LSTs, with two propellers on each ship.

We took great pride in racing our Mediterranean-based colleagues in how fast we could do this work, so we carefully timed each propeller changeover and radioed it to our competitor in the Med. Our Med colleagues made an infamous goof while trying to beat our time record and mistakenly interchanged two propellers (left-handed for right-handed) on one ill-fated LST. The skipper was mighty surprised when he ordered his vessel to get underway, only to realize that the LST was proceeding backwards when directed to go forward!

We also did a significant amount of under- or in-water maintenance of LSTs, including installing complete new propulsion plants worn out by the change in the use patterns of the vessel. We also patched up many hulls damaged by the rough conditions of constant use in the North Atlantic.

We were continually amazed at the ingenuity and sheer guts of the personnel onboard these underrated vessels. An outstanding example was one particular LST that was carrying a load of

Navy Construction Battalion personnel from the midwestern U.S., most of whom had apparently been recruited from farming communities. Rough conditions on their stormy North Atlantic transit had produced an alarming structural crack clear across the main deck of their vessel's hull. Since they had portable welding equipment with them, they had bravely welded the crack back together while underway. Our job was merely to inspect the quality of their work, further reinforce their temporary patches, and send them on their way.

A LOOK-SEE AROUND SCOTLAND

Unfortunately, since we were so busy, and since I was part of the primary functional group on board our ship, I did not have much opportunity to look around Scotland. However, I took a quick look inside of Glasgow, and made the required tours of the local lochs.

In one case, I had an unusual treat when the British brought a U.S. Army tugboat alongside our ship and asked for some diesel engine repairs. The Brits hastily left after tying up, without giving us a full description of the problem or what we were to do with the vessel. We quickly fixed the minor problems, and couldn't find any major ones. We then could not find our British friends to whom the vessel should be returned. I got permission from our Captain to take over the tug and to use it any way I wished.

It was a brand new, 60-foot-long river tug of a type which had been mass-produced for the U.S. Army and sent to Scotland as a deck load on a larger vessel. It was skillfully designed to be operated by one person on its bridge in that all engine controls were located at the steering position. It was an ideal setup, and I used it for all it was worth as my personal yacht/toy/motorboat. As a result, I had a chance to nose around the waterfront of the Firth of Clyde for over a week. It was a rare privilege, as this area is famous as a sailing paradise in peacetime.

PORTLAND/WEYMOUTH HARBOR

MOVE TO THE ENGLISH CHANNEL

After about a month tied up on the Clyde, the Melville was ordered to relocate to the English Channel in preparation for the anticipated Allied invasion of France. We took off from Scotland to proceed approximately 600 miles to Portland/Weymouth on the south coast of England. Being a slow, essentially defenseless vessel, the Melville was escorted the whole way by American and, I believe, British naval convoy escort ships plus an occasional blimp overhead. The trip took about three days. During that time I was assigned as a member of the ship's operating crew to watch duty in the engine and boiler rooms. It was an interesting experience since we were running a propulsion plant which was almost a nautical antique. Our voyage from the Firth of Clyde southwards to Land's End went without serious incident, although we had lots to learn about operating the ship since it had not been underway for several months.

Route traveled during my wartime service.

THE ABORTIVE "EXERCISE TIGER"

Once around Land's End, on April 28, 1944, while on the leg eastward toward our eventual destination, we crossed through a fleet of Allied naval vessels hastily moving due north across our path toward the south coast of England. They refused to divulge what they had been doing, and clearly indicated that something was amiss. We were warned by the vessels involved to get out of the way, to leave the area in a hurry, and to stay silent about what we had seen. We did as we were told.

We later learned that they were returning from an abortive rehearsal of the forthcoming invasion. They were practicing landings using a section along the south shore, just east of Plymouth, called Slapton Sands, an area whose particular beaches resembled the conditions which the Allies were anticipating. The training fleet had been set upon by several German E-boats, which were the equivalent of our own small, high-speed PT boats. The unexpected attack resulted in the sinking of two LSTs, the damage of a third, and, tragically, the enormous loss of 749 American GI's and 197 Navy personnel.

This particularly disastrous incident, code-named "Exercise Tiger," was hushed up for security reasons and not publicized until well after the end of the war. In fact, I never really appreciated the extent of the disaster until a few weeks before writing this chapter in 2009 when I was discussing the role of LSTs during WWII with a neighbor here in my retirement community. He not only had been in the aborted exercise himself, but had collected a lot of the later documentation, including official U.S. Navy records and local newspapers relating to the delayed divulgence of the hushed-up situation. Ultimately it turned out that the Allies were conducting a frantic search for the bodies of seven officers of one of the sunken LSTs, who had specific, ultra-secret knowledge of the invasion plans and proposed dates. The Allies had to confirm that the officers had not been captured by the Germans rather than killed in the attack.

GATHERING OF THE FLEET

Portland/Weymouth harbor is roughly one-half of the way from west to east across the 350-mile stretch of the south coast of England. A long arc of a sandbar, stabilized by rocks and a roadway, reaches southward into the English Channel from the city of Weymouth. At the end is the Isle of Portland, with its narrow southern promontory called Portland Bill. This C-shaped configuration cradles a very well protected harbor, perhaps two miles in diameter. It was strategically situated as a haven for the fleet gathering for the Allied invasion of war-torn Europe. The nearest logical invasion site was in France, slightly over 100 miles away. The 150 miles of coast between the cities of Portsmouth to the east and Plymouth to the west became the obvious focus of preparations for invasion, and Portland/Weymouth was right in the middle of it.

The USS Melville arrived to join a large fleet of ships already in Portland/Weymouth. At the southern edge of the harbor, a British Navy base provided a landing "hard" (a paved beach) which could accept four or five LSTs, side by side, or other beaching-style craft, grounding out to load and unload. Additionally, there was dockage to accommodate naval vessels and an extensive naval supply base. We lay at a British mooring half a mile off the base.

At the northern, mainland side of the harbor were the docks of Weymouth plus a test and development center for British naval torpedoes. A formidable breakwater to the east completed the circular harbor. The area of the coastline just east of the harbor was shallow and constantly patrolled so that a large number of vessels could spill out of the harbor to anchor there as the fleet built up for the invasion.

Portland/Weymouth Harbor, with the city of Weymouth on the left and the Isle of Portland on the right.

SITTING DUCKS

The distinctive shape and location of the Isle of Portland provided an unmistakable navigation marker over which outgoing aircraft formations could rendezvous and for returning aircraft to home in on. To further help them, the Brits turned on a powerful searchlight every night, pointing skyward as a beacon just inland from the harbor. Although the German aerial forces had been largely overcome by the Allies by then, we shuddered each night, as this searchlight could also direct a German bomber right toward us.

Protection of the fleet was provided by naval patrols outside the harbor, a significant number of anti-aircraft guns on the fleet itself, and extensive anti-aircraft batteries on the Isle of Portland. Barrage balloons surrounded the harbor, although they were at some peril of being shot down by Allied fleet gunners sighting in their own guns on them. At nearby airfields the British Air Force was training pilots to fly the new, high-speed jet aircraft.

As the invasion drew closer, the towns, roadways, and countryside for miles around were totally taken over by Allied troops, air bases, and supply functions, and it was obvious to us that decisions about when, where and exactly how to invade had been made. However, for security reasons, we were not told when or where it would happen.

DAILY SHIPBOARD LIFE

Once we were safely at anchor in Portland/Weymouth, we established new patterns of daily life. As in Scotland, it was clear to me from the outset that I was to be available 24 hours every day for responding to ship repair needs. Simultaneously, I had to do my share of non-repair duties as a member of the so-called "ship's company". My non-drinking status reduced my apparent "need" to go ashore, at least in the eyes of some of my shipmates. Accordingly, I found myself unusually busy. But I think that I had been well prepared for my status in the "old Navy" style of our NCOs at our NROTC at Michigan. The old-time instructors were "right out of the book" Navy-style, but we loved them and respected them anyhow. It does say something about the power of traditional Navy training!

The Melville intentionally had an over-capacity of many shipboard services so we could help other ships and their crews when they came alongside. We provided food from our oversized galley facility as well as health, chaplaincy, paymaster, and mail service to the crews, and electricity, fresh water, and sometimes even sewage service to the ships. We were, in a real sense, a "mother ship".

I was often on my feet as much as 12 hours a day, actually doing things manually and hence was in good physical shape. Luckily, I slept very well. So, outside of being continually concerned about being in a wartime situation, life seemed pretty good.

Because I was functioning much of the time in grease-prone locations when doing repair projects, I had to favor dressed-down uniforms that could tolerate the dirt. I had a certain amount of difficulty from my superiors from the fact that I had to fraternize with the NCOs and enlisted personnel in order to get the garage mechanic-type repair tasks accomplished. As a consequence, I found myself in some awkward social interactions with fellow officers. I guessed that was all part of the job under the situation that I was in. Luckily, nothing really serious came out of it all and, quite frankly, it strengthened my relationship with the repair crews.

Most ships requiring our repair services came to our vessel and tied up alongside us at our mooring. Our most frequent clients continued to be LSTs, but we also had many other interesting vessels to work on.

We continued to use the routine we established in Scotland for replacing the LSTs' cast iron propellers. The process was much more difficult here on the borders of the English Channel, however, since the surface wave action was considerably stronger than in the better protected Firth of Clyde. We were continually beat about as we clung onto the diving stage, protecting ourselves with our old-style full "hard hat" diving suits. This probably led to my post-war problem with claustrophobia.

Due to their hurried design and mass production, a number of LST maintenance problems continually cropped up. It was a lot of work to keep these vessels ready for the unexpectedly active duty that they inherited. As I had in Scotland, I found myself performing a lot of diesel repair and hull patch-up work.

Convoy vessels such as D.E.s (Destroyer Escorts, a scaled-down destroyer type of vessel) were also frequent clients. They worked extremely hard guarding large ship movements across the Atlantic. D.E.s presented a particular problem in that they had rather sophisticated propulsion systems, such as diesel-electric and turbo-electric power plants, requiring a considerably higher level of technical work than the LSTs. My previous experience working on destroyers at the Bath Iron Works put me in good shape to do this.

One day, rather unexpectedly, the remains of a severely damaged D.E. tied up alongside. She had lost about 50 feet of her stern in action, but was otherwise intact and in relatively good shape. Her diesel-electric power plant was functioning well. We wired her up, connecting her to our electricity distribution system, and the crippled ship thenceforth generated all of the electricity we needed to run our ship and attendant repair shops while also sustaining the several other ships tied up alongside us awaiting repair. At the time I was somewhat mystified about the adequacy of that whole arrangement, but I was just junior enough that I did not participate in those large executive decisions.

SOME UNUSUAL ACTIVITIES IN OUR HARBOR

The British Navy tested torpedoes in Portland/Weymouth harbor. Happily the weapons were not armed, but were constantly racing about, making us more than nervous and constantly preoccupied by the wakes as they flashed by our moored ship. When we first arrived, the floating remains of one of Admiral Lord Nelson's famous sailing warships was moored near us. It had ignobly been downgraded to a floating coal storage vessel to serve the last of the remaining coal-fired ships still in existence. One of the torpedoes under test hit the hull of the old sailing vessel, and it went down stern first, leaving an ugly bow sticking up in the air. Faced with an impending visit/inspection by British royalty, harbor authorities tried to clean up the mess. An LSM (Landing Ship–Medium, i.e., a smaller version of an LST) was assigned the task of ramming the partially exposed hulk repeatedly, trying to push it out of sight under the water. We watched this bow-butting process with glee for several hours until the whole mess sank–just ahead of the arrival of Their Royal Highnesses!

TRAGEDY ON THE FLOATING BREAKWATERS

Among the enormous, varied collection of vessels were several floating breakwaters. These were shaped like simple steel barges, configured so they could be towed, floating nose up. They had just arrived from the U.S., and were destined to be towed over for use in the invasion. Moored, these would serve as temporary breakwaters to create newly-formed harbors where no sheltered harbors currently existed.

Our assignment was to board the hollow breakwaters, which were designed to stay closed up and unmanned during their long tows, and check their structures in readiness for further deployment. Our ship's boatswain's department dispatched a group of deckhands to make the inspection, and they went down inside one of the vessels. Fellow crew members waiting outside soon realized that those inside the hull were strangely silent, and did not respond to calls from the men above. A second round of our crew mates was sent to check on the first. The hulls had not been aired out since their long trip, and, one by one, the crew members below had lost consciousness. The rescuers, in turn, were overcome. By the time those on the surface reacted, we had tragically lost five of our crew to asphyxiation.

A LESSON IN SEA LORE

At one point, a large, sea-going salvage tugboat tied up alongside the Melville, seeking respite and repair. It had located and towed back a cargo ship which had been completely abandoned and left to drift alone in the middle of the Indian Ocean. The ship had been carrying refrigerated cargo when its cooling system failed, causing the cargo to rot. The stench of the putrid goods was so hideous that living conditions were impossible for all on board. Her desperate crew deserted her.

The rescued ship, to my surprise, was the same vessel which had given us real problems as we launched her three years earlier at Bath Iron Works. As the most junior intern that summer, I had had to perform the most disliked part of the process. Standing waist-deep in the Kennebec River, at the outermost point of the launching area, my job had been to drive the most remote wedge into place to help jack the enormous ship up off the building ways, and onto the launching carriage.

As the launching started, the ship had become stuck. We struggled to get her started down toward the water, but to no avail. There was about a half-hour delay while the shipyard marshaled a "gooser"–a hydraulic device to push the vessel into sliding down the ways into the river.

While standing in the water, I remember looking up at the nearby railroad bridge and seeing Army troops swarming over it. President Roosevelt was on his way back to Washington from Halifax where he had landed after meeting at sea with Russian leader, Joseph Stalin. His train had been scheduled to cross the bridge on this day. We all worried as we waited for the launching. A strong southwesterly wind had come up that might push our ship out of control into the bridge. With great effort, the ship was finally "goosed," my remote wedge was driven correctly, and she slid into the water, in control and not hitting the railroad bridge.

Instead of shouting cheers, I remembered how our tired gang roundly cursed her as she finally slid past us into the river. Shortly thereafter, she ran aground, on this, her very first run. Capping her string of unlucky launch events, the poor ship was labeled forever as a fateful "Jonah"–the unhappy term from marine lore given to ships that bring bad luck.

Three years later, there I was, on the south coast of England, and the very same "Jonah" appeared, after being deserted in the middle of the Indian Ocean, suffering from rotting, reeking cargo. She had carried her curse!

Now, I am no longer at sea, and the name Jonah means something quite different. In April 2007, I proudly welcomed the birth of my great-grandson, Jonah Eric Lindstrom!

OLD FRIENDS COME TO PORTLAND

In addition to ships tying up to the Melville, I visited many anchored nearby which were waiting for our assistance. As a result, I came across a parade of NROTC friends from Michigan as well as a variety of friends and people of note. Of particular interest was the presence of a flotilla of PT boats commanded by John Duncan Bulkeley. John was the PT boat skipper who rescued General MacArthur in the Philippines. He was a cousin of brother-in-law Bob Bulkley (even though their last names were spelled differently). Accompanying John was Nat Benchley, a close friend of Bob's, whom I had met several times in New York City. (Nat later wrote the script of one of my favorite movies, "The Russians are Coming, the Russians are Coming.")

Peter Scott, son of the famous British Antarctic explorer, tied his patrol boat, the Grey Goose, up alongside the Melville to have some repair work done. Before the war, Peter was already known as one of Britain's leading illustrators of bird species. Peter had already achieved a brilliant war record in dealing with the German E-boats which had wreaked such havoc with English Channel shipping. The Grey Goose was a very fast experimental anti-E-boat patrol craft powered, of all things, by a steam turbine power plant. (After the war, the then-titled Sir Peter became a good friend as we raced against each other in the "International 14" high-speed dinghy sailboats. Later, he skippered Britain's America's Cup 12-meter-class challenger, *Sovereign,* in the 1964 race series.)

Also, from out of the blue, there came alongside a craft whose purpose I found sobering. It was skippered by one of the members of the Sierra Club hike that I had taken a few years before in California. This was a very small steel powerboat, perhaps only 40 feet long. It was fitted out as a control boat to coordinate by radio and visual signals the details of military movements during the forthcoming invasions. That assignment seemed to me to be one of the most hazardous tasks imaginable. I have yet to discover whether this friend did, in fact, survive the invasion.

As the invasion fleet assembled, four good friends from the NROTC turned up aboard various ships in a flotilla of new destroyers that had been badly damaged during the nasty fight to capture the French port at Cherbourg. I hope that I was able to provide them some solace after their rough time on the other side of the Channel. Ironically, their destroyers were the very vessels that I had been working on at the Bath Iron Works a year or two previously.

So, in some ways, it was a chilling "old home week" for me as we waited tensely at our mooring on the edge of the English Channel.

THE WAR ACTION COMES CLOSE

Being essentially right out in the English Channel, we heard gunfire and saw flashes of light from the intermittent naval action just offshore. In spite of the high level of defense of the harbor, German aircraft were able to penetrate the protection a few times. They dropped mine-like aerial bombs into the water which exploded *after* the aircraft had left, either through time-delay action or from acoustically or magnetically triggered ship movement around the harbor. This delayed-action bombing caused a lot of concern among all present, and resulted in a dozen or so incidents of damage to the ships, but only a handful of casualties to personnel. The Melville ended up with several of the resulting repair tasks.

SHORE PATROL DUTIES

The ships moored in the harbor took turns providing shore patrol officers to keep the unusually busy Weymouth landing areas running smoothly. Since we were one of the few ships permanently moored there, we drew perhaps more than our share of duty, and I ended up assigned to policing the docks more often than my less sober shipmates.

The dock was invariably a mob scene. Large numbers of "liberty launches" (very small boats that brought personnel to shore) lined up to take their turn at loading/unloading ships' crew members. The more vessels that arrived in the harbor in anticipation of the invasion, the more chaotic the shore scene became. Some men were in rather advanced stages of inebriation—quite smashed! The launches tied up side by side along the dock and it became a sort of a game to get returnees from shore leave back aboard their proper launches without having some of the drunks fall overboard. More than once the confused returnees scrambled across the nearest launches in search of their crewmates and ended up getting wet. I do not recall that we lost anybody through drowning, but I certainly found myself swimming in full uniform more than once.

THE NORMANDY INVASION

THE FLEET

There were already several hundred ships in Portland/Weymouth harbor when we arrived. We knew we were preparing for a large invasion of France, but we were not told exact details of locations or dates. As invasion time approached the fleet swelled to perhaps 500 naval combat and support vessels representing almost every Allied nation. They ranged from battleships ready for offshore bombardment of German fortifications down to very small beach invasion support ships.

The Melville was moored right off the stern of the two LSTs in this picture, perhaps half a mile out in the harbor.

Some very unusual vessels appeared, such as command and control ships for overseeing the landings, many convoy escort vessels, mine-layers, minesweepers, troop ships, dredges, and tugs. PT boats came to bolster the extensive British torpedo craft for which this harbor was home, in response to the recent history of intense German E-boat activity on the Channel. (However, not surprisingly, there were not many conventional surface combat ships, and no large aircraft carriers.)

Some of the vessels had highly specialized facilities for handling their important cargoes. For instance, the locomotive carriers were built to carry nothing but railroad locomotives and specialty railroad cars. One of these vessels had a locomotive permanently hanging over the side of the ship, irretrievably dangling from damaged loading cranes. Apparently it was the victim of some unique accident.

I marveled at the novel vessels that had been developed for the new challenges of invasion warfare such as the ships with monstrous coils of plastic pipe on oversized garden hose-style reels that would permit fuel tankers to lie safely off the invasion beaches or war-damaged ports while supplying critical fuel to the shore forces. Perhaps the most startlingly exceptional vessel was a large, very speedy side-wheeler, previously employed in the passenger trade along the southeastern U.S. coast. She probably was built before the year 1900, and had been recruited into war service after a long and peaceful life to be a decoy to divert enemy attention during the earlier invasions of North Africa.

We admired most the operators of a group of miniature two-man submarines. When seated inside, these brave souls were not able to see out well enough to properly "conn" their vessels around our harbor full of ships. As a result, the skippers rode, clad in hip boots, standing atop their little charges, piloting them in and out of the harbor. The skippers looked almost comic to us, as though they were walking on water. These little craft had done heroic work, however, especially along the Norwegian coast, by sneaking into the fjords and seriously damaging major German warships hiding from Allied attacks. I was fortunate to visit one of the little submersibles, and stood in awe at the guts of their crews.

The unique-looking, so-called Versailles Treaty British battleships (the HMS Rodney and the HMS Nelson) were in and out of the harbor, displaying their foreshortened after-bodies brought about by the limits in length imposed by the post-WWI treaty. (I went aboard them to help repair their American-built washing machines. I reveled in their luxurious officer lounges fitted out with fancy tea services while displaying a plentiful assortment of bottles of Scotch whiskey on their many tea tables. Even their engine rooms were a Gilbert & Sullivan show of polished brass fittings.)

Also of considerable interest were the several command and control ships which came and went. Among them was the USS Ancon, which carried the high brass of the armed forces.

The Melville's job was to keep the fleet vessels operational in an atmosphere of tension and high alert. At all times, we remained very concerned that we were an obvious target from sea and air. We were lucky that no serious attack took place.

D-DAY–THE INVASION

Every one of us who was around on June 6, 1944 can tell you just what they were doing on that fateful day. Looking back, I remember it well, in startlingly detailed visual images and with a lot of personal emotion. The imminence of the invasion was quite clear to us the day before as we lay at our mooring in the harbor. The level of activity in the ships around us markedly increased as hundreds of vessels prepared to get underway.

My roommate and I were sleepless during the dark hours of the night of June 5th. We strongly sensed the movements of the fleet, and were increasingly haunted by the aircraft noise building up overhead. By 2 or 3 a.m., the skies were crowded with Allied cargo planes towing huge passenger gliders. For security reasons no lights were showing from the fleet while vessels started their engines, noisily hoisted anchors, and headed stealthily out to sea–a totally spooky scene. We also knew that the patrol aircraft and surface ships in the English Channel that had been protecting the harbor must have turned toward the invasion area during the crucial night hours.

As it grew light, the plane traffic overhead, all headed south by east towards France, intensified as flyers could then see each other and avoid hitting the gliders and their long tow cables. Ship movement continued throughout the day, scheduled, precautionary, and sensible, stretching out as far as the eye could see.

On our side of the English Channel, the weather conditions were far from ideal and the Channel was rough and forbidding. Conditions aloft also appeared to be unwelcoming. It was later revealed that the exact timing of the invasion had been difficult because of the weather. Once troops were gathered for the assault, the weather took a turn for the worse, and it was predicted that fair weather would not arrive soon enough to permit rescheduling.

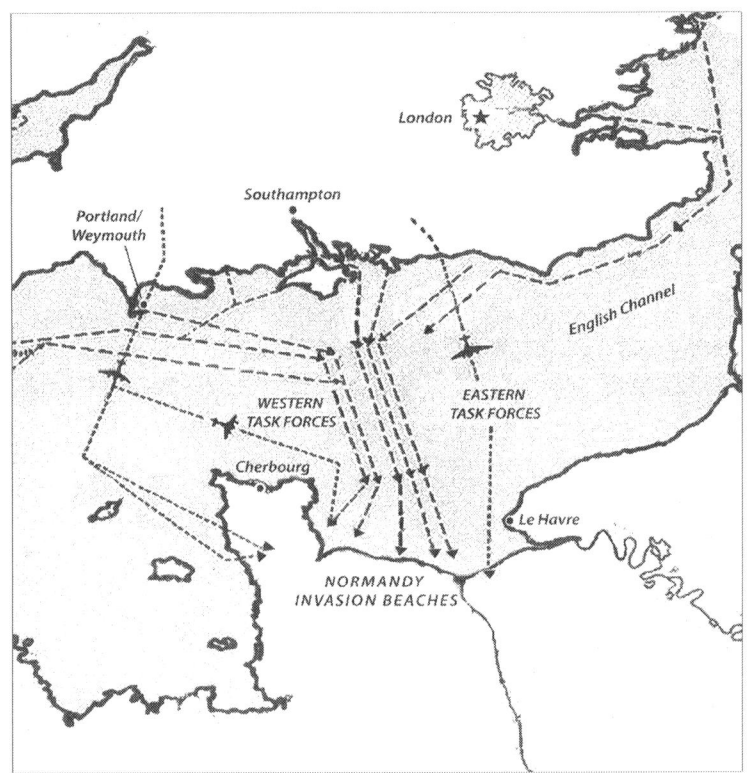

Allied Invasion Forces. Since my ship was in the distinctively-shaped Portland/Weymouth harbor, we were right under the route of invading transport aircraft, many of them towing gliders.

The Melville remained behind in the harbor, ready to repair vessels which, by the middle of the next day, were coming back from the battle front (which we by now had learned was the Normandy beaches). Returning ships were unloading the wounded, refilling with cargo, or being serviced in some way. All kinds of craft limped in, seeking help, and tying up alongside us. We repaired a wide variety of the smaller types of vessels–landing craft, service vessels, patrol boats, mine-sweepers, destroyer-escorts, destroyers, and the like. Occasionally, we worked on larger ships with urgent problems, essentially "applying field bandages" before they proceeded to the big shipyards in Plymouth or Southampton for more major repairs. The nearby British shoreside shipyards also worked straight out, performing some of the "heavy lifting" repair jobs.

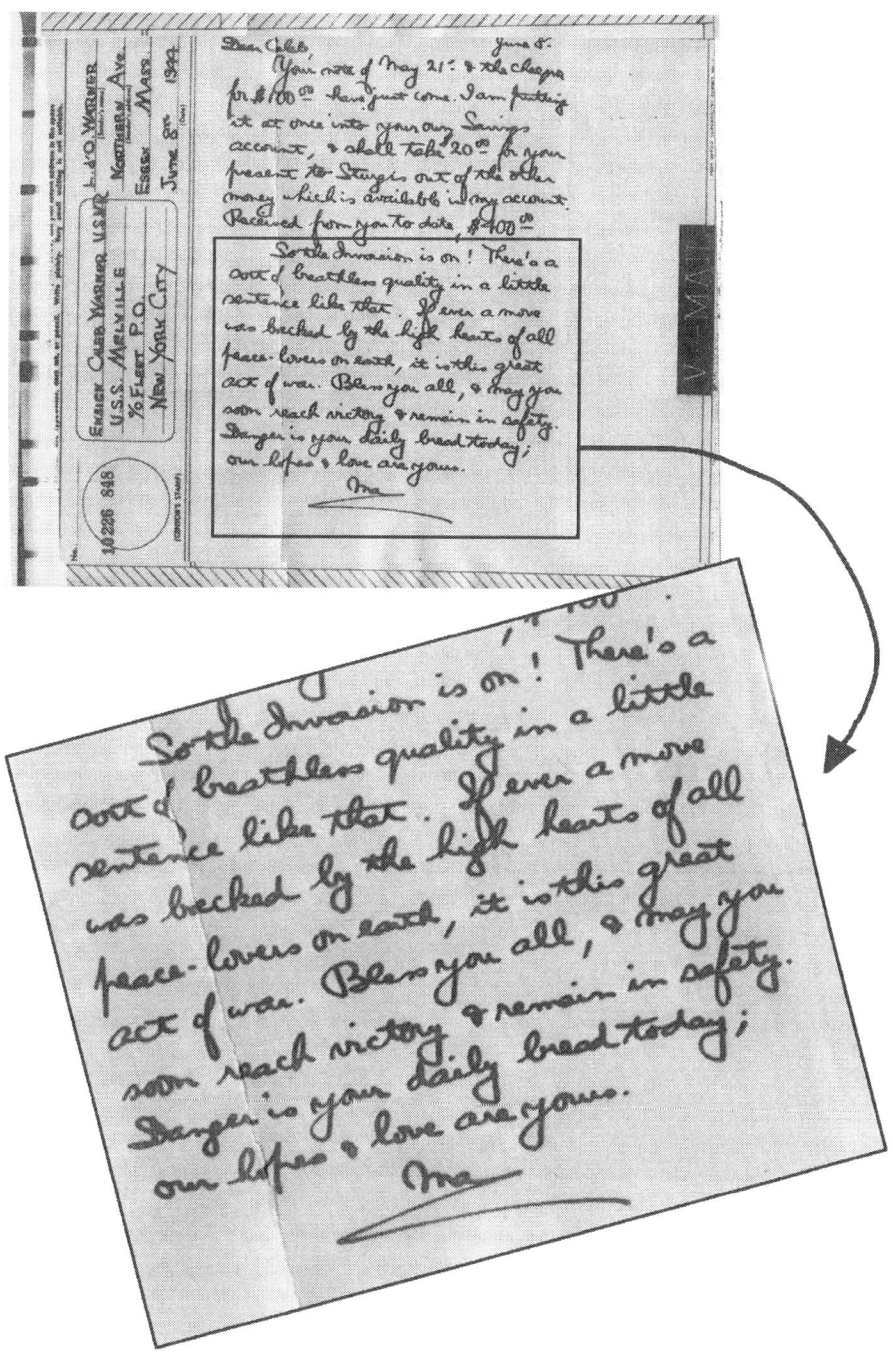

Content from a V-Mail from my mother, dated June 8th, 1944:
"So the Invasion is on! There's a sort of breathless quality in a little sentence like that. If ever a move was backed by the high hearts of all peace-lovers on earth, it is this great act of war. Bless you all, and may you soon reach victory and remain in safety. Danger is your daily bread today; our hopes and love are yours. Ma"

Our most frequent "patients" were needy LSTs. They continually tied up to the Melville, as many as seven at a time. Heavy-duty fenders kept the ships from damaging each other because of the continual wave motion in our exposed harbor. Rugged gangplanks bridged the gaps between the independently moving ships, providing ready access for personnel using two-wheeled carts to carry heavy loads of tools and equipment needed to conduct repairs. We did mechanical, structural, and electrical patch-ups, and virtually any maintenance for which vessel crews were unprepared.

With all this potentially confusing movement on and off the many ships that were tying up to us, we never lost track of our men or tools. We followed SOPs (Standard Operating Procedures), which prevented people or equipment from sailing off on another ship by mistake. Before the invasion, however, we had done a good amount of deliberate swapping of personnel. As men came aboard and we learned of their specific talents, we had some of them transferred to our ship to give us a hand. During the invasion and the weeks following, men from other vessels were also brought aboard with injuries, stabilized, and then taken ashore for further treatment.

The crew of the Melville was essentially acting as plumbers, garage mechanics and triage managers in the heat of the turning point of the war in the European Theatre. It was a time I will never forget. I seldom got off that ship, but that was fine by me. We were in the middle of everything, and I was quite happy to be doing my part. I was in the right place at the right time, and I was deeply satisfied with the duty.

However, many of the men whose vessels had been moored in our harbor before the invasion had been wounded or lost their lives, along with many more who had flown over us in the hundreds of transport aircraft. Approximately 15,000 Allied soldiers were killed or wounded during the first day of the invasion alone. We, and our country, were, and remain, grateful to all those men who gave their lives.

AFTER THE INVASION

Following the invasion, and for the next 11 months that I was stationed in Portland/Weymouth, that harbor continued to be a critical jumping-off place and refuge for ships from all around the world. It was an ever-changing, fascinating scene. It fulfilled my deep interest in the field of marine affairs. My engineering education, apprenticeships and internships were put to good work and more than proved their worth in support of the war effort, and give me a foundation for my career.

Eventually, as tensions eased a bit post-invasion, I finally had some time for non-garage-mechanic experiences.

RELATIONSHIPS WITH THE BRITISH

We had a tacit understanding with the nearby British naval facilities that we would help with work on their unfamiliar American-style equipment, from the British Admiral's American-built car to tricky maintenance on substantial ships' diesel engines. They, in turn, were generous in providing us with materials and supplies from their extensive marine stores warehouse.

At one point, I thoroughly embarrassed myself with the Brits. I was sent ashore to repair a British Admiral's car. Nobody had informed me beforehand exactly what the trouble was. I found out the hard way, much to my humiliation, as I crashed it soundly into the British Naval office building. The darned brakes did not work!

We generally got along well with our fellow British officers, and we were careful to include them in our holiday celebrations. A rollicking time was had by all on our own 4th of July party one night, when we wined and dined the British Admiral and his staff without their realizing what the celebration was about. At the end of the evening, it was time to divulge to them that we were celebrating our own Revolutionary War (against *them*, of course!), to which we all congenially gave a final toast.

DANGEROUS SHORESIDE EXPERIENCE

Although I was not drawn to the Officers Club activities ashore, it was very convenient to have the club there since it certainly attracted the date-seeking young ladies from the USO, WACs, and Red Cross.

Probably my most hazardous duty at the time was taking the ship's truck 600 miles north to Scotland to bring back a load of liquor for the Officers' Club. One of our ship's crew, while returning drunk after sampling the load, had been hijacked while on the road, robbed of the precious cargo, and subsequently murdered. When I was assigned to make that trip after the murder, I made sure I had an armed–and sober!–crew member along to ride "shotgun".

ENCOUNTERS WITH THE MOUNTBATTEN FAMILY

Among our officers, we had one man from a socially prominent New York family who sought socially prominent connections in Britain. Somehow, I don't know exactly how, our social climber managed to cultivate a relationship with the Mountbatten family and was often invited to its home at Broadlands. Broadlands was a marvelous summer estate, then inhabited by Lady Mountbatten and her two daughters, while Lord Louis Mountbatten was far away, serving in Southeast Asia. Broadlands was about 50 miles northeast of our harbor, just outside Southampton.

Our shipmate became good friends with one of the Mountbatten daughters. Several times he selected our Executive Officer and me to accompany him to Broadlands for a weekend away from the ship because, as he explained at the time of our first invitation, we were "acceptable representatives of Americans". Broadlands proved to be an absolutely stunning place. Lady Mountbatten was a charming and worldly person. Her daughters seemed to be quite taken with our shipmate's movie star appearance. Amusingly, we got quite an inside look at the swashbuckling Lord Louis, even though absent, as his family talked about him.

The side of a damaged LST from the Normandy Invasion fleet, badly in need of repair.

The same LST, tied to the Melville, during the repair.

MOVING TO PLYMOUTH HARBOR

By April 1945 the harbor system in Normandy had been built up and protected so that vessels could go directly to the French coast without involving us on the south coast of England. Our reason for being in Portland/Weymouth had virtually disappeared. Washington ordered us out of the area, and away from possible rogue attacks. Plymouth, less than 100 miles to the west, was a logical stop on our way home.

Plymouth was a fascinating harbor for me since it was a major base for the British Navy and, of course, a place of historic interest to any American as a jump-off point for many early immigrants to our country.

The local service craft were intriguing. There were a number of really old-style, steam-powered, coal-fired vessels still active, including several side-wheeler tugboats. I visited one and was amazed at the scene in the engine room where two monstrous, ancient reciprocating engines were located, one for each of the two sidewheels. When underway, the whole engine room was filled with moving steel arms, an almost terrifying atmosphere as one moved about on an elevated walkway, holding on carefully to handrails on either side. These tugs were amazingly fast and agile, able to spin about in place, with one sidewheel going backward and one going forward. The wake created by the side wheels was directed on either side of their tows, instead of directly back at them—a very efficient and effective scheme.

Also intriguing were the steam-powered ferries which pulled themselves back and forth across the harbor by a chain which was tied to each shore and lay on the harbor bottom.

VICTORY IN EUROPE

May 7, 1945 was V-E (Victory in Europe) Day. In celebration, and against the specific orders of our captain, we tied down the lever to activate the ship's whistle. It blew down the steam pressure in our boilers, perhaps dangerously shutting the whole ship down for a while.

We were moored near a railway bridge which sits high across Plymouth harbor. This was a partially tubular steel structure, well elevated above the water for tall ships to pass under. British fighter plane pilots dared each other to fly under it in celebration of V-E Day. These daredevils almost got their come-uppance because our ship, with its very high radio antenna masts, was right in their way as they hurtled out from under the bridge. I was deeply alarmed and frustrated since we were constrained to radio silence and could not warn the show-off pilots. Luckily no casualties were incurred.

RETURN TO THE U.S.

A few days after V-E Day, our ship received orders to return to the naval dockyard in Brooklyn, NY to be overhauled and made ready for assignment to the Pacific Theatre of Operations. Some major changes in the ship were necessary to make her fit for tropical conditions and to upgrade her repair facilities to meet the particular needs in that area. We were facing a major overhaul which would take a couple of months or more in the shipyard.

We had the luxury of crossing the Atlantic during the time of year when weather conditions are usually favorable. Thank goodness for that, because I am not sure what it would have been like to bring that poor old vessel across with a crew inexperienced at rugged conditions at sea. We had an easy trip for all of us, but for me it was made somewhat less interesting as I had to relearn watch-standing in the engine and boiler rooms while under way.

Since we were scheduled to go into drydock immediately upon reaching Brooklyn, we were ordered to lighten ship as much as possible on the way back. We were directed not to take on ballast water to replenish the weight lost from burning fuel since we might cause pollution in New York harbor if we discharged dirty ballast water after we arrived. The ship became increasingly unsteady as we proceeded homewards at the sluggish speed of about 12 knots (approximately 14 miles per hour). We noticed the increasing instability of the ship from one day to the next. As a student of naval architecture, I frankly became rather concerned about the danger of capsizing. However, we made it across the Atlantic without incident, in about eight to ten days.

I was very thankful to finally see the amazing Statue of Liberty as we drew near New York harbor. It made me imagine how our immigrants must have felt in years gone by.

REFITTING AT THE BROOKLYN NAVY YARD

As part of the ship's repair crew, I had some duties overseeing the restoration of the Melville, but I also had a lot of off-hours leisure time. Of course I was quick to update myself on the NYC jazz scene, both uptown and down in the "Village". Many of my Michigan friends were around and I learned of the fates of several of my cadet and school friends. I had the many cousins of my mother's family nearby, and I visited them as soon as I could. The city was welcoming to all returning servicemen. It was both a sad and a social whirlwind of an experience.

VICTORY IN JAPAN

Victory in the Pacific Theater was claimed by the Allied forces on August 14, 1945. We spent the daytime hours seeing how loudly and continuously we could blow the ship's whistle until our captain threatened to lock us up. He actually came down into the boiler room looking for the valve to turn off the steam to the monster whistle, but we never let on where it was. Our shipyard neighbors were none too happy about our noisy output!

Formal surrender aboard the USS Missouri in Japan took place on September 2, 1945 (V-J Day). We spent most of the day listening to up-to-the-minute radio broadcasts. That evening I found a date, a girl from school who lived in New York, and we went to the celebration at Times Square. There we found the most joyous crowd that I have ever seen. By 10:00 PM almost two million people had crowded into the square in a celebration unrivaled in American history.

Newsreels later revealed that one of our Michigan NROTC cadet leaders, a close friend of mine, had served as an aide to the senior officers aboard the USS Missouri. My friend kept appearing and reappearing in the newsreels, attired in snazzy full-dress uniform, in keeping with the dress code of the surrender pageant.

Amazingly, many of the employees in the Brooklyn Navy Yard who had been working on our ship just literally dropped their tools where they worked and walked out of the Yard, not to return. We were virtually deserted. Almost immediately, we came to realize that our planned transfer to the Pacific probably could not happen, certainly not in a reasonable amount of time.

HOSPITAL STAY, AND READYING THE USS MELVILLE FOR RETIREMENT

With our ship at least theoretically under intense refit for use in the Pacific, I got hit hard with bacterial pneumonia and languished in the St. Albans Naval Hospital for about a month. I shared a room with a marine officer who had been seriously wounded in the Pacific Theatre, and he needed a lot of support. I was not seriously ill, and helped him as best I could. It was a gut-wrenching time. While in that hospital, I saw or experienced situations similar to some played out years later in the popular TV series MASH, and I found myself unable to laugh much when later watching that show.

Meanwhile, I was ignominiously left behind in the hospital as my ancient ship finally limped down to Jacksonville, Florida, rather than to the Pacific. In Jacksonville it was placed into inactive status rather than being immediately scrapped, even though it was over 30 years old and technologically grossly outdated.

After my stint in the hospital, I traveled south and rejoined the Melville in Jacksonville, where she was moored near the harbor mouth. The ultimate plan, unbelievably, was that she would be moved up the St. John's River far enough for the water to be free of hull-eating salt. She would be tied up alongside a large number of much younger vessels, ready for reuse if needed.

The weather was freakishly freezing when I arrived at the ship. After my full month's stay in the hospital with pneumonia, I had been discharged and sent south immediately with no time spent on further recovery. My body must have been weakened by the illness, because I was not ready for such unexpectedly cold conditions. I was the coldest that I have ever been in my life, before or since.

Surprisingly, we had no designated duties in Jacksonville, not even instructions to ready the ship for retirement. I busied myself as best I could at the interesting shipyards and boatyards around Jacksonville. Our officer group tried somewhat unsuccessfully to be tourists, but it turned out to be a dull and unproductive several weeks.

TRANSFER TO DESTROYER DUTY: THE USS STRIBLING

The duties of the tired old USS Melville were about to end, and I really wanted to get some more time on a ship before leaving active duty. I sought assignment to a brand new destroyer. My brother-in-law was now Commander Bob Bulkley, with a very distinguished war record in PT boats in the Pacific. Through his good office, I looked around for an interesting berth. He helped me to get assigned to the USS Stribling (DD-867), a brand new destroyer that his cousin, John Duncan Bulkeley, was just commissioning. I happily became assistant chief engineer on the state-of-the-art ship which was then stationed at the naval shipyard at Norfolk, VA.

Our destroyer was assigned as tailing escort of the aircraft carriers in Norfolk which were readying for the atomic weapons tests at the Bikini atolls in the Pacific. Our job was to follow the carriers, right on their tails, and be ready to pick up any aviators or aircraft which missed their landings on the carriers.

We were quite concerned about the assignment. Many of the aircraft were drones (not manned, but remotely controlled) due to the hazardous conditions they would fly under during the weapons

The USS Stribling.

tests. We knew that those who remotely controlled the drones could not see us well enough to keep the abruptly-landing aircraft out of our way, and that this was a potential hazard to our ship. We were fortunate that no drones actually hit us.

During my stay at Norfolk, one particular job sticks out in my memory. Since the war was definitely over, many of those recruited into naval duty did their best to get out, leaving the navy yard quite low on men needed for many daily mundane tasks. The officers' club had lost all its helpers, including the pin setters in the bowling alleys. Being a very junior officer and, again, a non-drinker, I ended up as our ship's bowling pin setter. In those days, before the automated machines, pins were set manually. To do this, I was to stand right next to end of the alley and duck the pins after they were hit. Then I was to jump right in and set them up again. And, because of the dearth of junior officers, I had to set two alleys at a time.

One day, Lord Louis Mountbatten himself turned up. This energetic man required two alleys to himself, so he could bowl two balls simultaneously, one in each hand! Lord Mountbatten was not to be rivaled, and his performance certainly matched the image of him that we had received from his family during those earlier visits to Broadlands in England. I was saddened, years later in 1979, to hear of his assassination in Ireland from a bomb planted on the 30-foot boat on which he was traveling to fish.

We had only been in the Norfolk area for several months when we got a new assignment for our ship. We set off to Key West, Florida, for participation in a study for improvement of the art of antisubmarine warfare. The U.S. Navy had managed to get its hands on a relatively new, state-of-the-art German submarine, a fine specimen representing German ability to wage successful submarine warfare. After war's end, the U.S. immediately mounted a project to evaluate the captive vessel's capability and the latest developments.

Our ship played the role of U.S. antisubmarine forces in a simulated war game. This was a fascinating and challenging exercise. In my grunt job as assistant chief engineer of our brand new ship, I quickly felt right at home due to my experience building, testing, and trying out vessels at the Bath Iron Works before the war. The war game exercises proved to be intense, but very rewarding, like destroyer thrill rides.

THE EXTRAORDINARY JOHN DUNCAN BULKELEY

Service under John Bulkeley was full of surprises. He was a sort of a "damn the torpedoes" type, and some men called him the Navy's version of the Army's General George Patton.

We had a difficult situation each morning getting the ship underway and out to sea for the tightly scheduled antisubmarine experiments. Since the war was over, our crew was more than a little unruly and impatient to get out of the Navy and go back home. Each night after we returned to dock at Key West, the crew streamed off the ship and went downtown to the local bars. Needless to say, many were less than useful the following morning, and our skipper was often challenged by his ineffective early morning crew. One day he called the men together on the foredeck and announced that he was sick of sending his executive officer downtown each morning to bail men out of jail. He declared, "Men, from now on we bail out only those of you who won your fights the night before. The rest of you will have to stay in jail." He had made his point, and it did result in some improved behavior!

John was a man of many interests. He loved to tinker with high-speed cars. He thoroughly scared me one time by inviting me to test the performance of his rumble seat convertible. He asked me to build a special system which would inject water along with the gasoline into the cylinders, hoping to improve the performance of the engine. Thank goodness we were in Key West with a long straight road leading back over the keys toward the mainland, since we discovered that we could not turn off the over-stimulated engine, nor could we stop the car once out on the road. We had to let the car go at a high speed until running out of fuel, perhaps 30 miles down the highway.

When I later ran into him at my nephew Rob Bulkley's wedding, I reminded John of the Key West incidents. He was amused, and said that he had forgotten them, but would assuredly get them inserted in his biography, then being written.

John became commander of the Guantanamo Naval Base in Cuba just as the U.S. was having its first run-in with Fidel Castro. Once, in a newsreel, I saw Admiral John with an axe in his hand threatening to cut the pipe that brought fresh water from Cuba into the U.S. base. John was making the point that the base could take care of itself. I later had mixed emotions when I discovered that the U.S. Department of Defense had made John its representative to the U.S. Atomic Energy Commission. What a man to have his hand on our atomic weapons trigger!

Let us remember, however, that he was one of the most decorated men in the U.S. Navy in that he received the Congressional Medal of Honor, the Navy Cross, and ten other military honors. The first was for performing the courageous rescue of General MacArthur, his staff, and family from the Philippines in several 77-foot PT boats, bringing them over 600 miles, and through enemy fire, to safety. Another was for taking his destroyer into shallow waters inside the barrier beaches at Anzio in Italy, enabling him to pick off the enemy as it appeared over the dunes during the Allied troop landings. The book and the movie, both titled "They Were Expendable," did indeed paint a good picture of the man. I was proud to serve under him.

:MBER 8, 1944

Comdr. R. J. Bulkley Jr. Wins Medal for Heroism in Pacific

Former Herald Tribune Reporter Twice Cited as Head of PT Squadron

Special to the Herald Tribune

MELVILLE, R. I., Nov. 7.—Lieutenant Commander Robert J. Bulkley jr., U. S. N. R., New York Herald Tribune reporter, now in the Navy, received the Legion of Merit Medal here today for distinguished conduct recently as commander of a PT boat squadron in the South Pacific.

The award was made to Commander Bulkley in the drill hall of the Motor Torpedo Boat Squadron's training center, by Commander David J. Walsh, U. S. N. R., commanding officer of the center, at graduation exercises for 167 enlisted men and four officers who have completed training for PT boat combat service.

Accompanying the medal were two citations, one confidential and the other unclassified. The latter, signed by Vice-Admiral T. C. Kinkaid, commander of the 7th Fleet, was read by Commander Walsh. The citation follows:

"For distinguishing himself by exceptionally meritorious conduct in the performance of outstanding services while serving in the southwest Pacific. He has contributed outstandingly to the successful blockading and destroying of Japanese shipping. He commanded one of the first boat divi-

United States Navy
Lieut. Comdr. Robert J. Bulkley jr.

sions to operate in the southwest Pacific and aided in establishing bases. He labored untiringly to bring his organization to a high degree of efficiency and combat effectiveness, which resulted in the destruction of many enemy air and surface craft. He took part in many combat patrols and at all times displayed a coolness and exemplary leadership in the face of enemy resistance which was an inspiration to his men. His actions were in keeping with the highest traditions of the Navy of the United States."

Commander Bulkley, who lives at 60 East Fifty-fifth Street, New York, has been on leave from the Herald Tribune since March, 1941, and has served since then in various capacities in the Navy. For a time he was a press relations officer in the 3d Naval District.

Detached from public relations in 1942, he came to the Motor Torpedo Boat Squadrons Training Center here, and later served as commander of a PT boat in the Southwest Pacific. In 1943 he was made commander of a torpedo boat division, and from February, 1944, to April he was chief staff officer and operations officer of the motor torpedo boat squadrons of the 7th Fleet. He was detached as a squadron commander in August and is now awaiting further assignment.

Commander Bulkley is thirty-three years old, the son of former United States Senator Robert J. Bulkley and Katharine Pope Bulkley, of Cleveland. He was graduated from Harvard College in 1932 and from the Harvard Law School in 1935, when he joined the Herald Tribune as a reporter. He married the former Miss Lorraine Warner, of Cambridge, Mass., in 1933.

Two distant cousins, Bob Bulkley and John Duncan Bulkeley (with slightly differently spelled last names), both served on PT boats during the war. On the left is an article about my brother-in-law Bob Bulkley, upon receiving the Legion of Merit medal. On the right is a photo given to me by John Duncan Bulkeley, USN, my skipper on the S.S. Stribling and winner of the Congressional Medal of Honor and other decorations. His note says: "To Caleb Warner, with my admiration and friendship, from your shipmate, John D. Bulkeley Commander U.S. Navy."

DISCHARGE FROM ACTIVE NAVAL DUTY

I was honorably discharged from active naval duty in the fall of 1946 with the rank of Lieutenant, Junior Grade. I had served a total of about six years, less than two years as an NROTC cadet, and 4½ years on active duty, of which almost two years was overseas. Upon discharge, I elected to be in the inactive reserve rather than active reserve because I knew that I would be working on projects for the Navy where it could be inconvenient to be classified as active. In the long run, it might have been wiser for me to remain in the active reserve to pump up retirement benefits.

MY WARTIME DUTY

I was very lucky in my WWII duty in that I came out physically unscathed and perhaps mentally somewhat matured rather than tormented by my experiences. I was glad I had been really well-trained, experienced, and educated for the duty, and properly assigned and treated by the U.S. Navy.

I feel especially indebted to the Navy for the extensive financial support that I received during my college years. This enabled me to start my civilian life completely free of debt. I had been freed, also, from having to depend on my family for almost all of my college support.

I find it difficult to assess the value of my non-combatant war-time role or the effect that the experience had on my professional career and later life. During that period, I certainly learned a great deal about myself as a person, and also as an engineer. I think I was well-positioned to go into civilian life, and I was certainly ready to do so.

I was more fortunate than many. The war was life-changing for all of us, at home or in the service. It is with great assuredness that I came to believe that the accursed war had been a worthwhile and necessary effort.

It is with great sadness that I think of my many friends and colleagues, and of the thousands of my age group, who were wounded or died. As far as I know, the first casualty in my NROTC class was one of our cadet officers. He was swept overboard off a combat vessel in the Pacific. It was all the more sad because he had been the very first of our group to get married. To him, and to all those others in every branch of the service who did not survive the war, I am forever grateful to each and every one for giving their lives for our country.

*Right:Lieutenant, Junior Grade (at last!) I was finally
promoted from Ensign to Lieutenant Junior
Grade just before VE-Day.
Below: I wish I still had the names of these men, my
Melville repair operation colleagues. They were a great
bunch. I am standing in the second row, middle.*

The quartet that sang with the ship's dance band also sang for many other events. Above, we are singing for a memorial service in the cavernous below-decks of an LST. I am in front, fourth from the left.

Christmas card of unknown origin or date reflective of how everyone aboard the Melville was thinking of home.

My first car, purchased immediately after WWII. Impressed by the military jeep,
I chose the first available civilian version.

8

FINDING MY WAY, FINDING ALICE

DECOMPRESSION FROM MILITARY SERVICE

After discharge from the Navy, I returned to my parents who were then living in the very comfortable small wing of the family house in Cambridge. My father, then 64 years old, had retired from Harvard University, but was very busy teaching at Radcliffe, lecturing all over the country, and doing a lot of writing and revisiting Southeast Asia, pursuing his interest in Far Eastern Art. Mother was fully engaged in her musical activities as a choral conductor and teacher of music at the Buckingham School in Cambridge.

Sister Margot, who never married, was busily pursuing a career as a choral director, producer of musicals, and singing teacher, with a studio and living quarters in Boston. By this time, my parents had given the large main house in Cambridge over to Margot, and she, in turn, had sensibly rented the main body of the house out, reserving the smaller addition for our parents.

My sister Lorraine and her husband Bob Bulkley were living in the District of Columbia in the apartment belonging to his father (Senator Robert J. Bulkley, Sr., from Ohio). Bob had just returned from the Pacific. He remained on active duty in the Office of Naval History, where he researched and wrote the official Navy book on the WWII activities of PT boats, titled "At Close Quarters".

I concentrated on trying to understand what was available to me as a next step in life, and had long talks with my parents, relatives, and old friends.

CHOICES

I qualified for the G.I. Bill of Rights, in which veterans were offered financial help to continue their education, and it was obvious that I could go back to school for a higher degree, but I was eager to start an active and progressive life. I was rather fearful of returning to university without

---

immediately starting some sort of a more productive lifestyle, although, to be honest, I'm not sure I knew exactly what that might be. I started looking about for a good "starter" job, and put aside the opportunity to return to school. In retrospect, this decision may have been shortsighted. If I had it to do all over again, I think that I would turn to further education, judging from the fact that many of my age group did so, much to their later advantage. This was a classic fork-in-the-road situation, one of many that seem to litter my life story.

INTERNSHIP AT GENERAL ELECTRIC CO., LYNN, MASS.

Having rejected further schooling, I turned to finding an opportunity to kick-start a professional career. I looked around at the some of the leading firms in the marine engineering field such as the power plant manufacturer Babcock & Wilcox, Inc., plus several of the firms in the fast-emerging gas turbine field. I visited what seemed to be the leading shipbuilder in the nation–Newport News Shipyard, located on Chesapeake Bay.

The General Electric Company (G.E.) had always been in the forefront of my mind, a fascinatingly diverse leader in the general field of development and manufacture of sophisticated mechanical devices and the maritime propulsion field. They offered what I considered to be a singularly notable program of taking on young engineers and putting them through a sort of internship which gave the company a chance to evaluate a candidate before hiring. They labeled this program the *General Electric Test Program.* Candidates were provisionally hired on as "Test Engineers". The candidate engineers were trained and carefully evaluated as they moved around to various locations within the company, performing a sequence of quality control functions inside manufacturing facilities.

Since G.E. had a large facility in nearby Lynn, Mass., and since the company was heavily involved in building marine power plants, I felt that going there might be a good way to get started in my professional career.

G.E.'s Gear Works in Lynn made large reduction gears for naval vessels. This plant was specially built for the Navy. The plant had some unusual machinery for the sophisticated machining of the large reduction gears needed for steam turbines on board naval vessels. I am not sure what degree of ownership, if any, was retained by the Navy, but the facility was closely guarded and somewhat secretive. It had proved to be vital during WWII.

In any event, the local gear plant was about to be shuttered, but maintained as ready if needed in the future. It was not a facility in which to conduct the "Test Engineer" program, so I did the internship at a much less interesting manufacturing facility in another location in Lynn. This one manufactured specialized textile thread-spinning devices. The "Test" program did little toward exciting me to continue with the company.

I stayed in Lynn for the summer of 1946 while looking around for other options. This was a pivotal time for me, and for my career. Continuing on with G.E. might have been a wise road. This company might have been the one to give me a chance to pursue a career combining my keen interests in engineering and maritime orientation.

TEACHING AT TUFTS

My father had a close friend in the fine arts field on the faculty at Tufts University. He was one of the only senior members of his family running the Steinway company who was not currently engaged in its famous piano building empire. He was a close associate of the president of Tufts. One thing led to another, and an interview was arranged for me for a position in the engineering faculty which was seeking teaching help to handle the tremendous influx of G.I. Bill of Rights students.

The Tufts opportunity seemed like an ideal step as a career starter, and I very happily became an instructor in the Mechanical Engineering Department. I talked to my parents about living at home, and they were more than willing to have me. They were beginning to need some support, and I promised to do a lot of the work around the house. Thus, I could afford to take on the Tufts job, a potentially valuable experience which paid only starvation wages.

My first assignment was to monitor examinations to place students at the proper level of course work. Several hundred newly-arrived students at a time took each exam. Our job, as monitoring faculty, was to circulate, making sure that each individual was on the proper page and had understood the directions for taking the exam. It was about a three-hour test, and we became very familiar with its details, as we tested more and more groups of students. (Several years later, much to my surprise, my familiarity with the test had a tremendous influence on my qualification for the Central Intelligence Agency!) We reviewed the exam results and had searching discussions among our fellow engineering school faculty members on how to place incoming students in class sections in keeping with each individual's particular ability.

Shortly thereafter, the teaching load hit me, and hit me hard. Because of the enormous number of returning veterans hungering for an education, Tufts, in good conscience, had accepted many more students than it had ever handled before. It had enlarged its faculty and added more student residences at the remote location of Fort Devens, many miles northwest of the main campus in Medford, MA.

As a junior member of the Mechanical Engineering Department, I was assigned to teach the required introductory courses of drafting, descriptive geometry, and mechanical design. The descriptive geometry course proved important. It was a tool we used to identify who was likely going to survive the later, more difficult engineering schooling. We watched that particular course very carefully, making sure it was thoughtfully taught.

While teaching engineering at Tufts University during the G.I. Bill of Rights period.

Typically, I had 25 students in each class session. I taught about four or five sections, and I was in the classroom six days a week with, happily, no night classes. I brought home well over a hundred papers each night to grade.

My faculty colleagues were hardworking saints. They were especially teaching-oriented and not research laboratory-oriented or "publish or perish" academic types. They were solidly up to their tasks of handling the pressures imposed by the G.I. Bill. I developed a lot of respect for them. Our students were almost all older than I was, at age 24. This was a strenuous, but exceedingly rewarding time.

It was a real privilege to deal with a student body anxious to get an education and receptive to help from the faculty. I presume that these characteristics were typical of G.I. Bill students nationally. One facet of the situation bothered me, however. In our class of about 200 engineering freshmen, there were only two or three women students–a number much like at Michigan. There wasn't much I could do about it at the time, but I remember finding it troubling.

EXTRACURRICULAR ACTIVITIES

At Tufts, I centered my time on the Intercollegiate Sailing Team. Tufts had a long sailing history, a tradition of good participation by the student body, and good backing by a trustee of the university. During this period, I also had great fun musically. I played in Harvard's Marching and Symphonic Bands, as well as Tufts' Dance Band. I was very busy, and intrigued with every new thing I learned.

AUDITING CLASSES AT HARVARD: ROUND #1

A further advantage of teaching at Tufts was that I could audit graduate-level courses at nearby Harvard under the so-called "Special Student Program." This was for a non-degree status, covered by the G.I. Bill of Rights. In view of my vital, concentrated wartime engineering studies preparing me for overseas duty, I had not had the opportunity to take formal classes in diverse non-engineering subjects.

I chose a wide spectrum of courses at Harvard including Russian Studies, Agricultural Economics, Hydrologic Engineering, the History of Physics, Conservation of Natural Resources, and Introduction to Biology. As you can imagine, this was an intellectual broadening effort if ever there was one! It left me both forever intellectually curious, and cursed that I was never going to understand as much as I would like! I have a sneaking feeling that it also made me enduringly unsure about not knowing enough about an awful lot.

SKIP-BOMBING LESSON OVER NO MAN'S LAND

Once, when teaching at Tufts, I had a student, a newly-commissioned aviator, who had been sent by the Navy to Tufts for an engineering education. He was from the far south in the U.S. He was seriously and, sadly, obviously underprepared for college level engineering studies. I spent a lot of time with him to nurse him through my introductory classes, and he was genuinely thankful for the individual help.

One day he stood up in class, and said in his wonderful, classic, southern drawl, "Mister Wahner, do you-all like to flah? If so, wha don't you put yo uniform back on and ah'll meet you down at the gate of the Weymouth Naval Air Station, and we'll have a little enjoyment in the ay-yah." I eagerly accepted his invitation.

Dressed in my naval uniform illegally, I passed through the gate at Weymouth, which is just south of Boston. We climbed into a two-seater, propeller-driven, training plane and took off. First he asked me if I could stand high altitudes without using oxygen. Of course, I said yes... and he proceeded to fly us so high over Boston I was just short of passing out. Next he flew us to an area just off the southern coast of Cape Cod where the Navy operated a bombing training range, using an uninhabited island off the coast as a target. My young pilot friend then demonstrated the art of skip-bombing. Aiming toward the target island at high speed, the plane dipped down low, almost skimming the top of the waves. I found myself white-knuckled and holding my breath as he simulated the release of the bomb at wave-height, then zoomed up just in time to clear the island. After several of these demonstrations and more, I was thoroughly wrung out, but we'd had a great time!

We flew back to Weymouth and I managed once more to pass the gates in my Navy uniform without getting either of us in trouble. The memorable afternoon was done in the best of spirits; he was a solid citizen and a good candidate to have in our Navy.

FAMILY

My parents were slowing down a bit, but still active during these years. I am unsure when my sister Lorraine and Bob Bulkley moved to Long Island, where Bob worked in Public Relations for the Roosevelt Air Field. It was during that time, however, that they adopted a little girl, Laura, who was born in Washington D.C. in 1946. The family moved to rural Kennett Square, in Chester County, PA, in about 1950, and Bob went to work for the DuPont Company in Delaware. Their son Rob was born in 1953.

I am also unsure what year Margot began to teach music at Abbott Academy, the girls' boarding school in Andover, MA. In the many years to come, and in every place she lived, Margot was known for her dedicated organization of choirs, choruses, and stage musicals, as well as her skills in teaching voice.

SCANDINAVIA

OPPORTUNITY FOR INTERNING ABROAD

In 1947, during the spring term of my first year teaching at Tufts and auditing courses at Harvard, I kept an eye on the bulletin boards and news of what was going on in academia. I stumbled upon the mention of fellowships available from the American-Scandinavian Foundation (ASF). These looked particularly interesting since Scandinavia was replete in up-to-date marine engineering activities, and serving an engineering internship seemed a good way to advance my professional education. I had also come to know and like people of Scandinavian lineage while at the University of Michigan.

The American-Scandinavian Foundation stands as an educational link between the U.S. and Denmark, Finland, Iceland, Norway, and Sweden. As an American nonprofit organization, it works to build international understanding with an extensive program of fellowships, grants, intern/trainee sponsorships, publishing, and membership offerings.

I carefully applied for a fellowship by offering an extensive essay on my experience, future plans, and my hopes for the future. My Tufts bosses, and the very observant president of Tufts, were quite supportive of my interest in obtaining an overseas fellowship. They felt that it might be a good thing for Tufts for me to have this experience while on the faculty. I also had some assistance from a colleague and friend of my father who was involved in museum management and academic affairs in New York City, and who was also involved in ASF.

I was awarded a fellowship for July 1947 through August 1948. It provided enough funding to pay for transportation to and from Scandinavia plus modest living expenses for the period. The particular fund which supported me was endowed by Justus P. Seeburg, the jukebox magnate. Originally from Gothenburg, Sweden, he had moved to the United States in 1887 after graduating from Chalmers University of Technology, and used an Americanized spelling of his name for the very successful company he then founded.

I later learned that I was one of the few engineers that had applied for fellowships at that time. Most of the applicants and successful candidates had been student architects, budding research scientists, and aspiring academic scholars. The concept that I proposed of becoming an intern to industry, not merely a student, appeared to be an unusual approach and a good plan for the Swedish end of the international exchange organization. It fit me well, mostly because I was struggling with wanting to do more, rather than limiting myself to studying.

In seeking the fellowship, I had indicated to ASF that I would do some serious language preparation. I had no familiarity at that time with any of the Scandinavian languages. Fortunately, I found a great local tutor, who taught me one hour a day for about a month before I left for Scandinavia.

I was—and still am—far from a skilled linguist. The tutor was incredibly helpful. He told me that if I learned what he labeled as "Skandinaviska" (apparently a sort of nation-neutral version of the local dialects) it would be passable in Norway, Denmark Sweden and in much of Finland. He also explained that once I attained a vocabulary of about 1,000 root words, I could create the equivalent of 10,000 English words since the Scandinavians combine their root words to form complexes, such as is done in German. He pointed out, however, that the unfortunate initial result would be that I would readily be able to read the languages with a small vocabulary, but would be challenged to speak them since the complexes of the roots required a lot of language memory.

He further pointed out that the most serious shortcoming that English speakers typically have in making themselves intelligible in Scandinavia is that they do not learn the importance of enunciation. For instance, the common name of Anderson should be enunciated "an-ders-son", hesitating minutely, at the end of each syllable.

He made a comment which intrigued me—that I could measure how I was doing with my pronunciation of the language by whether I could pass off as being Finnish, not native-English speaking, in conversing with my Swedish friends. Apparently pronunciation of Swedish as spoken by Finns resembles an English speaker trying to learn Swedish.

He then proceeded to drill me on pronunciation and encouraged me to concentrate on learning the root word vocabulary. When I got to Scandinavia, I found that his analytical approach to my introduction was truly valuable, and inspired me to delve further into the language once I was overseas.

MY GREAT UNCLE'S CLASSIC SEND-OFF

Realizing that my Swiss cousins, the Wagnière family, were stationed in Copenhagen, I planned to visit them while in Scandinavia. As luck would have it, in 1947, about 15 years after marriage, Peggy and Jean Wagnière were posted to Denmark, bringing with them their young family of three sons. I looked forward to making them my first stop in Scandinavia. There, I could also link up with the Burmeister & Wain Company (B&W), a world-class builder of monster diesel engines used in powering large ships, located in Copenhagen. In preparation for my trip, I checked in with Peggy's father, one of my favorite relatives, Great Uncle Harry Warner, who lived in nearby Lincoln, MA. Still somewhat dismayed by losing his high-achieving, "glass ceiling-breaker" daughter to a foreign country, he warned me with an imperceptible smile, "not to be taken in by those darned foreigners!"

THE TRANS-ATLANTIC TRIP

Even though I had transportation support from the ASF, I was wary of expensive travel alternatives to get me to Scandinavia, especially as I was saddled with a significant amount of personal luggage to cover my needs. Crossing by freighter seemed a logical solution as I was not tight on time. Scheduled freighters with accommodations for no more than 12 passengers cost a fraction of airfare at that time, and of course I was not unhappy to find myself back on the open water. I booked passage on a freighter out of Bayonne, NJ that would land me in Amsterdam, a reasonable train ride from Copenhagen.

The crossing took slightly under 10 days. Luckily it was during calm summer conditions. I found myself in the engaging company of a group of eleven Dutch bulb growers returning home from the annual bulb auction in New York City. Overall, it was a very pleasant journey. Traveling on the freighter proved to be far better than most of the international travel I did later in my career.

Entering the long reaches into Amsterdam Harbor was haunting. A number of masts of sunken ships stuck up above the surface of the water adjacent to the harbor entrance, still there from the ravages of WWII. I now wish that I had looked around the Amsterdam waterfront more completely.

A Scare in Copenhagen

Arriving by rail in Copenhagen from Amsterdam, I taxied to the suburban residence of the Wagnière family located, if my memory serves me correctly, in Ballerup, several miles northwest of the center of the city. On the front door was pasted a large, threatening, temporary sign, boldly lettered "Mål". Since my only working foreign language was French and my hosts were multilingual but primarily French speakers, plus the fact that French was still the language of diplomats, I hastily figured that a very contagious illness had overcome someone in my hosts' family. I was devastated. I started back to the taxi wondering what to do. I was too ignorant of the language, and obviously too shaken to notice the small o-shaped accent above the "a", and I later discovered that the word merely meant PAINT. After several minutes of severe trepidation, I mustered my courage, knocked on the door and was warmly welcomed into a very affectionate and fascinating family.

The Wagnières

The Wagnière parents were worldly souls, very knowledgeable, and concerned about and involved in the workings of world affairs through their careers in international diplomacy. I welcomed the opportunity to get to know them and become better acquainted with their fields of expertise. They had just returned from a posting in Yugoslavia, and had much to say about it. Later, husband Jean became the Swiss Observer to the United Nations.

As they approached the end of their term in Yugoslavia, Georges, their oldest teenaged son, had been sent ahead by his parents to their next station, Denmark, to work on a farm for the summer, but, most importantly, to become familiar with the Danish language. Georges was already fluent in French, German, English, and Italian, as well as the Swiss versions of those languages. This would put Georges in the position of family interpreter, a position in which he performed well.

The Wagnières kindly made sure that I saw much of Copenhagen. They also took me around some of the beautiful northernmost countryside and dune shoreline of Jutland.

A Month at Burmeister & Wain (B&W)

Through the ASF in New York, I had arranged to visit the B&W manufacturing plant in Copenhagen. This company's largest engines, at over 100,000 horsepower, powered large ocean-going vessels, so a visit to the company might be a valuable marine engineering experience for me. Furthermore, B&W's contribution to achieving energy conservation through high thermal efficiency of their engines was of special interest and continued to be a focus throughout my professional life, as I have often worked on

Peggy Wagnière.

problems impacted by the increasingly short supply of fuels.

B&W responded helpfully by assigning one of their senior engineers to take me around and to explain what they were doing, how they do it, and what developments I was focusing on. This resulted in a privileged look at what was going on, and gave me a profound understanding of the role of the diesel engine in the increasingly problematic and critical area of energy production and conservation. My visit of a short month to their Copenhagen manufacturing plant, and my informative talks with their engineers, were valuable for me.

THE AMERICAN-SCANDINAVIAN FOUNDATION, STOCKHOLM

My objective was to get to Stockholm, the headquarters of my internship. I took the ferry from Copenhagen to Malmö, Sweden, then continued by rail to Stockholm where I was kindly welcomed. The Foundation was directed by a group of concerned Swedish citizens with interest in the U.S. They were based in a modest office suite in downtown Stockholm.

> ### PROTECTION OF DANISH INTELLECTUAL PROPERTY FROM INVADING GERMANS
>
> *I was fascinated to learn the sophisticated design of B&W's very large engines was a significant national asset, a treasure that could not be allowed to fall into German hands when Copenhagen was taken over during WWII. Accordingly, the wooden patterns used for casting various critical parts were deliberately altered by the company, making them ill-fitting if the Germans were to use them in attempting to build their own engines, and stored openly. The usable patterns were hidden away from the invaders, and put back in service only when the war was over.*

The vibrant Fru Adel Heilborn was the administrator. She was American-born and the wife of a prominent newspaperman, bilingual in English and Swedish, and extremely knowledgeable about Sweden, its industry, and its institutions. Additionally, she had many useful contacts. She was a veritable dynamo in her work. I felt that I had arrived at a well-organized and active place.

MY STOCKHOLM QUARTERS

My accommodations were ready when I arrived. Fru Heilborn had arranged a room in a student boarding house about 20 blocks north of the center of Stockholm, immediately across the street from the Olympic Stadium. It was a four-floor city apartment house with 15 boarders. Several of the boarders were students attending the nearby Opera School, while the remaining were recent college graduates just starting professional careers in downtown Stockholm. The owners were two resident ladies who had operated it for many years. It was its own institution, in a sense, apparently well-known around Stockholm. We ate all our meals there in a rather formal style, overseen by the two ladies, and waited on by a resident maid.

The Opera School students were especially enthusiastic in our house when the State Opera Company started each new operatic run. They would review the opera for us in considerable detail.

I remember, for instance, their description of Aida. They suggested that the person for us to focus on is the policeman in the center of the stage trying to conduct traffic: three elephants on stage left, city fire department brass band on stage right, opera school chorus running around the whole stage, opera professional chorus backstage trying to project their singing out front, and several soloists screaming on top of it all, with the pit orchestra trying to meld it all together. Of course we all streamed to the opera house as a group for performances, well prepared, paying 27 cents for a seat, and sitting way up in the third balcony, enjoying the opera with glee for being able to spot the policeman at his work.

I had arrived in Stockholm completely ignorant and somewhat wary of opera as a medium, but during my stay in that boarding house I surely became enamored. I remember arriving at Mozart's *Abduction from the Seraglio*, only to find my seat was behind a post on the third balcony. I was unable to see the stage well, but I must say I was still very happily taking in the beautiful music. I rapidly fell madly (but very remotely) in love with Eva Pritz, one of the second or third leads in the Mozart operas. I became an opera fan, buttressed by the Swedish folk operas celebrating national and religious holidays.

EARNING POCKET CHANGE

I had very little money, so I hit on an easy solution for earning pocket change. I went to the waterfront square, which is the assembly and meeting place for tourists. Swedish students with their classic student caps were always there, offering guide service to tourists. I gladly joined them on weekends, and with a slightly Swedish accent, allowed tourists to know that I spoke "a little bit of English." I also offered to chauffeur the tourists' rental cars when they were buffaloed by having to drive on the left side of the road. (Sweden finally switched to driving on the right side a short time later.)

Acting as a tour guide forced me to get to know a lot about the city of Stockholm and I came to appreciate it. When I returned home later, in fact, I realized I knew much more about Stockholm than I did about downtown Boston. So, I broke out my bicycle and systematically biked all around Boston, discovering a city I had lived near but had never really known well.

LIFE IN STOCKHOLM

There were several memorable aspects of living in Stockholm. Bicycling in winter was a personal craze of mine. Religiously, I bicycled all winter in spite of the dire warnings of my friends. I needed the freedom of getting around to get to work, as well as to take advantage of city living. This required a complicated series of junkets on bicycle, to get first to the commuter train, and then to the workplace.

Living across the street from the Olympic Stadium attracted me there every winter night to play hockey on their beautifully maintained outdoor rink system. Several teams systematically met there each night to play a series of games–very similar to the town games we play here or the intramural games in college. I found it great sport to play on two "foreigners" teams, one Finnish, manned by refugees from the USSR/Finland Winter Wars, and another manned by Hungarian refugees from some form of political uprising in that part of the world.

I found myself bothered by the drinking traditions amongst my ASF friends in Sweden. As an ASF Fellow, I was urged to attend parties and celebrations where the tradition was to drink toasts in the "Helan går" ("the whole goes") tradition in which an entire glass of their 180-proof national hard liquor drink is swilled down in one gulp, rather than merely sipped. This is often done while standing on a dinner chair. I still was a non-drinker when arriving in Stockholm, especially after my wartime experiences, and I found this "Helan går" routine to be really difficult to deal with at first, as I felt forced. Finally, I learned how to do it!

VOLUNTEER DIPLOMACY

At the request of the diplomatic service personnel in the American embassy in Stockholm, I attempted to help develop a way of assisting proper placement of Swedish students choosing to enter schools in the U.S. Since the Swedish high school system educates students up to the age and completion of the sophomore year in college in the U.S., it is difficult to determine where to place Swedish high school students when they come to America. I learned a great deal about the Swedish school system, and wrote a guide for the use of Swedish student placement over here. Also, at the Embassy's request, as well as the request of the American-Scandinavian Foundation, I held some seminars in areas near Stockholm on life and conditions in the U.S.

INTERNSHIP AT DELAVAL

AFS arranged my next experience, as an engineering intern in the DeLaval Company just outside of Stockholm. DeLaval was performing research and development in areas of significant interest to me–modern prime movers for ship propulsion such as gas turbines and fuel-efficient diesel engines.

Starting in the 1890s, Gustaf deLaval, often referred to as the Swedish Thomas Edison or Alexander Graham Bell, pioneered in the field of centrifuges, steam turbines, diesel engines, large reduction gears, and the like. Several companies attained a long history of diverse mechanical device invention, development and manufacturing. The best known results were the cream separator centrifuge, followed shortly by its attendant milking machine, resulting in what is today a substantial business and corporate structure found in several countries. A completely separate corporate structure evolved around prime movers. It had settled in a remote suburb of Stockholm, a half-hour ride for me on commuter rail.

As an intern in the diesel manufacturing arm of the company for the first several months, I participated in the industrial engineering functions in the division producing their brand of large engines. They were concentrating on improving fuel economy of their diesels, using methods to turbo-supercharge their two-stroke cycle engines to make them less fuel-hungry. I found this to be a valuable experience in the planning, manufacturing, and production of large, complicated mechanical devices. It also enabled me to further understand the role of the diesel engine in the prime mover field. Much of this industrial engineering experience became useful to me later in my career.

DeLaval had recently won a contract from the Swedish Navy to develop a gas turbine power plant for a new class of small, high-speed craft similar to our PT boats or the German E Boats. Their history of work on steam turbines, coupled with their unusual physical facility for testing high rotational-speed devices, made them particularly qualified to undertake the work. I was fortunate enough to qualify to work on this project.

In those pre-Sputnik days, many of us had heard of the technical advances being accomplished in Russia and I think that I had created a subconscious image of the personnel involved. I ran into the personification of that image–a fascinating Russian engineer who was overseeing the gas turbine development program. Working as the intern under this brilliant engineer taught me how to work and relate well with such significant people. Whatever success I had in this area later in life is due, in part, to my time at DeLaval.

Baltic Maiden was my stunning skerry cruiser, shown above in a peaceful cove off Stockholm.

Based on my experience on repair ships during WWII, an internship at the Bath Iron Works, and my degree in marine engineering, I was sent out by DeLaval to work with their field engineers, a task far more responsible than usually entrusted to an intern. My knowledge of English in the maritime field helped the Swedish-speaking field crew since we often were working on vessels where technical English was needed in order to accomplish the field mission. This field service experience provided me with a chance to travel to some of the major ports of Sweden and to gain skills in on-site service.

My Swedish Skerry Cruiser

Because of my overseas experience, as well as the work I was doing for the company that was above and beyond the typical intern's involvement, DeLaval started me on a modest salary. The small bit of additional cash was an enormous luxury for me and allowed me to buy one of the extraordinary skerry cruisers that I so admired. This boat became an important part of my Scandinavian experience. The type of boat enabled me to join an associated group of sailors, and I enjoyed their company and learned a lot. This fun group of people kept me busy all year, as they got me into skate sailing and other social activities.

AND THEN CAME ALICE...

At the beginning of the summer, an unexpected event took place. Both my father and my cousin Sturge Warner wrote me saying that a younger sister of his wife Hilda was coming to Stockholm for the summer as a participant in the Experiment in International Living student exchange program. I was asked by both men to be sure to meet her at the Stockholm Central Train Station, and take her to her host family's home in the city.

I did as I was asked. I met—and was quite delighted to welcome—a young, attractive and quite down-to-earth Alice Sizer at the train station. I oversaw the successful meeting between Alice and her new host family, and then returned right home to my boarding house in the city.

Several days later, I received a call from the parents of the host family. They invited me for a visit to their summer place on one of the islands in Stockholm's Archipelago. Happily, I discovered that island was a beautiful one-hour sail from where my little cruising sail canoe was tied up.

Alice Foster Sizer.

GETTING TO KNOW ALICE

It was a start of a terrific summer. As soon as Alice appeared in Stockholm, sailing took on a special role, as it was convenient and fun for me to sail out to the island where Alice was spending the summer. At first Alice was understandably a bit hesitant about sailing, as she had grown up with little experience or familiarity with sailboats, but eventually she came to genuinely enjoy our outings. For the final two busy months of my internship, we sailed often. We explored the country and other attractive islands in the Archipelago, and generally, got to know and genuinely enjoy each other.

ATTRACTION OF NORWAY'S WEST COAST

Before coming to Scandinavia, I had heard a lot about the west coast of Norway. This coast was famous for its mountainous island and fjord scenery, the area's environmentally controversial sealing industry, and the extraordinary ice-hardened small vessels so useful in Admiral Byrd's polar exploration.

The more I moved around Sweden, the more I kept being urged to visit the Norwegian coast. It was suggested by many that the way to see it really well with modest expenditure of my scarce cash was to travel on the coastal ferry system. Post-WWII Norway was similar to Alaska, in that a coastal highway system was either nonexistent or treacherous. The isolated coastal inhabitants had instead developed a very effective ferry system to support their needs.

My adventurous cruising colleagues also told me I could get less expensive passage if I were willing to forego a cabin to sleep in a sleeping bag on the fantail of the ship. Years later, I was also to do this occasionally on the Alaska ferry.

I took all of my friends' recommendations, and started out on an adventuresome journey. I went north by rail to Luleå on the Baltic Coast, about 360 miles from Stockholm. Then I took what is considered one of the most dramatic train trips in the country, upstream along the river which empties into Luleå harbor. That rail line heads northwest directly to Narvik, Norway, about 200 miles away. The rail trip was breathtaking. It paraded me through the dense forested banks of the lovely river. Then the scenery changed dramatically into a snow-covered mountainous country along the Sweden/Norway border. Finally, the train brought me down the steep hills into a harbor at the extreme end of a classic fjord nestling the small city of Narvik. Here I arrived at the start of my intended ferry trip south along Norway's coast.

Seeing Narvik had a poignant effect on me because of its critical role in WWII. As I left the harbor, standing on the deck of the ferry, I was haunted again by the ghostly masts of sunken ships sticking out of the water, just as I had recently seen when arriving by freighter in Amsterdam. As we traveled southward it was hard to deal with the recurring scenes of small, defenseless, coastal fishing villages showing their ragged wounds from the merciless shelling by German warships during the war.

Since we were several degrees of latitude north of the Arctic Circle, toward the end of the arctic summer season, the sun was below the horizon for only a short number of hours each night. I slept in my sleeping bag, outside on the ship's open fantail deck, shielded overhead only by the boat deck overhang. Each night, as I lay tired in my sleeping bag with the sun still up, I watched the breathtaking, panoramic view of the mountainous shoreline. Most dramatic were the scenes sliding by as we passed the string of the Lofoten Islands just outside the end of Narvik's fjord.

I was surprised and very pleased to meet several men on the docks of the fishing villages who had been crewing on the sealing vessels used by Admiral Byrd. Amusingly, I was able to carry their greetings back to the U.S. to our Essex neighbor, Ed Goodale, who had also crewed with them and Byrd.

As friends back in Stockholm had predicted, traveling the 360 miles by the ferry mail boat was, indeed, the best way to visit Norway's coastline. We stopped at innumerable small but regionally important places along the way. With great joy, some 30 years later, Alice and I traveled the Alaskan coast together on a similar ferry.

RE-AMERICANIZING...?

Shortly before I returned home, I was called in by a senior person in the American Embassy in Stockholm to answer some questions. He wanted me to supply him with information on how one of his senior staff was being received in local Swedish circles. I was able to duck his questions, though I was quite aware of why he was asking.

Suddenly, he stunned me with a remark. He said he was "concerned" that he had not seen me more around the embassy, and that he was "surprised" that I actually spoke Swedish. In defense,

I said that I was on a fellowship to get to know about Scandinavia, and felt my actions were completely appropriate.

He then said, quite flatly, "Warner, you need to be re-Americanized. Maybe we should help you return home." I am not sure to this day whether or not that was a threat, but my reaction is unprintable here. Later I was sure to monitor where he was posted in his State Department career, concerned that he might do damage elsewhere.

OSLO VISIT

Somehow, Alice managed to get me approved to return home with her Experiment in International Living group, which gave me the advantage of not only being with her but being able to return on a special charter flight leaving from Oslo. A further advantage was that I had a chance to get to know Oslo a bit, which I had not yet had the time to do.

With the image of the classic Viking double-ended sailing/rowing ship very much in mind, I concentrated on the marvelous museum in Oslo which featured the craft and all its travels in northern latitudes. I also did a bit of exploring around the extensive waterfront, enjoying the boats and coastal area.

In the process of waterfront exploration, and since I had raced against the Prince of Norway, who was a competitive sailor when I sailed six-meter boats in Sweden, I went with curiosity into the Royal Norwegian Yacht Club. I hoped to meet the prince, and discuss his sailing life. I walked up to the first person wearing sporty yachting garb and asked him if the prince was around. Much to my embarrassment, I found out from the stranger that I was already addressing the prince himself. My awkward social skills were still dragging behind me, halfway around the world!

Alice and I explored some of Oslo together, and both found it very attractive. Alice later often recalled our Oslo experience and hoped to return. I, too, wished many times that we had had an opportunity to return there again to get to know it better.

HOME AGAIN

Once home with my parents in Cambridge, I wrote a careful 50-page report, with a number of photographs, summarizing my activities in Scandinavia. This was distributed to the Foundation, my very supportive Sweden-American group in Stockholm, the U.S. Department of State, and to my boss at Tufts. In turn, I received a very rewarding thanks from the Stockholm group for my documenting efforts.

FLIGHT HOME FROM OLSO

On the flight home, Alice impressed me when she took over during a bit of a crisis. Young, mostly military, families had specifically been told that it was not necessary for them to bring diapers for the flight, as they would be provided by the carrier. Much to everybody's concern (phew!) we learned that the carrier had accidentally left the diaper supply behind. Alice ended up taking the situation in hand, and rounded up cloth napkins from the galley to be used instead!

I found myself dreaming in Swedish for almost two years after coming back. I also did all my calculations by converting the measurement quantities into metric. But I am most proud that I had become strong enough in the language that I was several times labeled as a Finn, not merely a native English-speaker!

My look back on this Scandinavian internship period rests solidly in vivid detail in my now rapidly deteriorating memory, and was certainly one of the most intriguing times in my life.

AND THINGS WARMED UP WITH ALICE

Most importantly, my trip to Stockholm had introduced Alice into my life. At the end of the summer, back in the states, our families became aware that Alice's and my newfound friendship might become something important. Although Alice and I both dated other people when we got back, we each found ourselves watching our emerging relationship, and eventually it began to take on a much more serious note.

BACK TO WORK

TUFTS AND HARVARD: ROUND #2

Upon returning to the U.S. at the end of the summer of 1949, Alice entered her senior year at Radcliffe and I took up again as an Instructor in the Mechanical Engineering Department at Tufts University, teaching essentially the same courses to the still overcrowded G.I. Bill classes. The only change was that I taught a more advanced version of the elementary mechanical design course, which helped my grounding in my subsequent professional life.

I also resumed my duties as sailing coach and did an increasing amount of work with the Intercollegiate Yacht Racing Association (ICYRA) by overseeing regattas all over the East coast.

To my growing excitement, I also joined the best dance band that I had ever played in. A Tufts undergraduate student had put together a 17-piece dance band, a group of highly skilled musicians, who worked beautifully together. I enthusiastically played in this band throughout my second year at Tufts.

I also picked up pretty much where I had left off at Harvard, except that I began concentrating most heavily on the profoundly fascinating conservation courses and their related activities. I came close to shifting my career goals to this discipline but found it impossible to see how to get into the field. I was frightened away because I did not have a sound enough background in the natural or social sciences. I found myself inevitably bound toward engineering. This was a difficult choice for me.

Simply, I was dazzled by the competent Harvard faculty and by the very select student body, but I remained somewhat terrified by the social atmosphere. I found Tufts to be a valuable place for my age group and I was very glad to see that the WWII returnees on the G.I. Bill had a college experience based around their needs available to them.

FALLING FOR ALICE

My social life finally blossomed at this point. I think that, at last, I had learned to present myself differently. Since returning to the U.S. from my internship in Scandinavia, I dated several Scandinavian girls here who were rather unusual people, daughters of various well-known citizens from back in the "Old Country". I was, however, quite obviously, slowly falling in love with Alice Sizer.

The fact that Alice was living at Radcliffe was almost too convenient to be true. I was living in my family's house, essentially on the corner of the Radcliffe dormitory quadrangle, and Alice was living almost next door. Also, of course, there was my wonderful golden retriever Karen who needed to be walked several times a day. Poor Alice was not yet exactly a dog lover. As for me, I was unbelievably busy with little time to walk the darned dog, so I screwed up my courage and asked her to walk the dog all by herself. I was doubly delighted that she agreed!

Karen had proven her loyalty when I first got her in that I erected a carefully constructed pen for her, complete with a safety feature consisting of a wooden plank, carefully buried on edge with a wire fence stapled to it surrounding the pen. The first day I left Karen in the pen, I came back after being away for the day to find that she had dug under the plank-on-edge, crawled under the barrier that was designed to keep her in, and was resting against the outside of the fence waiting for me to come home.

SUDDEN DIVERSION INTO THE CENTRAL INTELLIGENCE AGENCY (CIA)

Since being paid off from active Navy duty, I had been doing some special projects for the Navy on the side, to keep my hand in regarding marine affairs. So while at Tufts and Harvard, I occasionally went by train to Washington D.C. to check in with the Navy.

On one such trip, a Navy contact who was an old friend and academic colleague of my father's, asked me to take the evaluation examination given by the CIA. I declined, saying that I did not have time to take a three-hour exam starting that noon since I had a 3:00 p.m. train to catch to get back home. (The Navy wasn't paying me enough to afford to fly home.) He looked me straight in the eye, and changed his request to an order, and I had no way to back out.

I went across town to the CIA and took the test. The exam was exactly the same one that I had been monitoring at Tufts for

Alice and me.

125

our student placement in the School of Engineering! I easily did the three hour test, leaving on completion in two hours flat.

Almost immediately after I got home to Cambridge, I received a telephone call from the CIA asking whether I realized that I had scored in the 99th percentile in the test. I claimed that I definitely was not a 99th percentile type, as I well knew, and that I had known the test backward and forward from having to proctor it at Tufts. They claimed that the test had built-in features which could detect someone with prior knowledge, and that I, indeed, was in the 99th percentile. I suggested that they should look again at their built-in protection because it obviously was not working.

They offered me a job. We went around and around on the matter of my test score and they kept upping their offer to come to work for them. They finally got to the point that they were offering me so much that I could not refuse, especially after the starvation wages I had been paid at Tufts, so I gave in and agreed to further evaluation in Washington. Ultimately, they offered me an opportunity to enter their covert training program in D.C.

I, of course, knew that the CIA was just forming up and trying to get its bearings after WWII. During the war, the U.S.'s intelligence effort had tapped the services of an amazingly accomplished group of intelligence operatives by offering them the opportunity to serve in the famously successful, covert Office of Strategic Services (the OSS). After the war, these people wanted nothing more to do with such work, and many fled back to their more satisfying and less dangerous peacetime lives. This left a seriously stripped-down "extra-national" intelligence (meaning *outside* the country) force in each of the armed services, an inherent extra-national intelligence collection capability within the State Department network, and a technology-savvy facility dubbed the National Security Agency. Domestic intelligence continued to remain solely with the FBI.

The CIA was in its very infancy. It seemed like an interesting challenge, and I was attracted to join in, feeling a sense of urgency to do my duty and help fill the ranks in an important area of U.S. intelligence.

CIA COVERT TRAINING

When I started at the CIA, it was still located on the Mall in downtown Washington, D.C. It later moved to a more remote location. With the help of the CIA and my cousin Sturgis, I found an apartment within walking distance of the CIA headquarters, a boardinghouse for people in my general situation and age bracket. I shared quarters with an FBI agent who had recently returned from an operational assignment in South America. Alice, of course, remained at school in Cambridge–and continued to walk the dog, bless her!

For starters at the CIA, I was subjected to a number of tests, interviews, and examinations. As a result of this introductory processing, I was assigned to undertake covert operational training–a surprise for me since I had not yet known that was the way I was headed.

For obvious security reasons, I will not discuss the training in detail. All in all, I will say that I was given very specific instructions regarding what I could divulge and could not divulge regarding my status with CIA. I have followed those instructions to this day.

As a rather amusing aspect of my training rules and regulations, I was given specific directions on how to dress. This, unfortunately, involved my having to change my wardrobe to present myself as a typical business man, in Washington style, including the wearing of a fedora. Of course that style of dress was far from my usual habit–for one thing, I hate hats–and I was amused to note that whenever I ran into friends on the street they looked at my garb, shook their heads, and said, "You must be working for the CIA now."

The hat situation started a bunch of discussions that I kept having with my bosses. Probably the straw that broke the proverbial camel's back was that my bosses kept saying that we must emulate the British intelligence service. I knew a little about that service, and I made some remarks. In any event, I was put under some sort of watch and eventually eased out of the covert training program. The exact reasons were never told to me, but I landed hard but happily in the overt program in spite of my inauspicious start.

CIA OVERT OPERATIONS

I was welcomed into an overt section of CIA dealing with international intelligence on scientific/technologic matters. This group was just getting started and was participating in the emergence of the new agency. It was headed by a very bright and aggressive Army officer who may have been a West Pointer. (My memory fails me here, but he certainly was one of those people who probably should have been in the Marines, anyhow.) His type was badly needed by the CIA which, in its struggle to get started, needed aggressive management.

As you can appreciate, intelligence in the fields of science and technology was a truly hot area at that time, in view of the rapid progress that was underway in those areas throughout the world. It appeared that we had been assigned a very important task. Furthermore, since the CIA was just officially starting up, I felt that it was a meaningful slot to be in. I welcomed the challenge. Frankly, I think that I probably was unable to accomplish much, being so far down on the totem pole, but it was well worth a try.

ALICE

THE LONG ROAD BETWEEN D.C. AND HOME

After I had moved down to Washington, I intensified my long-distance courtship with Alice. Much was done by mail. I also left a lot of rubber on the roads, as well as wear on the train rails between D.C. and Cambridge. Above all, during that period, it became clear to both of our families that the stage was definitely set for us to get busy and establish a family of our own.

ALICE'S FAMILY

Alice's father was Theodore Sizer (no middle name), and her mother was Caroline Foster Sizer. Alice was the fifth of five sisters, Caroline (Cally), Hilda, Mary, and Elizabeth (Lib). They had one brother, the youngest sibling, Theodore Ryland (Teddy). It was a close-knit family, which included Anne-Liese Wellershaus, who lived with them for more than three decades. During WWII, Alice and Teddy grew up together while their older sisters married and moved on. The family lived in Bethany, Connecticut. Alice was schooled at the Foote School in New Haven, and briefly went to Chatham Hall School, where she found herself unhappy. She went on to Radcliffe at age sixteen and loved it.

The Sizer family, spouses, and grandchildren (1945). Back row: Teddy Sizer, Yorke Allen, John Ecklund, Sturgis Warner, Alex Cochran, Theodore Sizer.
Middle: Alice Sizer, Lib Allen, Mary Ecklund holding Hilda and Peter Ecklund,
Hilda Warner with Molly Warner, Cally Cochran, and Caroline Sizer.
Front: Gil, Teddy and Sandy Cochran.

I cringe a bit when I think back at the very serious lecture that I got from my father as I pursued Alice from afar and watched over her in the Cambridge and New Haven scenes. He told me in no uncertain terms that I was not good enough for such a wonderful person as Alice! That attitude shook me up a bit. It also reassured me that, at least, I had parental interest and genuine approval of Alice and her family for a possible marriage to take place. As for approval of me, I was not so sure!

I finally screwed up my courage to propose to Alice by, of all things, mail! I then stormed up to Boston as soon as I could, and on our next date, she accepted. The truth be told, Alice was not without other opportunities at the time, and I was both surprised and delighted with her decision.

Both sets of parents were happy with the engagement. That Alice's father had been one of my father's first, and probably best, students, delighted them both. The two had stayed close as they each pursued careers in museum affairs. My father had shown real joy over the wedding several years previously between Alice's sister Hilda and my cousin Sturgis, who was one of my father's favorite nephews. Happily, both of our mothers were also quite pleased with our engagement.

My father showed his support to Alice and me by loyally attending her inauguration celebration as she was taken into Phi Beta Kappa. He himself was an honorary member, but had not made the grade as a student. Later, Father again showed his support while I was still in Washington, by attending Alice's graduation from Radcliffe on my behalf.

Seeking New Opportunities

Excitement over our forthcoming wedding, plus the "no real success in sight" aspects of my job at CIA, as well as our joint concern about D.C. as a place to live, all indicated that I should seek a different job. My introduction to the world of natural resources, development, and conservation at Harvard had peaked my interest in the idea of working for a major company which was highly dependent on natural resources.

My older sister Lorraine and her thoughtful husband, Bob Bulkley, were living in Wilmington, DE. Bob was working for the DuPont Company in Public Relations, reporting to the upper levels of DuPont management. DuPont had attained an iconic position as a corporate entity in my mind and that led me to talk to DuPont about opportunities to practice in the field of natural resources.

Those talks led to a very interesting job offer working in DuPont's centralized procurement. This group was saddled with a series of problems regarding long-term supplies of critical materials. My familiarity with marine transport matters was to be useful since these materials were shipped in bulk from all over the world. I waited to accept the offer until I was sure it fit in with our plans.

Family Traditions and Expectations

Alice and I seemed to have much in common, in that our families had many similarities. Our fathers were both distinguished academics in art history, my father at Harvard, and hers at Yale. We each had strong greater families with lots of cousins, aunts and uncles. Financial accomplishments, aspirations, and inherited wealth were similar, as were the financial goals of attaining continuous adequate but not outstanding financial gains. Our parents' expectations about how we would live seemed similar as well, and the social statures were well-matched between them.

While courting Alice, I had become increasingly aware of the strong family traditions of the Sizer clan, and this was related to me both through cousin Sturgis and Father. The traditions of loyalty and closeness within the family practices were perhaps more in evidence in the Sizer family than they were in my own parental family, but were certainly in no way in conflict.

There were enough similarities in the religious outlooks of our two families that we were not facing insolvable problems. However, neither Alice nor I had ever been baptized. Reverend Sidney

Lovett, the Sizer's minister who would perform the wedding ceremony, promptly did the proper honors for both of us in the Congregational tradition at his church in the Yale Divinity School. This religious procedure bordered on being a bit sticky, given my Unitarian family's standpoint, but there were no family objections.

ENGAGEMENT CELEBRATIONS

We had two extensive engagement parties, one in Bethany, CT, and one in Cambridge. I recall the awesome nature of Alice's larger-than-life family as they flowed forth to greet us. Sturgis Warner had prepared me by sitting me down and explaining at length about who was who among the family, while all the time warning me that I darned well must get it straight. I hope that I did.

CONSIDERING WILMINGTON, DELAWARE

Alice and I wanted to live in a place removed from our families in the Boston, New Haven, or D.C. areas, yet near enough to our families so that we could see family when needed in our newly married life. That decision helped me decide to leave the D.C. area and my current CIA job. As I narrowed down my job opportunities, working for DuPont in Wilmington, DE seemed to fit our ideal location. We both liked what we saw of the lifestyle that we witnessed when visiting my sister Lorraine and family in nearby Kennett Square, PA, about 15 miles away from Wilmington.

On one of our visits to Lorraine and Bob, we found a relatively new garden apartment complex that was an easy bicycle commute for me to the downtown Wilmington DuPont home offices. It was just what we were looking for to start our married life. The complex consisted of about 15 two-story brick buildings, each containing four single-story spacious apartments in a community-like setting.

Mr. and Mrs. Theodore Sizer

request the honor of your presence

at the marriage of their daughter

Alice Foster

to

Mr. Caleb Warner

on Saturday, the first of July

at a quarter before four o'clock

Battell Chapel

New Haven, Connecticut

While staying at Lorraine's place nearby, we moved our belongings into our new-found apartment before the wedding, so it would be ready for us directly after our honeymoon.

The stage was set, and we were ready to tie the knot!

Alice, on her first day at Radcliffe.

Freshman year at Radcliffe (1946-7), with borrowed glasses

Alice's parents, Theodore and Caroline Sizer, in the living room of the house they built in Bethany.

Alice Foster Sizer.

The Sizer Family (1932).
Back: Teddy, Caroline, Lib, Theodore, Alice.
Front: Hilda, Mary, Cally.

Battell Chapel, New Haven, CT (July 1, 1950).

9

JUST THE TWO OF US

Wedding, Honeymoon and the Move to Wilmington

On July 1, 1950, we were married at Battell Chapel in the middle of the Yale Campus in New Haven. Alice's Maid of Honor was an American friend from the Experiment in International Living who had been on Alice's trip to Scandinavia. Another of the bridesmaids was a Swedish national whose family had hosted Alice in Sweden. My two ushers were long-time friend, John Ross, from Cambridge and sailing colleague, Dick Besse, from Syracuse, NY. The best man was Alice's younger brother, Ted Sizer. The three flower girls were our nieces, Molly Warner (Hilda's daughter), Laura Bulkley (Lorraine's daughter), and Hilda Ecklund (Mary's daughter). At the wedding, there were perhaps about 150 people in attendance.

After the wedding, a reception of several hundred people took place in the lovely orchard in back of Alice family's house in Bethany, ten miles north of New Haven. We were honored by the presence of our friends, including many from Cambridge, University of Michigan, Radcliffe, and Exeter as well as sailing team colleagues. Rice was thrown, the bouquet was tossed, and tin cans were tied to our car.

We ceremoniously drove off for a brief honeymoon, starting at the Roosevelt Hotel in NYC. This included a great meal at a New York Swedish buffet restaurant to memorialize the fact that Sweden had brought us together.

We then continued our way south, heading toward our eventual target of Wilmington, DE, to settle. Here is where my memory of details somewhat deserts me. I believe that we honeymooned on the way for about four days in Stroudsburg, PA, near the Delaware River Water Gap, a breathtakingly beautiful small town in the river valley. The honeymoon gave us time to ourselves, and gently pointed us toward our new quarters in relatively nearby Wilmington. We finally arrived at our new home, which stood ready for our arrival. Overall, the wedding had been a great success. The honeymoon had been just what we wanted, and we were ready to move into our new home.

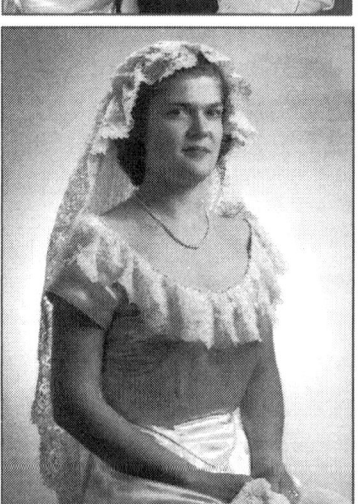

Top row: Alice and her mother, Caroline Sizer; Alice and her father, Theodore Sizer.
Second row: The bride; Laura Bulkley and me.
Front row: unknown, Ted Sizer, Alice, me, unknown, Dick Besse, Barbara Westerberg, John Ross.

Top row: Caroline Sizer, Alice and me after the wedding; Caroline Sizer and Lorraine d'O.
Warner, the mothers of the bride and groom.
Second row: Alice and me, with the flower girls, cutting the cake; Teddy Sizer, Alice and me at the reception.
Bottom row: Theodore Sizer with Molly Warner in front of him, Caroline Sizer, Lorraine Warner, Langdon Warner
with Hilda Ecklund in front of him, Alice, me, unknown, Barbaro Westerberg, unknown.

LIVING IN WILMINGTON

We were comfortable in our brand new garden apartment. The community was friendly and supportive. Community service started to emerge as an important factor in our lives as we participated in organizing the residents into a body to deal with management of the buildings and grounds as well as to establish regulations.

Our apartment was on the second floor in Monroe Park. It was built around one very large central room approximately 15 feet wide by 40 feet long with a nine foot ceiling. On one side of the main room was a kitchen, bathroom, large closet and a master bedroom. Two sides looked out over our neighbors. We subdivided the large room by placing furniture and books so that we had a dining zone, a living zone, and an entry zone. Office/work functions were housed partially in the bedroom and partially in a corner of the big room. It was a great setup for our lifestyle at the time.

Alice found a substantial outlet for her energies by volunteering almost full time for the Red Cross at the nearby Air Force Base just south of the city. She dealt with military family situations on base, and found that it was demanding work that she really enjoyed.

As for music, we both very much enjoyed participating in the well-known monthly chorus meetings at the home of Henry Drinker, Sr. in nearby Merion, PA, just our side of Philadelphia. (Henry Drinker was a well-known amateur musician whose translated texts of the Bach cantatas provided the source of title for this book.)

> ## SOCIALLY CORRECT BREEDING – WILMINGTON STYLE
>
> *One day, when Alice knocked on the front door of our neighbor's house, she heard a distant scream from the fourth floor as our neighbor wife pleaded for help. Alice let herself in, and tore up three flights of stairs. There she found her new friend stooped over a bathtub, with their pure-bred Golden Labrador in the tub, upside down, with feet up in the air. Our neighbor pleaded with Alice to help give the dog the kind of saline cleanse that I'd rather not mention here. Apparently, when the dog was last seen, she had just been amorously pursued by an aggressive local male dog of questionable pedigree.*
>
> *In the long run, our neighbor's beautiful dog produced a handsome litter of what appeared to be Golden Lab pups. Much effort had to be applied with the American Kennel Club to get the litter properly certificated. This was our introduction to social status in Wilmington—pedigree!*

Having just moved into our new quarters, I sorely missed not having a workroom or workshop included in the apartment complex. Thanks to one of Alice's sisters who had lived in Wilmington when first married, we were introduced to a fascinating couple who were fixtures in the Wilmington scene. The husband was a very successful young orthopedic surgeon, while the wife was the daughter of the local Episcopal Bishop. They lived in a large house on DuPont family property within walking distance of our apartment. Near the house was a barn into which I was invited to put my well-equipped workshop which included a full suite of power tools. Alice often accompanied me over there and visited with the wife as I worked in the shop.

THE WONDERS OF WINTERTHUR MUSEUM, LONGWOOD GARDENS, AND THE DUPONTS

In his role as Director of the Yale Art Gallery, Alice's father knew Henry duPont as a leading authority on, and collector of, antique Americana. Henry was, at that time, one of the three brothers who were the most senior, active members of the family. Unlike the other brothers, he was not intimately involved in operating the company, but was instead very active as the founder, developer, and operator of the singularly noteworthy Winterthur Museum.

Unbeknownst to us, Pa Sizer kindly tipped off Henry duPont that Alice and I were moving in just down the street from Winterthur. I was more than surprised when, out of the blue, there came a series of invitations to dine at Winterthur. At that time, Winterthur was still Henry's residence while simultaneously serving as a museum, a library and a research institution with somewhat limited access by the public. Later, in 1951, Henry built and moved into a smaller residence on the property. The main house then was opened to the public.

The Winterthur country residence had about 100,000 square feet of space, with over 200 rooms, and was, needless to say, well designed for entertaining. Henry and his wife threw awesome dinner parties each week, inviting 10-15 unusually interesting or distinguished guests. We were both awed and honored to be included at four or five of these dinners. Usually, some of the guests were invited to arrive late in the afternoon so that they might enjoy the swimming pool or the squash court before the pre-dinner cocktails. After dinner, there was the classic split up, whereby the women went to one ante room while the men went to another for the traditional gender-oriented discussions. Next came a special treat, a tour around parts of the museum-like house, and a detailed examination of one room selected to represent a particular period or function in American antiquity.

One particularly amusing situation took place at one of the dinners to which our new neighbors, the orthopedic surgeon and his wife, had been invited. The couple arrived early to play squash. Afterwards, they each stripped off their sweaty clothes and unceremoniously dropped them on the floor, then dressed for dinner and hurried to the dining room, leaving the mess behind them. During dinner, they were shocked to learn that the room in which they had messily left their clothes was going to be included on the tour after dinner. When the large touring dinner party got to the room, the embarrassed couple was relieved to see that the clothes had been picked up and carefully put out of sight. When, at the end of the party, our friends later returned to retrieve their dirty clothes, the garments had been carefully returned back on the floor exactly where our friends had originally thrown them!

This same couple, it turns out, had another interesting story to tell us about the duPonts. It was practice among many couples getting married in Wilmington to invite the Henry duPonts to their wedding in the silent hopes of receiving one of the *objects d'art* from the Winterthur attic. Under that procedure, our friends received a lovely Paul Revere-style silver bowl. Upon turning it upside down, they discovered that it was not an antique, but instead a modern trophy that had been won by Mrs. Henry duPont, at the Wilmington Tennis Club!

DuPont: Materials and Plant Construction Procurement

After the wedding and the subsequent move to Wilmington, I had started my new job at DuPont. My initial task was to work on a rather complicated situation–handling the raw materials that fed DuPont's ethyl alcohol plant located in a nearby manufacturing complex. The problem had all the aspects of dealing with natural resources (growing sugar cane), international political intrigue (feisty Caribbean governments), marine transport (tanker shipment into the U.S.), and the ups and downs of the U.S. economy (the somewhat wild commodity market for ethyl alcohol). This was an eye-opener for me and a privilege to work in such an eclectic field.

Another challenging part of my job was to deal with evaluating candidate contractors for construction of sophisticated chemical processing plants, then working with the lawyers, engineers and designers to develop the resulting complicated contracts needed to handle the projects.

I worked at this job for something under one year, covering a broad range of tasks while functioning in a very well-oiled organization in a corporate structure with which I became increasingly impressed. It proved to be a rare opportunity to understand business administration skills.

DuPont: Department Manager's Planning Group

My memory does not serve me well as to exactly how I lucked into my next step within DuPont. It probably was through my brother-in-law, Bob Bulkley. His public relations task involved getting a broad view over the internal workings of the enormous company. Somehow, I got wind of an opportunity to join a planning group in the office of the manager of one of the largest operating departments.

First of all, one must understand the rather uncommon overall organization of the DuPont Company. I had not known of other companies organized in this fashion. At this time in its history, DuPont was organized into 10 sections; nine of them were manufacturing departments, each concentrating on a narrow range of products. One was labeled "The Development Department"–a sort of "supreme court" consisting of a small number of very senior men devoted to steering the company through various areas of the chemical industry. Each of the manufacturing departments was managed by a General Manager (GM), which, in most other companies, might have been called a Vice President.

One GM distinguished himself by organizing a Planning Group which functioned more or less as a "brain trust" onto which he could unload the task of collection of information for making major managerial decisions. I was asked to join the group.

The department which had this novel Planning Group operated several plants located in West Virginia and in Texas. They produced the chemical intermediates which they then made into the now-familiar plastic "nylon", which in turn was both spun into textile thread and was also provided to plastic molders for molding into solid nylon objects. DuPont was a leader in the rapidly emerging area of structural and textile plastics. At that time, the nylon business produced the most income of any product made by the company.

The Planning Group was led by an MIT-schooled, PhD chemical engineer named Larry Dodge. He was a former technical leader and a senior operating officer of the old Explosives Division of DuPont which had been the major business arm of the company before the advent of nylon, almost dating back to WWI days. He was well-known throughout the company, and held in high regard right up to the top echelons. Larry turned into a mentor and was very influential in developing my career.

My working level colleagues in the Planning Group were unusually capable and had broad interests. Three were chemical engineers, all with graduate degrees from the University of Illinois. They had already achieved distinguished records at DuPont. Additionally, there was one man who was a research chemist and one who was skilled in banking and the financial aspects of business management. I was the oddball in the group. Apparently my marine orientation was the trigger that let me in since the group leader felt that it was an area where they had real problems and an area that personnel at DuPont did not cover otherwise. I frankly was flabbergasted that I was offered an opportunity to transfer into what I considered a really challenging position.

Our group was set up so that the GM of this pivotal manufacturing department could gather information for potential managerial decisions. We were to monitor sectors of the worldwide business scene. We were often further tasked to make presentations to the corporate Executive Committee to back up our GM.

In order to accomplish this amazingly broad-ranging series of tasks, we were assigned general areas of concern and assembled first thing every workday morning as a group to hear reports from each group member. By way of example, I was assigned to read the Commerce Business Daily, the Chicago Tribune, the shipping news press and several news magazines to report on the availability and activity throughout the world in the field of critical materials of current or possible future interest to DuPont. When important presentations were being prepared, we would critique each other's work.

I had always been intrigued with graphic presentations as a way of analyzing and communicating complicated situations. I gradually took over the job of developing visual aids to support the group's work, especially when we had to go before the Executive Committee personnel. As a result I became involved in most of the areas in which our group worked. I was encouraged by the positive way in which the upper management received the rather unusual approaches that we developed.

DuPont had been pioneering in the bulk shipment of hazardous chemicals via sea-going tankers. By the time that I joined the company they had solicited the help of a very savvy marine consultant to establish a regular monthly shipment of chemicals between their plant in the eastern-most port on the Texas coast up to the hazardous chemical port facilities of Carteret, NJ, and North Philadelphia. I had the privilege of working with this experienced individual and came to learn much about merchant marine affairs.

I was designated by DuPont to keep an eye on this process of shipping the chemicals. The operation was a bit quirky since we had to arrange for the vessel to lessen her draft as she came up river into the shallower waters of the Delaware River just north of Philadelphia. We also had to keep an eagle eye on our operations in the Carteret area, as there was an inordinate amount of hazardous cargo being handled dangerously close to the crowded city of New York.

I must admit that I found this situation to be the most stressful marine matter that I had run into. It was no fun when the director of Port Safety of the NY/NJ Transportation Authority lectured me on what to worry about. He made his point by showing me a dramatic set of photographs. One of our tankers had been sitting fully loaded with hazardous chemicals at the pier, next to a cluster of cigar-shaped natural gas storage tanks. A fire started between two rows of the tanks, and in one terrifying moment, they exploded, shooting up in the air like rockets. At the very same time, a small U.S. Army Aerial Intelligence Service light plane had been flying overhead, and the impact of the explosion literally flipped the plane upside down in the air. The pilot, in a more than miraculous move, was calm enough to get his plane under control quickly enough to start taking pictures in time to catch the tanks falling back down (from *above* him!), toward the ground. The other photos included the fiery scene right next to our ship.

A VALUABLE LEARNING EXPERIENCE

Larry Dodge organized and oversaw our investigations. He formalized the procedure by assigning one of us to head up each investigation and prepare a presentation of our findings. We then went through the excruciating process of testing out our presentation on our own group, where our colleagues evaluated us, tearing us and our presentation apart if necessary. Our group even played tricks on the presenter by simulating how the upcoming meeting before the Corporate Executive Committee might proceed, including the anticipated embarrassing questions that might be asked and the quirky behavior expected from the rather definite personalities on that committee.

All this reminded me of the stories that I had heard of the people going through the classic advanced management year at the Harvard Business School. By the time we actually stood before that "Committee of Grand Old Men" representing our local Division General Manager, we were really ready.

I was flabbergasted when our group boss reminded me not to be disturbed if a certain Corporate Vice President apparently went to sleep on us and even occasionally snored during a presentation. As it turned out, that particular guy usually asked the most searching questions and never missed a beat in spite of appearing to be "out of it". Our boss had predicted *everything* correctly during my first presentation before the assembled corporate bosses.

OUR FIRSTBORN, LANGDON SIZER WARNER

The location of our home was working well— far enough away from our families to learn how to live on our own, yet close enough to be able to get help when needed. Wilmington felt like a different place from the ones we had been brought up in. It turned into a good training ground for us as newlyweds.

Alice became pregnant early in our second year in Wilmington. There had been some question because I had been hit with mumps while in Scandinavia which might have damaged my potency. That turned out not to be the case.

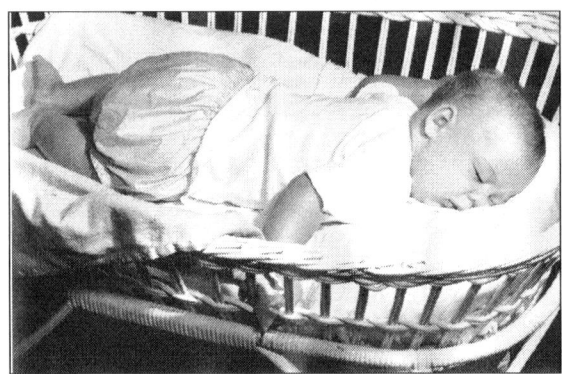

Langdon, our first-born.

Alice was quite happy and healthy during the pregnancy. When her time came, we rushed to the hospital only to wait for several hours because the obstetrician was unexpectedly delayed in getting there. We later learned that, just as he was trying to leave his house, one of his children vomited all the way down the main staircase of his house! The doctor had to clean up an unbelievable two-story mess before attending the birth of our first-born. The poor guy's task was additionally complicated by the fact that the stairs were of the spiral type–less easy to clean. When he finally arrived and explained the details of the scene at home, we developed real sympathy for him!

The baby proceeded to appear in the wee hours of April 20, 1952, neatly timed so that I had to go to work that day, after all, without having had any sleep for the whole night. Our son was named Langdon Sizer Warner, after my father. Both Alice and Langdon did very well. We were thrilled with our firstborn, and Langdon quickly grew into a happy, busy toddler.

THE LURE OF RETURNING TO NEW ENGLAND

After Langdon arrived, Alice and I began to feel the desire to be closer to family. We also wanted to return to the living styles of New England. Although my job at DuPont had been enormously challenging and intellectually stimulating, it was getting increasingly evident to me that I probably was not on a track at DuPont where I could move on, or up. Quite simply, my education, experience and oddball position bore very little resemblance to the established tracks toward success in this very fine company.

My father, Langdon Warner, holding his namesake.

Two of my close sailing friends were practicing industrial engineering in a small consulting firm operating throughout New England. They offered me a position. It seemed like a challenging opportunity, and would give me a chance to work in practical engineering.

We looked at our options. As my parents were in their Essex house for the summer, it was possible for us to move immediately into their Cambridge winter quarters on Linnaean Street. From there, I could easily commute to work. Alice would be essentially next door to where she had been living at Radcliffe, near friends and familiar activities. We could also be near many relations on both sides of our family, and could share our new son with his doting grandparents. The fenced-in area I had built (and rebuilt) was still in place for the other member of our family, our very important golden retriever, Karen.

So, in the spring of 1952, we made the relatively painless move from Delaware to Cambridge, into my parents' quarters at 64 Linnaean St. We spent a few months there while I had my first try at practicing industrial engineering.

BRUCE PAINE ASSOCIATES (BPA)–INDUSTRIAL ENGINEERING

BPA was founded in Westport, CT, just after WW II, and had been successful in offering industrial engineering services on a consulting basis to small manufacturing companies in southeastern New England. It consisted of between five and ten graduate industrial engineers who were skilled in operations management, management science, systems engineering, and manufacturing engineering.

In laymen terms, while engineers *make* things, industrial engineers are tasked to *improve the process* of manufacturing. Much of an industrial engineer's work involves detailed time and motion studies and the re-layout of a plant to improve manufacturing operations.

My assignment was to improve the manufacturing scene in a specialty textile mill located in Douglas, MA, about 45 miles southwest of our Cambridge house, and almost on the Rhode Island border. This plant was the only type of textile mill that had survived the recent disastrous flight of the textile industry from New England to the southern U.S. The secret of our client's mill was its high quality woven woolen cloth, produced in a facility that was flexible enough to meet the rapidly changing demands of the high-fashion clothing industry in nearby New York. Its success was further secured by meeting the very demanding specifications imposed by the manufacture of military textiles. Its inherently higher costs, when compared to the mills relocated to the south, were tolerated by a customer-based industry willing to pay higher prices for the products made in these specialty New England mills.

My workday was unusually long because of the 45-mile commute, and the days were strenuous because I was on my feet on the factory floor much of the time. I was keenly aware of the troubling manufacturing trends, and it was especially rewarding to me to be working with this textile plant. I felt a part of keeping manufacturing in my beloved New England by helping the plant to maintain a badly-needed edge when faced with the lower labor rates available in the south. I was to watch this problem become increasingly prevalent here in New England for many years; even more so, later, as the U.S. faced near insurmountable overseas manufacturing competition.

A BIG MISTAKE

The most significant problem the textile plant faced was the need to reduce the cost of manufacturing. We analyzed the factory layout, and came up with a way to increase the number of looms that each weaver could safely operate.

The weave-shed which contained all the looms was a long, very narrow building with floor-to-ceiling windows. Its width was limited so that natural light from the windows could enhance the loom operator's ability to keep a continual eye on the quality of the cloth being woven. The looms were placed side-by-side, four across, facing the long axis of the building. This layout limited the number of looms each weaver could conveniently operate. If the looms were turned 90 degrees, we figured, each weaver could easily operate more looms, a very inexpensive opportunity for significant labor savings. We called in the maintenance crew one weekend and had the looms swung around 90 degrees.

Unfortunately, as engineers, we had not fully thought out the results of our efforts. In order to minimize power usage, the electric motors that drove the looms ran at exactly the same number of revolutions per minute. To our horror, when we started up the plant on Monday morning, the whole building started to sway back and forth across its long axis. The looms, moving their heavy weaving arms back and forth in absolute synchrony, revealed that the long, skinny building was much less rigid across its length than it was along its length. The office area, tacked on to the end of the weave shed, rocked back and forth enough to produce complaints of seasickness from the office force!

To my dismay, I suddenly realized the purpose of the ugly diagonal metal tie rods that formed a large "X" across each of the enormous windows. They stiffened the building against swaying when the looms were as originally oriented, and protected the windows as a lighting source. Unfortunately there were no similar provisions to stabilize the building in the other direction.

Needless to say, Monday afternoon was a busy time, lasting well into the night, as we put the looms back to their old positions. The company then had to deal with the weavers, beseeching them to take on heavier workloads, even though they had to awkwardly run around the rows to oversee more looms. I was humbled.

RELOCATION WHILE IN CAMBRIDGE

While I was working for BPA, we ran out of our welcome at my parents' Cambridge apartment after several months. When they were ready to move back from their summer stay in their Essex house, we moved to a four-story walk-up apartment in Cambridge's Shady Hill Square.

Our new quarters were originally built as a "married Harvard student" cluster or young faculty residence development, probably just prior to the year 1900. It consisted of about eight or ten four-story walk-up apartment buildings, solidly built, forming a square, situated around a small parking circle.

The apartments were located next door to the large mansion and estate built for the Sachs family of New York City fame, and one of the Sachs family members was then a co-director of the Fogg Art Museum at Harvard where my father worked. The estate itself was owned by a trust that, I believe, was operated by Harvard University. My grade school, Shady Hill, it turned out, had been so named because of its location on the Sachs estate grounds when the school was founded in 1915. The school moved to the other end of Cambridge a few years later, carrying its original name

THE SACK OF POTATOES

Our Golden Retriever distinguished herself by attracting the male dogs in the neighborhood, especially the large poodle which lived downstairs with the owners of our fourth-floor walk-up apartment in Shady Hill Square in Cambridge. Alice discovered that she could always count on having the poodle along, uninvited, while walking our golden retriever. This proved challenging on one walk when Alice and our retriever, followed closely by the poodle, were buying groceries at Savenor's in Cambridge (the French Chef's favorite grocer). When Alice got to the cash register to check out, she noticed that the clerk had added a sizable dollar amount for a 50-pound sack of potatoes. Alice asked how come since she had not bought any potatoes. The clerk replied, "Your poodle lifted a leg on the sack, so you own it!"

with it. Later, the headquarters of the American Academy of Arts and Sciences was housed on the property.

AT THE SAME TIME...

While working at BPA, my professional exposure to the problems of established New England labor relations, managerial structures and human engineering had been useful. I found myself, however, increasingly attracted to the fast-emerging high technology opportunities that had suddenly blossomed in the Boston area. I was ready to take the next step in my still somewhat unfocused engineering career. Ultimately, I found a position at Arthur D. Little (ADL)–just in time to make yet *another* change.

LOOKING FOR OUR OWN HOME

As I was settling into my new position at ADL, Alice and I realized that living in Cambridge could be only temporary. We talked at length about what we wanted as a home to raise our family in, and embarked on an intensive search for a place to really settle down, to establish a realistic home base. It had to be a place with ready access to my job, yet inviting to Alice's lifestyle and inspiring as a neighborhood community in which we could happily bring up a family.

We started looking around in the emerging Boston suburbs. Weston looked promising, and we stumbled into an offer of some land there. One of Alice's sisters introduced us to the Janeway family in Weston. Dr. Janeway was head of Children's Hospital in Boston. His wife introduced us to the attractions of living in Weston and suggested that we consider a parcel of land next to their house that they owned, and planned to put on the market. It was a very tempting offer in view of the scarcity of available property in what many people considered to be a first-rate town. We knew that Weston schools were among the best around. I had a feeling that Weston was a bit "over our heads",

however, but the opportunity to build lit a fire under us to look even harder.

Alice was now pregnant with our second child and we knew, with the new baby coming, we would run out of space in our one-room, four story walk-up apartment. We turned our attention toward actively looking elsewhere.

At that time, Lincoln was generally held up as the best of all suburbs, with a terrific school system, a reputation for preserving open space, and adherence to exceptional planning. We found a sensational bit of property with a dramatic view over the Hobbs Brook Reservoir. We promptly bought a wonderful six acres on Tabor Hill in Lincoln.

Our building site in Lincoln.

We hired an architect to examine the rather challenging site. She came up with a design for a wing-shaped house which did justice to the view. We did extensive clearing of the property, and had a rather sophisticated driveway built to preserve the trees and to stabilize the steep hillside while it approached the house site. We spent many happy hours working on the land with great hopes of building there.

As Alice got further along in her pregnancy, however, we became increasingly aware that building the house in Lincoln was an unrealistic project—and also one that we really could not afford. We also came to realize that the house would have little community immediately surrounding it, making it a difficult location in which to raise a family.

Reluctantly, we sold the property. Happily, though, we sold it to a world-class scientist, the CEO and co-founder of a firm I later joined, the first "B" of BB&N, Dick Bolt. We felt that he would do honor to that splendid site, which in fact he really did. In the process, we turned down a candidate buyer who made a slightly higher offer because we did not feel that he would have developed the site in a caring way. We made a good, definitely deserved, profit which smoothed our way into the eventual purchase of a house—and happily even paid for our first sailboat.

A LUCKY STUMBLE: FINDING 546

Alice was almost full term with daughter Anne when she asked me to follow up on a real estate lead that she had run into, but was uncertain about. Even though far along in her pregnancy, and caring for our active toddler Langdon, she had been doing her loyal best to seek houses within a carefully determined circle of five miles radius from my new employment at ADL in Cambridge. I can still remember her halting remarks about a neighborhood organization called "something like Five Fields". She asked me to find out what it was all about when I inquired about the house. She also warned me to overlook the color of the house ("baby blue"), and said she believed the tiny home could be "easily fixed up".

This was a start to what became the luckiest break in our family life, as a pivotal piece of our family history took root at 546 Concord Avenue, Lexington, Massachusetts.

*Left: Alice and me leaving our
wedding reception.
Below, left: Alice in our first
year of marriage.
Below, right: Alice holding
baby Langdon.*

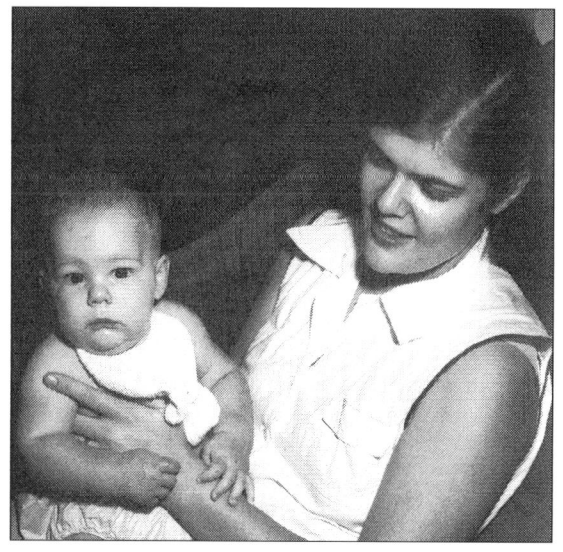

Above: Alice, pregnant with Nick, reading to Langdon, Anne, Wendy, and various neighborhood children.
Right: Me in the early years of our marriage.

10

A FAMILY EMERGES

*Here the chronological order of my saga changes. Langdon's birth and the
move to Massachusetts were a new beginning for Alice and me. In this chapter I do my best
to tell our family story from the birth of our three additional children through to the threshold of
our kids' adulthood, as well as the lives and deaths of my parents and sisters. Writing about
our children without Alice's assistance has felt nearly impossible. Nevertheless, it is with
much love and respect that I make this attempt.*

NEW HOME, NEW POSITION, NEW FAMILY

In August 1954, within a few weeks' time, we bought our house in
Lexington, I changed to a new position at Arthur D. Little, and daughter
Anne was born.

Our new house was quite small, considered by some "minimal", and was
mostly unfinished. It was post and beam construction with a flat roof. The
upper (street) level included a large living/dining room, a tiny kitchen, a
small office, a sizable master bedroom and a bathroom. The downstairs was
unfinished except for a roughed-out laundry/bathroom. The house was built
into a hillside, so the downstairs opened out at ground level in the back. It
was the smallest house in the immediate area, but as our family grew, so did
the house, paycheck by paycheck and hammer blow by hammer blow.

We would later come to realize that we had lucked into an extremely
good thing as far as neighborhood was concerned. We also learned that the town of Lexington
was a real find. During our search, I had worried about the various towns we looked at, and we

had decided to avoid some rather nice areas that we felt were overly influenced with the "town vs. gown" mentality, or where wealth or social status seemed to be deemed overly important factors. By the time Alice found the house in Lexington, however, we were pretty desperate to make a quick decision to buy and move in, as she was just about to give birth to our second child. Hence, we bought the house with little or no research into the town itself. In time I learned that I felt very comfortable in Lexington in its post-war era; we didn't need to build a "McMansion" to show that we had "made it." We lived in what had been a skinny little house for 47 years, and as we grew, we made it grow to fit.

A DAUGHTER – AND A HURRICANE!

Anne Elizabeth Warner was born on August 24, 1954. Alice and I named our new daughter after life-long honorary Sizer family member, Anne-Liese Wellershaus. Anne and Alice both did well during the birth. We all stayed with Alice's "Aunt Cath", Catherine Tappan, in Needham before and after Anne's birth, as we ultimately did for each of our additional two children.

On August 31, Hurricane Carol hit so intensely that it produced 500-year flooding levels, a near-calamity along the Northeast coast. Alice and I quite briefly thought of renaming the baby "Carol" after the storm, but wisely did not.

I soon realized that I had responsibility for storm cleanup at an unbelievable assortment of properties–my parents' houses in Cambridge and Essex, our Lincoln property (still only under sales agreement to the new owner), our quite recently purchased house in Lexington, and the machine shop at ADL, which was sited in the flooded Alewife Creek swamp. Aunt Cath also had a flooded basement and fallen trees which we felt responsible for as we were guests. Equipped with a four-wheel-drive Jeep station wagon, a chainsaw and several Shop Vacs able to pump out and clean up flooded areas, I was straight out busy for more than a week all around the Boston area. Toddler Langdon rode around with me in the Jeep, thrilled by the excitement and very easy to watch over while I worked.

A SECOND DAUGHTER: "WENDY"

In November 1955, 15 months after Anne, Alice Foster Warner was born, fortunately with better weather conditions. Named for Alice, and with Alice's mother's maiden name, we sought a nickname for the baby to avoid any confusion. Alice was reading a book about a girl named Winky, and so nicknamed our newborn for the first three days–until the girl in the book died. Alice quickly came up with the alternative nickname, "Wendy", and the name stuck. Some 40 years later, Wendy finally officially added it to her legal name.

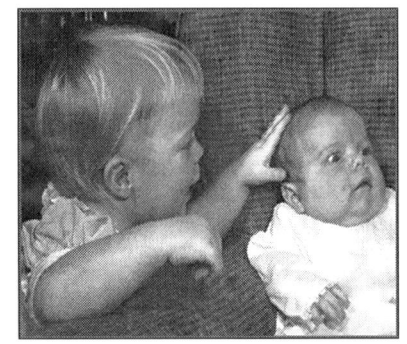

MY BEST BIRTHDAY PRESENT: NICK

On my 35th birthday on September 12, 1957, Alice gave birth again, this time to a son, Caleb Nicholas Warner (called Nick), honoring my mother's childless brother, Uncle Nicholas Roosevelt. I have never seen Alice so proud of herself for pulling off the birth on time to double-celebrate our birthdays! Nick was born with a club foot that required intense care, treatment, and later, much effort on his part. We all recognized that his ability to get around on his feet was important. His lifelong interest and achievements in soccer, hockey, tennis, skiing, and sailing, are ample evidence that his challenging start was definitely overcome.

"THE LAWN CLUB"

With four children, we decided that our family was finally the right size. Alice and I dubbed the children–Langdon, Anne, Wendy, and Nick–collectively, as "The LAWN Club", a name which is still used by some members of our family to this day.

MANAGING THE HOUSEHOLD

I do not remember ever working out with Alice exactly what our respective roles were going to be for family and household life. Someone had to work for a living, bringing in enough financially to support the family and, as it was the 1950s, that "someone" was me. It also went without saying that I would provide household maintenance and operational services that were traditional at that time for a man to provide. Alice took over running the household (an area that, at that time, was traditionally relegated to women, although that was soon to change) as well as participating actively in important family decisions and checking carefully on what I was doing for and with the family.

> ### ANNE ESCAPES
>
> *Anne, who was blessed with a higher-than-expected level of physical exuberance, had just learned to walk. To the busy Alice's horror, Anne escaped the house on several occasions. Once, she was brought home by the mailman. On another day she escaped again, and telltale evidence was quickly found: a sock (on our neighbor Kingston's driveway), another sock (behind neighbor Riffins' house), and a shirt, shorts and diaper, each in strategic locations. Alice, of course, followed the Hansel and Gretel-like trail to discover Anne at the neighborhood pool, quite safe and happily dressed in only her red sneakers.*

We chose not to hire household help such as maids, cooks or housekeepers which had been important parts of both of our parents' households. Quite frankly, we could not have afforded them anyway. Instead, wanting to help the family operate smoothly, we had *au pairs*, mostly from foreign countries, live with us, partly to lessen Alice's parental and household burdens and partly to offer the LAWN Club some diversification of adults in the house. The *au pairs* typically stayed for at least six months before moving on or returning home. Two women came from my Scandinavian contacts. Anne-Liese referred her German niece, who had been wounded in the war, to us, and a Dutch student in his 20s came through a student exchange program. The *au pairs* helped out significantly during the kids' earliest years.

SPECIAL FAMILY MEMBERS

As our family grew, so did the number of its special "members". Alice's siblings continued to be an important part of our family life. Sadly, her sister Mary passed away from Hodgkin's Disease late in our children's adolescence. The remaining sisters and brother continued their close bonds.

ROB BULKLEY

On November 23, 1962, when my 51-year-old brother-in-law Bob Bulkley died unexpectedly, his sudden passing was rough for everyone in the family. His death was the first in my generation, and it came out of the blue; he had had a heart attack. It hit all of us very hard.

As couples, he and my sister Lorraine, Alice and I had been close. I, of course, had a long-term friendship with Bob, who had been helpful to me during my wartime Navy service and also later linked me up with the DuPont Company to start my professional career. Lorraine and I had always been close as siblings, way back to my youngest days. Alice, too, happily found a sisterly friendship in Lorraine, which had developed early in our marriage while we lived in Delaware, close to the Bulkley's home in Pennsylvania.

Rob Bulkley joins us on a road trip with the family.
Back row: Alice, Langdon, and Douglas Cheek.
Front row: Nick, Wendy, Rob, and Anne.

Lorraine was left with the two children, Laura was in her later teens, and Rob was nine. We were in Massachusetts, and they were in Pennsylvania, so we all felt terribly far apart. Alice and I reached out as best we could. We made sure that we were there for them before, during and after the memorial service process.

In the following years, we wanted Bob and Lorraine's children to know that our home was theirs as well. Laura was growing into a young woman and naturally spreading her wings. Rob, however, was still quite young.

It was a natural fit for Rob to join our family during the summers and we all looked forward to his arrival. Our children welcomed him as one of their own and soon our gang of four turned into a gang of five; there was always enough room at our dinner table for Rob. About the same age as Anne, he was a congenial young person, smart, and steady by nature. He dealt quietly with the harsh blow of the loss of his parent. He swam at the pool, roamed the neighborhood with the children, joined us for various trips and cruises on our boat, and generally spent a great deal of time with us.He was good kid. I know that Alice had a particular place in her heart for Rob. We all loved him, and have always felt a special kinship with him.

ANNE "NANCY" MORRIS

Nancy is also an extended family member that became part of our primary family many years ago. Our daughter Anne's birth, along with Langdon's enthusiastic antics as a two year old, triggered the arrival of high school age Nancy Farlow. She was Alice's first cousin, once removed, and the granddaughter and next door neighbor of Alice's Aunt Cath Tappan in Needham. Nancy often stayed with us, read countless children's books out loud to the kids, took dozens of walks, and helped our toddlers drop an untold number of pebbles down the Five Fields street drains. In her college years she lived in our house for two critical summers. During one, she was accompanied by her college roommate, Anne Sprague. The two were lifeguards at the Five Fields pool, and also helped Alice in many ways, especially with babies Anne and Wendy.

Nancy Morris, special friend, family member, and editor of this book.

She is Nicky's godmother. Nancy has been an actively involved family member for decades. (She is, in fact, reading these very words for the first time as she edits this book for Wendy and me!)

DOUGLAS SOUTHALL FREEMAN CHEEK: "DOUGIE"

Douglas played a key role in all of our lives, and made an impact so strong it is still felt today by each of us–yet he was only with us for five short years. Around 1960, Caroline (Cally) Cochran, Alice's oldest sister, told Alice that Douglas Cheek, the son of close friends of the Cochrans from Virginia, was a student at Harvard and seriously ill with what eventually turned out to be terminal cancer. Cally felt that Douglas really needed a home and a family in the Boston area to help in what seemed to be an increasingly serious situation.

Alice and the children visited Douglas at Harvard's Stillman Infirmary. Alice went in to visit him, while the kids stood outside on the sidewalk below, waving up to the young man at his window, as children were not permitted to visit. On the way home, Alice delighted the kids with Douglas' story of hanging a full-size paper skeleton from the ceiling light of his hospital room the night before. The morning nurse had let out a loud shriek when she turned on the light, much to Douglas' glee.

Douglas Cheek, who we called "Dougie".

It was on that very first visit that Alice invited him to move in with us. I had never met Douglas before, but I knew that Cally had reached out to our family for good reason, and I also had great trust in Alice's intuition.

Douglas quickly became a special participant in the life of our family and a meaningful benefit to the kids as they were growing up. Dougie, as the LAWN Club called him, was involved with us while he completed his college education at Harvard and started training as an apprentice in the 4th grade classroom in the Shady Hill School teacher education program. Throughout, he swung back and forth between living with us, living as a student in his Harvard dormitory or, after graduating, living in an apartment overlooking the Charles River, near the Shady Hill School.

Douglas was an enthusiast by nature, and we now know he was battling his illness in silence. His death was quite sudden. We all suffered terribly from the loss.

It amazes me that Douglas chose to spend the final years of his life in our home. Another young man facing terminal cancer might have done quite differently, and rebelled at the thought of living in the Boston suburbs with four active kids. Douglas knew he was terminal, yet he quietly finished his schooling and began his chosen career as an elementary school teacher. While with us, he had a close relationship with each individual of the family, traveling with us on family vacations, driving carpools, helping out with kids' school projects, and generally making our home his home.

Dougie often bicycled with the kids, touring around Five Fields and the Lexington area.

To be frank, Douglas probably did a better job at fathering the kids than I did. More importantly, he helped Alice during a period which was more than demanding for her. Today I can look back and say that I, too, was very challenged as I was trying to get a new business off the ground. I was dangerously diverted from paying full attention to family affairs. I am everlastingly grateful to Douglas for filling in for me. Alice, too, was thankful for the family's involvement with this upbeat young man, and she benefited tremendously as well. All of us are grateful for having had Dougie in our lives. He was genuinely a good guy.

FOUR-LEGGED (AND SOMETIMES TWO-LEGGED) FRIENDS

THE GOLDENS

No story of our family life would be complete without the mention of our four-legged friends. Alice and I felt strongly that children should grow up with dogs. Animals were not only companions for the children, but also helped to teach them about caring and responsibility.

Our golden retriever Karen was still with me when Alice and I married. When Langdon was a toddler, we sought–and hoped we had found–a new pediatrician. The new doctor made a visit to our home to introduce himself (not done these days, but surely done then!). When I politely escorted him into the living room, I was somewhat horrified to see Langdon and the dog on the floor together, quite happily sharing a hefty dog bone. Alice and I collectively took in a breath, but the doctor didn't miss a beat. We hired him immediately!

The line of golden retrievers continued for over 50 years, involving a total of about eight dogs. This parade was aided by the fact that "Pagey" Elliot, a well-known golden retriever breeder, lived in nearby Carlisle. We were sometimes offered problem dogs that Pagey had taken back to the kennel from owners with various problems. (One dog had been forbidden by her previous owners to go upstairs, so had to be carried up and down the staircase of our four story walk-up in Cambridge until I could teach her how to go up and down on her own!)

Our goldens cruised up and down the Maine coast in our boat, slept in close quarters with the family, and even nobly suffered our awkward process of getting them to shore by dinghy to perform their much needed " natural functions".

I don't remember how long Veronica was with us. Phoebe, however, was our beloved family dog for 15 years. She was a close companion and friend to all of us. We also had birds, cats, mice, hamsters, gerbils, chickens, ducks, and yes, even skunk kittens. We had two house-broken rabbits, who would hide under the couch and then leap out in a dead run, to the surprised shrieks of our guests and family alike.

Phoebe, a faithful family member and friend for 15 years.

Wendy once arrived home with box of six skunk kittens. They had been born in a vacationing neighbor's cellar window well. Wendy reported that she had been watching the litter for several days, and a local dog had discovered them and had killed several, making the mother skunk abandon her remaining offspring. Our kids fell in love with the kittens, who enjoyed Alpo dog food. One skunk kit, almost all white except for the chin, belly and legs, made himself quite an attraction by sleeping only with his head in an empty Alpo can. I tried to find a vet who would de-skunk

A raccoon peeks into the dining room window from atop the birdfeeder. Note the paw print on the glass, right. This raccoon was a frequent visitor, much to my chagrin. Along with the squirrels, he did much to consume the birdfeed we put out each day.

kits, but was correctly informed by the vets that his wild nature would always overpower any taming influences. Once the kits matured enough to have the ability to spray, they were released. Phew!

For several years, Anne set up a hatching box for duck eggs. She raised the little ducklings behind the house. The ducklings, without a mother duck to turn to, "imprinted" to Anne. She is remembered walking to the pond in a bikini and Wellington boots, with a trail of ducklings walking obediently behind her (reminding us all of the famous "Make Way for Ducklings" book by Robert McCloskey). This was a "Kodak moment" but for some reason we never took a photograph!

We also had cats over the years. One kitten came into the family after Wendy had taken on the role of midwife at his birth. I was worried, as Alice had never been a cat lover, and did not take well to the young cat's presence in our household. Alice tried to start her car one very cold day and, to her horror, she discovered the cat had been under the hood enjoying the warmth of the engine compartment. One of the cat's legs had been caught in the fan belt and was quite seriously broken. Alice rushed him to the vet, who did a superb job of splinting the leg. Poor Alice felt so sorry for the wounded cat that she personally nursed him back to health, and in the process they became fast friends.

That cat was also known for trying to feed on our golden retriever, sucking loudly while kneading the dog's stomach. This created quite a stir amongst any visitors in the house, as they had to make an instant decision: ignore or make a comment? Another time, the cat and dog were discovered playing with a live mouse, with the golden retriever demonstrating her "retrieving skills" by carefully picking up the desperate field mouse to bring over to the cat again and again. The frantic mouse was teased back and forth around the living room, with family members hollering and running in between the animals.

The summer she was 13 years old, Wendy was hit hard by mononucleosis and spent two months in a cot as her sick bed on the porch. We were working on the training of a difficult golden retriever that summer, who, surprisingly, took only to Wendy and stayed close by her side. Also to keep Wendy company, we brought out the large parakeet cage out, along with its occupant, a very active and verbal parakeet. The bird promptly learned many of the bird calls he heard daily. When he and Wendy moved back in the house at the end of her illness, the bird and cage was came back into the dining room. We were all delighted to have our dinners accompanied by chick-a-dee, crow, dove, and many other bird calls.

FIVE FIELDS

THE HOUSE

If I remember correctly, we paid $11,000 for our house, or perhaps as much as $13,000. Most of the down payment came from making a reasonable financial gain from the sale of the property in Lincoln, which we had worked hard to improve. We probably took out a mortgage of about $8,000, and had enough also to buy our first trailerable, high-speed sailboat in which we cruised the Maine Coast for several years thereafter.

FIVE FIELDS

When we bought our house, we really bought much more than that; we bought into a community that ultimately served us well for almost fifty years. The concept of Five Fields grew out of the post-World War II pressing demand for residential suburban housing. The Architects Collaborative (TAC) in Cambridge, masterminded by Walter Gropius of Bauhaus fame, based its work on the social responsibilities of architecture. It sought to provide "starter houses" from which, it was assumed, the initial owners would move on as they progressed upwards in years and lifestyles. Undertaking all elements from finding a site to designing three standardized house plans, marketing, overseeing construction, and initiating a homeowners' organization to create and carry on the community, TAC settled on five contiguous farm fields in the southwest corner of Lexington as the location for this experiment.

The plan called for 55 small houses, each on about a half an acre, with an interior loop road and several commonly owned spaces to protect views of fields and stone walls. At the center of Five Fields was a three-acre open area eventually hosting a playground area, a swimming pool, picnic and fireplace areas, a frog pond/skating rink, and a large sloping field that could be used for any sport. Community members worked together over time to plan and develop these facilities for the use of all. Parties, "hootenannies", outdoor weddings, concerts, Five Fields reunions and anniversary gatherings, and other events have all taken place on this "Common Land". Other communal activities took place in the neighborhood, including annual meetings, Christmas caroling from house to house, Shakespeare plays given by the children, and an annual square dance on a flat place in the loop road. A good many years later, Alice and I were happy when daughter Anne decided on the community field as the site of her wedding.

When we moved to Five Fields, almost all the houses had already been built and were occupied. Our neighbors were professionals of one sort or another–psychiatrists, psychologists, doctors, architects, academics, and a few from the business world. I initially wasn't sure whether I would fit in, but I happily found it very welcoming. Although our community reflected Lexington generally, at various times over the years Five Fields was home to persons of various ethnicities, same-sex couples, and representatives of a variety of religious denominations. The diversity of our community was very important to us. Alice and I welcomed the privilege of these neighborhood experiences and exposures, and I believe that the LAWN Club members did too.

Almost all families had two or more children. We basically trusted our neighbors and they reciprocated.

The red circular staircase from the porch to the back lawn, a distinctive feature of our house in our unique neighborhood.

All neighborhood kids could go to any nearby household and be treated almost as a member of that family, and as the community developed, so did the co-parenting roles we all shared with neighborhood children. To this day, our children still feel as if they were "raised by a village".

The only way in which the Five Fields experiment did not turn out as originally conceived was that a large percentage of the original owners chose to stay in the community and build additions to their houses as their families grew rather than move out as originally anticipated. Living in Five Fields proved to be a tremendous boost to all of us and our subsequent lives.

The history of Five Fields from TAC's original ideas onward is well-documented in architectural and city planning literature. It is also available in the historical section of the Lexington Library.

THE LAWN CLUB IN THE NEIGHBORHOOD

Each of our children became fast friends with neighborhood kids. At school, each child also had a separate set of friends, who would in turn happily become involved with activities in Five Fields. All were welcomed in our house and at the dinner table. Alice had an impressive collection of cookbooks which she read avidly. But when it was time to cook, she ignored their specifics and created her own recipes, the most popular of which were roasted chicken, hamburger soup, lasagna, lamb with navy beans, meatloaf, salad with her own dressing "made right on top", and birthday cakes with pennies and a nickel, each individually wrapped in tin foil and slipped into the cake before it was frosted.

Sledding was one of the popular winter sports in the neighborhood. A veritable institution for our family and the community as a whole involved a steep slope running from beside the house next door down into the field below—a very exciting, 250-foot long, communal sledding hill, often with jumps and other enhancements built by older kids and adults. Parents could watch the children from our living room, while the children felt free from adult oversight. Neighborhood dogs, including our own beloved golden retrievers, would often jump into the festivities. Sleds, toboggans, flying saucers, and even an occasional waxed cookie pan was used. One year, Alice found the children vinyl sledding pants that needed nothing but a snowy hill to slide on directly. The children learned pretty quickly, however, that they'd rather have something more between them and that icy hill! I will confess that I earned a reputation as an avid sledder myself, and I know that I could make my sled go further than anyone else—almost all the way to the stone wall, and often with kids piled on top of me!

Nick tells of one especially bad ice storm that offered the kids the best sledding run of all. Field Road, one of Five Fields' internal roads located near our house, was normally

Nick, ready to take a dive into the Five Fields pool.

plowed, but this large winter ice storm left it impassable for a full day–long enough to have a cluster of neighborhood kids and their friends from surrounding communities take to the tall hill. This run was a full quarter-mile long, with a second hill two thirds of the way down and the opportunity to take a right at the very bottom to extend the distance and slow down. This amazing sledding day was never forgotten.

Yelling Rock was a large boulder down in the field behind our house. It was a great place to send the kids to sit and yell at the top of their voices when, as Alice said, they were "full of beans." This often happened when the children were ready for dinner before dinner was ready for them. Sometimes the kids were also assigned to let off steam by running around the house several times.

Our children learned to swim at the community pool built on the Five Fields Common Land. This was a 20-yard pool, four swimming lanes wide. It offered a diving board at one end, and adult wading depth at the opposite end. Nearby was a separate wading pool for toddlers. Paid life guards oversaw daily pool activities. Our kids participated in many years of swimming lessons, and they were allowed to walk to the pool at their will without parental oversight. Summer pool activities culminated in the swimming races held during the annual Labor Day Celebration. Swimmers of every age participated, racing not only the clock and each other, but also the records set by same-age swimmers of previous years. I believe Anne held the record for her swimming speed in one of those races for over a decade. Douglas also swam once in the infamous greased watermelon race. I, myself, was not a racing swimmer but a survival-type swimmer instead, and I appreciated the community aspect of the pool. So did Alice, who swam almost daily–the breast stroke always, with her head always out of the water.

The neighborhood offered many places to build tree forts. Capture the Flag and Freeze Tag were popular. The frog pond itself offered a wealth of activities for a kid to explore, an opportunity to get grounding in ecology.

In the winter, the pond conveniently became a two-section skating area, one for hockey, the other for general skating. All of our kids learned to skate on the frog pond, and at some point each kid tried his or her hand at ice hockey. I spent many a cold weekend lacing up kids' shoes on the benches next to the pond, and overseeing disputes over ice hockey vs. figure skating on the limited ice.

Nick really took to the game of hockey. This is when and where I was able to connect with Nick with what I considered to be my own sport. I had always loved skating and anything connected with it. I had played ice hockey hard throughout my life, especially during the year I lived in Sweden, so I found it a real privilege to unite Nick and the sport. Happily, he

A FRIEND AND DOCTOR

Five Fields neighbor Jock Robey was not only our kids' pediatrician, but he was also our friend. Anne recalls going to his house in excitement because there was a blue heron standing on one leg in the pond. The busy man stopped what he was doing to go right out to look at it with her. Wendy recalls the time her hamster was close to death and she called Jock up to come to the house and help her. Before he could arrive, the hamster died. Jock gravely took the hamster from the weeping child and put it in his pocket, telling Wendy that he would take care of burying her pet.

seemed to become similarly attracted to it. He started playing hockey at a very young age on the pond, played in leagues during his school years, and still plays ice hockey to this day.

I also remember taking the kids out to the Concord River, and skating for miles with my long Swedish skates. Whoever was tired would ride on a sled I pulled behind me, and I'd always keep a big rope on my shoulder just in case I had to rescue someone when the ice cracked. It never did.

The Five Fields playground was active all summer long. Several times a year, someone (often neighbor Sam Berman) would build a bonfire and start a sing-along "hootenanny", playing guitars and singing popular folk songs late into the night. Generally, I think we would all agree that Five Fields was a great place for kids to grow up.

ALICE AND THE FIVE FIELDS NEWS

The first neighborhood newsletter was started by two of our journalist neighbor's kids (Alison and Eric Wade) and was called *The Burning Bush.* After several years, Alice took on the newsletter, and announced a contest to rename it and design the masthead. Neighbor Eda Cascieri, wife of the sculptor Arcangelo Cascieri, won with a new design and the name of *Five Fields News.* Alice then wrote the newsletter for close to 40 years.

Five Fields News masthead.

The *Five Fields News* was a monthly two-to-four page circular. It became quite popular, with regular contributions from adults and children alike. It offered information pertinent only to Five Fields, and typical content included lifeguard position openings, square dance announcements, holiday gatherings, swimming pool race winners, death and birth notices for local gerbils and other pets, as well as notices for local house-sitting needs. Once a year it reported on the real-life sighting of a single box turtle's annual trek across Barberry Road, near the Robey's house, as it headed towards the pond area. Cartoons and quips from various sources filled some of each page of the newsletter, and both young and old enjoyed the read. Alice had regular "reporters", ages four to about 90, with whom she'd consult about the most recent "news". Alice delivered the newsletter herself, walking around the neighborhood loop, and putting the circular in a container installed under each mailbox–a requirement of the Post Office Service. As it turned out, there were many years when she also quietly planted flower bulbs at the base of many of those mailboxes–an anonymous surprise for her friends and a welcome to new neighbors.

As the years went on, and the popularity of the newsletter grew, people who moved away from the neighborhood began to request copies for themselves, as well as for their kids at college. Eventually, Alice found herself mailing newsletters to families as far away as California and Helsinki. Generally the newsletter was a hit and definitely useful for our neighbors.

After some years, Alice delivered copies of many of her past newsletters to Lexington's Cary Memorial Library for their Lexington History section, and then put the library on her mailing list. They can still be seen today.

HOLIDAYS

Dougie, as an important member of the household, made himself available to the kids for surprise projects for Alice and me. One Easter they gathered late at night and made an Easter bunny out of construction paper, as tall or taller than a human being, and snuck upstairs to hang it on the accordion-style door of our bedroom. The next year, they sewed together six sheets and spread them out in the big field below the house. The sheets were then folded into a bunny shape. We think Alice's sister Cally had taught them how to do that with a napkin.

Halloween was so enthusiastically celebrated in our neighborhood that our kids continually asked me why Halloween was not an official national holiday–which would then, of course, become a day off from school. I must admit that I had great difficulty justifying the fact that Halloween had never made the grade.

In Five Fields, Halloween trick-or-treaters of every age wandered from house to house just after dark on Halloween night. For many years, our children were haunted by a strange witchlike person who jumped out of the woods to scare them several times as they walked the Five Fields loop. It was years later that the kids learned that Alice sent the children out the door on Halloween, only to quickly put on her own costume (a black choir robe, witch's hat, and a nylon stocking pulled over her face, and haunt the neighborhood. (Did she also wear my mother's black mantilla? I am unsure.) I, of course, stayed on the home front to give pennies and candy to those who came to our door. (For several years, my job was to also refill the water buckets on the roof attached to the front door handle, to give select neighbors a wet greeting before I handed out the treats.) By the time the children came back home, Alice had quickly taken back my spot. Alice's secret was kept for many years, and all of the neighborhood children wondered who the strange creature was that ran through the neighborhood every October, screeching and leaving wishbones on people's car windows. Nick, apparently, was the first to figure out who the "witch" was, after it jumped out at him and his two friends, Harry Katz and Louie Pomeranz, one especially scary Halloween night. Nick was thoroughly embarrassed to discover "it" was his mother!

As often happens when a Halloween event is reputed to be a good one, our trick-or-treat night also attracted a group of kids from a nearby neighborhood who were known for being troublemakers. One dark Halloween night, Alice leapt from the bushes in full witch attire, forcing the group to jump back in fright. One young man hollered, "Jes** Chr***! It's Mrs. Warner! Let's get the he** out of here!" Alice arrived home a bit later, quite clearly satisfied with her night's work.

Then there was the time that 15-month-old Anne insisted upon dressing in her birthday suit and sneakers for Halloween. Alice brought her to our neighbor's, the Aladjem's, to trick or treat. As they opened the door to welcome the lively toddler, Anne reportedly proclaimed, "POOK!"

CHRISTMAS

As a family we all enjoyed music, and we certainly enjoyed community Christmas caroling each year. I would bring my flugelhorn, kept warm under my winter coat. A group of 10 -50 (in one year perhaps 100) neighbors of every age met at the top of nearby Field Road (the road that looped around the neighborhood) joining together to sing from house to house escorted, of course, by various neighborhood dogs. We supplied our neighbors with words to the carols on large cardboard posters and carried a search-light type flashlight so all could read the words of the carols. Later on we graduated to pocket-sized carol books.

Preparing for Christmas caroling. I hid my horn under my coat to keep it warm while walking between houses.

BOOKS, BLOCKS AND BOATS

All of our kids were ardent, almost ferocious, readers; this they learned from their mother, as I was never one to read books for pleasure but rather only for my profession. Alice, however, was an avid reader, and went to the library weekly, getting and returning large stacks of books both for herself and for the kids.

Langdon's L-shaped room offered the perfect place for a long wall of bookshelves of his own. He consumed book after book, with a keen interest in collecting and reading books about sailing and marine affairs. His avid interest in both books and boats continues to this day. Alice quietly kept a pile of library books on the window seat in the living room for many years, changing them weekly. She was careful to borrow books for many ages, and entertained visiting youngsters with books and her baskets of hand puppets and matchbox cars. We also kept our large collection of maple building blocks downstairs, where young people of every age enjoyed them. Over the years, Alice was also known to visit the library before overnight visitors arrived, leaving a carefully selected pile of books at the bedside in our downstairs guest room. She was also sure to provide a stack of well-thumbed paperback novels for the family to share when cruising on our boat, keeping in mind that it was perfectly alright for the books to get wet, fall apart, or even fall overboard (with or without a kid attached!)

The library also served as a display center for various projects that the kids worked on, including a display of boats made by Langdon and an elaborate troll house built with blocks by the whole crew.

SHAKESPEARE IN FIVE FIELDS

Kitty Miller, a Barberry Road resident, offered the neighborhood kids a unique opportunity as she rewrote several Shakespearean plays for use by children. Again, all of our children became involved several years in a row.

A reporter from Life magazine once came to write an article about this unique hometown experience for a human interest story. It was scheduled to appear late that fall in the magazine, and a picture that included one of our kids was slated to be on the cover. The week before publication, to our and our country's horror, President John F. Kennedy was assassinated, and needless to say the article about our small Five Fields production did not run. The assassination of JFK, and later of Martin Luther King and Robert Kennedy, affected us all, and reflected a time in both our country and in our personal lives of critical change and national turmoil.

If I remember correctly, the reporter that covered our production sent us a copy of the proposed article and its photographs with an apology we could share with the children of why the article had not been published. This letter only served, sadly, to drive home the horror of the assassination and its impact on our country. Alice kept the letter and the photos, several of which we include here.

LIFELONG FRIENDS

Many of the residents in Five Fields lived in their homes throughout their child-rearing years and well past retirement. The Katz's were fast friends of the family, as were the Robey's. None of us realized back in 1950s that we would come to know each other for over half a century.

In hindsight, Alice and I considered ourselves incredibly fortunate to have stumbled into the Five Fields community, as well as into the town of Lexington. It offered our children a great environment in which to grow up, and, as their parents, we found real community in both the neighborhood and the town.

THE KATZ FAMILY

Arthur Katz has been a long-term friend of mine, and was the person to whom Alice gave copies of each and everything she ever wrote "just in case". From my point of view, our children were really raised by "a village", and Arthur Katz was one of their many father figures. Arthur and Gladys's children—Jamie, Mara, Johanna, and Harry—are also the same ages and genders as the LAWN Club.

We all miss the house at 546 Concord Avenue. We lived it in for a rich 47 years, and it served us well. In 2001, when Alice and I finally moved to Bedford, we were happy–and fortunate–to sell it to another active, community-involved family with children. Since that time, our family has been happy to know that our odd-ball house remains in good hands.

SCHOOLING

As a parent, I found my role surrounding the schooling for our growing kids especially difficult. I worried then–and have been continuingly and increasingly haunted ever since–about both schooling choices and parenting during our kids' school years. I now reflect on the role my own parents played during my early years, and I can see that I was unusually fortunate as I stumbled through my own schooling experience. They made all the decisions up to my age of majority when I took over and virtually made all the decisions thereafter.

The importance of education had been drilled into Alice and me from young ages. We had surprisingly similar education tracks, in that we both attended private elementary and preparatory schools. Alice continued on to Radcliffe and I went to a state school, University of Michigan. Since both of our fathers' professions were in academia, our parents would have been severely limited in affording private education for us if financial help from the previous generation had not been generously offered in both cases.

THE SCHOOLING SHUFFLE

Preschool seemed like a necessary step for our children, especially since they were so close together–4 kids in 5½ years. We knew that a very busy Alice would appreciate the support and I was working many hours trying to get going professionally.

We were fortunate in two ways: there was an excellent private preschool in nearby Waltham and both sets of parents provided us with some financial support. Each child attended two years at the Green Acres School, which was only about five miles from our house.

When we purchased the house in Lexington, it seemed as though the town had a good school system. We hoped that the public schools would work well for our kids. By the time the LAWN Club was actually entering school, however, we realized that the system was undergoing a challenging period. Experimental team teaching was in place, and school administrative matters were in continual flux.

The saga of our children's orchestrated schooling shuffle started in elementary school and continued into the middle and high school periods. Langdon, Anne, Wendy, and Nick each traveled their own individual, carefully selected educational path. As each one of our children in turn went through preschool and entered grade school, we became increasingly involved. Fortunately, Douglas was available to help Alice with carpooling.

Langdon's attendance in a Lexington elementary school had a significant effect on our life as parents. Alice volunteered in the school library, giving us a much-wanted inside perspective of the school as an organization. We grew increasingly aware of the school system, as well as the broad complexity of our town and community. We developed a genuine interest and feeling of responsibility, and thus began a long-term involvement in town, community, and school affairs.

As is often true for so many first-borns, Langdon's schooling experience educated us as well as him, especially regarding getting help with his reading disability. It was clear quite early on that he was having problems. In those days, dyslexia was not well recognized and not well handled in many schools. Alice, an avid reader herself, was concerned, and stayed on top of Langdon's daily situation at the school. After much soul-searching, we pulled him out of the Lexington schools after third grade and enrolled him at the Fenn School in Concord. There, we discovered a wonderful and effective tutor, Diana Seamans. Her private tutelage focused on working *around* dyslexia, since a cure was not possible. Langdon learned to read, and a whole new world opened up for him. The work of this one woman made a life-long difference in Langdon's future, both as an individual and a professional. He is an avid reader, has earned his doctorate, and is now a teacher himself. I wonder if Diana Seamans ever knew how much she improved her young student's life.

At Fenn, our role was to listen and learn from their schooling methods. We welcomed their guidance rather than attempting to jump in ourselves. It was almost as if we were also going to school; we learned a great deal about a successful educational process and addressing individual student needs.

Anne's first two grade school years in the local Franklin School were also a challenge which Alice watched pretty carefully. Based on her observations as well as recommendations from the school faculty, Anne was moved into the Hancock School which provided Lexington students with an Advanced Program. Anne remained there for the next two years, during which the experimental educational spirit of the 60s took its toll on her. Wendy, in the meantime, had had an unsuccessful first grade in public school, and moved to the Belmont Day School to successfully and contentedly repeat first grade. For her fifth grade year, needing both a happier environment and to be closer to her sister, Anne moved to the same school as Wendy, where she thrived as well. Nick started in first grade there, and, generally, Belmont Day was a real success. Later, Nick joined his sisters at Shady Hill. Thankfully the kids' schooling was again made possible, in part, by financial help from our two sets of parents. (See Postscript for more detail about the LAWN Club's schooling.)

Anne, Wendy, and Nick spent several years each at Shady Hill School, the same school I had gone to as a boy. The school had evolved, grown, and thrived since my days there. Our kids were very happy, and the school successfully addressed the educational challenges that each child was facing. Nick skipped a grade and, as it turned out, this difficult decision was the right one and certainly did him well, thank goodness. Langdon continued on at Fenn and then went one year to Belmont Hill before moving on to Palfrey Street School.

As Langdon went through Palfrey, he was exposed in-depth to environmental issues, which were a strong suit of the faculty. This seems to have launched him on his later life's work in the environment field. I, too, found his studies fascinating, as I had done professional work in the natural resources field at DuPont and studied in the field at Harvard.

Anne entered The Cambridge School of Weston in tenth grade as a day student. She was heavily engaged with almost all aspects of the school, most notably drama (she played Lady Macbeth and Antigone, among other things) and modern dance, and was successful academically. She was definitely oriented toward a demanding college as a next step.

Wendy and Nick moved to the Lexington High School in the same year. Wendy entered in tenth grade, and had a troubled two years. Luckily, she continued to do exceedingly well in her classes, and she unexpectedly was able to graduate at the end of 11th grade. Nick entered the public school system in ninth grade, and went through to graduation from twelfth grade, seeming to take the school system in stride.

Alice and I believed that our kids each had a very good primary and secondary education, though it took much effort on our part to make it so. Each kid also had his/her share of difficult as well as excellent school years.

HOCKEY DAD GONE MAD

Five Fields was conveniently located close to Boston and to various good athletic facilities. One of those was Hayden Recreation in Lexington, which offered both ice skating and swimming to local children of every age. Nick was very involved in hockey, and often his team practiced in the wee hours of the morning due to scheduling difficulties with the ice rink. I was the parent to drive him to these practices and to attend his games.

When Nick was about 15, he started playing on the Midget AA All-Stars ice hockey team. The team had only played several games together that year when they played a home game at the Hayden rink against a strong, rival team. Only one referee was working the game, where there were supposed to be two, and he was struggling to keep the teams in check with little help from each team's coaches. A fight broke out and the teams were out of control. Both coaches were over the top, screaming at the kids to fight harder. The ref made only a weak attempt to stop the fight and then simply walked off the ice.

I'm afraid that that's when I stepped in. I came over the wall and started picking up kids by the scruff of the neck and the seat of their pants, throwing each of them over the wall into the seats. Eventually when things slowed down, the head of the league promptly kicked Nick off the team and informed me that I was no longer allowed in the arena. It was several days and many phone calls later before Nick and I were finally allowed back.

Years later, the start of that fight was revealed by Nick. What I had *not* seen was that it had all started when Nick had the puck, and came out of a corner only to lift his head straight into the fist of an opposing team member. He landed flat on his back on the ice, and both teams piled on top of him with fists flying. Nick had successfully fended for himself. My involvement was only due to the fact that the ref had no control over the teams, unaware that my son was at the bottom of the pile!

THE PALFREY STREET SCHOOL COW

One major school project involving Langdon lives on in infamy even after some 40 years. The real story is that, apparently, Langdon had a crush on a girl at Palfrey during the January that they were required to do a Senior Project. For reasons none of us can recall, Langdon, the girl, and their imaginative teacher decided to produce a full reconstruction of the skeleton of a cow from a cow carcass itself. They then (of course) planned to mount the school's (artificial) human skeleton on the back of the cow's skeleton as if riding it.

The teacher had contacts with someone from a local suburban zoo, where meat was provided in bulk for the animals. A cow carcass "became available", and the two students and their teacher went to the slaughterhouse to pick it up. With the students' help, the teacher removed meat from bone. They were assured that the meat would be fed to the tigers, and consequently, they later arrived back at school with buckets full of extremely messy bones. They spent the next several weeks boiling the bones in sodium hydroxide.

As soon as they attempted to join the bones up, a distinct problem arose. They simply could not manage to hold all the bones together in place, due to the weight of the skeletal structure. The darn thing was just too heavy to stand up on its own.

This is, of course, a father's saga, so my own story starts here.

Since we were the only family with a pickup truck and a workshop at home adequate for the necessary assembly and stabilizing of the beast, I was duly elected to help out. Although I have vague memories of transporting the beast's bones home, I do have a clear memory of working on a lot of large odoriferous animal skeletal parts before it all came together. My engineering feat was made possible, it turned out, only with a good amount of epoxy. After an inordinate amount of time and effort, the enormous cow was ready to go, and was attached onto a base. For added flair, Langdon ceremoniously affixed longhorn bull horns to the skull.

We managed to get our beast into the pickup truck bed for transport, and posted young Wendy in the truck bed with the cow, instructing her to bang on the window, should calamity occur. As we drove slowly to the school, a local reporter clicked a picture, and we were a hit in our small town's local newspaper that week.

This project certainly symbolized the unusual but intriguing aspects of Langdon's school's approach to education!

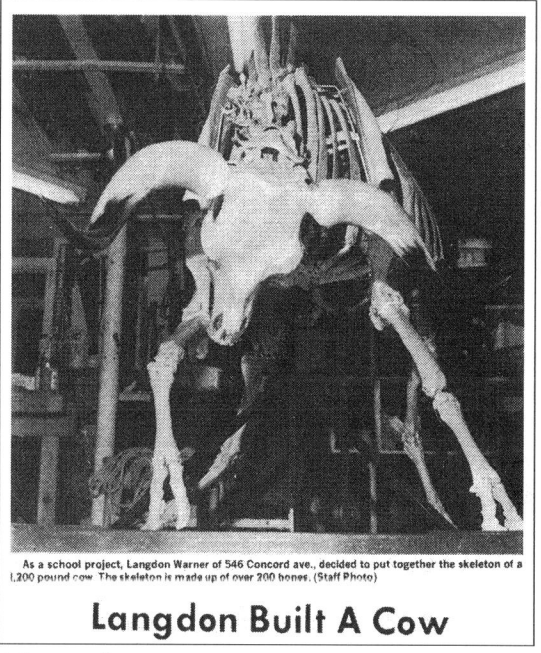

As a school project, Langdon Warner of 546 Concord ave., decided to put together the skeleton of a 1,200 pound cow. The skeleton is made up of over 200 bones. (Staff Photo)

Langdon Built A Cow

The cow that Langdon, a friend, and his teacher built for Langdon's senior project at Palfrey Street School, as shown in the local newspaper.

STICK SHIFT OR AUTOMATIC?

As each of our kids became old enough, learning to drive stick shift cars and trucks, as well as how to tow trailers, became inordinately significant. My business required that I have a pickup truck, and my love of boating required me to have boat trailers around. Alice needed to have her car continually available, and was understandably reluctant to let our kids share it. The result was that each member of the LAWN Club was forced to learn on the stick shift truck. Because of our tight driveway, the truck, and often the trailers, had to be moved around.

Although this situation caused a bit of difficulty when the kids took driving tests or required driving lessons in school in automatic shift cars, it stood them in good stead later. When Langdon was at Southampton College on Long Island, NY, his truck savvy enabled him to set up a recycling effort within the school's local county. He also was heartily welcomed as the only student able to drive the stick-shift college vehicle while on a student exchange in the U.S. Midwest during his undergraduate days. Anne's truck driving skills resulted in her driving the Yale University rowing shells to Florida and back. Nick's truck driving started early and he has always favored having a truck in his "stable" of vehicles in Burlington, Vermont, where he went to University of Vermont and has lived ever since.

FINALLY, COLLEGE

Alice and I played a role in the critical process of college selection and application only with Langdon. At Palfrey Street School's suggestion, we sought the good services of a professional experienced in advising students in the college selection process. Following his lead and assistance, Southampton College of Long Island University seemed a fit. Langdon graduated after four years. Next he earned his Masters degree at University of Rhode Island in Marine Affairs, and eventually went on to earn his PhD in Geography at Rutgers, with a concentration in Environmental Science.

Anne, Wendy, and Nick decided things on their own, and we, as parents, did our best to keep up. Although Anne was accepted to several of her target colleges, she was initially put on the waitlist at Yale, which was her first choice. She then elected to spend a year in Finland studying Marxist Leninist theory and working at the Marimekko Fabric production line in Helsinki. Happily, she was accepted at Yale for the following year. Wendy, too, took a year off, due to her unexpected high school graduation in 11th grade. She followed up by going to Middlesex Community College. Nick, in turn, went to the University of Massachusetts for two years, before transferring to the University of Vermont, in Burlington. To this day he lives and works in Burlington, VT.

AN EPIPHANY FOR ALICE

Perhaps the most significant and unexpected lifelong impact on our family of Langdon's struggles with dyslexia was that Alice experienced a true epiphany as a result of her involvement in his school's library, where she volunteered simply to be closer to his situation. Librarianship became both her passion and, later, her profession. She volunteered for many years helping to start mini-libraries in Boston neighborhood schools and companies. She collected book donations, and processed books in small libraries in the Boston area, and generally began to immerse herself into the library world.

We received continued financial help from our families to pay for college tuition and costs for Langdon, Anne, and then…Alice! Alice happily decided on a career in Library Science, and graduated from Simmons Graduate School in 1973, the same year that Anne entered Yale and Wendy entered Middlesex.

THE FOLLEN CHURCH

FINDING FOLLEN

In the early 1960s, when our children were of grade school age, Alice and I felt strongly that exposure to religion was an important parental responsibility. Neither of us had a strong orientation to a particular religion beyond agreeing that Protestant denominations were our best places to look. My father inherited an inclination towards Unitarianism, and my mother towards the Episcopalian practice, but they never pushed me one way or another. Our family's resident cook in Cambridge had exposed me to Catholicism which had proved to be very useful while I was serving as an assistant chaplain in the Navy during the war. My high regard for Catholicism has since caused me some difficulties with the Unitarian/Universalist denomination. In college my girlfriend, who had become disenchanted with her Lutheran upbringing, and I systematically sampled diverse Christian denominations. All of this left me somewhat informed, but not soundly committed. By the time I became a parent, I was ready to get more involved, as was Alice.

Together we looked over the wide variety of houses of worship in Lexington, a town which offered religious and ethnic diversity. Eventually we chose the Follen Community Church (then Unitarian, now Unitarian/Universalist) as the place for our family to get started. We became members in 1965, daughter Wendy was married there in 1976, and we remained members for many years. Alice's memorial service was held there in 2006.

FOLLEN AND THE FAMILY

Traditionally Unitarian churches do not hold summer Sunday services. In Lexington, the Follen Church typically gathered with congregation members from the First Parish Church for a series of summer services provided by an assortment of people. We volunteered to present a summer Sunday service one year, celebrating the start of our new membership. Each family member actively participated, including Douglas, and we led the service from beginning to end, leading the responsive readings, announcing the hymns, leading the benediction, and, playing the handbells with the Seven-Fold Amen and the Harmonic Change. My sermon, which was based on Unitarianism as a bridge between many beliefs, reflected some of the reasons we had chosen the Follen church. Even Nick, who was only age eight at the time, helped light the candles, announce the meditation, and then led the congregation in the Lord's Prayer. As a family, we led the congregation in a musical round that resonates with all of us to this day, *Dona Nobis Pacem*. We led other services over the years, but this one best represented the culmination of our search for a church and commitment to Follen and its community. The last and most important service we presented was Alice's memorial service in June of 2006, which again included the *Dona Nobis Pacem*, sung by all. Several of my children have since told me that they felt Alice's spirit quietly exiting this world, down the aisle of the church, as we sang.

Over many years, our kids were very active in Follen's music, holiday celebrations, yearly Gilbert and Sullivan operettas, and some of the church's religious education programs. In the summer, Alice and I continued our connection to our beliefs by welcoming Sunday mornings with the brief, and beautiful early morning prayer service at Lexington's Episcopal Church of the Redeemer.

All of us sang in the Follen choir at one time or another. A very active group, it presented a wide variety of music, exposing us to many different forms of religious and secular works at a high standard of performance. One of the most interesting was when our choir presented a Latin mass in the Catholic Church immediately across the street from Follen. The Vatican had just decreed the church was to shift their mass from Latin into English. As a result, our offer to perform it in Latin was warmly received! I also did a lot of recorder and trumpet playing for our own church services. Much of it was with organ accompaniment, and also in conjunction with other instrumentalists.

Thanks to our very talented and ever-patient music director Louise Curtis, the children's musical season was capped by a Gilbert and Sullivan operetta at the end of each school year. The production also involved children from other churches and local temples. Rehearsals were organized to fit into school schedules, culminating in an open dress rehearsal and two performances. Our kids participated for almost 10 years, with adults of the congregation involved in scenery, costumes, and any other help that was needed. Alice helped with the cast backstage. These performances, and the friendships the kids made in choir, were central to all of their young lives.

VOLUNTEER INVOLVEMENT

I was very involved with administration at Follen, serving on the Parish Council, on and off, for most of the time we belonged. The Council was elected to oversee church operations–raising money, conducting searches for new ministers as needed, budgeting, hiring and firing employees, and caring for and maintaining our historic treasure of a building.

At the time we joined, Follen was "church-mouse poor." Its budget was $50-70,000, and grew almost three-fold by the end of the century. The church itself is an octagonal structure, constructed out of lumber salvaged from blown-down barns in about 1838. It was an antique architectural showpiece for Lexington, listed on the National Register of Historic Places. We stabilized a leaning steeple and a choir loft threatened with collapse as well as the quarter-ton bell which was on the verge of crashing down into the entryway. In later years cell phone antennae were installed in the steeple, yielding substantial annual income to the church from the telephone companies. Altogether, there was a constant parade of updating and repair. We also built a new pipe organ, and we added office and other spaces to make the church a full-service community function center, which it had never been before.

A SYMBOLIC PROJECT–THE FOLLEN CHURCH MODEL

At one point, it became increasingly obvious that our family finances were becoming challenged as I was getting my own business under way. Supporting our church proved to be difficult. Surprisingly, the Follen Church model project became a way for us to help. Trading on Lexington's image as a significant part of local history as well as the attractive appearance of the historic octagonal landmark building, we developed a model of the church that we could build ourselves to be sold to tourists and given as awards to financial donors to the church.

We put together a good group of volunteers for the project, consisting of two architects to perform the design plus a team to assemble the models. We were further aided by a cooperative local architectural woodworking shop which produced the odd-shaped wood stock which was needed to make the models from the unusual types and natural colors of various special woods. My small, home business's prototyping workshop gave us the facility to go into modest production. We built about 1500 of these models, enough so that they could be offered for sale at the tourist shop next to the Green in Lexington Center as well as fill the needs for mementos for the church congregation. This was a rewarding project.

Follen Church Christmas tree ornament models, fabricated in our home-based shop and sold in the church annual tree sale and the Town of Lexington Visitor's Center. We built about 1500 of them.

HANCOCK CHURCH

In later years, I also became a member of the Hancock United Church of Christ, which offered me a more conventional religious experience as well as civic connections and additional musical opportunities. Follen Church was especially fulfilling for Alice, while I remained involved in both churches.

FAMILY LIFE

VISITORS FROM NEAR AND FAR

Throughout the years, Alice and I tried to expose the LAWN Club to as wide a range of experiences as possible. Each child became increasingly aware of the world around him/her and intellectually sought to understand it. We brought them along to various seasonal activities and included them when entertaining local and international visitors. Each of our children developed very close friendships with kids who seemed to meld into the family to the extent that Alice and I often felt as if we had more than four offspring when we did things as a family, and Alice was sure to make every child welcome in our home. Various

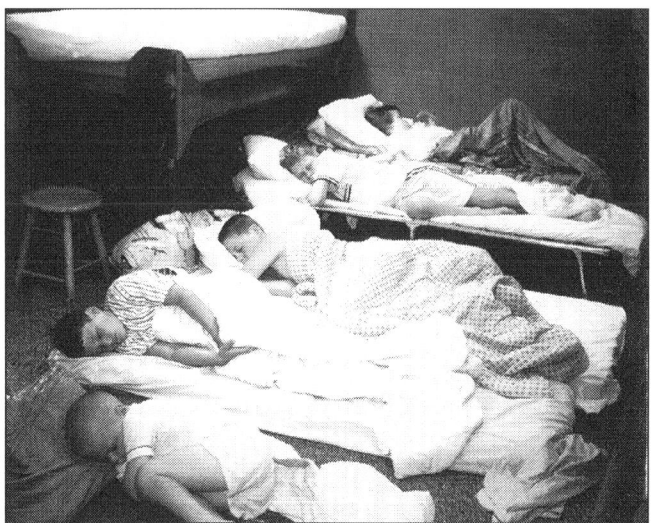

There was always room for extra kids at home. Here, on a sleepover, from the bottom are Nick, Richard Souza, Langdon, Rob Bulkley, Anne.

members of the Sizer family were also very receptive to our children as we made a point to visit or exchange children with Alice's family members on a regular basis. This perpetuated a tradition in Alice's family that happily continues to this day.

Through her ties to Radcliffe, Alice plugged us into a program which offered family-based experiences to foreign notables visiting the Boston area, giving them a feeling of welcome by providing dinner experiences with representative American families. The result was that we had a series of really fascinating people perhaps 10 or 15 times over a five-year period. These visits were fun and interesting for us, but an added benefit certainly was the exposure of our kids to persons from all over the world.

One visitor, a close assistant to the Premier of Australia, came to the U.S. to study our handling of the drug problems with American youth. Our Department of State had carefully laid out an itinerary for him to visit chiefs of police all over the country. He was slated to meet with our Lexington police chief the day after dining with us.

After he explained his mission to our assembled family, Alice and I winked at each other and carefully withdrew on the synthetic excuse to "wash the dishes," which we did–at length! As our guest reported to us later, the LAWN Club, without the questionable benefit of parental presence, then filled him in on what was really happening with youth and drug use in this country, apparently much better than any of the official contacts that had been arranged for him. He was most grateful to Alice and to me for the opportunity of getting a more relevant and realistic story from our kids.

A charming, French-speaking priest turned up as our dinner guest, complete with his interpreter. The LAWN Club struggled with the foreign language they were learning at school, and seemed to really enjoy the back-and-forth with this exceptionally sensitive visitor. If I remember properly, our guest later became a national leader in Madagascar.

Another visitor, a blind woman and member of the Royal Family of the Maldives, spent an evening with us, a fascinating and enlightening experience for all of us.

Another intensive program, overseen from Washington, was designed to establish relationships with the constabularies of emerging countries. A group of six or eight police chiefs from several African countries were visiting representative U.S. police forces, including Lexington's. In gracious keeping with tradition, they brought a present for their dinner hostess. We were all impressed as they ceremoniously presented Alice with a spray canister of Mace. They proved to be a fascinating group, and highly communicative with our kids.

FRIENDS AND FAMILY MEMBERS

A slew of people, young and old, came and went in our household, and, over the years, some of them became life-long family friends.

Jim Niccolson was a keyboard recitalist and was introduced to me by friend and colleague, Eric Herz. His genuine attraction moved him right into the family! He was originally from Washington DC, and ultimately we introduced him to the woman who was to be his wife. During his musical career, he went to Germany every year for a performance tour. We became quite close with our common interests not only in keyboard instruments, but in my harpsichords and his expertise in Baroque music, especially the clavichord. He has been a family friend all these years, and our adult kids all have felt a connection with him throughout their lives. Jim attended Alice's memorial service and reflected on his friendship with her and with our family.

We met **Paul Hopkins** when he was just a teenager, delivering our daily newspapers. I first noticed his involvement as a Ham Radio operator with First Responders–people who are trained to be first on the scene in emergencies. Ham radio operators are an interesting bunch, and are traditionally innovators and concerned people. They are, quite literally, plugged into world affairs and events. His ability to function as a shop technician also proved very useful during my years of building instruments and self-employment. Living nearby, he became a good friend, and was considered a member of the family.

Poochie (Sarah Bradshaw) and Wendy.

On weekends, Anne often brought fellow students to our house, many of whom were from far away and seeking a home-like experience. Generally, they were an interesting bunch. One of those students was **Michael Tackie**. Michael is from Ghana, and we later came to know his family when they were visiting him in the U.S. We struck up an immediate friendship with him and he soon was also counted as an honorary family member. We tracked him as he finished Yale, continued on to Syracuse University for an advanced degree in Chemical Engineering, and then went to work in the chemical industry in Pittsburgh. Michael has been awfully good to me over the years, and was especially supportive to me after Alice passed away.

Anne also introduced us to **Julie Snyder (Thompson)** whom she met at the age of 11 in the Follen Junior Choir. Julie, a good-hearted young person, was always welcome in our home. She remains Anne's best friend to this day–more than 40 years later.

Another special family member was **Sarah Bradshaw**, from Belmont. Nicknamed "Poochie", she was Wendy's best friend and playmate for many years. The two of them loved Five Fields, swimming in the pool almost daily. She was among the guests we invited during an extended summer vacation. Alice used to tell the story in one simple sentence, with a big grin: "Poochie came for the weekend and stayed for six weeks!"

DINNER IS SERVED

Poochie and Wendy were known for "running away" on any given summer night. Alice was so accustomed to this that she often packed them a picnic dinner. The girls would wait until dark and then quietly dash out the door. They'd get to the closest field and pitch a tent with a blanket over a tree branch and then settle down to have their supper. They never made it any further away, and would "sneak" back in the door quite content after several hours. Poochie was a happy kid and a welcome friend of the family. Poochie now teaches shop at Shady Hill, the school where I and three of our kids spent many happy years!

FAMILY SUMMERS IN THE 60s AND 70s

DUXBURY

As the LAWN Club was growing up, we intermittently sought out summer camp activities for them. Then, in the early 1960s, we attempted to work out a scheme for making vacations really meaningful for everyone. Having heard a lot about Duxbury, MA, as a good site, which was also near enough to where I was then working, we rented a modest summer cottage from our old Shady Hill Square landlords and moved the family down there for the summer. To make sure our children had friends, several close friends and family of the proper ages were invited. To take advantage of the marine scene, we also took our rather extensive fleet of sailboats, a rowing shell, and other miscellaneous small craft. We even added a Boston Whaler outboard motor boat to the fleet.

This turned out to be a wonderfully worthwhile family summer. Douglas Cheek played a large role in its success.

While we were in Duxbury, I had a single rowing shell which I rowed religiously about two miles each morning, circumnavigating an island immediately adjacent to our cottage. The only reason I could afford such an expensive shell was because it had been given up for hopeless by its former owner since it had warped into a slightly curved shape. It wanted only to go around clockwise in a large circle. By chance, the size and shape of the local island near our cottage fitted the oddball characteristics of the shell, so all was in order for a regular two-mile daily row for me.

Langdon and a close friend who was visiting us conducted an overnight "cruise" from Duxbury to Plymouth and back, sensibly all within the limits of Plymouth Bay, in "Spirita," our 12½ foot sailing dinghy. At that point, the boys were each about six feet tall. How they managed to sleep, cook their meals, and perform the necessary living functions in that craft, I will never know, but they were justly proud of their accomplishment. Alice and I were properly impressed.

Although not yet aware of the imminence of the computer age, Alice insisted that all four of the children attend Duxbury's excellent intensive two-week summer typing school for kids at the start of our summer stay. She knew that typing skills would be important, even though several of the kids strongly objected. Anne remembers being told that she had to wear "something on her feet" to attend this summer class, and so she covered the soles of her feet with bandaids–but she learned to type! Earlier, when I was dating Alice, she had similarly insisted that I go to typing school, believing that it was too late in my life not to be comfortable with what we now call "keyboarding." We now, of course, realize the value of her emphasis and thank her for her prescient approach.

SAILING

Following our happy, busy summer in Duxbury, our family took to the water for many more summer experiences. All six of us, along with various friends and relatives, sailed in a series of boats. Our boats grew in size, much like our house, according to the size of our family. We sailed along the coast of Maine for several summers.

At a relatively young age, Langdon developed a seaworthiness in his swimming abilities; he could function safely in the water for relatively long distances in rough conditions. Once he used those newfound skills to help the family during a rather frightening sailing experience. We had to seek shelter from a storm while cruising in Buzzards Bay. All six of us were in our small 19-foot boat (the smallest of our Crouton series of boats), the children at relatively young ages. In the confusion, we lost gear overboard in the rough waters. Langdon cool-headedly jumped overboard and swam through the choppy waves to retrieve it. He then swam further to assist us in picking up a mooring buoy. (It is interesting to recall that Langdon's godfather, environmental scientist David Barnes, was a rough water swimmer and, during David's civic service as a conscientious objector during WWII, he swam across Boston Harbor to test the development and effectiveness of "greases" to help shipwrecked swimmers survive in frigid waters.)

Later, as our brood grew, we graduated to sophisticated family cruising on a large, fast catamaran, aptly named Crouton II. Photos of putting Phoebe (the golden retriever) in the bosun's chair to lower her over the side into the dinghy should have been kept in our family archives, but unfortunately were not!

On those long overnight sails from Maine to Cape Cod, the game of "Crummy" was invented. It was originally based, of course, on Rummy 500, but soon graduated, first to Rummy 5000, then finally to the infamous Crummy. Alice was an avid card player, and as time wore on, the scores rose into the thousands, with all the kids participating in the competition. The game could be played with almost any size group of players using multiple decks of cards. As the occasional card was lost or blown overboard, the decks continued to be used, regardless of whether or not they were complete. Russian Bank – an endless game for two that filled many a long rainy afternoon—was also a favorite with family or friends. I admire Alice for livening up our family gatherings in this way.

For those of our readers who are unfamiliar with boats or ships, a catamaran is essentially twin vessels, attached together, side by side, with a common area suspended above the water in between. Generally, they are well known for their speed. Larger cruising catamarans, such as our 38-foot sailing version, are also known for their stability in turbulent water, and are spacious enough for a family to sail on with more cabin space than is offered in single hull sailboats.

One pastime our children enjoyed in particular was the use of a seaman-style hammock slung between the two bows of our large catamaran, and suspended over the rushing water. The kids would sit in the hammock, holding a safety rope while we were under sail, and occasional waves would hit their undersides. It was a wild experience, and one that consistently thrilled the

WIGGLY LEGS

Anne had her share of getting wet when cruising on the family boat. After days when she clearly felt particularly cooped up in the cabin all day (she called it having "wiggly legs"), I would, with some frequency, either (literally) throw her overboard or else put her into the dingy to row around the harbor, which of course is when she first learned to row(!) Nick, too, was thrown overboard more than once for misbehaving. Says Nick now, "Hey—I deserved it!"

LAWN Club. The hammock was used hard, and one day Wendy and Poochie were seated in it together, holding safety ropes, while we were fast under sail. The hammock, rotted by use and too much salt water, split down the middle and the girls plunged through it. They found themselves under the boat, in the air space between the hulls, heads above water, holding tightly to their safety ropes and being dragged through the rushing water with great force. Their screams could not be heard from above, and eventually, the force of the water was such that they had to let go. It was not until they suddenly appeared behind the boat that the rest of us realized what had happened. Rather than reeling from the terror of their experience, thank goodness, the girls were pulled aboard unhurt, giggling nervously, then telling us excitedly about their adventure.

We later replaced the hammock and it soon ceremoniously dumped the headmaster from one of our kids' schools into the water as we sailed in to Cuttyhunk Harbor, south of Woods Hole. We

We often hung a hammock (being folded, at right) on the bow of our catamaran (left) when we were under sail, motors safely raised out of the water. When lying in the hammock, one could see directly under the boat and out the other side.

were all duly embarrassed and did not use the hammock again for other important guests!

As we traveled near and far, Alice's stack of paperbacks was read by all. Spam in all its iterations, tomato soup with hot dogs floating in it, or split pea soup out of a can will never taste as good as they did on chilly late Fall days of sailing! Friends and family alike traveled with us, and we made good time sailing up and down the coast of Maine.

Langdon, Anne, and Nick enjoyed learning the nautical and technically arcane aspects of sailing the boat, while, generally, Wendy was more interested in riding high on the one of the two bows looking for lobster pots. I fondly remember Wendy's reaction, however, when I finally turned over to her the job of being responsible for piloting. Wendy wowed us as she came up with the solution to our much-awaited estimated time of arrival as we proceeded along the coast of Maine. She loudly exclaimed, *"That's* what Mr. Lawler was trying to explain in math class!" When I looked at her chart-plotting job and her calculation notes involving current effects, direction bearings of significant land features, and distance-made-good, I realized that she was getting a very useful workout!

LEXINGTON GOES TO THE NEW YORK WORLD'S FAIR

"THEY NOBL'Y DARED"

Lexington takes its Revolutionary Era role quite seriously. In keeping with its annual tradition of reenacting "the shot heard 'round the world" scene every April 19th on the Town Green, it was inevitable that some sort of stage show be developed. In 1964 an operetta titled "They Nobl'y Dared" was written by D. L. Pullen, with music composed by D. MacFeeley, and put to stage. Alice enthusiastically joined the cast for its several performances. The show was then invited down to the 1964 World's Fair in New York, and Alice was a member of the expedition. She arranged for the LAWN Club to be included. Happily, Douglas Cheek volunteered to help. Dougie, Alice, and the kids proceeded to Queens to see the fair and participate in the performances and parade. I was able to join them after a day or two.

Nick and Alice preparing for the parade at the New York World's Fair, where Alice was involved with "They Nobl'y Dared", a production about the town of Lexington during the start of the American Revolution.

This was a memorable trip for the kids, as they were able to enjoy the World's Fair as both performers and guests. After the show, when faced with keeping track of four kids in the large fair crowds, Alice came up with the great idea to dress the children in matching red striped shirts so they could be easily spotted in a crowd if lost. The family stood in awe together one late evening when the nightly fireworks, bursting over the enormous world-globe fountain, were joined by a thunder and lightning storm—an unforgettable experience to watch. Overall, we had a lot of fun.

After we got back home from the NY World's Fair, while exploring Boston Harbor with the whole family in our 18-foot outboard-powered Boston Whaler boat, Alice had the kids in their red-striped shirts and life preservers. The kids spotted the USS Constitution tied up at her pier in the Charlestown Navy Yard, crawling with the usual crowd of tourists, and pleaded to go aboard her. I quickly put our boat alongside the public dock next to the Constitution and they jumped out and hustled over to the gangplank leading to the deck of the sailing ship, still wearing their striking shirts and life preservers. They created a sensation as they flocked aboard the ship, and both tourists and guides asked us if we were concerned that (*seriously!*) our children would fall overboard or (jokingly) that the USS Constitution would sink.

THE BELLS

THE HANDBELL PURCHASE

Handbells came into our family life in an interesting way. To this day I am unsure as to what my ever-patient wife *really* thought about it.

In mid-1960s, I went to the Music Manufacturers' Association Trade Show in Chicago, followed shortly by Alice, Douglas, and the LAWN Club. I occupied a booth next to that of the Schulmerich Company, the larger of the two manufacturers of handbells in the U.S. The art of ringing handbells had been ingrained into me by Margaret Shurcliff, the person who had brought them to the US from the UK in the early 1920s. She had kindly included me in her iconic Beacon Hill Christmas Eve ringing activities in the mid-1930s.

Years later, at the Trade Show, I found myself drooling over the gleaming sets of handbells. At the end of the show, the salesman complained that he was not looking forward to lugging the heavy cases of bells back home to suburban Philadelphia. He made me a very tempting offer, well below the normal price. I succumbed and snapped up the 25-bell, two-octave set housed in its two fitted and hardened transport cases. In the process I had to lay out an unmentionable number of thousands of dollars in cash. The family then started on a vacation trip to visit Sizer cousins on the Northern Peninsula of Michigan.

I am ashamed to admit that I made a secret deal with the LAWN Club and Douglas that the bell cases contained a surprise present for Alice, and hence we should not divulge to her what was in them until getting to Michigan. Frankly, I was pretty darned sure that she would not be happy in view of our rather shaky financial situation at the time. I had hoped to reveal the bells in the presence of Alice's relations, and thus I might become quickly excused for my clear financial gaffe. We covered the cases with furniture moving quilts and I encouraged the kids to hide the bells from Alice's sight by sitting on the cases in the station wagon,

There was a great ceremonial unwrapping when we arrived up north. I was scared stiff about what Alice's reaction would be. In truth it appeared, however, that she, egged on by her cousins, might actually have been secretly thrilled. I must admit she didn't have the opportunity to say, "What the *** did you do that for?" I was surprised that she clearly seemed to take it in stride and never talked to me about it afterwards. Later Alice became a true and genuine supporter of handbell ringing.

I immediately began to write a lot of bell music parts, and the family was introduced to playing handbells in the peace of Michigan's Northern Peninsula over the next two weeks. The family's bell involvement grew quickly over the years.

One of the pieces I wrote was the Harmonic Change Ring, which has become sort of a "theme

The kids learned to play the handbells at a young age, and played for many years. From left to right: Nick, Wendy, Langdon, and Anne.

song" of our ringing activities. It allows the minimum number of people to ring in a celebratory mode. It helps to train newcomers as well as to warm up skilled ringers. I must admit that by now—decades later–our family has rung it so often that they are understandably sick and tired of it and justifiably resistant to playing it. I can't blame them!

Once the family was involved with bell ringing, it was a little easier for me to get away with spending a large amount of money to add half an octave at both the top and bottom of the original set. This finally resulted in a complete, three-octave set (37 bells), which is the optimal minimum number for playing worthwhile music. For this, we really needed at least eight players, so our nuclear family of six needed only several others to get us going. Ten to twelve players gave us full capability and the flexibility to handle the three octaves.

Typically, on Christmas Eve nights, we'd play at as many as three different churches, and we admittedly broke some traffic speed laws hustling between them. We played by the steps outside the first church at the beginning of a service, in the foyer during the service at the second church, and then we formed on either side of the narthex, allowing congregants to exit right through us at the end of the service at the third church.

The family played in various events and celebrations over the years. We participated in one of Bud Collins' Christmas shows on National Public Television, and we did several sessions at holiday times in the schools attended by the LAWN Club. The bells reside with me still, and I currently lead a bell choir with residents from my retirement community.

MY PARENTS AND SIBLINGS

Throughout the years, as our children were born and grew up, my parents and sisters experienced their later lives, which were full of interesting work and family.

LORRAINE AND MARGOT

Lorraine never remarried after the sad and early loss of her husband, Bob. She and her children remained in Kennett Square, PA, and Laura and Rob led full young lives. Margot continued her career teaching music, lived in Boston in a succession of several houses on Beacon Hill, and eventually was given my parents' Essex summer house. She lived in the large, well-preserved historic house for some time, using the small house on the same property for her studio, as our mother had done. Eventually, she sold the Essex property and moved into a small home down the road from the original house.

Margot on the cover of a program at the New England Conservatory of Music (1953).

FATHER'S LATER LIFE

In his retirement, Father had served in the Arts and Monuments recovery and protection operation as a so-called "**Monuments Man**" during, and just after, WWII. This group was involved in the worldwide protection and recovery of significant artifacts impacted by the war. This fascinating collection of almost all men and a few women were art historians, museum curators, conservators, and directors from the U.S. and several other countries. Alice's father had also served in Europe in that operation.

My father is credited for keeping Allied strategic bombing away from Kyoto and Nara, Japan, to preserve those sites as Japanese national treasures. His wishes were always that those who helped in his efforts be lauded, not just him, for this work, yet he alone has been credited for it. He expressly told me this before his death. After the war, a beautiful small garden was built just outside one of the shrines in Kyoto memorializing his efforts to save the city from total destruction.

MOTHER

My mother gradually retired from active music except for piano practicing, which remained an important element. She took great care of my father as he aged and became increasingly frail. She took over the operation of the household and family business matters, utilizing some help from outsiders for heavy cleaning and details of fiscal management. She remained my father's chauffeur until his death.

FATHER'S PASSING

Father passed away in 1955, at the age of 75, after several strokes. His memorial service was held at the Appleton Chapel in Harvard's Memorial Church, conducted by his friend, the Dean of Harvard Divinity School. It was well attended, and honored well his life and work. He is buried in the Warner family plot at Mount Auburn Cemetery in Cambridge, MA.

Langdon Warner, painted by Charles S. Hopkinson (1955).

MOTHER'S PASSING

Several years after my father's death, when I was busily pursuing my professional engineering career, my mother suffered a number of minor strokes that gradually took over her speech and general functionality. This was her entry into what would become dementia.

My sister Margot increasingly took over Mother's care, for about eight years, assisted to some extent by Mother's French cousin, Germaine Arosa. When Mother finally needed more care than was possible for Margot to provide, she entered a nursing home in northeast Lexington, MA. This was a very unhappy situation for her, and consequently she was a difficult patient for the nursing home to handle. That phase lasted about a year before she died there in 1965, at the age of 77.

Looking back, I am somewhat ashamed that I found it very difficult to be of much assistance to my mother during that unhappy period, and I am everlastingly grateful for the consideration, care and support that Margot unselfishly provided Mother through that trying time.

My mother's memorial service, similar to my father's, was very moving. The service was again inside the Appleton Chapel, again led by the Dean of Harvard Divinity School. In the middle of the service, we paused for an interval in which the organist played J.S. Bach's prelude from the Organ Prelude and Fugue in A-minor (BWV543). This was the original version of Liszt's piano reduction which Mother had played loudly on the piano every day of her life, as a 6:00 a.m. "wake up" call for our whole family. To her this was a challenging finger exercise and to Lorraine, Margot, and me it reminded us that we had better get up and *stay* out of bed!

We scattered Mother's ashes near our Essex, MA summer house, at the clam-diggers' landing in the back creek of Essex, during an outgoing tide.

*Mother in her later years
(date unknown).*

THE LAWN CLUB GROWS UP

TEENAGE YEARS: OUR FAMILY STRUGGLES

At the time that our children began their high school years, our family was generally struggling with many issues, and as a result, the period surrounding our children's teenage years proved to be rough for the whole family. Alice, who had gone back to school for her Masters degree in Library Science, was busy working in a new business information venture, Warner Eddison Associates.

I had changed my career to become self-employed, and, as parents, it worked well as we also considered it a good idea if one of us were in the house all the time to participate in the daily activities of our growing family. Our children were teenagers, naturally spreading their own wings, exploring the world around them and becoming quickly more and more independent. We had lost Douglas, and the impact of his passing had left a deep wound both in us as a family, as well as in each of us individually.

All six of us were experiencing individual personal challenges and troubles which affected our family as a whole. This was confused even further by the fact that, as a family of both adults and teens, we were also enmeshed in the times of the late 1960s and early '70s, an era of deep societal change. Alice and I had a very hard time understanding how our children perceived both their present and their futures, and they, I am certain, must have had a very difficult time understanding us. All six of us struggled to realize each others' needs. We made mistakes, and it may be safe to say that we all have found ourselves relieved to have those years behind us. I know I tread on sensitive ground here but I do so with the blessing of the LAWN Club.

Now, when I talk to others who were parents during those tumultuous years, they remind me how many families suffer through tough times when their children become teens, and many families experienced additional upheaval during the pivotal decades of the '60s and '70s. But this does not set right those years in my mind and heart.

THE LAWN CLUB HERE AND NOW

Nothing I write here can fully or successfully describe the early lives of our children. Langdon, Anne, Wendy, and Nick have since grown to become intelligent, value-focused adults, and have married and are nurturing their own families and careers.

As of this writing, in late 2012, Langdon and his family live in South Carolina, and he and his wife Susan have two adult children, Nathaniel and Megan. Anne lives in Connecticut with Dan Paul, another important and special family member. Anne has two adult children, Ali, who lives in California, and Hannibal, a student at Harvard. Their father, Cliff Taubes, is still a valued player in of all of their lives. Wendy lives in Massachusetts and her adult children, Becky and Jake, who both live in Pennsylvania, have families of their own. Becky and Cory Schreiber have three children: Elijah, Zechariah and Simon. Jake and Julie Lindstrom have four children: Brooke, Jonah, Aiden and Emelia. Nick and his wife Holly live in Burlington, Vermont, and as of this writing, their son Caleb is eleven years old.

Alice and I were blessed with a great group of enjoyable and lovable kids. They grew up on us when we weren't looking and I'm only sorry that Alice didn't have the privilege in recent years of seeing as much of them as I have. I wish Alice were here.

Our Boston Whaler.

Anne-Liese Wellershaus, between couples Alice and me, and Teddy and Nancy in the mid 1950s.

Years later: Ted Sizer and his wife, Nancy Faust Sizer. On the right, the Sizer sisters (Lib Allen, Alice, Hilda Warner, Cally Cochran). Missing is Mary Ecklund, who died in 1973.

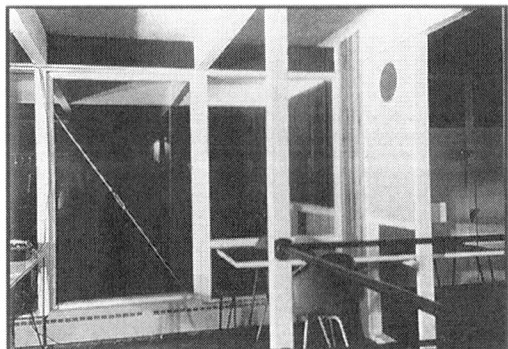

546 Concord Ave, Lexington, Mass., as purchased in 1954. Exterior and interior.

Our house grew as our family did.

Above: The wall of our dining room. The natural trumpet and handbell rack are above the print of an owl by Albrecht Dürer and three portraits by Theodore Sizer: self-portrait, Caroline Sizer, and Alice Sizer; silhouette of Nick Warner, and photo of me. Right: Closer look at the profile of Nick and the photo of me, showing our similarity at similar ages. Below: Layout for Five Fields community, as later submitted to the Lexington Historical Commission in 1984. Pool, playground, and pond have been added here, and our house was number 546.

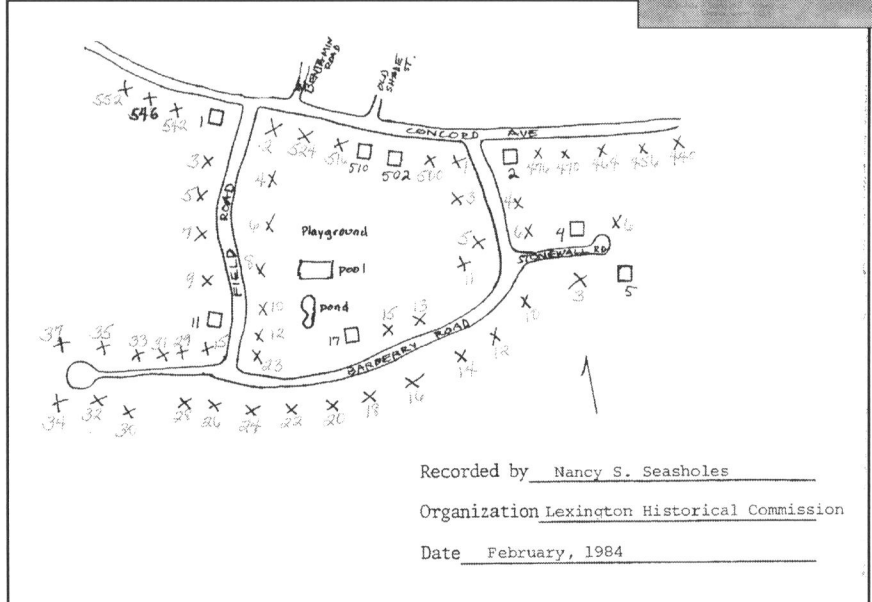

Recorded by   Nancy S. Seasholes

Organization Lexington Historical Commission

Date   February, 1984

Above, left: Alice and me, with Wendy, outside the house
in Duxbury. Above, right: Alice and Wendy (1956).
Below: Shakespeare community productions. Upper left:
Langdon and a neighbor reading before the show started.
Upper right: Alice, carrying a drum to play in the
community orchestra. Bottom: Anne singing a solo.

Above, left: Crouton, our first family boat, looked like this when we purchased her. I made considerable changes to the boat over the years, including extending her to accommodate our growing family. It is hard to imagine that this little craft was extensively enlarged so that it eventually slept six! Above, right: Langdon and Anne-Liese sailing in Spirita. Langdon sailed skillfully from a very young age. Right: Crouton, with Langdon riding the bowsprit, a favorite spot for all of our kids.

Yelling Rock.

Left: The kids in Alex and Cally Cochran's Japanese bathtub, Baltimore, Maryland. From the left, Langdon, Rob Bulkley, Anne, Wendy, and Nick, with the paddle!

The LAWN Club

Right: This bookplate, designed in memory of Douglas, was placed in books donated in his name to the Shady Hill School.

Given in memory of
DOUGLAS SOUTHALL
FREEMAN CHEEK
*An apprentice teacher
at Shady Hill School
September-December
1966*

Below: This memorial was erected in honor of my father, Langdon Warner, in Kyoto, Japan. He helped prevent Allied bombing of areas of ancient and cultural art and architecture in both Kyoto and Nara, Japan.

I learned to play the handbells with the Shurcliffs when I was a teen. Here, we play at 66 Mt. Vernon St, Boston, on Christmas Eve. (Boston Herald, December 25, 1937)

Alice and I in front of the portraits of her mother and my father.

ALICE SIZER WARNER'S
HONORS AND BOOKS

Alice earned her degree as a Master of Library Science in 1973 at Simmons College. She later became a member of the college's Library Science Executive Board and a faculty member. She received the Distinguished Alumni Award in 1993.

Alice wrote throughout her adult life. A large number of articles and briefings can be found in various publications, mostly pertaining to libraries. Her papers are available for review through the Archives Office at Simmons College in Boston. Her Five Fields Newsletters are available at the Lexington Library, Lexington, Massachusetts. Six of her seven books, listed below, are available at Amazon.com.

Her seventh book, a brief memoir about growing up during World War II on a farm in Connecticut, is entitled "Bethany." It was distributed privately to family members in 1995, and revised in 1998. After Alice's death in 2006, daughter Wendy found an envelope labeled "Illustrations for Bethany" in Alice's distinctive handwriting, in which were dozens of photographs Alice had intended to use for her book's final printing. The illustrated version of *Bethany* will be available on Amazon.com in 2013.

BOOKS WRITTEN BY ALICE

Volunteers in Libraries (Library Journal, Special Report No. 2) (July 1978)

Volunteers in Libraries II (Library Journal, Special Report) (July 1983)

Mind Your Own Business: A Guide for the Information Entrepreneur (March 1987)

Making Money: Fees for Library Services (May 1989)

Owning Your Numbers: An Introduction to Budgeting for Special Libraries (February 1992)

Budgeting: A How-To-Do-It Manual for Librarians (February 1998)

Bethany (1995, 1998)

11

STARTING THE PROFESSIONAL PRACTICE OF ENGINEERING

Here, then, is the chronological link between this chapter and the end of Chapter 9, "Just the Two of Us."
Now we return to 1953, when I started in my first position at Arthur D. Little.
(The hurricane in Chapter 9 hit one year later, when I changed divisions within the company.)

A NEW JOB: ARTHUR D. LITTLE, INC. (ADL)

My first cousin, Roger Warner, Jr., had just emerged from his work in the Manhattan Project. He obviously had a "nose" for what was developing in the high technology field. He was working for Arthur D. Little, Inc., as a somewhat mysterious corporate officer dealing with starting a subsidiary corporate entity relating to his past work at the Atomic Energy Commission.

ADL was an international consulting and development firm, founded in 1886 by Arthur Dehon Little, an MIT chemist well known for developing acetate as a structural plastic. The company was headquartered in Cambridge, MA, and was still closely associated with MIT. ADL had pioneered the concept of contracted technology research and development and, uniquely, had elected to perform such services on a for-profit basis. It had already played key roles in the development of the petroleum refining field, fiberglass, operations research, the first synthetic penicillin, and many other products and services of a highly technical nature. The company was one of the world's leading consulting and technical development firms, working closely with large firms and governments across the globe. By the time I joined in 1953, the company had grown to perhaps 300 employees.

After Roger explained to me what the company was all about, I believe we both felt uneasy about my approaching ADL (potential nepotism and all that) but when I was hired, we were able to clear up those complications.

My Term in ADL's Business Research Division

I somehow managed to survive the rather demanding job application and interviewing process which unearthed my limited experience and education in business practices. The Business Research Division in which I landed was a group of about 15 technically oriented professionals, most of whom had formal business degrees or experience in business administration.

The work involved market research, initiation of diversification, and management consulting. Our clients were primarily rather large corporations, spread all over the world. Our main competitors, at the time, were "not-for-profits" like Battelle Memorial Institute in Columbus, OH, Stanford Research Institute (attached to Stanford University in California) and, of course, MIT itself.

Typical of the situations we addressed was our service to Harley Davidson Co., which was seeking diversification. We examined the possibility of getting them into the burgeoning air conditioning/refrigeration field since their considerable manufacturing expertise was in making high quality motorcycle reciprocating engines, devices which were very similar in principal to refrigerant compressors. This was, in part, a market research task and, in part, a manufacturing engineering task. Both required rather profound understanding of technological issues.

I spent a rather unhappy period in this sort of work at ADL, feeling ill-equipped to present myself as a cock-sure management type – characteristics that my colleagues seemed to have almost to excess. This work was my first real failure in achieving satisfaction. I wanted a more "hands-on" environment and I am sure that the ADL management saw that.

Luckily, ADL was making a radical change by moving from their location on the banks of the Charles River in Cambridge to a new location in the fast-developing industrial section in North Cambridge. The new location was called Acorn Park, because the public relations posture of the company was that "large things from small acorns grow". I became a member of the Mechanical Division, headed up by Alan "Jack" Latham, ADL's Vice President of Engineering. Included in the move was the construction of an extensive prototype machine shop and mechanical engineering laboratory. That activity was more to my liking and happily the ADL management was in complete agreement with having me move.

A House, a Daughter, the Storm and My New Position at ADL: 1954

I was relieved to join the Applied Mechanical Engineering Section, even though the timing was chaotic, to say the least. With newborn Anne's arrival, Alice was recovering, and toddler Langdon was in his glory at our temporary digs, the Tappan's. I started the job just as we were about to move into the Lexington house, and, as you know, we were hit with Hurricane Carol.

Post-storm, after cleaning up the new ADL facilities, as well as our other family properties, I could finally settle down to work. This division was a triumvirate, consisting of a mechanical design engineering group of perhaps 50 professionals, plus a mechanical analytical group of about 10 professionals, plus a proprietary laboratory equipment group of about five professionals, plus a full-blown machine shop of perhaps 20 skilled machinists/technicians. Together with support personnel there were something over 100 people involved in a new combined office and shop building in a flood-prone location at the headwaters of Alewife Creek on the Cambridge/Belmont line.

I was assigned the number two position in the applied end of the Mechanical Division which consisted of the machine shop, mechanical laboratory, and device assembly areas. Elwin "Tilt" Tilton was my boss. He was a very intelligent person who had come up through the skilled machinist route without a lot of formal academic education, but with a tremendous amount of practical experience and capability. I found very much to like and revere in him and I hope that we effectively complemented each other with our differing skills and capabilities.

We had a highly supportive relationship with the group of mechanical engineers on the floor above. Among the many diversified areas of this technology development effort were three world-renowned areas of special note: cryogenics (ultra-low temperatures), ultra-high field magnetics, and blood donation/preservation equipment. The work in these areas blossomed over the next half century into such significant fields as MRI (magnetic resonance imaging), LNG (liquefied natural gas), IBM (intercontinental ballistic missiles), superconducting electrical energy devices, and blood fractionation/preservation.

In this job, I was on my feet on the shop floor virtually full time, involved in all aspects of a highly varied spectrum of mechanical research and development. For me, it was a very happy change.

ADL's Proprietary Laboratory Equipment Operations

As I worked in ADL's machine shop and assembly area, it became obvious that we should pay special attention to our proprietary laboratory equipment business that was becoming increasingly lively. I gradually became involved not only with improvements in the devices, but also with marketing efforts in that field. I had the luxury of delivering these esoteric laboratory tools to some of the top physics laboratories at home and abroad, installing them, and finally nursing them into working order while instructing the physicists in their care and feeding. That assignment led me to two particularly fascinating situations — one month's work each at Iowa State University in Ames, Iowa, and the Bavarian Physics Research Laboratory just outside Munich.

Munich Visit

On a similar delivery/installation trip I spent almost two weeks at one of Germany's premier physics research laboratories, about 35 miles southwest of Munich, on the shores of the Ammersee.

It was a sociologically fascinating exposure to Germans impacted by WWII, some of whom remained very sensitive about the U.S. and its relations with Germany. My contacts included quite a cast: several renowned German professors, and a sweet, shy, sympathetic Ph.D. who had apologetically been in the occupation forces in Norway and was repeatedly welcomed back for summer vacations by the Norwegians. A distinguished physicist kindly whisked me all around the area, painting Bavaria as the "ante-bellum" Germany. There was also an angry Prussian veteran who had been wounded and lost an eye on the Russian front. It was quite a cross-section of the German populace at the end of the war.

The Ammersee was a beautiful lake located almost in the foothills of the Alps. It reminded me of the significant writings of Dr. Manfred Currey who had done pioneering work on the aerodynamics of sails in his earlier boating days on that lake.

I found wandering around Munich a real pleasure. The emblematic rebuilding of the war-damaged churches was quite moving. At one of them, I was surprised to see a large crowd waiting patiently to get in to a concert. Out of curiosity, I joined them only to be introduced to the playing of that superb organist, Karl Richter, whose Handel Organ Concerto recordings I have since come to revere and listen to often, even today.

MY ROLE IN ADL'S SERVICES TO THE MILITARY/INDUSTRIAL COMPLEX

In the late 1950s, ADL's Mechanical Division had established itself as a leader in the field of applied cryogenics — the handling of liquefied gases. Liquefied Natural Gas (LNG) was becoming an important source of energy around the world. Liquid oxygen and liquid nitrogen were also becoming important in medicine and in many emerging manufacturing processes. Liquid hydrogen and liquid oxygen were used as fuels in the emerging development of intercontinental ballistic missiles (IBMs), space exploration, satellites, and more. Liquefied helium and hydrogen were important in research efforts in physics. Its specialty in LNG gave ADL an entrée into working with significant defense contractors as well as the U.S. Department of Defense.

With my Navy and CIA background, I knew my way around Washington, DC to some extent, so I found myself caught up in technical sales, proposal writing, and all that goes into working in the military/industrial complex. I was also a constant visitor to the West Coast.

Several times during my time at ADL I was given the uncomfortable job of being a courier for classified material. This pattern continued later when I worked for other companies involved in the defense business. My stint at the CIA qualified me for the duty. I had a leather sack or briefcase locked to my wrist to assure that I would not lose the material, and was allowed to sit only in the rear, most uncomfortable seats of the airplane to increase my chances of survival in the event of accident to the plane. These deliveries involved long flights and very short recovery times at the destination so that I could quickly get back to more productive work. I remember several round trips to the Mojave Desert from the East Coast in which I stayed at my destination for less than an hour. I endeavored to free myself from this kind of life, and the threat of courier assignments played some role in what I chose to take on in the way of future projects.

ADL'S NEW ENGLAND SMALL BUSINESS SERVICES

ADL management realized that their success in providing technical business services to large firms might become of value to smaller firms if remodeled to suit the smaller firms' particular needs. A senior member of ADL, Dr. Austin "Bud" Fisher, began to organize and market a small-firm service. I voiced genuine interest in the idea and was taken aboard the project.

I signed up with the New England Council, a well-recognized public relations group which had a lively program for attracting firms to New England and promoting the industries in the region in general. From them, I got leads as to which companies might be candidates for the type of technical services we might provide. I then engaged in intense activity to visit these candidates. I spent about a year and a half developing the service and participating in its projects. It was convenient to draw on the highly diversified pool of skills available in ADL, and the small business clients were generally enthusiastic about the results. I found it a very satisfying endeavor. However, top management of ADL was wary of applying high-quality services to small businesses since the potential profits were limited. "Bigger fish" seemed more attractive. It was time for me to move on.

My experiences getting to know and understand emerging New England firms proved unexpectedly valuable to me as I next welcomed the opportunity to participate in the startup of a small business. Still later, it triggered me to become self employed by forming the Instrument Guild as my own small business.

CALEB WARNER INSTRUMENTS

During my tenure at ADL, I found myself fascinated with the role of the harpsichord in the fast re-emergence of Baroque music. Harpsichords had been around for centuries, but they always had their limitations. The complexity of construction historically caused high building costs, and the instrument's inability to reflect a performer's expression using touch sensitivity had long been an issue. The added problem was the harpsichord's carrying power, which, especially when played as a solo instrument, quite often could not be heard well.

I began to experiment at home in my shop and, throughout about 20 of my professionally productive years, my fascination held. On and off, I dubbed my effort Caleb Warner Instruments, and worked on it at night and on weekends.

I built a succession of harpsichords out of materials not traditionally found in the instruments. My first experimental prototypes were built using a welded, harp-shaped frame made out of extruded aluminum channel, serving as both the structure and the body/cases of the instrument. The aluminum surfaces were sand-blasted to give a warm and even finish. I hoped that these novel materials would help to stabilize the instrument's tuning so that it was not sensitive to the inevitable changes in temperature and humidity which had long plagued harpsichords. As I continued to experiment with soundboards, I varied back and forth between fiberglass-reinforced epoxy (actually thin electric circuit boards), strikingly colored red to overcome their

LIFE magazine, Sept. 1962
"The Take-Over Generation" issue

Using modern techniques to update an old instrument, Boston development engineer Caleb Warner in his spare time builds and sells harpsichords with aluminum frames and electronic amplification. They are more rugged and reliable than conventional types.

drab green native color, and various wood laminates, with and without fiberglass stabilization. The instruments were occasionally topped with a clear Plexiglass lid that could be raised, both to attract the observer to look into the intriguing decorative workings, and to eliminate the annoyance of blocking the line of sight among surrounding players.

Later, when I returned to working on a second generation of my own line of instruments, I steered away from the rather severe looks of the exposed metal. I shifted to fiber-reinforced plastic body/structure, colored a comforting forest green, plus what earlier experiments had proven to be the best soundboard material, glass-reinforced epoxy. Throughout the twenty-year period of dealing with these plucked string instruments, I continually addressed methods of amplifying, modifying, and generally handling the plucked string sound, not only to deal with the issue of amplitude/volume, but also to deal with its effective quality/timbre. Quite obviously, the plucked string, like the whistle or wind-excited pipe, is a substantial and fundamental candidate source of a musical tone. When picked up electromagnetically, or with an accelerometer (that detects and measures sound vibrations), I was able not only to deal with the volume problem but also experiment with a wild variety of sounds, some of them quite new.

To many people, this was an insult to the instrument; harpsichords have always held a strong and faithful following in support of their preservation and traditional past. Accordingly, I was labeled as treading on thin ice with those folks. As I began to show my harpsichords to musicians around me, however, I found there was a certain amount of interest.

Over time, the construction of new and innovative plucked-string instruments was an underlying presence in my activities, and opened many doors for me in the years to come.

MAGNION, INC.: A STARTUP LABORATORY EQUIPMENT BUSINESS

In 1962, a group from the faculty of MIT realized that ADL had several proprietary products that it was not pushing hard in the evolving marketplace, and that these products might be the basis for a new company. One was ADL's ultra-high-field laboratory magnet, the so-called Bitter High-Field Magnet. This device was already contributing to research in nuclear magnetic resonance, on the edge of the emerging medical imaging field that became today's familiar Magnetic Resonance Imaging (MRI). (Notice that the word "nuclear" is tastefully removed from today's label to soften the fear that the word often triggers.)

Another product of interest was ADL's adiabatic demagnetizing refrigerator, on the edge of the emerging electrical superconductor field. This research is important today in highly efficient electrical power devices and distribution systems.

The MIT group made arrangements with ADL to take over the Magnet, named for its designer, Francis Bitter, and the conceptual design of the refrigerator. They attracted venture capital to finance the startup of a new firm they named Magnion, Inc., located near MIT. I was recruited as General Manager and design engineer of the new firm, which already had three or four physics-oriented engineers, a cadre of consultants from MIT, a shop crew of two or three technicians, and an office staff of another one or two more souls. Our potential customers were a small list of major, highly sophisticated physics laboratories thinly scattered all over the world.

Marketing was going to be primarily word of mouth — relatively straightforward because these potential customers all talked to each other and gathered several times a year at their professional meetings.

I struggled with the situation for a little over a year and we got our two main products up and going, but it was clear that I was not the kind of person to make this firm really tick. The professional staff was head and shoulders beyond me in their technical capability and I did not have the proper disciplinary orientation to keep them focused. Eventually, I was fired, but in a friendly way. (This was the second time I was fired. The first was while at ADL when I left my first assignment and landed more happily in the Mechanical Division). I am glad to say that removal from Magnion was the last "firing" in my life. Frankly, I remain in complete sympathy with those who fired me!

With that less-than-happy-experience behind me, I figured I ought to seek professional job-hunting help. This approach was really worthwhile. I went to what many in the job search field fondly called a "body snatcher" who had a reputation for being both thorough and aggressive. He worked me over in the practice of being interviewed and in directing my job-seeking efforts. He pointed me toward Edgerton, Germeshausen & Grier, one of his regular clients, and the process went smoothly from start to successful finish.

EDGERTON, GERMESHAUSEN & GRIER, INC. (EG&G) — MILITARY AND CIVILIAN PROJECTS

By 1964, EG&G had grown beyond Harold Edgerton's pioneering work in developing the xenon flash tube (a lamp that could produce a flash of very high levels of light for a very short time). The flash tube started as a device to produce illumination for taking photographs in low light conditions and in stopping motion instantaneously so that the nature of the motion could be comprehended. Out of this capability came the stroboscope, flash photography, and aerial night photography. Not so well known is that certain aspects of flash technology are also heavily involved in the triggering of nuclear explosions. EG&G was a development company, and then a manufacturer of high-energy flash systems, and an operator of atomic weapons test and field facilities for the U.S Department of Defense and the Atomic Energy Commission (AEC). In 1964 its headquarters was on the Charles River in Cambridge, with manufacturing facilities in Salem, MA and California, field operations at AEC sites around the U.S., and weapons test sites in the Pacific.

When it came time to get high level clearances to permit me to work on classified matters, I came close to having a problem when the FBI performed their usual investigation into my background. I was surprised to find out that my father's position during the Spanish Civil War as well as his choice of close friends in academia during the 1950s McCarthy era had made him look questionable in the eyes of the FBI, hence potentially throwing cold water on my clearance. Furthermore, the agency was apparently not fully informed of, and thus mistrustful of, my statements regarding my prior service in the CIA. I gave them a rough time by refusing to give them details about my CIA experience in concert with the directions dictated to me when I left that agency. I also pointed out that their claim against my father was definitely inaccurate. I am afraid that I did not handle the situation well in dealing with the FBI. In spite of all the difficulties, my clearance finally came through.

The bulk of my work at EG&G centered on night aerial flash photography and the emerging field of satellite imaging, so important today in weather forecasting. We also did a lot of very interesting work on navigation aids that used light flashes. We set up a test range for assessing the conspicuousness of various configurations of flashing buoy lights when viewed against lighted land backgrounds, during varying weather conditions, and under varying conditions of sunrise/sunset. The test range that we set up to evaluate the performance of these navigation aids transited Salem Bay from Marblehead Neck to the Beverly Farms shore. This allowed us to evaluate the effectiveness of buoy lights viewed by mariners approaching the shore in relation to other interfering sources such as street lights and car headlights.

THE CANNON GUILD, INC.: A STARTUP COMPANY

In 1967, even though extremely busy with my work, I realized that I was more than just fascinated with the experiments I had been doing on stabilizing the tuning of harpsichords and amplifying their sound for use in the current Baroque music scene. I had been doing these experiments for about a decade out of my home, in my ever-expanding workshop. I had tried to use electric guitar string magnetic pickups, microphone techniques, electronic vibration sensors, and modern manufacturing techniques using up-to-date materials to effect the needed improvements. I had even gotten as far as demonstrating an experimental instrument back in 1957, under the name of Caleb Warner Instruments.

While at ADL in the late '60s, I was approached by Jim Cannon, the scion of the highly successful Cannon electronic connector family, who had heard about my efforts. He felt that perhaps the harpsichord was ready

A BRILLIANT SOLUTION

During the 1960s, when I was continually chasing or participating in Defense Department work, I did a lot of business flying, and was subjected to many infamous snafus connected with business travel. One time, when returning to Boston from Cape Canaveral with Alice, we had a stopover in Atlanta for a connecting flight back to Boston. As was typical in those days, airline ticket desk personnel refused to explain the delay of a plane that was scheduled to take us on our next leg.

Two reporters from the industry magazine Aviation Week happened to be with us on their way back from the same conference I had been attending. They started plotting how to get back at the uncommunicative ticket desk people, and came up with a brilliant solution. They got on the telephone with the Associated Press news line, identified themselves as being Aviation Week reporters, and then spun a story about a flight that was "overdue and unaccounted for" that was supposed to have arrived in Atlanta. That action produced a lot of scurrying and name-calling on the part of the ticket desk personnel. We politely moved away out of earshot, so I am not sure what really happened next. By the time Alice and I returned to the ticket desk for further information, we encountered a lot more cooperation, and the plane was promptly boarded.

to emerge as a commercially viable instrument. Since he had several million dollars in hand after just selling his family company to a much larger electronic components firm, Jim propositioned both me and the established traditional harpsichord builder, Eric Herz, with the idea of starting up a musical instrument development and manufacturing company to build updated harpsichords. Jim was to run the company as CEO. Eric was to provide intimate knowledge of existing instruments' construction and musical capabilities, while I was to bring modern technological design and manufacturing processes into the effort. This all looked so good that we decided to undertake the new enterprise.

The original work site was Eric Herz's existing workshop in West Concord. Jim Cannon added a second space in Cambridge well-suited for housing a modern development company. We ended up in Cambridgeport, on Howard St., about five blocks from the Charles River, close to the eastern extremity of the Harvard campus. The building had been a church and was ideal for our operation, with a large clear basement which could house noisy woodworking and metalworking machinery, a high-ceilinged former sanctuary as our main assembly area with almost concert hall acoustics, an upstairs apartment in which Eric could live, and various spacious rooms to house demonstration instruments. We eventually took over space across the street and moved the modern instrument construction there, leaving Eric Herz's antique reproduction shop in the old church building. We had five or ten production employees, half of whom were specialists in harpsichord construction, while the remainder were skilled in general manufacturing trades.

The first product we tackled was to establish ourselves as a modern competitor, building modest-flexibility harpsichords with quality sound when compared to the better antique-style instruments then being made throughout the world. Our instruments featured improved tuning stability and modern production techniques that might lend themselves to a growing market and which could be priced below what was then being charged. To improve stability, we used steel framing and experimented with fiberglass soundboards. To improve manufacturability and control prices, we used modern furniture building construction details. To retain sound quality, we used proven designs from some of the better antiques. We built and sold five or ten of these instruments to demonstrate the processes and test the market. Eric Herz paralleled the efforts of the modernized instrument program by bringing out a line of modest capability instruments, moderately priced, but of high musical quality, using established techniques, with the anticipation that those instruments could meet what was hoped to be an expanding market.

As we progressed, however, it became increasingly clear to Jim Cannon that there really was not a burgeoning market for harpsichords as we had hoped. So there was a real need to take a careful look at the potential viability of the total effort of the Cannon Guild.

Meanwhile, the strident electric guitar was becoming increasingly evident in the field of popular music. It looked as if there might be a market for a keyboard electric guitar, based on some of the principles inherent and already proven in the harpsichord. Accordingly, I developed such an instrument based on my familiarity with applied magnetics and my experience in mechanical design and production, using what we already knew about harpsichords. Perhaps a better name for the instrument at that time (taking advantage of electric guitar terminology) might have been "solid-body harpsichord". I received some really good consulting assistance and actual manufacturing service from an electronics-oriented friend who was also skilled in applied magnetics, so development of the instrument became relatively straightforward.

The appearance of the 61-key instrument was greatly enhanced by its harp-like curvaceous body, scaled down from the classical harpsichord, constructed of space age aluminum structural materials, set off by a bright red fiberglass-reinforced plastic soundboard. Supported on natural-finish red oak legs, it used a contemporary-style guitar amplifier, an airplane cockpit-style dual floor pedal for volume control, with timbre selection by an array of toggle switches above the keyboard.

This instrument was a real attention-getter, with just enough originality of sound to attract some powerful musicians, including Hank Jones (formerly Benny Goodman's pianist, then a standout in the New York cabaret scene) and Henry Mancini of "Pink Panther" theme fame. Additionally, several rock music groups picked it up here and in Britain. Various musicians made some records featuring the instrument.

There seemed to be enough initial interest in the instrument that Jim Cannon sought an established musical instrument manufacturer to take over our instruments. The Baldwin Piano Company, headquartered in Cincinnati, already well known for their pianos and electronic organs, was heavily engaged in diversifying their product line. They agreed to buy us out and move the operation to their Fayetteville, Arkansas manufacturing operation.

It was, in fact, the timing of our efforts that was our fatal flaw. Electronic generation of sound had not yet progressed far enough to produce the class of sounds from a keyboard such as we were able to produce. We were operating just at the end of the 1960s, when the electronic organ and synthesizer were just short of bursting forth. As soon as their sounds reached the marketplace and demonstrated that they could pretty much do what we were doing musically with a much less expensive and simpler instrument, there remained no role for our products. Baldwin realized that fact, so we folded our collective tents after a rather interesting three-year scramble. Poor Jim Cannon obviously lost much of his investment. Quite frankly,

"LUCY IN THE SKY WITH DIAMONDS"

Son Nick has kept an "ear" out for my solid-body electronic harpsichords' use over the years. It garnered an initial spurt of interest but soon thereafter had only a very small following. It came to life right before the family of all-electronic synthesizers, which came close to producing the same sound. As a result, we'll never know how much my instrument was actually used in recorded music. A short list includes use by Hank Jones (in the recording session in New York City, above), solo work by Rick Wakeman of the band YES, the Beach Boys in live versions of California Girls, and in a brief interlude in the WHO's Live at Leeds *album. "By far the most gorgeous use I've ever heard, however," says Nick, "is in the Beatles' song Because. It starts the piece hauntingly, and then supports the song throughout. The electronic harpsichord is also quite beautifully featured in the Beatles' Lucy in the Sky with Diamonds."*

I am sure that the world is not much ahead because of what we accomplished in the two or three years in which the Cannon Guild was alive and kicking. But quite selfishly, I had a really fascinating time in the process. I returned to Caleb Warner Instruments, on the side, for any other future instrument development and fabrication.

MY WORK AT BOLT, BERANEK & NEWMAN, INC. (BB&N)

Having been strongly oriented toward acoustics and sound, with the demise of the Cannon Guild in 1969 I sought a place with Bolt, Beranek & Newman. Initially BB&N was internationally noted for leadership in many areas of acoustics. Dick Bolt was famous for his work in the field, most recently for his detective work on the infamous Nixon tapes as well as his forensic analysis of the recordings of the shots fired in the assassination of President Kennedy. He had been a high-profile performer in the emerging field of applied acoustics. Leo Beranek, along with the cofounder of the firm, Bob Newman, had been a pioneer in the architectural design of highly publicized projects such as the rebuilding of Carnegie Hall. I joined the applied acoustics end of the firm, concentrating in building and operating the laboratory facilities as well as working on acoustic aspects of antisubmarine warfare.

More recently, the firm had become a leader in computer sciences, most importantly in the interconnection of larger computer facilities, the initiation of the Internet, artificial intelligence, operations research, and so forth. Since those areas of technology were far from my training, experience or know-how, I did not work in those fields at all.

As I knew my way around DC to some extent, I found myself once again

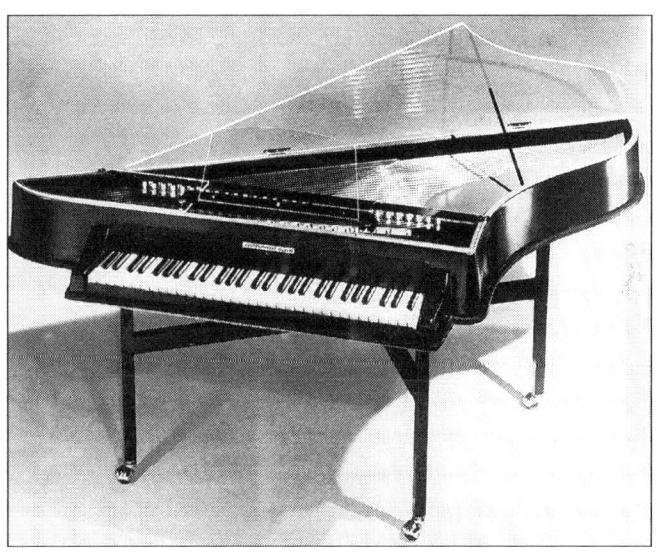

This modern "classical" harpsichord, sold under the name of Caleb Warner Instruments, had a fiberglass body, with an epoxy reinforced fiberglass soundboard. It was the only harpsichord I continued to make after Baldwin bought out Cannon Guild. To this day, it is my favorite for its classical antique sound.

PHISH AND BAD TV

"Trey Anastasia," says Nick, "who was the lead guitarist for Phish, used to live next door to me and would come over just to play my dad's electronic harpsichord. This was long before he was famous—but he loved playing it. CBC (Canadian PBS) studios, back in the 1970s, also had one and used it for background for TV shows. I used to watch bad TV just to hear it. And, interestingly, the early Yamaha electronic keyboards had a preset called 'Lucy' which was from a sample of the electronic harpsichord."

caught up initially in technical sales, proposal writing, and all that which goes with working in the military/industrial complex.

In a parallel manner to what happened earlier at ADL, I became increasingly involved in applied acoustics, especially in the rather extensive laboratory facilities such as the large, low-speed wind tunnel where we studied aircraft noise reduction, for which I built operational models.

I also built extensive models of downtown building clusters for test in the wind tunnel at Boston University. An infamous Boston skyscraper, the John Hancock Building, set an example of natural wind damage when its windows were blown out, showering pedestrians below with broken glass. Pedestrian injury and annoyance in dense city building clusters had emerged as a significant problem.

GENERAL OCEANOLOGY, INC. (G.O.): A STARTUP SUBSIDIARY OF BB&N

In 1970, BB&N initiated a subsidiary company in a diversification move to provide field services in the emerging environmental science field. BB&N assembled a group of employees who had a practical bent, plus a few new hires, and set them up as General Oceanology, Inc., across the street from the BB&N corporate headquarters in North Cambridge. I was part of that group.

G.O.'S FISH PROTEIN CONCENTRATE PROJECT IN CHILE

One of our most meaningful projects at G.O. involved a contract with the U.S. Agency for International Development (USAID). We looked at the availability and use of certain relatively unmarketable but plentiful fish stocks to upgrade the availability of high-quality protein to stave off starvation and improve dietary quality in developing countries. This was primarily through the harvesting, processing, distribution, and ultimate use of a protein concentrate made from Chile's plentiful fish, the hake.

This project involved travel to Chile twice, for about a month each, for me. We were lucky that Alice could come to Chile on one of the trips to perform an independent professional library science-oriented mission that she had arranged.

G.O.'S FISH PROTEIN CONCENTRATE PROJECT IN KOREA

Our fish protein experience in Chile opened the door to go to South Korea for about a month. I worked with the fishing fleets in the south of the country to initiate a similar program there. South Korea had just started to emerge as an industrial powerhouse in the worldwide marketplace. I found it personally educational to get a view of that though we were working in a non-industrial area. This trip also gave me the luxury of stopping over in Japan on the way so I could visit the memorials that had been built in both Kyoto and Nara in thanks for my father's work to preserve ancient art and culture during the war.

G.O.'s Frustrating Antarctica Opportunity

There was one special project at G.O. that might have taken us on a field service program in Antarctica. It was an opportunity we ultimately lost; this was a major disappointment and still haunts me to this day.

With increasing concern about the role of Arctic and Antarctic regions in postwar international affairs, the National Science Foundation (NSF) undertook an upgrade of the U.S. outpost at Palmer Station in Antarctica. A significant improvement to the station operation was to be a specialized ferry to make travel to and from the station more adequate. The program was to provide the operating crew and home base support for the ferry service between Punta Arenas and the Palmer Peninsula using a specially designed ice-hardened

Work in Chile and Korea was an important part of our Fish Protein Concentrate program. I found this project to be particularly satisfying.

small vessel. This service was to be contracted out to a qualified firm, rather than provided by the U.S. government, with NSF scheduling and generally overseeing the operation. BB&N wanted G.O.'s mission to include this kind of business, a service we would have liked very much to perform.

It turned out that the vessel was almost completed and was just about to be launched from a Maine shipyard that I was familiar with. I hustled up to the yard to familiarize myself with the vessel, and then actually attended the launching ceremony, hoping to demonstrate to NSF that our firm was definitely interested in what was going on.

I was fascinated to observe the features of the vessel's unusual structure. It took many of its ice-hardening features from the structural designs of Norwegian sealing vessels. The design work had been done by Boston's Porter & McArthur Associates, naval architects. (Interestingly, as a result of getting to know that firm during my trip to look at the NSF vessel in Maine, I was invited to become a director of that firm several years later when I was in business for myself.)

The competition for the Antarctic services contract was considerable. Much to our sorrow, however, General Oceanology proved to be too much of an unknown entity to be selected. It was a sobering experience, and I believe that it was a major factor in the decision by BB&N to terminate General Oceanology as their subsidiary.

Wind Tunnel Models

My tasks for BB&N expanded into making models for aircraft noise reduction to be used in the company's in-house wind tunnel. Construction of these modestly sized models was readily accomplished in my workshop, which was gradually growing larger in our Lexington house. (One year, when doing the taxes, we claimed that our businesses, between them, utilized 70% of our home's space. This was, I'm afraid, quite correct. As you might easily guess, it was not *Alice 's* business that was taking up so much space!) I also built extensive wind tunnel models of proposed downtown Boston building clusters.

BB&N had been contracted to determine whether the infamous kind of wind-induced window damage previously suffered by Boston's John Hancock office building might happen again if proposed new, large office buildings were constructed in downtown Boston. In performing the wind tunnel tests, we were also looking for other wind conditions which might cause difficulties for people at street level. One of those annoyances included a downright embarrassment for ladies: winds that could lift women's skirts could crop up if incorrectly designed large buildings induced drafts in the downtown Boston area. The actual testing of the building cluster models was performed by BB&N using the sophisticated slow-speed wind tunnel at Boston University.

G.O.'S EMPLOYEE STOCK OWNERSHIP SITUATION

The startup of General Oceanology, Inc. had originally put employees in line to receive stock in the newly formed corporation. When BB&N finally decided that G.O. was not going to continue, we were automatically transferred back to BB&N. This was the fourth time that I was involved in the failure of a new high-technology corporate structure. The first was ADL's slide downhill, next was Magnion's demise, then the sellout to Baldwin of the Cannon Guild, and fmally this fall of General Oceanology.

I was shaken hard enough to be convinced to seek another mode of earning a living. The possibility of becoming self-employed so as to be clear of the corporate shenanigans that I had witnessed was tempting and could offer me a chance to be rewarded for what I myself could do rather than what somebody else's organization could do for (or against) me. This seemed attractive. It is a difficult feeling to describe at this point, but it was certainly a powerful force that urged me to give self-employment a try.

LOOKING BACK

Today, with some perspective on those first 20 years of professional work in the Boston area, I realize that I was privileged to work both with and for some extraordinary people in several truly fascinating areas. The feeling of my own professional accomplishment was, quite honestly, not up to my own expectations — but who knows, ahead of time, which expectations will point one in the direction that will be best for him and his family? My financial performance was adequate to support a good lifestyle for my family. Luckily, we were all also generally healthy and content, the growth of the family and family relationships were good, and our social lives seemed definitely rewarding.

BASIC
ACOUSTIC
HARPSICHORD

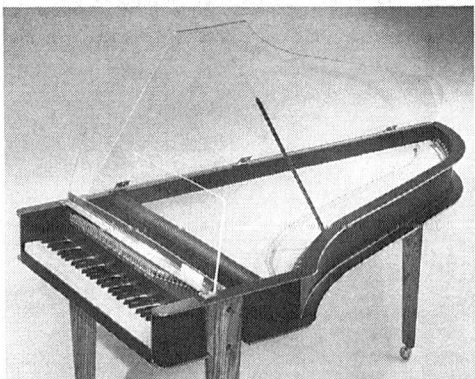

With Optional Sound Reinforcement Through
The New **TRUE-TIMBRE-FIDELITY**™ System.

TRADITIONAL in tonal excellence,
whether unamplified or
electronically reinforced.

MODERN in styling,
yet tastefully adaptable
to any surrounding.

INNOVATIVE in design,
using latest materials to
assure tuning stability
and reliability.

PRACTICAL in its portability,
ruggedness and ease of
maintenance.

FLEXIBLE in usefulness,
since it can be reinforced
electronically, without tonal
degradation, to volume levels
heretofore unattainable.

UNIVERSAL in acceptance,
by a variety of players
— professional • amateur
— classical • popular • jazz
— beginners • advanced
— individuals • group.

The Cannon Guild

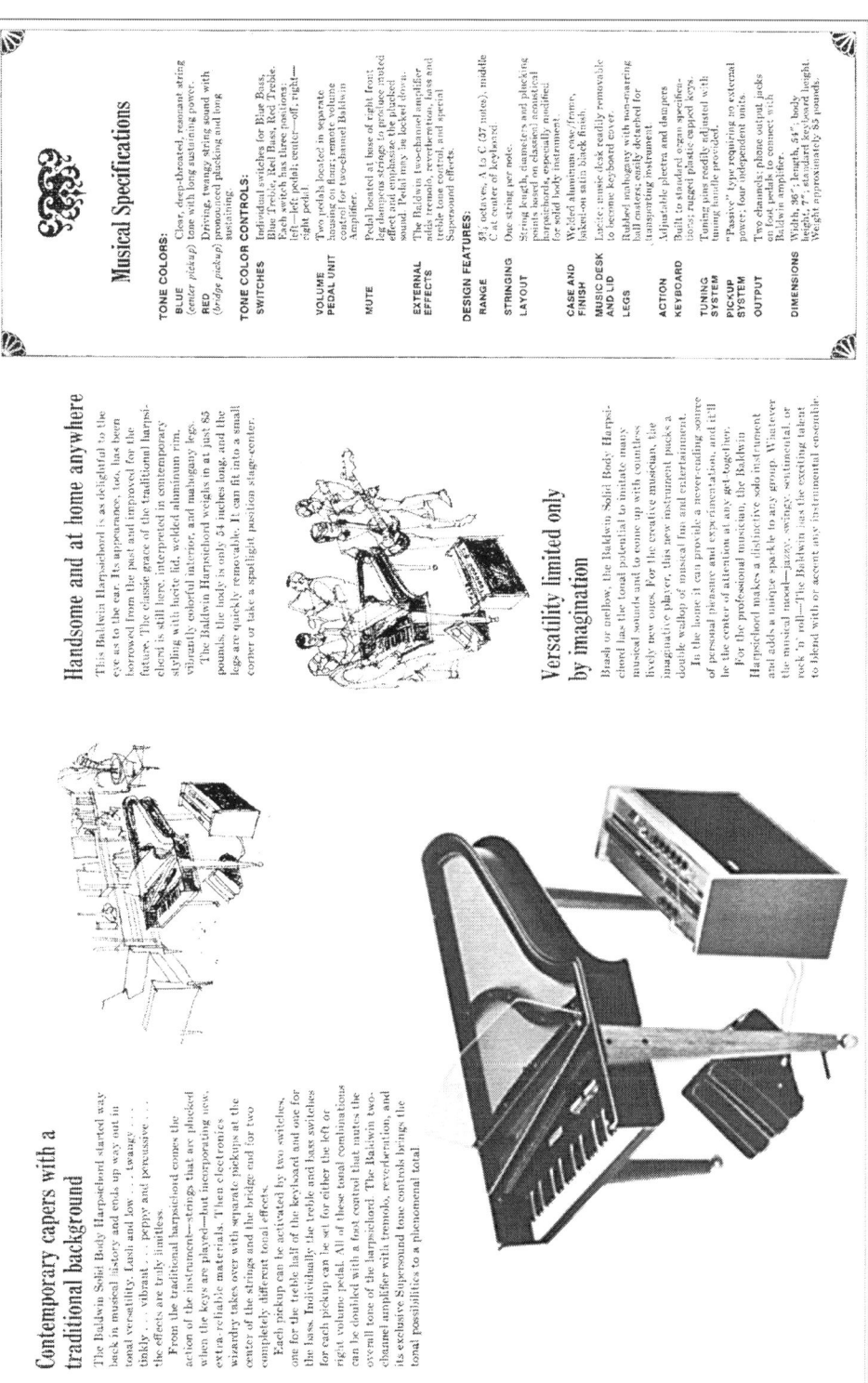

A Baldwin Piano Company marketing brochure featuring our electronic solid-body harpsichord, the rights to which had just been sold to Baldwin.

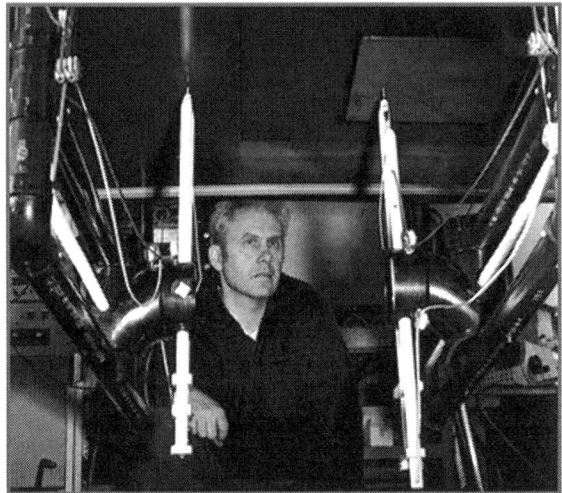

At left, a noisy fan in a large truck engine. At right, quieting an aircraft engine.

Measuring the actual sound of tires in use for reduction of the din of public traffic. Eventually, this
BB&N work led to the development of noise barrier walls found today along many large suburban highways.

CALEB WARNER
– Experience Profile – May, 1976

PROPRIETOR — Prototype Shop Services (Mechanical); Proprietary Product Business (Musical Instr'ts); Consulting Practice (Mechanical Design, Materials)

ADMINI-STRATION — Founding Group; Operating Management; Planning, Acquisition, Diversification; Project Direction

OPERATING RESPONSIBILITY — Mechanical Prototype Shop Management; Small Lot Production Management; Vendor Liaison; Direct Sales of Technical Services

MARKETING — Product Sales; Market Research, Promotion Development

TECHNICAL DISCIPLINES — Mechanical R&D, Design, Styling; Industrial & Production Engineering; Applied Sciences R&D

ARTISAN SKILLS — Models, Prototypes, Patterns, Molds, Tooling; Plastics (Adhesives Selection, Fabrication, Lamination)

DOCUMEN-TATION — Proposal Preparation; Industrial & High-speed Photography; Drafting Layout, Design & Detailing; Technical Writing, Editing, Manuals

FIELD OPERATIONS — Equipment Installation & Troubleshooting; Operator Training

TEACHING — Field Survey

Companies (top): TUFTS, C.I.A., du PONT, ARTHUR D. LITTLE, INC., E.G.&G., INC., BOLT, BERANEK & NEWMAN, INC.

EDUCATION & HONORS –
Grad. Level: Harvard, '48–'49, Non-degree program in eng'g., physics, biology, gov't, economics.
B.S.: Marine Engineering, Univ. of Michigan, 1944.
HONORS: American-Scandinavian Foundation Fellow in Sweden. Elected Tau Beta Pi, junior year. Registered Professional Engineer, Mass., 1969, #9673 (now inactive)

PATENTS & PUBLICATIONS:
Recent Papers: Marine Safety, Fishery Fleet Economics, Musical Instrument R+D.
Proposals & Reports } Samples
Promotional Material } Report
Patents: 15 Musical Instruments

PERSONAL DATA –
Born: Sept. 12, 1922, N.Y. City. Health: Excellent.
Family: Married, 4 children, 18–24 years old.
Wife: President, (Warner-Eddison Assoc., Information Specialists)
Clearance: Top Secret (current), AEC "Q" (expired). Job opportunities for community involvement. School parent comm., church renovation, students, musical education in local school system.
Hobbies: Musical Instrument R&D, high-speed sailing.
Director: Potter & McArthur, Inc., Naval Architects.

REFERENCES –
On request

ADDRESS: Business — The Instrument Guild, Box 254, Lexington, MA, 02173. Home: 546 Concord Ave., Lexington, MA., 02173. Tel (617) 862-9278

FACILITIES PROVIDED –
- Light Metal Fabrication
- Wood working
- Plastics Handling (Vacuum, Oven, etc.)
- Finishing & Coating (spraying, etc.)
- Dimensional Inspection & Quality Control
- Light Rigging & millwrighting
- Materials & Supplier Reference Library
- Photographic Darkroom (Black & White)
- Secure Facility for Commercial R+D

Caleb Warner 546 Concord Ave, Lexington, Mass., 02173 (617) 862-9278

My resume. My headhunter informed me it should never be given to a prospective employer in this oddball layout, and refused to use it. I felt that it served as a tool to sort out the kind of people I actually wanted to work for! I used it, and it worked!

215

CALEB WARNER

Mechanical Development
of
Products & Processes
through
Turnkey Services

The INSTRUMENT GUILD INC.

Box 254
Lexington, Mass. 02173
(617) 862-9278

12

THE INSTRUMENT GUILD:
SELF-EMPLOYMENT

TIME TO MAKE A CHANGE

It was 1971, and I was eager to be self-employed, to work in an environment based less on bureaucracy and more on my own ideas of meaningful work and know-how. I also wanted to work from home, allowing me to be around and more available to both my wife and kids. The kids were spreading their wings, and Alice, who was considering going back to school for her master's degree, was already starting to do some consulting work in the field of Library Science.

I was surrounded by a cadre of really competent men who were doing what they really loved on the side while working a regular job each day, as I was. In fact, my colleague Byron Blanchard had already started his own small business. I thought I could pull together these clearly skilled friends, who were ready to take on more work of their own, to form a new business. Happily, BB&N supported my idea and pressed me to remain available to do contract work for the company.

I honestly cannot recall Alice's first reaction to my idea, but she believed that I would do my best to support the family. I decided to start the Instrument Guild, and Alice decided to go back to school. The kids' lives changed as well. We modified our schooling decisions and the two younger kids shifted from private to public high schools. None of these changes were to happen, however, until my fledging business idea was mapped out.

WHAT ABOUT A BUSINESS PLAN?

When preparing to start a new business, one normally first determines that a market exists, and then a business plan is carefully crafted before jumping in. Toward the end of my full-time employment period, it had become apparent that there might be a market for the various kinds of services that I could provide. However, planning it in any formal way with a classic business plan, I reasoned, might be better accomplished by first "testing the waters".

I felt that I should set up a strict set of financial performance goals before wading into a self-employment style of business. Accordingly, I set up rules for levels of billable hours per month that I must achieve and standards for proper payment performance that I must receive from clients in order to work for them. I set goals on levels of cash flow and capital requirements. I did the best I could to establish supporting forms and documents to permit adequate accounting, estimating, and contracting. My target was to support the lifestyle that we were practicing as a family and I set the hope that I could attain a reasonable but not necessarily overly substantial upgrading of lifestyle for the future.

My departure from BB&N to initiate my self-employment status was a truly satisfactory move for both sides. BB&N welcomed me as an immediately available, on-call subcontractor. That was more than helpful for me because it meant that our family could continue to eat! I could go into business with work immediately in hand.

It was clear that my target clients were going to be the technology-oriented firms then blossoming around Boston in what was then referred to as the "Route 128 Technology Cluster". It was also obvious that I was *not* going to be useful to firms oriented toward the skyrocketing field of information technology since that was an area in which I had virtually no background or skills.

In view of my unhappy experience with the bureaucratic structures of the big-time research and development (R&D) firms where I had worked in the recent past, I made what now, looking back, was a non-traditional decision. I would organize my business as a one-person enterprise with no full-time employees beyond myself. Then I would flesh it out with a cadre of contractors with highly diversified technological skills. I would provide the less interesting functions such as marketing and project management. This would free up my contractors to concentrate on practicing their technical skills. I would have a hands-on involvement in all aspects of the project, arranging to contract out in the areas in which I did not have a high enough expertise.

In the long run, I was correct. My arms-length contractors were glad that I took on the marketing and project management tasks for them, and our division of effort was, in fact, generally welcomed. It worked quite well.

THE GUILD CONCEPT

I puzzled for some time over the name for my new business. I was wary of forming a statutorily correct <u>corporation</u> since <u>in</u>corporation would inevitably involve legal and tax issues, the complication of which I was desperate to avoid. I further suspected that if the proposed organization had my name in its title, some of the people that I hoped to involve might have their egos dented. If the term "associate(s)" was in the name, there also might be some ego problems, and I favored not having employees in my future organization; I wanted to operate as a sole proprietorship.

I puzzled over selecting a name since it was important to steer away from what it *was not,* but it was difficult to find an established generic rubric which fitted what the enterprise *was to be.* It was easy to appreciate Jim Cannon's ingenious name for our previous startup venture, the Cannon Guild, Inc., since that name had a nuance of history or early days, and was attuned to the fact that we were dealing with, of all things, harpsichords. But I was naturally wary of some of the negative aspects of the ancient guild structure, and I was further concerned about the perhaps "antiquarian ring" of the word itself.

However, one dictionary cited a definition of the word "guild" as "an association of people with similar interests or pursuits," and another defined it as "a forum for developing competence". Those definitions sounded hopeful. Perhaps naming our proposed effort a "guild" was appropriate after all, especially if it were organized as described above. "Collectivism with a common goal" was exactly what I was trying to get across.

Further, attaching the descriptor "instrument" to the new enterprise had a two-pronged purpose in that it hinted at my demonstrated musical instrument interests while also producing a slight sense of technical matters, a plus when marketing our collective services.

Thus, the business became "The Instrument Guild" (I.G.). Since I was soon to be the founder, sole organizer, and manager, my job was to do the marketing, planning, and promotion, and work hands on, actively, on the anticipated technically oriented projects, contracting out anything that needed further expertise to my pool of experts.

FINANCING CONSIDERATIONS

I set up a scheme to limit cash flow and to remain unencumbered if outside financing was needed. My agreements with my clients required the client to pay my Guild contractors <u>directly</u> rather than <u>through me</u>. Instead of taking add-ons to the costs of participating Guild contractors, I openly required clients to pay for my time as a project manager, planning and overseeing the efforts of the contractors.

GUILD FACILITIES

As I continued to plan my business, it was clear that I needed more shop and office facilities to support it (another of a continuum of changes in our house layout to fit our ever-changing living and working needs). I took over an upstairs bedroom, and an overly commodious two-car carport attached to our house became a separately heated and insulated workshop with its own door to the outside. In the process of redefining the space in the house, we had to rebuild and rework the whole lower floor to make additional individual bedrooms for our kids. For years thereafter there were continual room reassignments, both upstairs and downstairs, to accommodate the ever-changing needs for Instrument Guild functions and changing lifestyles of our growing children.

INSTRUMENT GUILD CLIENTS

Since, for the preceding two decades, I had been around many of the founders of the burgeoning Boston high technology industry during its formative years, I set out to market I.G. services directly to those founders. Quite often, they said they wanted me to help them get back into working directly on development of new products or processes. In other cases, they wanted to find a way to parallel what they were already doing, by using a different or more inventive approach. Quite typically, they chose to enlist I.G. services to buttress their innovative ideas. Consequently, I often ended up working directly for the corporate founders themselves.

Three of my earliest clients were people who had been singled out by the Boston Museum of Science as the region's top pioneers in starting up technologically oriented new companies. One by one, Alan Latham, Arthur C. Ruge, and Henry Kloss each had been labeled by the Museum as "Inventor of the Year".

MY STRUGGLE WITH GETTING INTO INFORMATION TECHNOLOGY

Keeping in mind that I started my business in the early 1970s, as the age of the information technology (IT) industry was truly dawning, I found myself purposely ducking the effort to learn to use some of these important IT tools. I was not so naïve as to ignore that I needed to learn to use them in their application to my projects, however. I struggled to get up to speed in computer-aided engineering design software, or "CAD". I did not have enough time and money to take formalized training, so this was a stressful self-teaching effort.

ASSOCIATION WITH PAT (PASQUALE) PEPPICELLI

Early on, in the process of attending all the local machine tool auctions to build up my machine shop capability, I stumbled into a man who was doing exactly what I was doing—breaking out of working in the research and development industry and starting a business similar in some ways to what I was building. We established a rather useful routine of working the auctions together by bidding for machine tools together rather than competitively.

Pat had a stellar history of machine shop experience (apprenticeship and all that goes with it) plus a thorough education in machine design via night schooling. He had a small, well-equipped machine shop in his garage with really good, well-set-up, well-maintained tools. His shop included the classic indicator that this was a "for real" machine shop in that he had a full-size, fully tooled Bridgeport Milling Machine. We subsequently performed as partners, although we did not formalize or legalize the relationship as such. The arrangement was all on a handshake basis.

He gradually built up a substantial contract machine shop and engineering design service. Called Innovative Products and Equipment Co., it was housed in one of the rehabbed mill buildings in Lowell, occupying perhaps 2,000-3,000 square feet of factory floor space, with 10-15 employees. Initially, he built almost everything that I designed, and gradually went far beyond me in designing as well in developing an engineering staff. I brought him much of the work that got him going and he became increasingly self-sufficient.

Recent Projects   1977-1978

The INSTRUMENT GUILD INC.
Box 254
Lexington, Mass. 02173
(617) 862-9278

for HAEMONETICS CORP.
a pioneer in blood fractionators
- Innovating disposable plastic systems for blood recovery and clean-up
- Introducing new plastics fabrication & assembly under sterile conditions
- Fabricating prototypes of new blood processors
- Styling, tool design and tool fabrication for thermoformed devices & packages

for A MEDICAL INSTRUMENT COMPANY
pioneering in medical osmometry
- Styling and conceptual mechanical design of the next-generation body fluid osmometer
- Detailed mechanical design and fabrication of prototype osmometers for market evaluation
- Conceptual design, tooling and prototyping of a novel, disposable plastic osmometry chamber

for BOLT BERANEK & NEWMAN, INC.
nationally known for acoustics research
- Design and fabrication of scale models for wind tunnel and acoustic studies
- Consulting on materials selection and fabricating techniques for noise control
- Industrial still and high-speed technical photography

for GREGSTROM CORP.
a prominent thermoformer of plastics
- Development of improved production tooling techniques for vacuum forming
- Fabrication of unusual production tooling using high performance plastics

for NEWPORT METALS
a newcomer in international gold trading
- Styling of enclosure for gold bar impurity detection device
- Development of thermal control system
- Mechanical design and prototype fabrication of initial prototypes for test marketing

for McCLELLAND ENGINEERS
prominent west coast geophysical surveyor
- Next-generation electro-magnetic sound source for off-shore sub-bottom surveys
- Improvement in fieldworthiness, acoustic output and reduction of spurious outputs
- Fabrication of fieldable transducers involving high-performance plastics and elastomers

for E. A. KELLEY ASSOCIATES
a leading local pipe organ builder
- Construction of mechanical components for updating large tracker (mechanical action) organs
- Consulting on new materials and fabricating techniques

for A BOSTON LAW FIRM
active in occupational safety law
- Technical investigations into the cause of industrial accidents
- Expert witness services in occupational hazard court cases

for A LOCAL MEDICAL INSTRUMENT COMPANY
manufacturing diversified instruments
- Research into methods of building a new disposable plastic blood oxygenator
- Demonstration fabrication of prototype oxygenators

for A PLAY EQUIPMENT MANUFACTURER
a leader in quality outdoor products
- Styling and design of outdoor children's slide to meet upcoming consumer safety standards
- Development of low-cost tooling system for large, short-run laminations and moldings

plus continuing PROPRIETARY PRODUCTS & PROCESSES under development for the Instrument Guild
- Process for reducing mold costs and styrene air pollution in match-mold laminating of glass reinforced polyester parts
- High-speed, off-shore rowboat
- Packaged, portable pipe organ

—Caleb Warner, January 1979

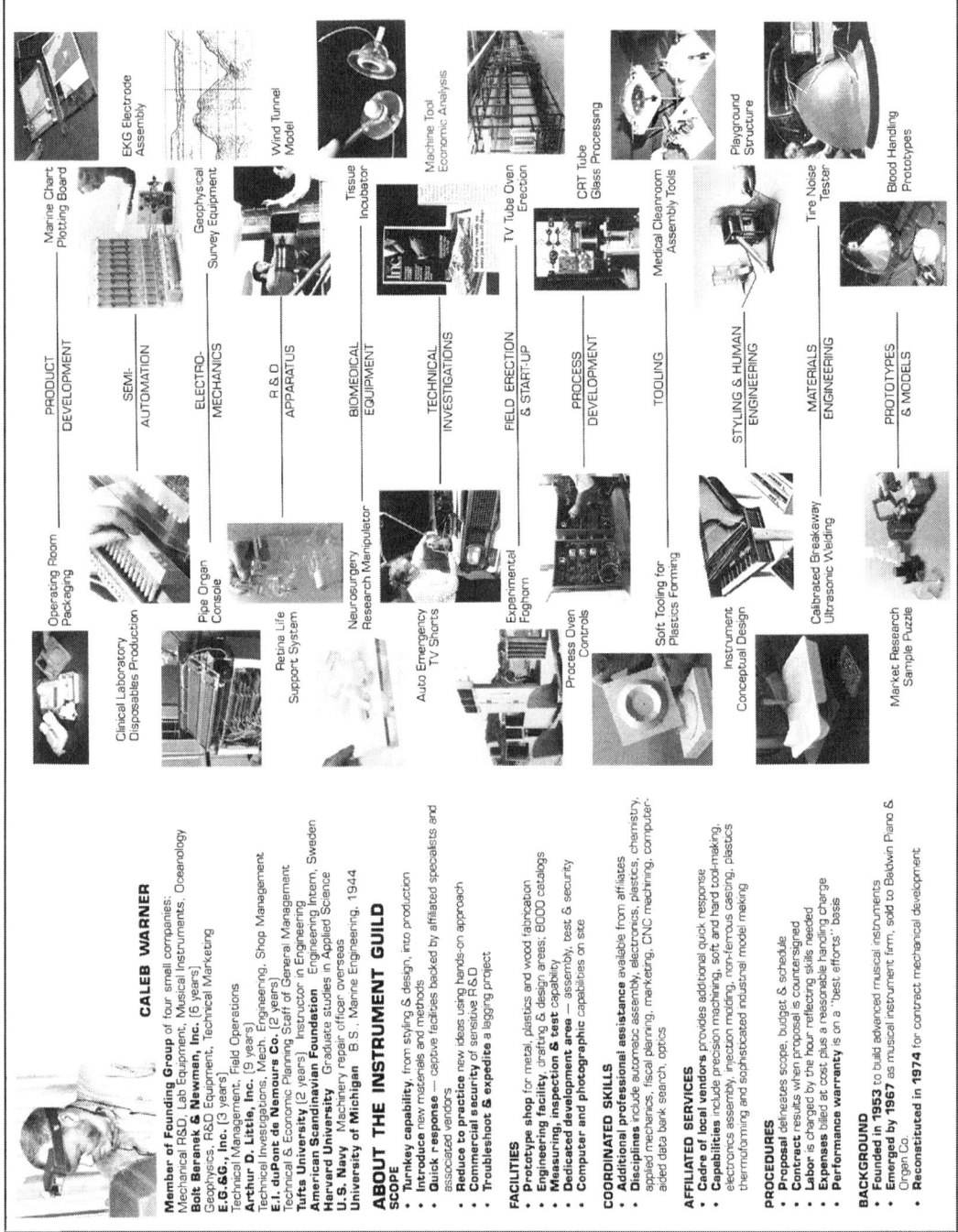

CALEB WARNER

Member of Founding Group of four small companies:
Mechanical R&D, Lab Equipment, Musical Instruments, Oceanology

Bolt Beranek & Newman, Inc. (6 years)
Geophysics, R&D Equipment, Technical Marketing

E.G.&G., Inc. (3 years)
Technical Management, Field Operations

Arthur D. Little, Inc. (9 years)
Technical Investigations, Mech. Engineering, Shop Management

E.I. duPont de Nemours Co. (2 years)
Technical & Economic Planning Staff of General Management

Tufts University (2 years) Instructor in Engineering

American Scandinavian Foundation Engineering Intern, Sweden

Harvard University Graduate studies in Applied Science

U.S. Navy Machinery repair officer overseas

University of Michigan B.S., Marine Engineering, 1944

ABOUT THE INSTRUMENT GUILD

SCOPE
- **Turnkey capability,** from styling & design, into production
- **Introduce** new materials and methods
- **Quick response** — captive facilities backed by affiliated specialists and associated vendors
- **Reduce** to practice new ideas using hands-on approach
- **Commercial security** of sensitive R&D
- **Troubleshoot & expedite** a lagging project

FACILITIES
- **Prototype shop** for metal, plastics and wood fabrication
- **Engineering facility,** drafting & design areas; 8000 catalogs
- **Measuring, inspection & test** capability
- **Dedicated development area** — assembly, test & security
- **Computer and photographic** capabilities on site

COORDINATED SKILLS
- **Additional professional assistance** available from affiliates
- Disciplines include automatic assembly, electronics, plastics, chemistry, applied mechanics, fiscal planning, marketing, CNC machining, computer-aided data bank search, optics

AFFILIATED SERVICES
- **Cadre of local vendors** provides additional quick response
- **Capabilities** include precision machining, soft and hard tool-making, electronics assembly, injection molding, non-ferrous casting, plastics thermoforming and sophisticated industrial model making

PROCEDURES
- **Proposal** delineates scope, budget & schedule
- **Contract** results when proposal is countersigned
- **Labor** is charged by the hour reflecting skills needed
- **Expenses** billed at cost plus a reasonable handling charge
- **Performance warranty** is on a "best efforts" basis

BACKGROUND
- **Founded in 1953** to build advanced musical instruments
- **Emerged by 1967** as musical instrument firm, sold to Baldwin Piano & Organ Co.
- **Reconstituted in 1974** for contract mechanical development

PRODUCT DEVELOPMENT

SEMI-AUTOMATION

ELECTRO-MECHANICS

R & D APPARATUS

BIOMEDICAL EQUIPMENT

TECHNICAL INVESTIGATIONS

FIELD ERECTION & START-UP

PROCESS DEVELOPMENT

TOOLING

STYLING & HUMAN ENGINEERING

MATERIALS ENGINEERING

PROTOTYPES & MODELS

Marine Chart Plotting Board

EKG Electrode Assembly

Geophysical Survey Equipment

Wind Tunnel Model

Tissue Incubator

Machine Tool Economic Analysis

TV Tube Oven Erection

CRT Tube Glass Processing

Medical Cleanroom Assembly Tools

Playground Structure

Tire Noise Tester

Blood Handling Prototypes

Operating Room Packaging

Clinical Laboratory Disposables Production

Pipe Organ Console

Retina Life Support System

Neurosurgery Research Manipulator

Auto Emergency TV Shorts

Experimental Foghorn

Process Oven Controls

Soft Tooling for Plastics Forming

Instrument Conceptual Design

Calibrated Breakaway Ultrasonic Welding

Market Research Sample Puzzle

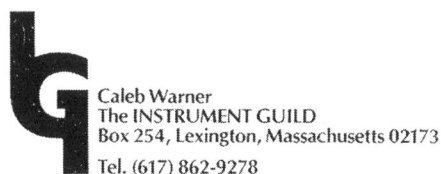

Caleb Warner
The INSTRUMENT GUILD
Box 254, Lexington, Massachusetts 02173
Tel. (617) 862-9278

"Hands-On" Technical Support
for Industry and Laboratory

1.

2.

3.

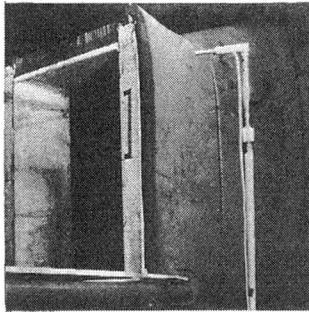

4.

5.

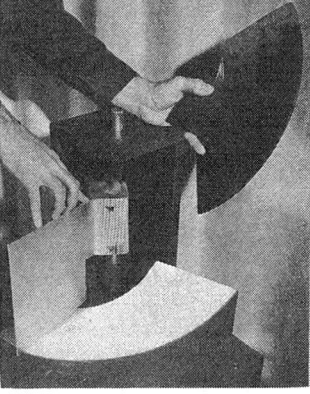

MATERIALS SELECTION, ANALYSIS & APPLICATION   May, 1976

1.STRUCTURAL PLASTICS APPLICATIONS where static, dynamic & chemical properties critical; shown is tensile test of geophysical streamer.

2.MEDICAL MATERIALS SELECTION involving toxicity, reliability & tailored mechanical properties; simulated skull tests shown here.

3.TAILORED ADHESIVES to improve fabrication & to join difficult materials; shown is test of adhesive to terminate nylon rope.

4.UNUSUAL MATERIAL USE TECHNIQUES: uncommon combinations of fabrication & material; pictured is wood laminate used to improve fairness of curves in large nozzle.

5.MATERIALS FOR "SOFT" TOOLING: castable filled plastics, waxes, bonded fibers & controlled expansion plaster; example shows helical ramp generator and resulting propeller pattern both using glass fiber reinforced tooling plaster.

Caleb Warner
The INSTRUMENT GUILD
Box 254, Lexington, Massachusetts 02173
Tel. (617) 862-9278

"Hands-On" Technical Support
for Industry and Laboratory

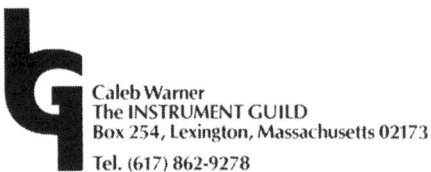

1.

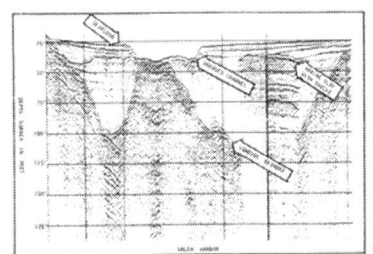

4.

2.

5.

3.

6.

FIELD OPERATIONS

May, 1976

1.SUB-CONTRACTOR LIAISON: fabrication oversight & QA at vendor's
plant; large steel weldment shown,
built outside under supervision.

2.FIELD SITE INSTALLATION & start
up of sophisticated equipment;
pictured is erection of one of 4
test foghorns at remote site.

3.VENDOR SEARCH & SELECTION: computer-aided New England Manufacturers Exchange provides detailed
capability data on local vendors.

4.ENVIRONMENTAL SURVEY: planning,
staging & operating geophysical &
related data collection; chart
profiles sub-bottom of harbor.

5.FOREIGN ASSIGNMENTS: familiar
with methods, operations & some
languages abroad; shown is Chilean
fish resource & processing study.

6.FIELD EQUIPMENT R&D: calibration
& tests leading to evaluation of
fieldworthiness; shown at sea is
calibration of underwater devices.

In the process of developing his own skills in computer-aided design, he inspired me to come along in that field also. Altogether we worked on an informal basis for about 20 years. Unbelievably, we seemed to get along really well for the full length of our two-decade association!

BB&N had an unusual contract with the U.S. Coast Guard to develop a neighbor-friendly foghorn. As we all know, coastal foghorns are a vital part of the marine safety system, and are both a haunting fascination for coastal tourists and a significant noise annoyance to year-round neighbors. There was a real need for retaining the safety role of the horns while at the same time quieting them for people living nearby. A horn system with *directional sound* was needed, to concentrate the sound offshore while lessening the sound that would "leak" inland.

Foghorn prototype for reduction of noise annoyance.

BB&N proposed a solution which involved adding wing-like walls to the foghorn which would not only direct the sound seaward, but absorb the sound headed inland. The manifestation of this idea was a full-scale test model consisting of rigid tubes stacked up in wing-shaped walls on each side of the horn. This proof of principle was going to require some heavy construction supported by an adequate workshop and lots of erection space. The shop that I was pulling together for my upcoming business, located immediately alongside our driveway in Lexington, was preferable for the job when compared to what BB&N could provide in their Cambridge facility.

I built the large experimental model in modular form and then filled a large rented trailer in the driveway with the pieces, which son Langdon helped me transport and set up alongside the monstrous sewage plant on Deer Island in Boston Harbor. Langdon considered this project to be an ideal activity for his emerging interest in coastal matters. We then tested and evaluated the performance of the system for ships entering Boston Harbor. The test was very encouraging. I believe that the first actual installation by the Coast Guard was at Cape Porpoise, Maine, so positioned to make the inhabitants of the large swank hotel there somewhat happier during the frequent fogs.

Happily, the neighbor-friendly foghorn was successful, and provided a model for how my newly formed Instrument Guild could do business with BB&N. Luck was with me. I continued to have a good base load of work during what otherwise might have been a difficult startup period.

MISSED OPPORTUNITY, OR THE CURSE OF GOVERNMENT BUREAUCRACY?

In the process of working on the Coast Guard sponsored directional foghorn problem at BB&N, Chuck Malme, the highly imaginative and inventive BB&N project manager, had an ingenious, potentially useful idea. Possibly, a system of two foghorns, one on each side of a harbor entrance, could be arranged not only to warn approaching marine craft but to guide skippers into the harbor. Such a system was not part of the scope of the contract with the Coast Guard, so corporate BB&N took a chance to establish a proprietary product and funded us to perform a proof of principle demonstration which we might then take to Washington in the hope of selling the Coast Guard on underwriting further development.

We cobbled up a test routine to try this guidance scheme in the Hull Gut section of Boston Harbor. The system seemed to go well in actual practice.

Unfortunately, we then got a lesson in bungled bureaucratic governmental reasoning when we got to Washington with the idea in our back pockets. Upon demonstrating the concept to the Coast Guard with live acoustic recordings of our experiments, they informed us (in their own way, of course) that the Coast Guard's mission was to keep mariners <u>away</u> from harbors during foggy conditions rather than guide endangered mariners <u>into</u> harbors! We could not begin to appreciate their line of reasoning. We returned to Boston with our collective tails between our legs.

> ## THERE'S A FOGHORN IN THE DRIVEWAY?
>
> *Wendy was hit quite hard with mononucleosis at age 13. She spent all summer recuperating on a cot on our screened porch, which opened fully to both living room and dining room. Too young to be aware of the intricacies of my business, she recalls, "Dad woke me up late one evening while I was still quite sick. He needed help moving a newly painted, eight-foot-tall foghorn in the driveway out of the rain. Apparently, I was the only other person home at the time. Do you know how big a foghorn looks to a barefoot, 13 year old sick kid, in the dark, in her nightgown, in the rain? And what was a foghorn doing in the driveway in the first place?"*
>
> *My kids were very accepting of my work!*

GEOPHYSICAL SURVEY FIELD WORK

On several occasions during the first two years after leaving BB&N, I was invited back to work with Bill G. Watters (familiarly known as "Bilgey") in BB&N's continuing geophysical field surveys. These were a form of seismic survey of the immediate sub-bottom of the ocean, downwards from the ocean floor for the first several hundred feet. We were determining whether offshore drilling for oil and natural gas might produce oil leaks into the ocean, as had historically caused severe environmental damage, most notably in the Santa Barbara Channel off southern California.

The most intriguing of these projects had been a month's work just off Sable Island, east of Nova Scotia. Our techniques involved using an acoustic seismic "boomer" system built by BB&N under license from my former employer, EG&G. The survey party and their equipment were carried aboard a large survey vessel which steamed in a systematic grid pattern over a several hundred square mile area surrounding an offshore drill rig. It was an enlightening and even thrilling experience for me to be aboard the drill rig and to man the survey system aboard the survey vessel. It was definitely a hands-on task; I drove the equipment-laden ten-wheeler truck to Halifax, rode the long-distance cargo-carrying helicopters out to the drill rig, operated the survey gear once aboard ship, and participated in the interpretation of the survey data in real time, in the field.

I had previously participated in another type of survey using the same equipment to determine how and where to build structures such as bridges, dam foundations, tunnels, power transmission cables, and pipelines just below the ocean bottom. One of the most interesting was to find a satisfactory route for a large pipeline to conduct sewage from the lower two-thirds of the state of New Jersey out to sea for disposal several miles off the Barnegat shore. This involved chartering a commercial fishing boat to take our survey gear out to sea, then operating the boat over a carefully designed grid for about a two-week period. Again, it was a strictly "hands-on" task, and one that I found fascinating. Happily, Alice was able to come along on that particular Barnegat, NJ, field trip. She had a wonderful time volunteering in the local library ashore every day while our team was offshore surveying.

PROJECTS FOR RUGE-DEFOREST, INC. (RDF)

From my wanderings throughout New England's intriguing small businesses during my ADL days, I had come to know the Baldwin-Lima-Hamilton Corp. (BLH) electronics firm. I stayed in contact as it became a successor firm, Ruge-DeForest.

In 1939, Arthur C. ("Proff") Ruge and his colleague, Alfred deForest, both at MIT, started to produce a most significant invention: the strain gauge. Strain gauges are critical electronic sensors that can measure extension of materials when they are under load; hence strain gauges are vital elements in many weighing scales and in a multitude of systems that require the sensing and measurement of force, stress, and weight. By 1955, the fast-growing strain gauge company had been bought out by the enormous Baldwin-Lima-Hamilton Corporation (BLH), famous builders of locomotives, home-based in the Philadelphia area. BLH had recently diversified into electronic devices. Once the original Ruge-deForest operation was within the BLH corporate structure, it became BLH Electronics and further diversified into the closely related temperature measurement field. When I linked up with them, they were just starting to extend into gas pressure and vacuum sensing and measurement. They became increasingly independent, and were then breaking away from their BLH connection to become RdF.

My work with RdF was to develop marketing strategies and to generate supporting technical literature as they reconfigured their original profile and re-emerged as an independent company. My memory is a little cloudy regarding the details of ownership, product profiles and change in names. However, my work for them was a relationship that lasted about a year and a half on a very part-time basis. It was a generally worthwhile involvement, and helped get my Instrument Guild underway.

PROJECTS FOR HAEMONETICS CORPORATION

At Arthur D. Little, I had worked under Jack Latham and came to respect him highly. If I had to assign relative rankings of the technically oriented icons in my life, I think that I would rank Jack topmost. By the early 1970s I was able to reconnect with Jack Latham. Thanks to Jack, Haemonetics became a client of the Instrument Guild for about four years.

In the surgical practice of the 1960s, human blood was being centrifuged into its component parts (platelets, plasma, and red cells) in stainless steel bowls that had to be painstakingly disassembled, sterilized, and reassembled for each use. While a vice president of ADL, Jack worked with scientists and doctors from Harvard University and MIT to develop an alternative way of centrifuging the much-needed blood. He developed the concept of a relatively inexpensive plastic chamber in which whole blood could be centrifuged into its components at between 3000 and 6000 revolutions per minute. The used centrifuge bowls could then be disposed of, saving time and costly cleaning labor.

The disposable processing bowl became known as the Latham Bowl. It revolutionized the way blood was collected and processed, and continues to be universally used to this day.

Jack's blood processing machine was marketed for a brief period by Abbott Laboratories. When Abbott decided not to pursue this activity any further, the Haemonetics Company was formed and subsequently became an independent private company. Jack gradually shifted from ADL to full time at Haemonetics. The company subsequently built an extensive manufacturing and research facility readily visible from Boston's Technology Highway (Route 128) in Braintree.

At Haemonetics I helped develop manufacturing techniques for some of the disposable plastic elements of the blood handling system. I further assisted with the autologous blood collection systems whereby a patient's blood could be collected during surgery, cleaned of byproducts of the surgical procedure, and immediately recirculated back to the patient. This permitted the patient to be less dependent on a donor for replacement of lost blood.

Haemonetics was my first really significant client after finishing up my residual employee tasks for BB&N. It was, quite frankly, a very difficult period for me since I was working directly for Jack and hence somewhat in competition with some of his in-house employees.

A valuable by-product of the Haemonetics work was that I reconnected with George Feick who was, like me, a refugee from Arthur D. Little. Since George was an infinitely wise man of broad technical skills and a sound authority in both organic and inorganic chemistry, he became increasingly useful to us as we formed up our Guild. He was involved in many of the I.G. projects up to the time of his death in about 1995.

Autologous blood centrifuge bowl. It enables a patient's own blood to be processed and returned to the patient, thus reducing the need for donated blood.

A Disappointing Near Miss: The Vincent S. Bach Co.

This missed opportunity was, perhaps, one of the more frustrating of my professional life. Many of us who are trumpet players looked on instruments built by the Vincent Bach Company of Mount Vernon, NY, as the "Stradivarius" of trumpets (excuse the mixed metaphor). My first trumpet teacher, Georges Mager, was very much involved in getting the Bach company going. Vincent Bach had graduated in mechanical engineering from the technical institute in Vienna and was a brilliant trumpet player when he landed in the U.S., just after WWI. He gained the first chair trumpet position in the BSO, and was succeeded by Georges Mager who enthusiastically promoted Bach's instruments throughout the emergence of the firm.

I was fascinated by the reputation of Vincent Bach and awed by the fact that he had achieved the remarkable feat of producing instruments of consistently high quality and sensible price–a feat seldom attained in the characteristically archaic musical instrument manufacturing and marketing field. He attained a world-class position in his industry.

I had also heard rather extraordinary tales about Bach's plant in Mount Vernon, so I eagerly arranged a visit. I toured the plant in considerable detail under Mr. Bach's watchful eye, and was fascinated to witness that he had done some unusual things in setting up the facility. He assuredly was conducting the business in a progressive fashion. It was an ultra-modern plant with advanced machine tools being run in an orderly manner. He had worked out how to build consistent quality into the instruments without requiring inordinately high levels of highly specialized artisan-like skills.

Mr. Bach invited me back to his house where he showed me the very well-organized and beautifully rendered designs of his instruments as well as the specialized tooling that he had developed. After high tea with his wife and daughter, his wife pulled me aside and said that her husband was seriously looking for somebody to buy the firm so he could finally retire. She was very interested in having him do exactly that. They were hoping that I might be a candidate to take over since I appeared to be an engineer, experienced in musical instrument construction, an enthusiastic brass instrument player, and, in addition, a pupil of Vincent Bach's friend and backer, Georges Mager. Mr. Bach really did not want to give in to the several competitors that were drooling to buy him out, and his wife was pushing for something to happen. I must admit that this was completely unexpected by me and it totally floored me. Obviously I became excited about pursuing the matter.

Looking for someone who could advise me on the subject, I immediately sought out brother-in-law John Ecklund who was, at that time, very successfully practicing law in New Haven and was intimately connected to the business community there, as well as being wise in business finance matters. (This was just before John became Treasurer of Yale University.) John was very discouraging about the possibility of my being able to raise the money to buy the Bach business. He pointed out that venture capital at that period was generally limiting itself to opportunities in the electronic or information technology field. The musical instrument business was classed as archaic and not an attractive target for speculative investment.

**Caleb Warner
The INSTRUMENT GUILD
Box 254, Lexington, Massachusetts 02173
Tel. (617) 862-9278**

*"Hands-On" Technical Support
for Industry and Laboratory*

1.

2.

3.

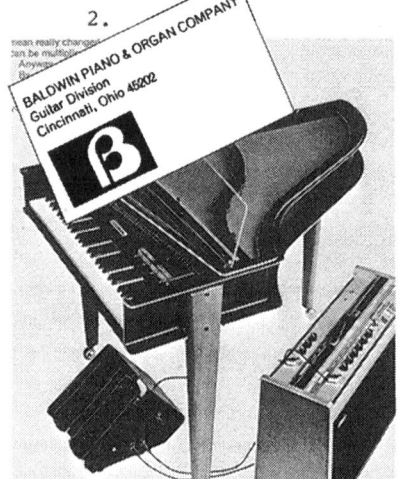

4.

5.

6.

MECHANICAL DESIGN & STYLING

May, 1976

1. WOODEN MODEL SOUVENIR styled for volume sales to raise money for church. Designed & tooled for quality production by unskilled volunteers. 750 built.

2. KEYBOARD ELECTRIC GUITAR conceived & prototyped for Baldwin. 1,500 built under license.

3. MODERN DULCIMER developed to improve tone & benefit from modern materials. Currently being test-marketed.

4. ULTRA-MODERN SPINET, fiberglass throughout. Features tuning stability & highly efficient soundboard. Economical to build, yet uncompromising in musical quality.

5. ALUMINUM HARPSICHORD of latest materials, styling & fabrication methods. Formerly sold by Baldwin.

6. SLIDE PROJECTOR SYSTEM for public lobbies; 6 projectors, 3 screens & sophisticated electronic control. (Conceptual model shown).

Caleb Warner
The INSTRUMENT GUILD
Box 254, Lexington, Massachusetts 02173
Tel. (617) 862-9278

"Hands-On" Technical Support
for Industry and Laboratory

1.
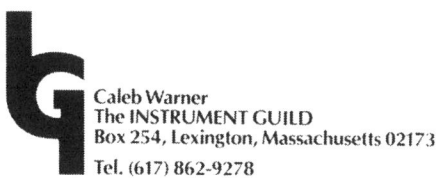

2.
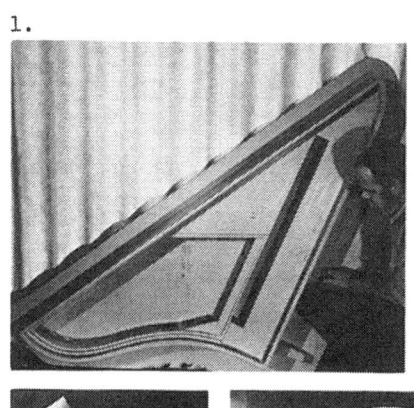

3.

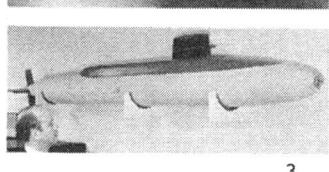

4.
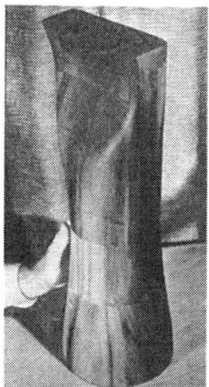

5.
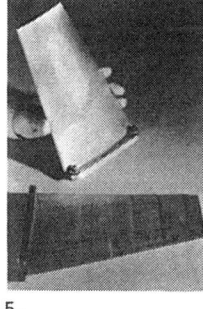

6.
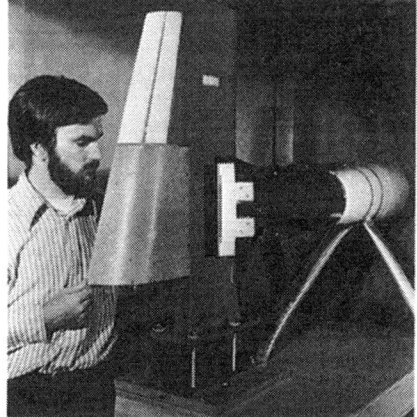

7.
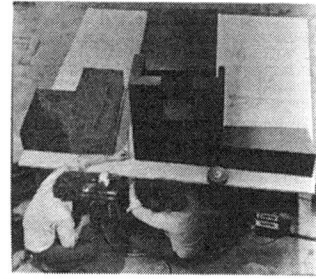

PRECISION MODELS, PATTERNS & MOLDS   May, 1976

1.WOODEN MASTER PLUG for 3-piece FRP molding; features rigid fairness tolerance for complicated curves, high-gloss finish.

2.COMPUTER-DERIVED FAN BLADES for quieted Ford truck; master pitch-block, pattern and cast aluminum blades shown here.

3.MODEL SUBMARINE with inter-changeable appendages for flow tests; foam core, FRP skin & precision stabilized wood fins.

4.PRECISION MALE MOLD for FRP wind tunnel model of jet engine nacelle; offsets derived from flow requirements.

5.PATTERN & ALUMINUM CASTING for measuring vibration in control fins; precision sections derived from NACA airfoil series.

6.STOL WING/ENGINE MODEL for noise tests in wind tunnel; precision fiberglass, aluminum casting & sheetmetal techniques.

7.MODEL OF N.Y. CITY BLOCK to predict impact of traffic noise; acoustically "hard" materials simulate brick.

231

John, being a truly sensitive soul, did not accuse me of being unqualified to do the job, but I knew that I probably was, in view of my lack of business experience and, of course, my lack of personal wealth. It was a heartbreaking situation for me, but in reality I am not sure I could have pulled it off successfully. I do not hold a grudge about John's stance, as he was undoubtedly correct. This was another of those cursed "fork in the road" situations that seemed to challenge me often as I zigzagged along on my somewhat hazardous career path.

PROJECTS FOR KLOSS VIDEO CORPORATION

While at ADL, I came in contact with a brilliant yet eccentric British engineer and inventor named James Hosken ("James," as he insisted on being called, never merely "Jim"). He had successfully served several of the area's most innovative entrepreneurs in development of their novel ventures.

Among them was Henry Kloss, most noted as the "K" in the pioneering high fidelity equipment firm of KLH. Kloss co-founded KLH back in 1957. Its brilliant success was often cited as an example of Boston's stellar high-tech firms. James had previously supported Henry Kloss by prototyping several of Henry's products. He suggested that I might be of some assistance to Kloss's latest venture, Kloss Video, Inc.

Kloss Video had developed, and then was manufacturing and marketing, the first generation of large-screen projection TV sets. These TV systems consisted of a projector with three telescope-like projector tubes that could produce a bright 5'x 5' TV image on a movie-style screen placed six to eight feet away. The new systems were catching on fast in the market place.

My new relationship with Kloss Video developed into the first really big job for my fast-expanding Instrument Guild practice. My assignment was to build various pieces of process equipment for Kloss's rapidly-growing company.

Usually Kloss conceived the device to be manufactured and suggested the general concepts of how it might be made. I typically counter-proposed what I thought might be an alternative, perhaps a better way of accomplishing that particular process in the plant. We went back and forth about how to proceed, often aided by several wise friends, such as George Feick or a colleague in Kloss's extensive group of experts. We had a consistently novel give-and-take, and it was always a fascinating process, which generally produced a solution that really worked.

Once we settled on a concept, I finished off a set of shop drawings for the manufacturing process equipment, and often enlisted Pat Pepicelli or one of the local contract machine shops to build the actual production plant equipment, the installation of which I often performed or oversaw. I was often involved in testing and starting up production.

The Kloss Video production plant was located in the section of Cambridge surrounding MIT that contained many of the flowering high-tech firms which had grown out of MIT itself. The area had historically been a helter-skelter location characterized by a continual parade of manufacturing firms that grew and ran out of space. When the initial occupants moved out into new and more spacious plants on the Route 128 corridor, space then became available to succeeding generations of new firms. The turnover was rapid. Today the area is a crowded maze of firms constituting one of the national centers of the U.S. biotech industry.

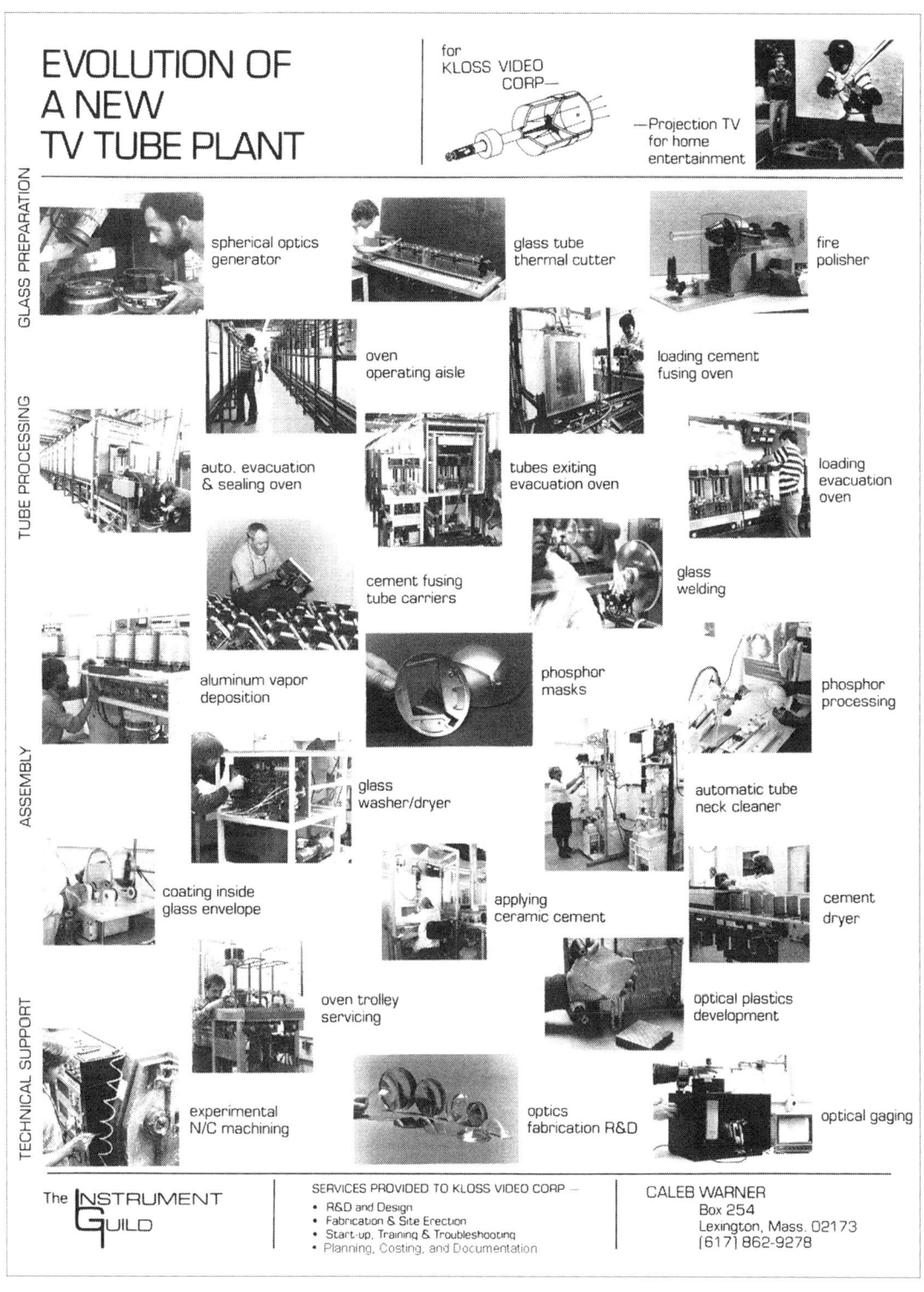

My first major project for Henry Kloss.

The labor force lived immediately nearby in Cambridgeport. It consisted primarily of an ever-growing group of immigrants, primarily from the Cape Verde Islands and Haiti. They were typically still communicating in their native old-style French (Haitian) and more modern Portuguese (Cape Verdean) languages. Laborers passed the word back to their countries of origin, encouraging relatives and friends to come to the U.S. and take advantage of the fast-growing opportunities for work at firms such as Kloss Video.

The *patois* style of French was easy for me to understand. Unfortunately, I knew no Spanish at that point, and had absolutely no knowledge of Portuguese at all. I found myself increasingly thankful for schooling in the Romance language tradition, however, because I could often sense what was being said, even in Portuguese.

I found Kloss's approximately 100 production employees generally cooperative and eager to learn the skills involved in the rather intricate manufacture of projection television tubes. The pervading attitudes seemed rather more healthy than those I had witnessed in the manufacturing workforce of the New England textile mills. I think that Henry Kloss's intense desire to succeed in manufacturing in the U.S., as opposed to giving in to overseas manufacturing, probably had a lot to do with the high quality of the labor/management relationship at this plant.

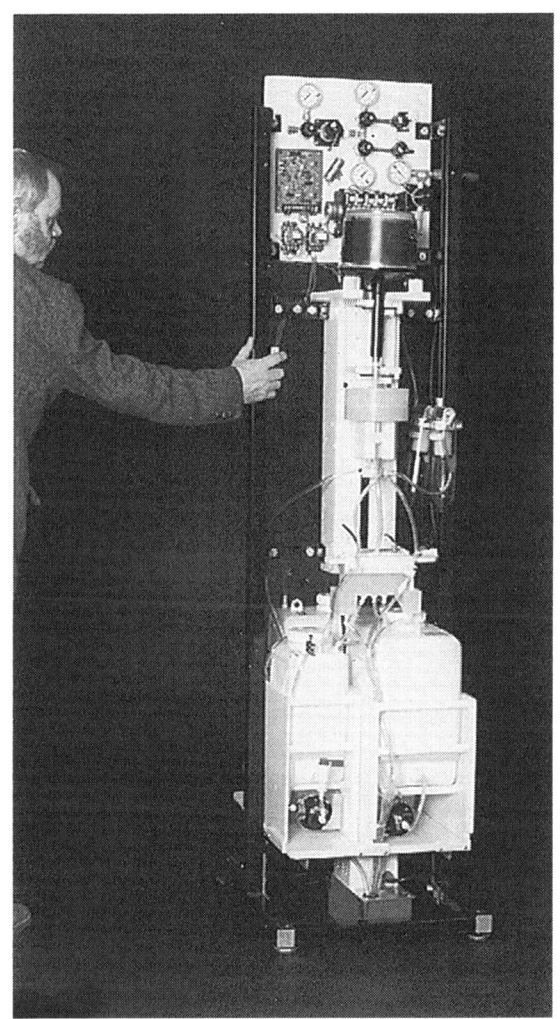

A Kloss Video production station that readies tubes for the furnace.

BREADTH OF THE TECHNOLOGY INVOLVED IN DEALING WITH THE KLOSS VIDEO PLANT

At Kloss Video, I had the great experience of coming to understand a whole new (to me, at least) group of technologies. The tubes were very advanced, miniaturized, astronomic telescopes (so-called "Schmidt" types), light-sourced by electronic vacuum tube light emitters, subsequently focused by sophisticated plastic corrective lenses. The process involved manufacturing and assembling large high-vacuum glass structures, electronic vacuum tube-like innards, and high-precision plastic corrective external lenses. This process required highly specialized manufacturing equipment that the Instrument Guild was tasked to build.

I also became involved with the design and production of the "package" of the product: the projector cabinet and its attendant projection screen. Luckily the electronics were the concern of others more skilled than I.

I had the good fortune to work with a broad collection of vendors and specialists to put together the required manufacturing facility. It turned out to be a really enlightening, thoroughly challenging, rewarding and generally enjoyable experience.

Eventually Kloss Video was put out of business when its TV configuration was surpassed by single-cabinet units built by others. However, just under 10 years of intense successful activity by Kloss gave my Instrument Guild substantial continual

Long fusing furnace for making projection television tubes.

business. Henry Kloss ultimately moved on in 1988 to form a new company in the high fidelity audio field. He already had significant reputation and knowledge based on his previous experience with a parade of firms such as Acoustic Research Corp., KLH, and Advent Corp.

PLASTICS PROCESS EVALUATION AND DEVELOPMENT

In dealing with Gregstrom Plastics Co. in Woburn, MA, one of the important vendors who produced the projection video screens for Kloss Video, I ran into an interesting neighbor from Lincoln, Mass. who was in need of help to produce a line of very rugged children's plastic outdoor play structures. I worked with him on a no-charge basis because I foresaw a possible opportunity for a proprietary position in the fast-developing reinforced plastic fabrication processing field.

The goal was to make large structures using high performance materials such as fiberglass-reinforced plastics (FRP) without incurring excessively high mold costs. We perfected a very early version of what is now known as resin transfer molding (RTM) or vacuum infusion molding in which an open (or single-sided) mold could produce the high quality products that only closed, expensive, double-sided molds could produce at the time. Our new process could cut the expensive mold-making costs in half.

We conducted a proof-of-principal demonstration but were unable to see how to pursue what was then a new technique in view of our limited financial resources. Perhaps we should have gone forward into that new world, but that road seemed out of reach. Subsequently, this process has become an important technique in the commercial world of fiberglass reinforced plastic molding.

In my work with Kloss Video and Gregstrom, I had the great good luck of being inducted into, and schooled in, the complexities of three other major areas of structural plastics processing: thermoforming (now universally used in packaging those annoying rigid plastic bubbles protecting precious consumer items), blow molding (the great quandary of plastic bottle-making), and rotational molding (producing wonderful modern kayaks, fuel tanks, etc.). Of course, all this brings to mind that classic, but very dated scene in the 1967 movie, "The Graduate", in which *plastics* are touted as "the all important future"!

PROJECTS FOR MASSACHUSETTS GENERAL HOSPITAL (MGH)

Adelbert ("Del") Ames, Jr. approached me to help construct laboratory apparatus for his neurology research laboratory at Mass. General Hospital (MGH). I had known Del for a long time, first as the son of my father's roommate at Harvard, next while we both attended Phillips Exeter Academy, later as he married one of my favorite cousins from Long Island, Judith Derby, and still later as a neighbor in nearby Lincoln, Mass. When I casually told him about starting up the Instrument Guild, he confessed that he needed help in building specialized laboratory equipment.

In theory, this equipment could probably have been built by the very competent in-house shops at MGH, but Del had difficulty getting rapid and flexible response from those facilities and wanted the kind of services that perhaps the Guild could provide. Apparently, his funding for this was from outside the hospital, and so could be used without going through time-consuming bureaucratic procedure. Furthermore, the local in-house MGH machine shop teams seemed delighted not to be hounded by Del's tight schedules.

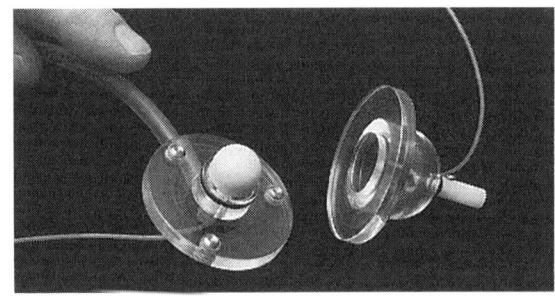

Laboratory equipment for eye research lab at MGH.

Del would, for example, describe what he wanted to do in performing neurological experiments on human brain functions in the general area of the eye. He needed rather small devices which could readily be made in a small machine shop such as mine. He would often sketch up the rather specialized apparatus, and I would reduce the concepts to machine drawings and build the apparatus rapidly.

Del was a very hard-working person, and also a world-class skier. I got urgent jobs from him, typically on Friday afternoons when he was "on the way to the slopes". He often requested that I build the equipment for him over the weekend so that it would be ready for him early on Monday morning. He would pick it up as he passed our house in Lexington on his way in from Lincoln to attend morning grand rounds at MGH.

This arrangement worked well for a period of about five years. It was just the type of business that I wanted to do. I did a total of about ten jobs for him in that period. He passed me on to colleagues in his department of the hospital, and to brain-surgeon colleagues doing similar work at Beth Israel Hospital in nearby Brookline.

PROJECTS FOR BETH ISRAEL HOSPITAL

Similar to what I had been doing for Del, I supplied the surgeon group at Beth Israel with quick-response services in building tools for their research. At the time, they were operating a very up-to-date Magnetic Resonance Imaging (MRI) setup. They wanted to improve the techniques and accessory hardware.

As an example, I was tasked to provide devices for immobilizing the head of a patient so doctors could get a good image while he was in the MRI machine, and then help the surgeons guide their long surgical tools to the desired location within the brain. The intent was to help surgeons go to the correct "brain latitude, longitude and depth" to perform their surgery or to place a sensor to detect brain function. The devices that I built had to be tolerant of the extreme magnetic fields common to MRI while not disturbing the quality of the MRI images. This meant working in wood or in one of the high-performance structural plastics. This, again, was just the sort of fabrication I could do in the somewhat limited shop facilities that I had at home. I welcomed the challenge of translating their needs and ideas into three-dimensional utilitarian hardware, often on a tight time schedule.

The brain surgery group was also developing electronic sensing tools for monitoring brain function. These monitors were worn by the patients for hours or days at a time to pick up patterns of brain functions as patients went through their daily activities. These were especially useful in diagnosing various types of epileptic seizures as well as in the understanding of the bodily control functions of the brain. The proponents of the monitors were attempting to develop a proprietary product around which a business could be formed. I helped with the mechanical and packaging (housing) design and guided the inventor to vendors who could build prototypes as well as manufacture initial quantities for introduction into the market.

I gained a lot of help in the electronic aspects of this work from my valuable electronics colleague, Byron Blanchard, one of the most valuable members of the Instrument Guild's cadre of technical savants. Beth Israel was one of the most attractive environments that I ever worked for or with.

MEETING THE CHALLENGE OF OUTSOURCING

Henry Kloss's newest venture, Cambridge SoundWorks Corp., was located in a restored mill building in Newton, MA, almost on the banks of the Charles River, adjacent to Watertown Square. His new line of high-performance, modest-budget, high fidelity audio equipment was attracting a rather broad consumer market.

In about 1989, I reconnected with Henry. His philosophy about creating an operation that could succeed in the face of, or even in spite of, foreign competition was still his driving force. Being able to accomplish the manufacturing that he required under U.S. conditions was difficult. Manufacturing in the U.S. was becoming more costly than manufacturing abroad, and this situation was a challenge to both our regional and national economy.

Manufacturing technology was a primary factor in Kloss's new venture. It controlled both product conception and design. My task was to aid in optimizing the production process. Although challenging, thanks to Henry's continual participation and enthusiastic backing, it seemed to go forward. It became what might be termed "micro-industrial engineering" for me. (That may be coining a new term, but it is truly *apropos* in this case.) I was on the manufacturing floor a substantial amount of time to tighten up the various manufacturing processes, under Henry's close direction and cooperation. Thankfully, I participated with the various teams involved with product design and marketing, so manufacturing decisions were taken into consideration as the products emerged. This phase of my Instrument Guild era went on for about five years.

ACTIVITIES WITH POTTER & MACARTHUR, NAVAL ARCHITECTS

Back in about 1970, when I was involved in trying to obtain a contract to operate a ferry service between Chile and Antarctica for BB&N, I became familiar with the firm of Potter & MacArthur, who were designing and overseeing the construction of the new ferry.

Well after the Antarctic ferry vessel was in service, the Potter & MacArthur firm dissolved and the practice was taken over by its former employees. I was asked to become a director of the succeeding naval architecture firm. I did so only briefly, and frankly was able to do very little to assist the new version of the old firm. I did, however, participate in the design of an updated version of the smallest class of powered U.S. Coast Guard surf boats. The aim was to develop a craft which could survive in the severe breaking-wave conditions found over the bars across several river mouths in the U.S., most prominently in the mouth of the Columbia River as it meets the Pacific Ocean.

The powered surf boat shown above represents the design that we started with and reconceived to meet the challenge of difficult surf conditions that would prove it otherwise unseaworthy. It was self-rightable and launchable by men without the aid of large equipment.

The new surfboat was intended to replace the classic oar-propelled surfboat. It had to be small (about 25 feet long), light (trailerable), self-righting, survivable after capsizing, with an extremely shallow draft (less than about 18 inches), and capable of taking a severe beating, yet powered by motor (to eliminate the hazards of rowing). Water-jet propulsion was used to eliminate an exposed propeller and damageable rudder, all in a rugged hull built of reinforced composite plastics. The prototype was to be built at the Coast Guard shipyard in Baltimore and evaluated in an East Coast river mouth which had Columbia River-like conditions. Luckily, such nasty conditions were available at the mouth of Barnegat Bay in New Jersey on carefully selected bad-weather days.

I wish that I had been able to participate more intimately with this project but there were not adequate funds and I probably was not really qualified. However, it was a great experience just to be on the edge of the project.

This small naval architecture/marine engineering firm designed and oversaw construction of many oceanographic research ships as well as several innovative fishery factory ships and specialized coastal vessels. If I had entered a firm like that, I might have practiced marine engineering, but it was not a sound career path for me at the time.

Using the special drafting tools of naval architecture. The tool on the lower right is called a "duck". It aids in the drawing of curves.

PROJECTS FOR THE VON HUENE WORKSHOP (VHW)

While working on harpsichords in the Cannon Guild, we were involved with the whole early music scene in the Boston area. The Cannon Guild's Eric Herz was especially prominent in that he was running ancient musical instrument festivals in Boston. Similarly important was the von Huene family, since their workshop was probably the world leader in building recorders, or blockflutes, and almost considered "royalty" in the worldwide faction of recorder players, early music lovers, and the like.

Friederich von Huene, the senior member of family, was watching our attempts to update design, manufacturing and marketing processes. He himself had been working hard along such lines and had achieved a lot of progress. After the demise of the Cannon Guild, he invited me to tackle some of his production problems, which I was happy to do on his behalf.

My initial task was to help get the Von Huene Workshop's production tuning equipment in order. The shop was dependent on electromechanical tuning devices built perhaps 20-40 years previously, in which a mechanically adjustable tuning fork was listened to by a magnetic pickup, processed by old-fashioned vacuum tube electronics, and displayed by stroboscopes. The "care and feeding" of those devices was not within the know-how of a group of skilled woodworking instrument makers, nor was the archaic electronic technology any longer available from the local electronic repair shops. So my Instrument Guild's oddball collection of know-how was applied and I provided the musical orientation to their problems, importantly aided by colleague Byron Blanchard.

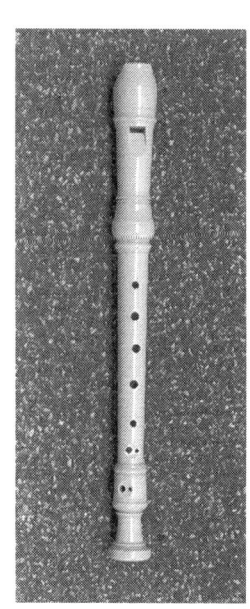

A Von Huene recorder (blockflute) of classical design.

We next introduced modernized CAD techniques for upgrading VHW's dealings with outside vendors and for producing adequate documentation to reduce skill levels needed on the production floor. This was a classic case of applying up-to-date tools to an age-old, artisan-oriented procedure and was a prototype for what was to come for the Instrument Guild when von Huene turned us over to two world-class flute makers located nearby.

PROJECTS FOR THE WILLIAM S. HAYNES FLUTE COMPANY

A series of tasks for the Instrument Guild resulted when Friedrich von Huene helped me connect with the Haynes Flute Company. By the last quarter of the 20th century, Haynes flutes were ranked very high, just below Powell flutes, which were the Cadillac of the instruments.

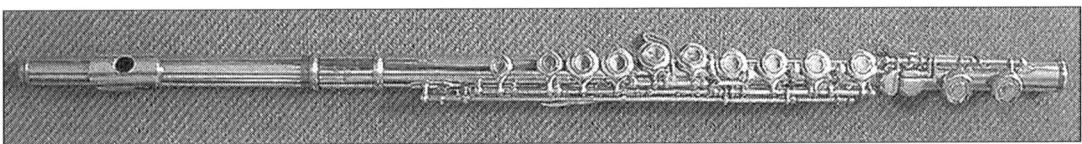

A Haynes flute of modern day design.

I made a sales pitch to the top man at Haynes. He felt that there was room for improvement in the manufacturing, but he was not definite as to details, nor was he especially concerned with the gentle art of manufacturing his product. He was an excellent figurehead for the business and had managerial skills fitting the business. He directed me to get together with his operations manager, and asked the two of us to come up with a plan of action for his approval. This turned out to be a surprisingly workable arrangement.

Haynes flute-making was a striking example of the problems facing much of the musical instrument industry. They did exceedingly fine quality work but were almost completely dependent on the skill of their production people. Those skills were highly particularized to the product, and required a long time to develop. In short, it was a craft industry requiring specialized artisans, using some archaic practices. There was a lot of room for updating manufacturing practices. The fact that I was not very "high-tech" in some way fitted the needs of this client, and it was relatively easy to be useful under these conditions. Happily, the employees were inordinately cooperative with, and supportive of, my efforts.

I worked for about two years for this client. I provided a useful service to an appreciative client group, but the work did not provide opportunities to achieve much progress in my professional skills nor did it lead to significant new marketing opportunities. However, I am glad to have served in a truly significant corner of the musical instrument world.

PROJECTS FOR THE VIC FIRTH COMPANY

I do not recall how I tumbled into the connection with this client, who was the first chair timpanist of the Boston Symphony Orchestra. Perhaps our initial connection took place after I had met his director of marketing at one of the trade shows held by the Music Manufacturer's Association in Chicago. Vic Firth is still the owner of a truly successful company making drumsticks and mallets which are exported to 50 countries worldwide. He has also been a real innovator in the development of percussion instruments.

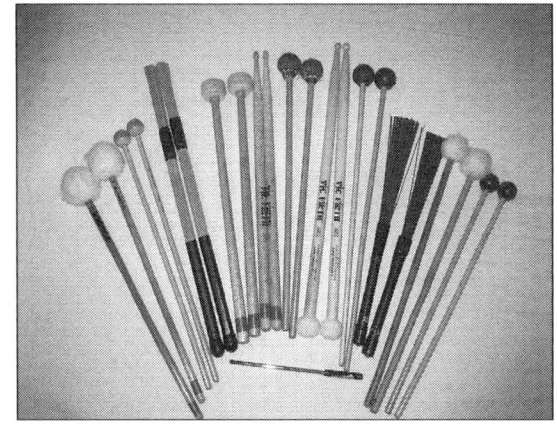

I remember vividly my first meeting with Vic in his office in Dedham, Mass. He blurted out something like, "I know your classical music background, Caleb, and we must get one thing clear from the start. If you see a man here with green hair, don't be flip. Be real good to him. He is a big time rock star, and we eat off of his type in my organization."

Vic got his start in popular music as a highly reputable jazz drummer in the studios in New York in the big band era. He became a leader in pioneering the tools that enable rock percussionists to make such unbelievable sounds. He has since become something of a legend as a symphony orchestra percussionist.

Assorted percussion sticks and mallets of Vic Firth design and manufacture.

Vic is most famous for developing the drumstick to an unbelievably fine degree. One of the secrets was the special shape of the bulb on the end of the stick (he produced a variety of shapes from which a drummer could choose). Another secret was the accuracy with which the stick shapes were then reproduced, plus the consistency of the wood, so the drummer could be assured that he would receive the expected performance each time he replaced his inevitably expendable sticks. An unexpected aspect of Vic's production process was that he carefully matched the "tuning" of the two sticks in each pair. He accomplished this match on his production line by striking each individual stick on a massive stone block and recording, with sophisticated electronic measuring devices, what musical pitch was produced by the blow. He then had his production workers sort the sticks into matched pairs of similar pitch, packaging them to be sold as a pitch-matched pair.

This care and detail of manufacture produced real opportunities to introduce updated manufacturing technology. I introduced the concept of making really accurate CAD drawings of his full line of sticks to ease up tooling, simplify quality control, provide input to patent information, and guide tool construction and tool maintenance. (One might be surprised at adding such a very simple element to the manufacturing process, but the musical instrument industry often cries out for this sort of cleanup job.)

I also did some new product development for Vic, most prominently in the adjustable wire drum brush that is in general use today. It is an updated version of the "brush" which for years was used for making subtle drum sounds, unlike the more strident wooden sticks. Brushes consisted only of a bunch of straight, light piano wires fanned out of the end of a handle. The development conceived by Vic Firth made it possible for the percussionist to vary how far the wires extended out of the drumstick-like handle so the sound level could be adjusted by the drummer to suit the musical conditions.

Admittedly, this is a mechanically simple device, but is quite difficult to design and build so it can survive the rugged conditions experienced in the hands of an intense rock music drummer. I repeatedly sweated out the test routine for the product, as Vic sent the prototypes that I made down to a brutal rock drummer star in the New York studios to be intensely survival-tested. That guy could really bust them up in one single night!

Vic Firth bought a serious wood-turning production plant in Newport, ME, famous for making lovely, large wooden pepper grinders seen in fancy restaurants. The plant had special capabilities that lent themselves to conversion to highly accurate, mass production of wooden drumsticks. I enjoyed and was amazed to tour the plant and work with the local, highly competent plant personnel.

Working with Vic Firth was a genuine privilege and pleasure. I am not sure what it did for me professionally or what position it has on my *curriculum vitae,* but it was truly productive and almost a vacation for me from the otherwise fractious industrial world.

PARTICIPATION IN THE CONTROLLED DEMISE OF AN EXERCISE EQUIPMENT MANUFACTURER

I was asked to look in on a manufacturer of exercise equipment that had been in business, I believe, since the end of WWII. Although historically successful as pioneers in walking, running, and step-climbing machines, it had been unable to keep up with modern competition. I took a look at their designs, their plant, and what the competition was offering to the marketplace. I did some of what they requested, and then more or less helped them ease out of business. It was a sad scene that occupied me on and off for several months. I do not feel right in naming the company here.

FIBER OPTIC CONNECTOR PROJECT

The Guild often received valuable sales leads from companies from which the Guild was buying services–as many as several dozen in our three decades in business. We could not afford to advertise, and the usual route of technical papers and professional society meetings was not necessarily open to us since we did not have a true specialty. Sales leads generated through our vendors were important.

One of the important providers of service to the Guild, the Lavelle Machine Shop, manufactured fiber-optic cable connectors for a local firm which was an international leader in their field. The metal connector that allows cable lengths to be connected is one of the critical parts of any fiber-optic cable system and its manufacture requires unusual precision and quality control–just the kind of work Lavelle excelled in. Lavelle's customer also made a line of installation tools, and that line was giving Lavelle's customer trouble in the marketplace.

Since the connector must readily and consistently align the fiber extremely accurately if the cable is to function properly, the tools for installing the connectors on ends of the fiber optic cables are truly critical. The connection must be rugged and able to be installed correctly under difficult conditions in the field–for instance by a worker, without powered tools, down a manhole, standing perhaps in 18" of sewer water, under all kinds of temperature and weather conditions.

Our job was to understand the aspects of connector installation and help in improving field installation tools to assure proper performance and reliability as well as to ease the job of the installer.

This task introduced me to several new fields. I became familiar with high-precision glass fabrication, through which I came to know Gerhard Finkenbeiner, who lived and worked in nearby Waltham. He was world-famous as the resurrector of the Mozart-era glass armonica (also known as the glass harmonica, bowl organ, hydrocrystalophone, or simply the armonica) as well as the developer of the modern, electronically-synthesized church steeple chimes. Both of these mysterious wonders are dependent on the art and science of high-precision glass manipulation, otherwise known as glass blowing. Tragically, in 1999, Gerhard Finkenbeiner disappeared in his small airplane, never to be found. It was a serious loss to modern science laboratory operations as he was one of the best makers of sophisticated glassware for research laboratory use.

While working on fiber-optic cable problems, I also became acquainted with the fast-emerging field of high precision, computer numerically controlled (CNC) machining since this manufacturing process was needed in the fabrication of metal fiber-optic cable connectors. Thirdly, I was introduced to the field of fiber-optic technology. The total project lasted about six months and wound up when the firm could get underway with an increasingly viable installation tool business.

PROJECTS FOR DIETRICH GROUP, INC. (DGI)

Several years before becoming self-employed, I came to know Chuck Dietrich, an accomplished practitioner in the fields of automotive and industrial safety as well as applied physics. He formed his own business, called the Dietrich Group, Inc. By the time that I established my Instrument Guild, Chuck Dietrich's practice was solidly established with law firms scattered about the U.S., to supply technical backup for their court cases involving industrial and automotive hazards. I provided services to his practice several times, including the three projects discussed below. (We have remained in contact for several decades, even up to the present day when I am in retirement.)

Example of a hazardous industrial tool problem that I worked on with Dietrch, Inc. Pictured is an apparently innocuous, yet highly dangerous common tool. Note the natural placement of the finger, unprotected, near the blade.

DGI supplied technical support to a Boston law firm for a complicated suit regarding a fatal automobile/truck accident on U.S. Route 495, the outer circumferential highway around Boston. The accident site was in the Lawrence, MA area. Required for the accident analysis and courtroom presentation were physical models of the accident scene plus some carefully constructed maps and charts showing the dynamics of the accident in a form that could be readily understood by the court, especially by the jurors. I used CAD techniques to generate large-scale charts, maps, and three-dimensional physical models to support demonstrations of the accident scene. Thanks to Chuck Dietrich's capability, I was spared having to appear at the trial. This was a substantial and very interesting task for the Instrument Guild that took several months to complete.

DGI was also called in by a Boston law firm on a case involving hazardous industrial hand tools, in this case a powerful skill saw. The saw was in use on a wool warehouse floor covered with slippery lanolin grease oozing out of the stored raw wool. The objective was to dramatize the inadequately anticipated hazards in an everyday work situation. This was an especially rough situation for me since the opposing lawyer was gunning for me, even to the threat of locking me up if he did not approve of how I conducted Instrument Guild business.

He demanded that I produce the original written records that I normally keep for other clients. He even had the nerve to require that I submit a list of my clients, together with statements of exactly what services that I had supplied in the past. I claimed that his demands were unethical and threatened my reputation regarding confidentiality of my client's situations. Luckily, the lawyer on our side went aggressively to my defense and a lawyer vs. lawyer verbal battle broke out.

I went away from that case thoroughly shocked by the inner workings of the legal process and the behavior of the opposition lawyer. It turned out that the opposition's lawyer was a political bigwig in Portland, ME, municipal government. I finally had to threaten him through our lawyer with the possibility of stirring the political pot in his home town in the upcoming elections. Happily we ultimately won what we had sought in the industrial accident trial.

My last project before I retired, for DGI, involved discovering the cause of a major flood in a low-lying part of the City of Boston, which is essentially at sea level. The basements of the buildings normally remain dry due to the fact that their walls are waterproofed. In the event of a significant amount of rain, the impacts on basements are mitigated by an extensive storm-water drain system serviced by a monster of a pump driven by a gas turbine. The pump is automatically activated by a water level-sensing control system that fires up the turbines as needed.

The fuel for the turbines is stored in large tanks located above the turbines and the fuel is turned on and off by electrically activated valves located just above the turbines. During a particularly severe rainstorm the fuel valves had failed to open, starving the turbines of fuel, allowing a major flood with severe property damage. The initial detective work identifying the valves as the culprits was done by the city's public works engineers.

The valve manufacturer was being held responsible and hence liable for the considerable financial losses experienced by the community. My job was to analyze the cause and nature of the failure and to determine whether the fabrication, quality control and testing of the valves had been adequate. I also was tasked to build a working model to demonstrate the nature of the failure.

The situation was about to go to trial in a local court. Lawyers, politicians, manufacturers, city engineers and victimized citizens were involved in the preparation. The project stretched out over about three years of back-and-forth activities between the many forces at work on the problem. It was a long and arduous process.

In summary, my three-decade relationship with the Dietrich Group was intriguing, stimulating and educational. I did the final work on the valve project in the shop here at Carleton-Willard Village. But since I am not allowed to engage in any profit-making activities on these premises, it was no-charge charity work, strictly for the benefit of the City of Boston, and to salve my conscience in view of the fact that Alice's unexpected accident, her illness and our move to Bedford had prompted the timing of my premature retirement.

THE INSTRUMENT GUILD ERA: THE BALL SCORE

While there were many high points in my experiences during the era in which I was self-employed, there inevitably were some low points, and luckily only a few real disappointments.

Of special note were my colleagues, an extraordinary group of people that I could really count on to help get the jobs done, and also enable me to broaden the development services the Instrument Guild was offering.

This era of self-employment gave me much needed and much welcomed opportunities for profession progress in activities of interest to me. Some of these were new to me, while in others I had some capability but needed updating or strengthening.

My personal satisfaction was considerable since I received some personal reward, such as an increased knowledge or understanding, even when a project did not go altogether right. In addition, I welcomed the freedom from bureaucratic structure common in contemporary corporate life where my progress often depended on whether I could step over the person on the rung just above me. The rewards of being self-employed were more directly responsive to what I actually accomplished than they would have been in a "normal" corporate environment.

If I had to give myself a performance grade on this era, I probably would give it a "ball score" of 750–i.e., about three quarters of the clients' problems (hopefully more) were resolved. I think that that my clients were typically satisfied.

It is somewhat difficult to analyze the financial performance ultimately achieved by the Guild. Over

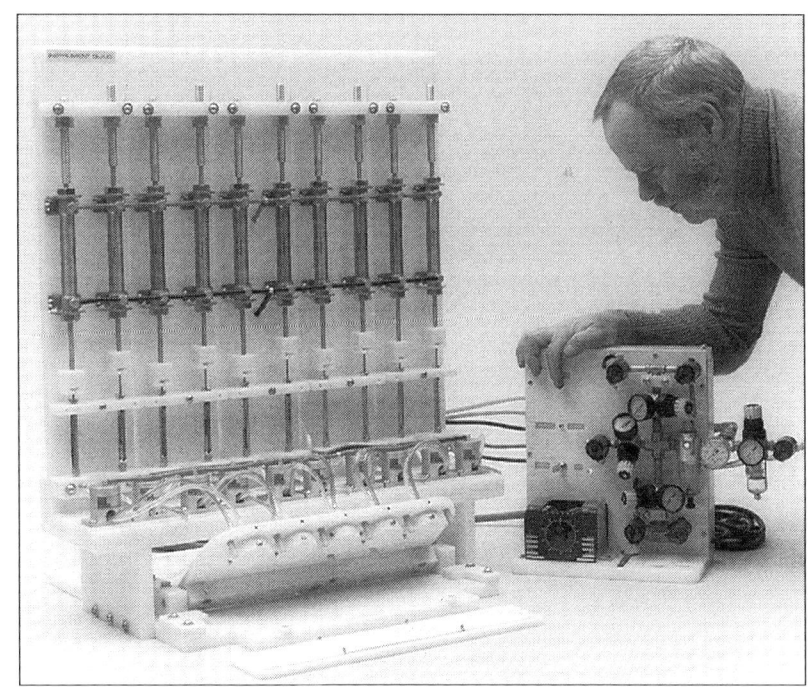

Development of medical products.

the three decades during which it was in operation, the monthly cash flow swung widely. The maximum flow was as much as three times the minimum flow. My net income was comparable to what I probably would have been getting if I were an employee of a sound firm in the area. Self-employment and proprietorship were neither a financial disadvantage nor a significant advantage. It most certainly led to a more contented lifestyle. Alice kept a close and constructive watch on how things were going financially so as protect the family finances.

Where I obviously missed out was that my scheme did not build a saleable capital value to my venture. Hence, in order to prepare for survival after retirement, Alice and I had to rely on putting away savings in a serious way. Thanks in part to her watchful eye, annual savings were religiously attended to, and retirement has become possible, although inheritance for the next generation has not been well-favored.

I sincerely hope that my chosen mode of employment was not a drag on our family life. I remain concerned that my contribution to the upbringing of the family was diverted by the fact that I had to pay a lot of attention to my professional duties. Alice, bless her, realized all of that, and tried valiantly to make up for some of my inattention as a parent.

Alice, I believe, got a certain satisfaction from this era in her own way. She was certainly supportive, encouraging, and did a great deal to make my self-employment possible. I remain grateful to her for her contribution and encouragement.

Tooling a mold to make unusual fiberglass-reinforced plastic products.

From my promotional brochure for Town Meeting representative for our Lexington precinct.

13

VOLUNTEER INVOLVEMENT

COMBINING INTERESTS

I think it's safe to say that my "civic responsibilities" simply encompassed some natural interests on my part, making my contribution to our community both fun and happily challenging. I volunteered in various capacities. My contributions were always a reward to me personally, as they were both educational and interesting to me throughout my entire adult life.

LEXINGTON'S MUNICIPAL SCENE

I believe that Lexington had something over 18,000 souls when we moved there in 1954 and thus was designated as a town as opposed to being designated a city. The principal governing body was the usual New England-style elected but non-salaried Board of Selectmen, backed up by a full-time salaried Town Administrator who primarily operated the town under the direction of the Selectmen.

Lexington had recently graduated from an open Town Meeting form of government to a representative Town Meeting. Thus, whereas any registered voter could previously vote at the meeting, the new form designated that each of the nine precincts of the town elect representatives, resulting in a body of 110 voters at the meeting.

By the time we moved to Lexington, the reconfigured meeting seemed to be actively working. The Town Manager claimed that the amazingly large number of 1500 volunteers were manning, or had been recently involved with, the standing committees of the town. I was obviously attracted to this scene, which offered volunteering opportunities on a wide variety of municipal tasks.

FIVE FIELDS' CLASSIC PROBLEM

When the whole town is mapped, a bubble-shaped area off the southwest side appears, known as South Lexington. Consisting of less than 10% of the total area of the town in the early 1950s, it contained about 3-5% of Lexington's total population. It is somewhat isolated from the center of Lexington by a major highway, Route 2. Our community of Five Fields lies within that bubble.

This physical location contributed to the social and even political separation of our community. A rather self-contained lifestyle for the neighborhood evolved which became a strength rather than a weakness throughout our stay there. This sense of unity enabled us to accomplish things as a solidified neighborhood, both to our local benefit and for the benefit of the greater town.

Just after we settled in Lexington, our Five Fields Community was faced with a classic community situation. Route 2 needed to be widened, and its connection with adjacent Concord Avenue improved. The Federal Highway System designers in charge of the widening proposed an intersection with our Concord Avenue which would have made the local street on which we lived into a heavily traveled, high-speed threat to our neighborhood.

EMERGENCE OF THE SOUTH LEXINGTON CIVIC ASSOCIATION

Four of us called more than 100 of our concerned neighbors. We all demonstrated loudly against the proposed new intersection while systematically proposing changes that would benefit life in our neighborhood. We gathered together as a large group, meeting the road designers/surveyors/field agents when they appeared at the site. In the process, the South Lexington Civic Association (SLCA, fondly referred to as "Slicka") was born, and we became a going concern. Shortly thereafter, I became SLCA's president.

Various Lexington neighborhoods have since copied our model and, at last count, eight more local civic associations have emerged in Lexington. Such associations thus became a going part of the municipal procedures.

When the matter of the Route 2/Concord Avenue intersection came up for approval at Town Meeting, we organized an aggressive action to drive home our disapproval of the federal design, and to have our suggested design improvements heard by the Selectmen. We made sure that one of SLCA's officers attended every Selectman's discussion of the intersection. We then organized a chain-like telephone network which could instantly activate our neighborhood if needed. During the Selectmen's meeting, we stationed two SLCA members at the two public coin telephones just outside the Selectmen's meeting room, ready to act. This kept the telephones immediately available to respond to our meeting room observer's alert. One phone was used to alert our SLCA network, while the other was used to contact our lawyer in downtown Boston for instant legal advice. (Remember, this all took place before cell phones were available.)

The Selectmen's procedural rules permitted a 20-minute citizen-requested recess to halt a meeting. When our matter was about to come up in the meeting, we requested the recess. We telephoned an alarm to our network and informed our lawyer about what was going on, keeping him on the line so that he could advise us when to back down in order to remain within the law.

Before the end of that requested recess, we were able to provide a continuous stream of SLCA residents into the meeting chamber, chatting loudly with each other about the issue at hand, so that the Selectmen could clearly overhear.

We certainly got our point across, and our alternative road design proposal was taken into immediate consideration. In subsequent meetings of the Board, we made it known that we were ready to repeat the process if need be, and we were always given attention to our needs. Our proactive approach was deemed a success.

We formalized SLCA by establishing an organization with a membership of about 100 households, a stated mission, and regular meetings. We worked with the various town statutory committees which held sway over our area as well as organizations operating or about to operate here. For instance, we closely followed the planning and startup of nearby Brookhaven, an extensive continuing care facility. I participated in SLCA for almost 25 years and it was probably the most meaningful of my volunteer, politically oriented civic activities.

SERVING AS AN ELECTED MEMBER OF THE LEXINGTON TOWN MEETING

For 15 years, I worked from the balcony during meeting sessions to get our South Lexington problems before the Town Meetings via SLCA. When the political significance of a regional Civic Association was finally accepted by the Town Meeting, I decided it was time to join the representatives on the floor, so I ran for election in the early 1970s, and happily won a seat that I maintained until Alice and I had to move from Lexington to a continuing care facility in nearby Bedford, just short of the year 2000.

Those years were full of developments and changes in the town, many of which were addressed and fought out on the Town Meeting floor. Lexington was dealing openly with many significant changes of the era: growing schools, ethnic and religious diversity, town planning, and administrative issues, youth culture changes, municipal/state/federal interrelations, increasing wealth disparities, emergence of cyber culture, civil rights, and more. Lexington was a microcosm of what was going on in a larger scale all across the country.

PUBLIC ADDRESS SYSTEMS FOR LEXINGTON TOWN MEETING AND ELSEWHERE

In watching town functions from various seats in Cary Hall (Lexington's Town Hall) I realized the severity of the damage to intelligibility of speech in the town's public meeting places. This, I quickly realized, was due to the public address systems. In some cases the system equipment was inadequate, and in more cases the use or operation of the systems was at fault.

Building on my experience in audio recording and amplification over many years of dance band activities and working at Bolt Beranek & Newman, I sought to improve the intelligibility situation in the local public assembly. I voluntarily took over the task of upgrading the public address equipment and I installed myself to operate many of the systems–the so-called "front-of-the-hall" man (a term commonly used by commercial acousticians, show business, etc.) in several public meeting places.

The new system in the Town Hall chamber had a control board which could be manned for both concert performances and meetings. For Town Meetings, I was allowed to interrupt speakers to help them with microphone management and usage. The situation was accepted, surprisingly, and became a fixed feature of the meeting process in Lexington.

I then found myself, over a period of perhaps 15 years, reworking the public address systems and their operation to three churches–Follen (UU), Hancock (UCC), and First Parish (UU)–as well as at the Lexington Public Library meeting room. Amusingly, I also helped to equip the horseback riders and Minutemen for Lexington's annual reenactment of the midnight ride of Paul Revere. I used remote microphones so that the several thousand spectators usually present could hear what was going on. This, to me, was great fun.

LEXINGTON CABLE TV ADVISORY COMMITTEE

Once I was established in the Lexington Town Meeting, and demonstrating an interest in public communication, the Lexington Selectmen asked me to chair the Lexington Cable TV Advisory Committee. I did this for about five years, as the liaison between the town and the cable TV provider. This assignment proved to be a veritable hot-seat for me since there were continual difficulties between the cable TV providers, the town management, the cable customers, and the state and federal regulations. The position introduced me to new political, technical and community relations areas which I found really troubling. The complicated details of this activity are beyond the scope of coverage here, but I found them fascinating and continue to be involved with them even to this day.

LEXINGTON SCHOOL MUSIC DEMONSTRATION PROGRAM

Typical of our imaginative home town, a group of Lexington parents who were accomplished professional musicians offered a volunteer service to the schools. They put together a well-thought-out music demonstration which was programmed into each of the town's several lower-grade schools. They had been doing this for a few years when they invited me to join them. I decided to demonstrate some things about musical instrument acoustics and construction. Such an approach could also reinforce the education of physics, and of making and designing things.

In my sector of each demonstration, I started with a 45-second rousing bugle-call-like blast on the little G-pitched trumpet, a brief showpiece by Telemann, seldom heard these days, aptly titled "Air de Trompette". (In some ways, it reminds me of those fight cheers that we used to play at football games!)

With the bass fiddle, I showed off the largest of the stringed instruments. With a jump rope I demonstrated the principle of harmonics by making the rope into one, two, three, and four successive waves. I next combined a garden hose, a metal funnel, and a trumpet mouthpiece to make a bugle, then drilled holes in the hose to make a keyed trumpet. Next came a cobbled-up trombone–all of this directed toward explaining the inter-relationship of acoustics to music and musical instruments. My sector lasted no more than about 15 minutes, leaving plenty of room for some fun music, always including a wide variety of instruments like the bassoon, oboe, flute, and various stringed instruments played by my professional musician colleagues.

It was both fun and a rewarding experience. We got a surprising amount of press coverage regarding our efforts.

LEXINGTON HIGH SCHOOL INSTRUMENT BUILDING PROJECT

Our teenaged daughter Anne became interested in the Appalachian dulcimer as an elementary instrument, pointing out that there seemed to be a renewed and growing interest in the instrument. At that time, the country music genre was coming to life to a broader audience. I had been looking for an activity to allow local high school kids to work with their hands, to gain after-school employment, and to experience the "new venture" of the small business world. I latched onto the idea of building a line of modernized dulcimers based on the Appalachian dulcimer.

The traditional Appalachian style of instrument had been made from a variety of locally grown woods, styled in a wide variety of locally preferred shapes, using a number of different schemes for producing the sound: two vs. three vs. four strings, various tunings of those strings, and a variety of layouts of the fret boards. In effect, each instrument reflected the traditions and the needs of the particular locale it came from, which was completely the opposite of what had historically happened to most other musical instruments.

That peculiarity seemed to offer us an opportunity to develop a truly modern instrument, reflecting modern practices. I had been working on developing vacuum-injection reinforced plastics for one of my Instrument Guild clients, and I thought that perhaps this technology could be used in making the body of a modern dulcimer. After a bit of market research, it looked as if these various aspects might be put together into a going operation.

Mr. Warner creates some sounds that could be made through a six foot copper pipe.

Caleb Warner demonstrates some basic sound concepts for Diamond students in a culminating portion of a sound and music unit.

Music demonstrations in all levels of the schools in Lexington.

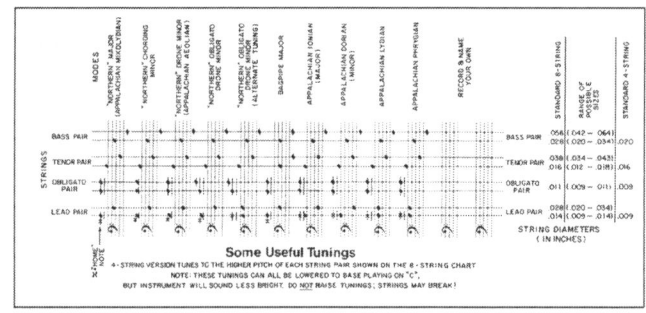

STANDARD FEATURES

· Available in versions with 4 & 8 strings to match player's skill and musical needs

· Interchangeable fretboards so player can choose most desirable fingering

· "Active soundboard" acoustic design delivers large tone to balance other instruments and singing

· Modern materials throughout, including stabilized wood sound-board, hand lay-up glass fiber body, horizontally laminated wood fretboard, and rugged aluminum neck/tail bar

· Action adjustable through variable height bridge and fretboard curvature

· Worm gear tuning and adjustable friction

· Finish: rubbed natural sound-board, dark green body, red trim strip and rosettes, satin-rubbed aluminum neck/tail bar

OPTIONAL ACCESSORIES

· Cases
  – Over-the-shoulder style of heavy corduroy with decorative strap
  – Hard protective tube style transporting container

· Interchangeable Fretboards
  – Northern Style (Standard) "Home" = open string
  – Appalachian Style "Home" = third fret
  – Chromatic
  – Fretless with Nut
  – Blank Board
  – Extra-Width Northern Style (To facilitate chording)

· Custom colors, fitted cases and special features such as amplification available on special order

Specifications and prices subject to change without notice.

Nov. '74

Why Modern Designs?

MORE SOUND — Separate bridge and fully active sound-board produces louder and fuller tone than traditional instrument in which finger board is usually fastened to soundboard.

BETTER INTONATION — Stable materials maintain instrument in tune. Worm-geared zero backlash tuning system makes tuning simple and accurate.

Workhorse Wanderer and Student Model

Deluxe Rosette Model

Kits – All Models

The dulcimer project, offering employment and small business experience to local high school students. Wendy is the model for this photo.

I signed up a small group of high school students and we started to work. Taking a cue from the burgeoning guitar world, we added amplification to our instrument, offered it in both 4-string and 8-string versions, and reinforced it to permit it to survive rough use. The project ran for about a year and involved about ten students who moved in and out of the project as time would permit. They were paid at a level that was in keeping to what they might have received doing conventional jobs. We made and sold almost a hundred instruments and developed a marketing network of about a dozen musical instrument retailers around New England to handle our line of dulcimers.

SAILING

While on the engineering faculty at Tufts University, I sought engagement in community activities by working on the development of sailing on the nearby Mystic Lakes. I helped oversee the design and construction of a new fleet of racing dinghies for Tufts. I coached the college sailing team and became increasingly involved with the fast-growing sport of intercollegiate racing and the ever-expanding development of community sailing on the nearby Charles River.

While working at the CIA, following my time at Tufts, I also coached sailing at two colleges in the District of Columbia. I then continued helping the Inter-Collegiate Yacht Racing Association (ICYRA) run college regattas at East Coast locations for about 10 years. Gradually, the ICYRA's work resulted in an increase in community and school sailing. Working with community sailing was a rewarding way to combine my maritime and civic interests.

SHOP CLASSES FOR FIVE FIELDS NEIGHBORHOOD CHILDREN

Realizing the significant boost that Margaret Shurcliff's summer shop classes and Shady Hill's shop program had given me, I sought a way to provide a similar opportunity for the children in our own neighborhood. Since we had a very complete workshop in our Lexington house in the middle of that 55-house community, we had plenty of children nearby, and the communal nature of the neighborhood made the program immediately feasible.

I felt strongly that it would be important to get the parents involved alongside their kids. I included a strong role for the fathers/mothers in the scheduled classes and accepted only children who had a parent that was willing to attend.

It was important that the participants be able to do some of the shop-like work at home, even if they did not already have tools and a workbench. Accordingly, as our first task, each parent/child team built a readily transportable, combined workbench and tool storage box. It looked quite similar to the "shoe-shine" kits which had been legion in public places in previous days. It consisted of a wooden box, perhaps 30" x 12," x 12" with a universal metal vise fastened on top. The box was capable of housing an assortment of basic tools inside, while providing small but usable workbench surface outside.

Between five and ten of our neighbor families participated in the classes held on Saturday mornings at our house. If I remember correctly, we did this for perhaps two years, meeting relatively often.

These classes meant a lot to me, as I had the opportunity to pay forward to the next generation of children what had been given to me by Mrs. Shurcliff in Ipswich, so many years before.

New England Council

The final phase of my nine-year stint at Arthur D. Little consisted of starting up the newly formed New England Small Business Services. Part of the job involved participating in many of the activities of the New England Council (NEC). Founded in 1925, the Council is the nation's oldest regional business organization. It is a non-partisan alliance of businesses, academic and health institutions plus public and private organizations, formed to promote economic growth and a high quality of life throughout the six New England states.

After leaving Arthur D. Little, I continued volunteer activities with the NEC, since I felt that it was a useful regional function in the burgeoning local small business scene. The format consisted of regular meetings with groups of managers of small companies in eastern Massachusetts who were in search of sharing experiences in running small businesses.

Minuteman Career and Technical High School Advisory Committee

Elected representatives in the Lexington Town Meeting were encouraged to participate in the sessions of the multi-town committee advising on the operations of our regional vocational high school. The committee was tasked to represent each of the town's concerns and desires to the school's administration and, in turn, represent the school back to the town leaders. Additionally, the committee was tasked to inform the town's educational and civic leaders, parents, and students about the school's objectives, attributes and accomplishments. The committee was also responsible for understanding the finances involved.

The task became increasingly complicated by the fact that there were students in attendance from 16 towns, and all matters had to be addressed to all the towns by working with the committee of community representatives to accomplish school goals. This proved understandably difficult because of the widely different viewpoints of towns involved.

Since recent state public school attendance laws permitted parents to choose schools for their kids regardless of where they lived, students from municipalities outside the Minuteman region were attracted to the very successful Minuteman School and attended in significant numbers. Costs per pupil for Lexington skyrocketed to levels far above those of our normal non-vocational high school.

This was an eye-opening experience for me and enabled me to get an increasing perspective of the strength and weakness of state controls over municipal operations. It was also a useful experience for me in understanding some of the practical problems of handling inter-municipality matters.

At one point I am afraid I took a stand which caused some controversy. The administrators of the school repeatedly boasted of the fact that they had an unusually high percentage of students entering college compared with other regional schools providing similar types of education–in the past called vocational, trade school, artisan-oriented, or some such, all terms not currently favored. I questioned whether their claims were short-changing the important fact that they were filling a much-needed and highly valuable service enabling non-college students to get a useful start toward what would become their vocations. I feel strongly that the school was doing an exceptionally good job and I was glad to be associated with it.

ASSISTING HIGH SCHOOL STUDENTS CONSIDERING THE UNIVERSITY OF MICHIGAN

I must admit that attending Michigan turned me into an enthusiastic recruiter. Through the Alumni Association and the School of Engineering, I learned that there was a need for assistance from graduates in helping with recruitment and serving as information sources for high school students facing college. I was asked to perform some admissions/placement interviewing for the university in several public high schools in the greater Boston area over about a ten-year period. This had two benefits for me: I was able to get a look at several interesting high schools, and this recruitment process kept me somewhat abreast of what was currently happening at Michigan. I welcomed the continued involvement in university matters.

CAMBRIDGE WATER BOARD

As the crow flies, our Lexington house was slightly over a half mile from the shores of the Hobbs Brook Reservoir, the main source of water for the city of Cambridge. The reservoir and its outlet stream and pumping station are on land which is part of four adjacent municipalities, Lexington, Lincoln, Weston, and Waltham. It was situated about 5½ miles from Cambridge's water treatment and pumping station, located on Fresh Pond in Cambridge. The City of Boston and many of its suburbs are on another system–The Massachusetts Water Resources Administration facility–a holdover from a long and complicated history of inter-municipality conflict (including shots being fired between Cambridge and neighboring Belmont!)

During my last decade of living in Lexington, I was appointed to represent the town on the Water Board of the City of Cambridge, along with representatives from the other three towns. Happily, this assignment proved an enlightening insight into some of the better aspects of municipal bureaucracy since it was manned by highly competent people from the surrounding municipalities and was doing a competent job for the common good. It also met my desire to participate in handling important, increasingly challenged, natural resources.

There was some interesting technology involved in the field of hydrology for which I had some formal training while studying at Harvard. My engineering experience with power plants and moving water around in the marine engineering field proved to be useful. Completely new to me, but quite fascinating and educating, was the field of potable water treatment. It was also the first time I had become involved with public health matters.

In practice, a group numbering eight or ten of us gathered each month, usually in an historic gem of a meeting room in Weston. My term on that committee lasted for something over five years. I found the experience both informative and very rewarding.

LEXINGTON TOWN MEETING SPECIAL RECOGNITION

For almost three decades I had been increasingly involved with the Lexington Town Meeting. It was an important part of my life and provided some significant experiences in practicing democracy in action. I learned a lot from what I like to call the "loyal opposition"–those with leanings quite different from mine, but with the good sense to do their homework and stand up for what they believed in. I found the experience valuable and broadening.

Having been turned down for entrance by Lexington's continuing care facility, Alice and I were facing a move out of Lexington. Accordingly, I had to resign as a Lexington Town Meeting member. Much to my surprise, the Town Meeting members organized a recognition ceremony for all of my services to the town. As part of the surprise, they saw to it that daughter Anne escorted Alice, who was then ailing, to the event. I am grateful they were present for a very nice public celebration.

COMMUNITY WORK IN BEDFORD

Once Alice and I moved to Carleton-Willard, I wanted to really get to know our new home town. It may seem strange that I did not feel well enough informed about a town immediately adjacent to Lexington, but Bedford is a different sort of place. Becoming an active attendant of Bedford's open Town Meeting (in which all citizens of the town are eligible to attend and vote, in contrast to Lexington's representative Meeting, in which only elected representatives can vote) was a start. I made a point of attending many of the meetings of Bedford's elected Board of Selectmen as well as several of the volunteer Town committees such as the Planning Board and Conservation Commission.

After sampling these activities, I was ready to approach the Chair of the Board of Selectmen to ask her where I might be useful. Much to my surprise (and somewhat to my horror), she headed me toward the Conservation Commission and the Board of Appeals, two committees that I never would have dared to try to serve on in Lexington as a result of my somewhat combative position with them in my SLCA days in Lexington.

Appointment to the Board of Appeals, in a position that dealt heavily with legal issues, made me feel ill at ease. However, since I respected the judgment of my informant on Bedford's Board of Selectmen, I accepted and ended up really welcoming the opportunity to try a new aspect of civic duty. It turned out to be truly informative.

I had heard of the outstanding reputation of Bedford's professional conservationist and I really looked forward to working with her. She was exceedingly well informed and had accomplished a lot for the town. I learned a lot from her.

I was the only member of the Committee who was not working for a living, so I was available to work on some projects during business hours. I also had some equipment that could be used, including cameras and surveying equipment. Serving on this committee was a good experience and helped me markedly as I came to know the town of Bedford.

Based on my rather long tenure on the Cable Advisory Committee in Lexington, during which we had worked closely with our sister committee in Bedford, it was logical for me to offer to serve on Bedford's committee which I did immediately. Lexington and Bedford had previously been tied together by a common cable TV provider so we had been drawn into cooperating across town borders.

I found the local Cable Committee to be well manned with very competent people. By then the cable TV provider had changed over to a more reasonable firm than I had been previously dealing with in Lexington, so my brief service on the Bedford committee was a relief after my tedious Lexington experience.

WRAPPING UP CIVIC ACTIVITIES IN BEDFORD

Unfortunately, as Alice became increasingly incapacitated by her dementia, and as Bedford's committee meetings seemed to pile up and last until later hours at night, I reluctantly withdrew as a useful civic volunteer and turned, instead, to our emerging problem: my struggling efforts to care for Alice.

Volunteering for the town of Bedford was, however, a wonderful way to get to know this very well-run municipality.

Inscription: "Caleb Warner for his many years of service to Lexington".

Sailing on Crouton II, our catamaran.

14

MARITIME ACTIVITIES

My interests and activities in maritime matters ran parallel to my professional, familial and community-oriented life, from my pre-teen summers through the University of Michigan, wartime service in the Navy, and then throughout the rest of my life.

PRE-TEEN SUMMERS – GETTING THE MARINE CRAZE

My parents' summer house in Essex, MA, bordered on and overlooked the much-loved Ipswich/ Essex salt marshes. A classic winding creek meanders through the marshes, edged on the far side by the barrier sand dunes of Crane Beach. Sailing, rowing, clamming, tidal flooding/receding were all part of the scene. It was here that I caught the craze for all things maritime.

Essex is famous for the building of wooden fishing vessels dating back to the 1700s. The town abuts Gloucester, MA, historically one of the most significant fishing ports on the east coast, and is conveniently connected by sheltered, shallow salt water creeks (virtually "marine roads") to Gloucester.

Our house was a short distance from the shipyard site. My parents made a point of taking me to the shipyard often to watch the wooden wonders being built. Two of the photographs here show the structures of the shapely hulls growing on the launching ways, immediately above the creek into which they were launched, down which they were towed to Gloucester to be fitted out and rigged.

Whenever there was a keel-laying, a ceremony was held at the boatyard involving the community, yard workers and representatives of the future owners. Again, my parents made sure that I attended and came to know about the people involved, and especially about the skills involved, such as the arcane use of the adze, broad axe, spoke shave (cutting tools used to shape wood) and the caulking iron.

The launchings were true events, essentially town holidays, attended by the whole community, and I assuredly was present, too. Historically, but long before my time, the townspeople actually were put to work at some of the launchings. Apparently, as the main shipyard area had grown in earlier, busier times, it ran out of space and a second building area was developed further inland from the waters' edge. This new site was on the *other* side of the hill on which the town center buildings sat. Come launching time, logs were put under the hull keels as rollers, and the heavy hulls were hauled tediously by yoked oxen up and over the hill down to the water's edge. This task took considerable manpower, and town members always turned out to help. Incentive was always assured, however. A full keg of rum, unreachable from ground level, was securely tied to the deck, keeping it safe for the uphill trip. At the top of the hill, the keg was ceremoniously unpegged, and distributed generously among the town citizens in great celebration.

The mystique of the whole wooden shipbuilding scene became unparalleled for me. One can understand why, in very early life, I came to revere the town for its shipbuilding status. In many ways, it helped nurture my fascination with all things maritime, and later influenced my professional career.

AN INTRODUCTION TO SAILING: MY FIRST BOATS

As a youth, as I crossed the mile of salt marshes on foot to reach the bustling summer activities of my Uncle Roger's summer house in Ipswich, I found myself involved firsthand in a kind of summer fun that, to me, became unrivaled. My two cousins, Roger and Sturgis Warner, were young, hard-core sailing enthusiasts, and they got me going in the maritime field.

Cousin Roger gave me my first boat when I was about 12 years old. It was a nice wooden sailing dinghy about 12 feet long, built locally by one of the men in the fishing boat shipyard in Essex. Next, when one of our neighbors was away for the summer, she lent me her "MontyCat", a rather unusual boat designed for the winding creeks and shoal waters of the marshland. It was about 14' long, 7' wide ("beam"), a shallow draft (the depth of the boat as she sits in the water), and was equipped with a centerboard to accommodate the shallow water. It was ruggedly built of wood with a simplified hull shape, well-decked to form a protective cockpit, simply rigged as a (one sail) catboat.

I then graduated to a beautiful and able Manchester 15 (15-foot length on the waterline, 18-foot length overall), a sloop (two sails), which had been designed as a class boat by the well-known naval architect John Alden for the nearby Manchester Yacht Club. I was lucky enough to find a storm-damaged hull, and was old enough to be able to salvage it. It was a thrill to work on my own boat and sail it, in working order, up and down the local shoreline. I was hooked.

Newly built vessel's overland transport from construction to launch site. Rum keg is out of sight, tied to the deck, ready to be tapped for community celebration.

Fishing vessel under construction in Essex, MA.

Vessel is ready to be launched into the creek, in background.

SERIOUS TEEN SAILING

I sailed that Manchester 15 alone, hard, and all over the place. I had no qualms about taking her outside the local creek and the attendant bay into the ocean, circumnavigating Cape Ann to get to Marblehead, and sailing up and down the New Hampshire coast. I gave sailing lessons to teenagers in nearby Annisquam. My cousins supported my interests by drilling me hard on boat maintenance and repairs. Their barn and workshop became a veritable boatyard.

APPRENTICE BOAT BUILDER

Thanks to my fascination with the woodworking and metalworking opportunities I found in Ipswich, by the summer of 1936 I was ready to get serious about working around boats. I was welcomed into the shop of a local production builder of small wooden boats. I was an unpaid apprentice–a win-win deal for both me and the shop. I agreed to turn up at the shop every weekday at 8:00 a.m. and stay through until the end of the workday at 4:30. At first, when I walked in the shop, the crew gathered around me and told me they wanted me to mix the putty all day. Luckily I fought it, and learned how to build boats instead!

The shop offered a line of two basic rowboats and a 14-foot basic sailboat. These were built on a production basis by a shop crew of about six people and were distributed for sale to a number of boat shops around the Massachusetts and New Hampshire coasts.

Once we got past the putty idea, I began as a "go-fer", but soon graduated to being a true production hand, assisting the one real pro who nobody else could get along with but who was the highest producing person in the shop. For some reason, he was an S.O.B. to fellow workers but treated me really well as long as I worked hard. This was my first experience requiring real work skills. It taught me many lessons that proved useful later. I ended up very happily apprenticing for three successive summers while in prep school at Exeter.

This experience must have gone well, since a few years later I unexpectedly was offered a chance to run that shop. The father of the current boss was an up-and-coming executive in the burgeoning IBM Company. He had financed the startup of the small boatbuilding business as an outlet for his boat-loving son who needed a career. The son became impatient with the business and went to the Caribbean to become a charter boat captain, leaving the business unmanaged. As I passed through New York City on my way to college, I stopped in at IBM to visit the father. He asked me if I would stay around to run the business in which I had apprenticed. I thanked him profusely and explained that I really had to pursue another course. This was my first experience with one of those thought-provoking forks in the road that continued to appear throughout in my career.

I traveled alone to Bristol, RI at age 15, and stayed with family friends while I explored the fascinating scene of the America's Cup racing. I visited the boatyard and got a good look at several of the Herreshoff boats close up. I then got passage aboard a small fishing vessel (turned tour boat) to watch the races from the water.

A Frightening Experience in San Francisco Bay

During the summer of 1938, while my parents were staying in Berkeley, CA so that my father could take charge of the Pacific Rim aspects of the San Francisco World's Fair, I visited the San Francisco Yacht Club looking for a chance to do some sailing on the bay.

I was invited aboard a 40-foot racing yawl to help crew the boat in an evening race. The owner was inexperienced and the boat was new. After the sun went down, the wind increased and we ended up finding ourselves in dangerous trouble. The crew members, also inexperienced, lost control of themselves, causing the skipper to lose his nerve. He radioed the Coast Guard for help.

One of the Coast Guard's high-speed 60-footers arrived and started to tow us toward shelter. The rescuer's boat was ill-suited for towing ours, however. The helm on their boat was positioned way forward, where their helmsman could not see how we were doing. His crew member posted to watch over us astern had to stand way aft, essentially at the stern of the Coast Guard boat. Communication between the helmsman and the crew member was virtually impossible at that distance, especially at night, with a strong wind to boot. This alone was a setup for potential disaster.

Further complication was that the engines of the rescue boat could not run slowly enough to prevent wild yawing (swinging back and forth widely, rather than following straight behind) of our sailboat. The result was that they had to stop engines periodically, in an attempt to straighten us out. At one point, we simply over-ran the rescue boat. Our bowsprit pierced their transom. Our bowsprit was sheared completely off, starting a leak in our bow. The rescue launch suffered a hole in its stern, and it, as well, also began to take on water. The rescue boat then towed us, both boats limping, about 10 miles that dark night, back to shelter at the yacht club mooring basin, where both boats were docked for repair, and the crews staggered home. It was a terrifying experience but I learned a lot.

Shipbuilding Internship

During the first of my two summer breaks while at the University of Michigan, I served as an intern at the Bath Iron Works (BIW) in Bath, ME, which is described in the College Era chapter. This, indeed, was a captivating experience for me as a student studying Marine Engineering. I learned a great deal about the real-life process of building large Naval ships.

Intercollegiate Sailing Racing At Michigan

Since Michigan had courses in naval architecture, it attracted students from all over who were seriously interested in sail racing. We had an excellent sailing team and participated in intercollegiate racing all around the country. I found great pleasure in that program and continued to race for many years after graduating from college.

WWII Navy Repair Ship Duty

As originally planned when selecting the University of Michigan, my college studies qualified me for assignment to repair ship duty. My participation in the NROTC program produced immediate commissioning as an officer. I was therefore able to serve overseas after graduation without the delay of extra training as was required for the non-Naval Academy graduates entering the Navy as officer candidates.

COAST GUARD COMMITTEE DUTY

Immediately after returning from war duty, and because of my marine training and orientation, I was assigned to represent DuPont on a Coast Guard committee. We oversaw the safety of hazardous cargo shipping of chemicals on inland waterways and ocean routes. At that time, DuPont was shipping these substances in bulk between their manufacturing plant on the Gulf Coast and their storage facility in Cartaret, NJ, using a specially-fitted-out tanker.

Several other chemical companies were also shipping hazardous chemicals throughout the inland waterway system. The U.S. Coast Guard organized a technically savvy oversight committee. I found this task very interesting and at the same time quite worrisome, especially since our main objective was to watch over the extensive shipment of chlorine over the inland waterways–a disaster waiting to happen, in my estimation.

While serving on this committee I learned a lot about the workings of the Federal Government and got to know and appreciate a lot of the activists in the chemical industry. I sometimes regret that I did not follow up on this field of maritime safety. It could very well have provided a continuation for my maritime interests.

ON THE SUBJECT OF YACHTING...

I can hardly complete this recounting of my maritime activities without discussing "yachting" as opposed to "boating". Looking back at the maritime sector of my life, I concentrated my professional activity on the operation, design and construction of working craft, and engaged seriously in the high-speed sailing of small boats as my chosen competitive sport and recreation. I consciously avoided being part of the "show and tell" scene, so-called yachting.

Perhaps the recent bestseller "Mine's Bigger–Tom Perkins" (one of the Silicon Valley boys) and "The Making of the Greatest Sailing Machine Ever Built" describes some aspects of modern yachting. The much publicized America's Cup events and the show-off gyrations of the yachting world in general were not what I wanted to get involved in, and never did, although many of my International 14 sailing companions and University of Michigan schoolmates did.

BECOMING AN UFFA FOX DISCIPLE

As I got into serious sailing in the pre-WWII period, I watched with fascination as Britisher Uffa Fox introduced sailboats that were ultra-light. Their hull shapes lifted them up onto the surface of the water, out of the displacement mode where they had been limited in speed, and into the planing mode where they could go very much faster.

Richard Besse, chairman of the Essex Yacht Club international 14 foot dinghy class, won the Roger Sherman Warner trophy in the two day regatta held May 27 and 28 by the club on the Connecticut River. Presentation of the trophy was made by Vice Commodore Stuart Squier at the clubhouse Sunday afternoon. Shown left to right are: Squier; Richard Carter of Yale who placed second and his crew, John Carter; Besse and his crew, Ted Carter; Colin Ratsey who captured third place, and Capt. Henry Rotherham of Great Britain who crewed for Ratsey. (Photo by McCabe)

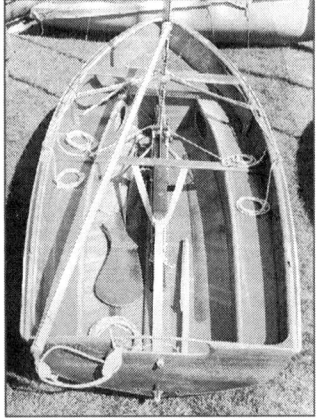

Uffa Fox's International 14-foot Dinghies. Top row: A friend and I sailing out of Manchester Harbor; crewing for John Carter in the Roger Sherman Warner Trophy Series in Manchester Harbor; my International 14-footer. Middle photo: Another competition for the Roger Sherman Warner Trophy, with Dick Besse, winner! Bottom row: Racing in Montreal against the British and Canadian teams; a typical International 14-footer.

The epitome of Fox's work was the so-called International 14-foot dinghy, usually referred to by sailers simply as a "14". These boats were superb racing machines requiring two highly athletic, highly sailing-savvy individuals to sail them. They were built like fine wooden furniture and included every modern "go fast" feature imaginable. They attracted serious sailing enthusiasts worldwide because they were an "open class design", in which each new boat could be altered to make it faster (as opposed to "one-design class", boats in which every new boat was the same). The 14's became things of consummate nautical beauty and a continual naval architects' challenge. At that time, they were mostly built in England. They attracted a following in the international small boat racing world and developed a reputation for hotly contested regattas in England, Bermuda, Canada, and both coasts of the U.S. I found one available in Buffalo and happily joined the U.S. group headquartered in Essex, CT.

The American group became almost an extended family for me. One man was an usher in our wedding, another became our family pediatrician, two of them became my bosses in an industrial engineering firm, and two of them became members of U.S. Olympic teams and participants in America's Cup races. We raced year round, shifting into frostbite sailing mode in the winter. This type of sailing lasted for me for about five years, starting in 1947. Getting married and starting to work seriously for a living put some sense into my head and made me put sailing into a more sensible perspective. But it was tremendous fun to be a part of that intense activity surrounding designing, building and racing internationally.

MARITIME EXPERIENCES IN SCANDINAVIA

Most of my time in Scandinavia, starting in 1946, revolved around my maritime interests. During my first month in Copenhagen at the Burmeister and Wain plant, I was introduced to their enormous diesel engines, designed to power large ocean-going vessels. Next, in Stockholm, where I interned at the DeLaval Company, I was introduced to the development of large marine gas turbines for use in the Swedish high-speed Naval patrol craft. My participation in field repair for the company furthered my experience with ships built in surrounding countries. During my time off the job, I sailed in my very own sailing canoe and did a lot of single-handed sailing in the famous skerries east of Stockholm, and later on with Alice.

I also had the luck of sailing in the Olympic tryouts in one of the local six-meter boats. This was the most strenuous workout I had ever had on a sailboat. I was the bow-man, responsible for working the foredeck of the boat.

I then found a rather unusual job. I was asked to help train the Swedish small boat skippers who were completely unfamiliar with the new boats designed by Uffa Fox which were being introduced into the Olympics for the first time. My experience with the International 14s back here in the U.S. was just what they needed. I worked with very competent Swedes who soon would be competing against the U.S. squad. I did a bit of worrying about whether this activity fit my ethical standards of allegiance to our own U.S. Olympic sailing team, but the experience of working with the Swedes was done in the spirit of good sport and was a valuable one for all of us.

SANDY DOUGLAS—"AMERICA'S UFFA FOX"?

In some ways, Sandy Douglas was an American version of the UK's Uffa Fox. Headquartered on Lake Erie in Painesville, OH, he helped arrange building Fox-designed International 14 sailing dinghies by a U.S. boat builder in the Midwest, who was skilled in molded plywood techniques.

In 1945 he designed an enlarged version of the 14 which was 16 feet long and named it the Thistle, over 4,000 of which have been built. I had the privilege of being his crew in several Thistle national championship regattas. Cousin Roger Warner owned a Thistle (and son Langdon has since inherited it). Sandy then enlarged the very successful Thistle design into the 19½-foot Highlander, still maintaining many of the features introduced by Uffa Fox. Alice and I bought a Highlander some years later, which we happily sailed all over the East Coast, then lengthened its hull twice to become our "ultimate mobile marine home".

Sandy's next step was development of the Flying Scot, sized between the Thistle and the Highlander, but built out of fiberglass. Almost 6,000 of the Flying Scots have been built to date and they are among the most successful sailboats ever produced.

I had the great privilege of being a good friend and regular crew for Sandy Douglas in regattas all over the Eastern U.S. I rate this as a significant part of my total marine experience.

FOX'S ATALANTA

Uffa Fox had been on a team with Cousin Roger Warner, working on amphibious vessel development during WWII, but I am not sure of the details. It is clear, however, that Fox did work on special small craft for the unusual littoral warfare facing the Allied Forces in WWII.

Roger described to me Fox's attempt to develop one such small boat. This craft was designed to be attached to, and carried under, a small airplane to be stealthily flown into a remote location. The boat would be dropped surreptitiously from the airplane with the special operations skipper already aboard, ready to gather intelligence, rescue behind-the-lines combatants, place damaging explosives, or rescue sailors and airmen from the sea. Fox's subsequent "Atalanta" was a unique, post-war, 26-foot, trailerable, high-performance cruising boat based on that extraordinary stealth craft. Cousin

THE BOAT THAT DROPPED FROM THE SKY

A scary story comes to mind about Uffa Fox and his stealth craft. The boat was designed to be transported by an airplane and dropped into the water with the skipper aboard. It has been reported that Fox built a prototype boat and volunteered to test it with himself as the skipper. The British Navy brass refused to allow him aboard for the first test drop. Everything went well in the drop, until the heavy iron ring on the harness that attached the boat to the bottom of the airplane crashed right through the bottom of the boat upon its impact with the water. The test boat immediately took on water. Fox would have been right under that ring when the boat was dropped, and it was quite obvious that he would have been instantly killed. The harness was promptly redesigned. The record does not show whether this amazing craft ever saw actual use. However, Fox's ingenuity and guts were definitely exhibited, and the basic design of the hull reappeared after the war in his design of the "Atalanta".

Roger, being an admirer of Fox's work, acquired an Atalanta, and I had the opportunity to sail on it with him after WWII.

CROUTON

Sailing was part of Alice and my relationship from the very start, as we sailed around the coast of Sweden the summer we met. It was not until we were married and about to have our second child, however, that I dared to buy our first boat. Following the sale of our land in Lincoln, Mass., we used most of the profits for the down payment on our new house and used the rest for the purchase of a small boat–a Highlander.

Over the years, Cousins Roger and Sturgis Warner had informed me of some of the old "good luck" traditions of maritime lore and insisted that I honor them. One of these was that a boat's name must be seven letters long and one of its vowels must be repeated. We duly struggled with these requirements and finally came up with the name "Crouton", which properly conveyed the image for the kind of boat we wanted to have!

Our floating tent.

We outfitted Crouton for cruising along the idyllic coast of Maine. It was a type normally classed as an "open boat", i.e., without a cabin or attached shelter of any kind–just an open cockpit. To make it fit for cruising, it needed a shelter. The most rudimentary solution was a so-called boom tent–weatherproof material held up by placing it over the boat's boom once the mainsail is lowered, and tying it snuggly down to the deck surrounding the cockpit. Landlubbers might term it a nautical version of a "pup tent".

This was our choice for shelter, and the design of the Highlander was ideal for it. We did a bit of fancy fitting of tent flaps and insertion of Isinglass portlights plus super-secure fastenings for the flaps to make the tent really habitable and comfortable.

As the children grew, and family members offered to babysit them for some summer weekends, Alice and I started our Maine cruising trips. We had our boom tent ready for shelter, and, as a final touch, we decided to hang a camping "mantle" lamp inside it, giving us warmth in the cold Maine nights while providing light bright enough to read by.

The boat was transported by trailer, so the first year we drove to Casco Bay, the part of Maine where the best cruising starts. Launching from Falmouth Foreside (just east of Portland), we could safely leave the car and trailer. We then sailed eastward, usually as far a Schoodic Point or Winter Harbor, just beyond Mt. Desert Island, where the coast suddenly becomes less friendly. Our cruising trips were a wonderful way to spend time together while exploring every nook and cranny along that wonderful 120-mile coast.

THE EVER-EVOLVING "CROUTONS"

Alice, bless her, had started out being somewhat wary of boats, and over the years to come this wariness was to wax and wane. After experiencing our first elemental "cruising/camping" routine, however, she came to rather enjoy our outings. That was my signal to get busy and improve the scene. I first lengthened the basic 19½-foot Highlander by adding about three feet to her stern to give us more room. I then took an inspiring message from Alice's grandfather, Charles H.W. Foster, and converted the sail plan to his new and original design of a staysail ketch or yawl: a rig on a single mast in which the aft sail slides up and

The family, sailing on an early version of Crouton I.

down on a backstay rather than on a separate mast. To round out the conversion, I added a clipper bow plus bowsprit to give us a larger jib. To house our fast-growing family, I added cabin structures both forward and aft.

The net result was that we could now accommodate the whole family in our cruising/camping vacations. Another result was that our rather unusual craft caused a lot of comment when we sailed her around the coast, especially when all six of us were aboard. Her unusual appearance resulted in her being featured on an official colored postcard of the town of Manchester, MA, our home port. We sailed her hard for about three years, both in Maine and all around Cape Cod. She eventually ended up with the Girl Scouts on Chesapeake Bay when we bought our next, much larger boat.

MULTI-HULL CRAZE

The next chapter in our marine activities was a venturesome story. In my participation in the International 14 dinghy group, I came to know John Hughes, a brilliant

Alice, an avid writer, always found a space and time to work. Here she is on the deck of the boat, with her hand-written notes carefully balanced against her foot!

Morning aboard Crouton II. Top: Nick, asleep in the cockpit; Alice and her sister Cally Cochran playing Russian Bank. Bottom: I needed good light to shave each morning; Langdon, checking one of the rudders at the stern of the boat. Middle: My trumpet-and-initials burgee (family flag).

student in the MBA program at Harvard. John was heavily engaged in high-performance sailing. He commissioned the design and construction of a catamaran (a boat consisting of two parallel hulls), 38 feet long with about a 24-foot beam, by Prout & Sons at Covey Island in England. He wanted to sail it back to the U.S. in the hopes of challenging the speed record for crossing the Atlantic east to west. When the boat was completed, he went to England and made a test run across the Bay of Biscay to Portugal. He judged that the boat was not capable of making the trans-Atlantic crossing after it damaged itself when heading into steep, short waves. So he had her shipped by freighter to the East coast. Still wanting to cruise in Europe, John had the catamaran laid up on Martha's Vineyard and returned to Europe to cruise for about a year in a mono-hull.

I became curious about the catamaran and found that John's lawyer was watching over his affairs here in the U.S. When I asked him about the catamaran, he said, "Make me an offer". I suggested about 20% of what the boat must have cost, and suddenly I owned it! So here was our next Crouton. I will admit that I gave Alice no chance to participate in this decision, and, again, I found myself trembling in my boots when I told her!

Inside the main cabin.

As we sailed Crouton II from Martha's Vineyard to her new home port of Manchester, I immediately observed the boat's inability to survive short head seas. As we approached the exceedingly steep seas caused by the interaction of wind and tidal current in the southern entrance to the Cape Cod Canal, she slammed the underbody of the wing connecting her two hulls on a wave top so hard that the wing opened up and threatened to do serious damage to the boat's structure. I vowed to "baby" her in the future when operating in similar circumstances and came to appreciate John Hughes' wise decision not to sail this catamaran across the Atlantic.

TOOTSIE MELT

Anne and Wendy were sometimes in their cabin, often hiding candy in the vent above their shared bunk. I learned the hard way to bring a putty knife on our longer trips. Tootsie Rolls melt in heat and moisture!

Crouton II was an excellent solution to the problem of accommodating our whole family. Believe it or not, she could sleep 10 people comfortably, provided eight were in sleeping bags below decks while Alice and I slept luxuriously in the cabin on the main deck. This meant that each of our kids could bring along a friend when we cruised. There was even room enough for our golden retriever, who was not a pet, but an important member of the family.

Crouton II enabled us to take real family vacations. We sailed all over the place, on both day trips and longer vacations. These were vacations for the family, but were hard on Alice, who had a great deal of preparation and hands-on work to do to feed our many family and friends on board. Appetites ran high and she was feeding an army.

The food preparation area, or galley, on board the catamaran was a physical challenge for Alice. Space was constrained by the tapering dimensions of the walls of the pontoon-shaped hulls of the boat. The available space was only about 5½ feet at its ceiling (the beam or width of the hull) and sloped down toward a single plank floor area. Its length, although a full ten feet, was also tapered to one narrow end to allow for the shape of the stern, with the other end an adjacent waist-high bunkroom. Fortunately, the galley had adequate headroom and good ventilation.

The utilities included a hot/cold water sink, a two cubic foot, gas-cooled refrigerator, a two-burner gas stove, and a 1½ or 2 cubic foot oven, and a small dish storage and food storage locker above a two-foot long food preparation counter.

In spite of the tight quarters and limited facilities, Alice found it possible to feed up to ten of us very well, sometimes with the help of another person squeezed into the limited space. Admittedly, she initially started out quite concerned about the challenge of the galley (she often suffered from sea sickness), and I admire her for learning to accommodate those limitations.

On one such trip, we sailed directly from our home port of Manchester, MA, to a mid-coast point in Maine, above Casco Bay. We then started "gunk-holing", going in and out of the islands, for about a week. Our daily routine involved requiring each person to go swimming just after waking up in the morning to keep us all clean. At the end of a week everybody was annoyed by the cold water, and we turned around and sailed south, back past Manchester to spend a few days in the warmer waters south of Cape Cod. The boat was so fast that we could accomplish these distances quite readily.

The 200-mile, non-stop trip from Eastern Maine to south of Cape Cod was a fascinating family expedition in that we had to shift into a real sea-going mode. The family was organized into watches and performed some real at-sea piloting, planning courses, taking radio beacon bearings, plotting compass courses on marine charts, making allowances for currents and tides, and calculating ETA's (Estimated Times of Arrival), while all the time keeping an eye out for weather conditions broadcast by the marine weather service and monitoring marine distress radio frequencies. It was an eye-opening experience for the whole gang. I found it a real challenge to stand back—to try <u>not</u> to act like those nasty Hollywood sea captains, yet make sure that all things that needed attention were being properly (and safely) performed.

Alice.

When not on vacation, we often spent weekends on the catamaran sailing around the north and south shores of the Boston area with the whole family (usually including Rob) plus friends. Alice and I even occasionally arranged for an overnight baby sitter for the family so we could go up to Manchester and spend the night on the catamaran, moored immediately outside the harbor.

We had one near tragedy when the catamaran was stolen off its mooring in Manchester. The thieves ran her aground on the Coast Guard seaplane launching ramps in Salem harbor, then deserted her, leaving all the sails up and showing signs that those that took her did not know how to handle her unusual nature. She suffered a hard grounding which resulted in puncturing both hulls. This took place at the end of the sailing season. So, while bailing her hard to keep her afloat, we took her around to the boatyard in Essex where she was patched up and laid up for the winter.

We had this sizable catamaran for about five years, and used her hard. In the end, as our kids began to grow up and to have their own lives, we realized that she no longer satisfied our needs. It was also apparent that a boat that large was going to cost more than a sensible amount to hold onto. Langdon was ready for college, so we sold her for exactly what we had paid for her five years previously. She sold in a matter of hours and her happy new owner took her immediately down to Florida where she disappeared from our lives after having given us much pleasure, excitement and learning.

THE ULTIMATE MOBILE MARINE HOME

When we sold Crouton II, I sought a more practical multihull for our next boat. Ian Farrier, an Australian multi-hull designer/builder, had developed what looked like a sensible family of trimarans which were foldable so they could be readily trailered. His smallest model was the Eagle, a 19½-foot craft, which folded to meet the eight-foot maximum width allowable on U.S. roads and designed so I could readily launch and retrieve her by myself. In the mid-1980s one of these unusual boats was in stock in Annapolis, MD. I picked it up and towed it home to Lexington. Crouton III was a welcome new member of the family.

A trimaran is a three-hulled boat. This one's design had been attractive to me as I could, on my own, fold the two outer hulls up to prepare it for its trailer. At the time, we had a pickup truck onto which we could put a slide-on camper and behind which we could tow the folding trimaran. This array produced the ultimate mobile marine home.

The first time Alice and I used Crouton III on the Maine Coast, we stumbled into a campground in Southwest Harbor

Launching Crouton III, the trimaran, in Essex, MA, with Hog Island in the background.

that we found to be the ideal spot to summer. I made arrangements with the harbormaster to rent his personal mooring, which was near the launching ramp. This way, once the boat was in the water, I did not have to take it out until the end of our vacation. One by one our adult kids and their friends turned up with their tents and pitched them near us in the campground. The camper had a really good galley and a head. It also had two luxurious bunks just for Alice and me. We placed a commodious picnic table at the rear door of the camper, occasionally shaded by a pop-up tent, to provide a dining facility for the extended family and friends. Alice, as usual, produced continuously simple yet elegant meals for us and for our guests in the camper's tiny kitchenette.

Our daily routine was quite pleasant. Echo Lake was immediately adjacent to the campground. It was about 1½ miles long, so it provided an ideal course for a three mile row for me first thing every morning. I brought a so-called Alden ocean shell on the top of the car which provided high-grade rowing with competition oars and a sliding seat. (Luckily this time, it was not one that wanted to go in circles!) Then Alice and I generally had a half-day expedition driving or hiking/exploring together, after which I usually took a half day of sailing, occasionally accompanied by Alice.

During Alice's typical half day back at the campground, she found much to do. She was fully and happily occupied doing a lot of productive writing. She rewrote her autobiographical book entitled Bethany, an account of Alice and her brother's early childhood days on the family farm in Bethany, Connecticut, during WWII. She also worked on articles and several other books for her professional field of Library Science. She spent time at the local library and enjoyed her daily visit to the local farm stand for "the best tomato" or "one perfect zucchini" to enjoy with our evening meal. Alice made fast friends with various fellow campers and we enjoyed "neighborhood gatherings" at the campground each year. Often, she also entertained visiting family members camped nearby.

The trimaran was so fast that I was able to explore the waters around a lot of the beautiful islands in an ideal area for sailing. She was fitted with an outboard motor so I could keep a reliable schedule for meals and activities.

We found ourselves enthusiastically returning to Southwest Harbor yearly, and did so for almost 15 years. One summer, we went all around Nova Scotia and Prince Edward Island and another summer we sailed and camped on the Great Lakes using our mobile maritime home with a boat both summers. I even drove the rig to Florida for a Sizer family wedding where we had a memorable family sail in celebration of the event.

THE ULTIMATE "STINKPOT"!

For years, sailors have tried to explain why it's "more fun" to trim the sail, chart a course, and work every aspect of a sailboat on the way to a destination–even on a pleasure outing with nowhere to go in particular. As large motor boats speed past sailboats, leaving a big rocking wake and the smell of exhaust behind, many a sailor has remarked, *"Stinkpot!"*

When I got to be 70 years old, the Harbor Master in Southwest Harbor told me that it was time for me to graduate to a motorboat. He was right.

I looked around for a suitable craft. My requirements were that it be an outboard of modest enough size to be trailerable, with two quiet, non-gas-guzzling motors (one high horsepower for decent speed and one of lesser power for safety and leisurely travel), with a cabin to keep me out of the skin cancer-inducing sun, with some sleeping accommodations, and an enclosed head, a boat styled to be acceptable in appearance to both me and my "boating snob" neighbors in Maine. An advertisement in the back of the National Fisherman Magazine provided the answer: the C-Dory 22. There was a used one available on Cape Cod. I took a look at it, bought it, and named it Crouton IV.

THE END OF OUR SUMMERS IN MAINE

Crouton IV was a mixed blessing. For the two summers that we had it in Maine at the campground in Southwest Harbor, it was just what we wanted and needed. I found it very satisfying, and welcomed the newfound capability of traveling more widely around that beautiful coastal Maine.

Sadly, however, at the end of the second summer, it was involved in Alice's terrible rollover car accident, as she was towing the boat on the way home from our summer in Maine. It was the end of our boating days, and poor Alice never fully recovered from the dreadful accident.

MARINE ACTIVITIES IN MY LATER YEARS

Since Alice's accident and our move to our retirement community, I've tried to keep up some marine activities. Son Langdon and I share three radio-controlled, one-meter model sailboats that can be raced and enjoyed by young and old alike.

Carleton-Willard has a well-equipped workshop for use by residents, into which I had moved a significant number of machine and hand tools from my Lexington shop. It was a real retreat for me, and I often went there to release some of my tension caused by my concerns about Alice's ever-worsening condition.

I became increasingly interested, in fact fascinated, in the recent development of very effective tugboats, the work-horses of the maritime industry. One of the most sophisticated designs is the Ship Docking Module (SDM), a marvel of a weapon in the continuing battle to take care of large vessels as they are moved around in port.

The SDM can pull or push in any direction with tremendous force. This flexibility comes about through the use of azimuthing drives, propulsive devices at each end (bow and stern) of the vessel, that can be trained in any direction. The result is that this unique vessel can pull or push *sideways* (left/right, port/starboard). The "oxen" of the maritime industry,

One of our remote controlled sailboats.

they can pull or push an almost immovable larger vessel, and can do so with tremendous force.

The unusual capabilities of the SDM produce a tugboat, the control of which is understandably counter-intuitive to many skippers who must operate it. I thought a radio-controlled scale model might be useful to one of the Maritime Academies where skippers are trained. Accordingly, I have built a radio-controlled model that is about three feet long. It is my hope that it will be donated for use at one of the Maritime Academies.

MARINE INTERESTS OVER THE YEARS

Over time, I was able to involve my maritime orientation in several phases of my professional career. I owe a lot to the fact that I had been bitten by an early interest in marine matters since that eased me into my first job as an apprentice in the boatbuilding shop where I found the manifold benefits of having a job and having a direction in which to grow. I am also very glad that I was oriented toward, and thoroughly trained in, things nautical as I was preparing for WWII duty. It was truly satisfying to be able to perform in the maritime field during the war. My shift away from the maritime field as a profession after the war leaves me a little sad and even a bit jealous of some of my Michigan colleagues who have made some real contributions in that area.

I, of course, wonder if I should have pursued a more marine-oriented career. Marine safety, along the lines of the Coast Guard Committee on which I served while at DuPont, might have been a worthwhile effort. I would very much like to be involved with the evolving Littoral Combat Ships (LCS) program in the Navy, since I am convinced that the LCS program offers an opportunity to bring the Navy into optimal focus in today's world. I also would have liked to join Rhode Island's Luther Blount and the Australians in developing the resurgent small multihull cruising passenger ships and ferry systems.

However, using maritime activities as my principal enjoyment rather than as a career after WWII was a luxury which has shaped my adult life.

Alice.

Above: My Manchester 15, ready for launching.

Left: My mother's cousin, Paul Hammond, saw the need for a new medium-sized sailboat. He turned to his good friend and boat builder Nathanael Herreshoff, whose design and building techniques were internationally known. The S Boat was born and the first was built for Hammond himself. Many S Boats were later built, and raced seriously up and down the East coast. The S Boat was my favorite conventional sailing craft.

Right: Launching of the USS Frank Knox at the Bath Iron Works, Bath, Maine, on September 17, 1944.

Left: Alice in Crouton I at the dock. Note the round chart table I made, with a compass set above it, forming a pelorus.

Alice, ready to help launch the recently enlarged Crouton in Camden, Maine.

Crouton I in her final phase. Top photo: Alice. Middle photos: Note the staysail ketch rig, patterned after developments by Alice's grandfather, C. H. W. Foster. Bottom photo: Young Wendy and Crouton I in our driveway at home.

Our second family boat, Crowton II, a catamaran, before and after being painted.

Tel.
451-1850
(business)

CALEB WARNER
546 CONCORD AVENUE
LEXINGTON, MASSACHUSETTS 02173

Tel.
862-9278
(home)

"CROUTON II" IS RELUCTANTLY
FOR SALE

Our family has grown up. She needs
a special kind of new owner -- skillful
enough to master her whims, tolerant
and mechanically oriented enough to keep
her alive. She sleeps 8-10, and is as
fully equipped as any floating tent.

Our camping gear and boats for summers in Maine, dubbed collectively our "summer estate".

15

MUSIC

MUSIC FROM THE START

Since music was the primary focus of my mother's existence, it surrounded me from the start. It has been, and still is, a core part of my life. Not merely a hobby or a peripheral activity, it became increasingly important over the course of time. I do not qualify to be labeled a "musician", so much as to be called "music-involved". I have never been an accomplished or highly capable performer, but music in its many forms has been tremendously enjoyable, satisfying, and happily demanding.

LEARNING TO LOVE MUSIC

For me, it was important to have an understanding of any and all types of music, rather than to label a particular style or piece as "liked" or "disliked", an approach that has served me well.

Late in my self-employed era, I did some development work for Vic Firth, the iconic principle chair of the percussion section of the Boston Symphony Orchestra. When introduced to him the first time, as you've read here, he let me know in no uncertain terms that if I saw anyone around his shop with green hair I was to be especially kind to him, because he represented the type of musician that Vic's company served at that point. Green hair, in those days, of course spelled rock musician. Vic assumed that I was not a lover of rock music, and he was right. But he made sure that I understood the importance of the genre before taking me aboard to work on his products.

Another example of when my musical tastes were "challenged" by someone important also occurred in my Instrument Guild era. My largest client, Henry Kloss, was respected worldwide as a developer of high fidelity audio systems. Henry wanted to develop speakers for rock bands to amplify their low notes to an ear-splitting level. He asked me if we could apply the techniques used in the old-fashioned nautical foghorns–the type that could produce swooping, two-pitch growling tones, technically called diaphones. Henry himself despised the rock music, but he was open-minded enough to devote his energy to reproducing alternative music forms, whatever they might be, in the best possible way. In the end, however, his foghorn project proved to be technically impractical.

My first organized musical experience was singing choral music. Once hooked, I was then continually involved in choral and small group singing my whole life. Singing in choruses allowed me to witness the performance of some of the great leaders of the musical world, both conductors and soloists. Throughout the years, I sang under Serge Koussevitsky, Eugene Ormandy, Leonard Bernstein, Nadia Boulanger, Harvard's G. Wallace Woodworth, and Michigan's Thor Johnson. The most personally satisfying choral experiences that I had, however, were at my own home town churches–Follen Community Church and Hancock Church–where I found truly inspiring music directors and music projects.

Throughout my life I have been in and out of playing, developing, and constructing a variety of kinds of musical instruments, including brass, strings, woodwinds, percussion, and keyboard. The trumpet family of brass instruments was my primary instrument-playing focus. My secondary instrument was the recorder (more accurately termed the blockflute). I rang handbells, starting at prep school age playing Christmas music on Beacon Hill. The interest in handbells became increasingly serious when our family finally owned and used three octaves of the bells in later years.

I did a small amount of self-taught acoustic string bass playing in order to sample the great satisfaction of playing in small-group jazz. I even took up the oboe, taking lessons in the late 1950s, thinking that I might be able to expand my participation in Baroque literature. I quit when I found out that it damaged my embouchure for playing the trumpet. The recorder then gave me the satisfaction of playing a woodwind.

Playing double bass in a small jazz group.

GETTING STARTED IN PLAYING AN INSTRUMENT

Although choral music came first in my musical development, my mother insisted that I start studying a musical instrument at the age of about 11 years. She chose the violin since that instrument is a mainstay of the classical music genre. Somehow, she instinctively realized that I probably was not a candidate to tackle her own particular instrument, the piano. How she knew that mystifies me, and it certainly demonstrated her prescience. It turned out to be a particularly

288

apt decision since, as I grew older, I demonstrated an almost crippling inability to deal with the kind of multi-tasking playing of more than one note at a time (obviously a basic requirement for playing a keyboard instrument!). I now sadly realize that I should have tackled keyboard playing merely to support basic music skills. It is a little like learning to type at an early age so that one can survive the current information technology age.

I had absolutely no love for the violin. I had become awed by the trumpet's role in the Boston Symphony concerts that I was required to attend by my mother every Friday afternoon. Happily, by about 12 years old, I was allowed to shift allegiance to that instrument. I had the great privilege of taking lessons for about three years at the nearby Longy School of Music, taught by the first chair of the Boston Symphony Orchestra (BSO) trumpet section, M. Georges Mager. He was an extraordinarily accomplished musician and an inspiring individual, but I obviously was not accomplished enough for his expert level as a teacher. He was a kind individual, so there was no undue friction.

Eventually, he made a very wise pronouncement to me and to my mother that I was really not a candidate to become a trumpet player, and he essentially fired me as a student. He was busy with really good students such as Roger Voisin (who later succeeded him as principal in the BSO), Adolph Herseth (later principal trumpet in the Chicago Symphony), and Renold Schilke (later an important trumpet maker). My turndown by Mager did not seriously upset me because I realized he was right! I never really dared to find out my mother's reaction. However, I was now reset onto a more realistic and productive course. I realized that there was a difference between having the capacity to become a dedicated amateur and having the talent to become a true professional. I sought to attain an adequate proficiency as a trumpet player, as I still wanted to participate in instrumental music.

At Exeter in 1937, as previously mentioned, I found the help that I needed to address the apparent block in trumpet playing. I obtained the good services of a brass and woodwind teacher at the school who gave lessons in a variety of instruments. This man was a skilled troubleshooter, a rather unusual type of instrument teacher. His careful analysis of my problems and his suggestion of highly systemized drills gave me what I wanted: a working level of proficiency. The experience set the stage for a very important part of my music activity throughout the rest of my life.

Exeter gave me my first in-depth exposure to marching bands, dance bands, and choral singing. All three areas of music involvement also made a significant contribution to my social life since I was drawn together with young people from perhaps five other schools each year to give joint concerts, and to participate in dances and marching band events.

Certainly, my one high school summer as a "go-fer" for the Benny Goodman Band at the World's Fair in California was also an eye-opener for me into the inner workings of the big band era. It was a real music education to boot. Exposure to Fletcher Henderson's role as arranger and pianist was most fascinating. As I watched his career over the years, he became an early icon as a leader in introducing what was then called the "black sound" into mainstream popular music, which had been mostly represented by "white" styles up to that point. The chance to get to know Henderson was an experience I will never forget.

Music thus definitely became a large part of my preparatory school lifestyle, and was an area in which I could attain some degree of achievement. This was valuable since other phases of my Exeter schooling were far from distinguished. By the time I graduated, I was convinced that I wanted to continue to be "musically involved", but music definitely should not be my primary life's work, and certainly <u>not</u> my profession as a performer.

Left: Fletcher Henderson plays piano. Benny Goodman is to the right of the drummer.

MY EMERGENT CLASSICAL TRUMPET NICHE

The most common type of trumpet, pitched in B-flat, became my basic instrument. I played it in marching bands, symphonic bands and orchestras, celebratory bands, small brass groups, and dance bands. Drawing on my experience of watching Georges Mager play Baroque music, I also used a high trumpet pitched in G and very occasionally a four-valved piccolo trumpet pitched in A. Under circumstances where it was vital to preserve the Baroque atmosphere, I reluctantly played a "natural" (valveless) instrument pitched in D when asked to do so by fussy Baroque-addict conductors. While at the University of Michigan I used a cornet pitched in E-flat when playing the Sousa marches, as well as a mellophone, and occasionally a heraldic trumpet when participating in a showy parade. I used a flugelhorn to lead community singing, primarily outdoors at Christmas time. When in symphony situations, I played a trumpet pitched in C. I did a little bit of low brass instrument playing–bass trumpet, mellophone or baritone horn–as a fill-in when a band found themselves to be short in these instruments.

Post-WWII, an unexpected development in the Boston music scene turned out to be a real opportunity for me. Choral groups seemed to be everywhere, significant in the amateur concert scene. I wonder if, perhaps, the constraints on residents imposed by WWII triggered the movement. Literature for these choruses included the great Baroque oratorios and other works of Bach, Hayden, Handel, Purcell, Telemann, and Vivaldi. Many of these featured prominent trumpet parts, and many vocal arias and cantatas had wonderful trumpet obbligatos.

For some reason, there seemed to be a dearth of trumpet players who could (or perhaps wanted to) perform this type of music. It required playing in the instrument's high register and in a rather unusual style. It did not, however, typically require advanced playing techniques, in part because the music had been written in the era of the "natural" trumpet which is limited in its technical capability.

Taking a cue from Georges Mager, I obtained a French-built trumpet of higher pitch than usually played, pitched in G rather than B-flat or C. Many people who were playing the Baroque literature used piccolo trumpets pitched an octave above the usual B-flat trumpet in order to make it easier to play. I felt that those piccolo trumpets had a timbre (tonal quality) which was too thin and "squeaky" which, in my opinion, does not do justice to the beautiful music of the period. My G-trumpet, although perhaps more demanding, was closer to my ideal in timbre and one that very few players owned. I believe the sound of that particular instrument was the reason I was asked to play extensively in the Baroque music scene.

My high-pitched E-flat cornet playing of original Sousa March arrangements at Michigan gave me a real start at playing these special types of instruments. Furthermore, playing in the big dance band era had given me the endurance and range to meet the challenges of playing the Baroque literature. I very happily became a "niche" player in the classical musical scene, not only in Boston, but in many eastern cities.

My classical repertoire on trumpet eventually included works by J. S. Bach—the Mass in B-minor, Christmas Oratorio, Magnificat in D, many cantatas, chorales and arias featuring trumpet obbligatos, as well as his Brandenburg Concerto #2. I also mastered works by Handel— the Dettingen Te Deum, the Messiah, and Israel in Egypt—plus works such as Hayden's trumpet concerto, Hummel's trumpet concerto, Purcell's Trumpet Tune and Trumpet Voluntary (recently re-attributed to Purcell's copyist), as well as Vivaldi's Gloria.

THE BAND SAGA

Once underway with the trumpet, bands of all sorts became an obvious outlet for my playing hunger, a veritable saga of band playing developed. Exeter got me going in the marching/symphonic band genre, much of which is detailed in the Prep School chapter. Similarly, my intense exposure to, and participation in, very advanced marching and symphonic band playing is cited in the College Era chapter.

TOWN, DANCE AND REGIONAL BANDS

The institution of the town band has always attracted me. Playing in one is akin to joining a universal club like the Rotary. I occasionally took my trumpet with me on business trips and sat in with local town bands at night while my fellow travelers were at the local pubs. I also became an unofficial visitor/member of the bands of Huntsville, AL, Bath, ME, Dover, DE, and Lexington, MA.

I want to register a very strong "Thank Goodness" here for John Phillip Sousa. He wrote in a universal language that I had learned well and came to respect and love. Sousa's work might almost be deemed as "music Esperanto" since it was, and hopefully still is, "spoken" universally in every town band in the country. His work has, indeed, become a national treasure.

I now realize that dance bands came on the music scene after WWII, in some ways similar to the older town band organizations. Happily, I got caught up in that trend too, and played in such bands in Lincoln, MA, Wilmington, DE, and Bath, ME. I played in regional dance bands almost continually from about 1940 up to retirement.

NAVY SERVICE DANCE BAND WHILE OVERSEAS

In my continual attempt to diversify my efforts while aboard the repair ship during WWII, I organized a 12-piece dance band consisting of four saxes, four brass, and four rhythm instruments. With a lot of effort, we also put together a quartet of singers from within the band. We were inspired by the ever-present U.S. Armed Services band, fronted by Glenn Miller, who was broadcasting to us all the time over the British Broadcasting Network and Armed Forces Radio until his untimely death in plane crash in the English Channel. Through pure luck, we had qualified personnel in the existing crew for a band of this size and instrumentation.

I did a lot of music writing and arranging for our shipboard band as well as for the Army band that I also became associated with. We typically rehearsed aboard ship a couple of times a week and played for dances ashore several times a month. We also served as a sort of "symphonic band" to support chapel services and to play at various celebrations, both on board ship and ashore. We were more than a little short of "professional grade", but served an honest and well-received function.

ARMY DANCE BAND

While our dance band played at the inter-service officers' club ashore, I was invited to meet the Army sergeant who headed up the local Army dance band headquartered at a nearby field hospital just outside Weymouth. This was a no-nonsense group of about 16 members, including several professional musicians from the New York City studio scene, fronted by a well-known jazz harmonica player from the NYC radio studios. They were short a trumpet player so I gleefully joined them.

It was an eye-opening experience for me since I had never been around the U.S. Army before. I spent nights after each dance in an enlisted men's tent in spite of some hesitation on the part of my ship's captain. My tent mates put me through all the classic treatments famously used on newly enlisted Army recruits, such as the old routine of dropping only one shoe from the bunk above me to haunt me into sleeplessness. I even ate in the enlisted mess, all the time being razzed by my band mates. But it was a truly enjoyable time, and the musical standards and music quality were both good. The fellowship was outstanding.

Playing in the Army Dance Band. I am in the back row, third from the left. I was the only Navy man, and the only officer!

THE INTERCOLLEGIATE BIG DANCE BAND AT TUFTS

While teaching at Tufts, I played in what was probably the best dance band that I have ever been in. A Tufts undergraduate student had put together a 17-piece intercollegiate dance band, with four trumpets, three trombones, five saxes, four rhythm instruments, and a singer. It was made up of students from the New England and Boston Conservatories, plus students from Harvard and Tufts. I was the only non-professional-grade member, and thus I really had to sweat.

I played 4th trumpet, which was a challenge because the 4th chair generally played at the bottom of the trumpet register, only called upon occasionally to shift to the top or screaming end of the register to reinforce the unison parts played by my section colleagues. We played arrangements from the top-flight big bands of the era, such as the bands of Stan Kenton and Count Basie. In addition, the Conservatory students were doing a lot of writing in the super-big-band genre, so we were continually challenged. I did a little arranging, primarily in the Benny Goodman and Glenn Miller styles, which was rewarding because we had a good enough group to play it well.

HARVARD MARCHING AND SYMPHONIC BAND

While teaching at Tufts, I also had the joy of joining Harvard's marching and symphonic bands. I tried very hard to bring some features to Cambridge from my Michigan experience such as spirited fight cheers to be played at sports games by a brass choir. As I did while I was at Michigan,

I also made an attempt to introduce the marching band to the popular big band sound via special arrangements. That created something of a conflict with the Harvard academic band management (although my attempts to do the same with the University of Michigan were even worse!)

I had varied musical experiences playing in the Harvard band when it shifted into symphonic band mode for playing outdoors in the Harvard Yard at graduations, in holiday parades, and even performing occasional choral and instrumental concerts in Sanders Theatre. I performed the adagio movement of the Hayden Trumpet Concerto as soloist, where I found myself experiencing an especially grand feeling from the wonderful acoustics of Sanders Theatre's chamber. It was fascinating to become familiar with the story of those acoustics when, much later, I was working at the acoustics firm of Bolt, Beranek and Newman.

After struggling with notation taken from the original recording, I made a unsuccessful attempt to resurrect Bunny Berrigan's iconic big band theme-song "I Can't Get Started With You" for use with the Harvard Symphonic Band. We were never able to get it up to concert performance standard, in part because it was beyond my own soloing skills (in spite of those phrase-swapping sessions we practiced in the Michigan dormitory in years previous), and there was nobody else at Harvard who could or would play that wonderful Berrigan solo.

Playing with Harvard's band in its various modes (concert, marching and celebratory) certainly was gratifying, but it lacked some of the inspiring thrills I had experienced in my days at Michigan.

MUSIC SOIRÉES

SOIRÉES AT HOME AND IN THE COMMUNITY

Informal gatherings to make music are an important, long-held tradition in our family's musical life. The typical music soirée format was to invite competent musicians to gather, sight-read one or more significant works, rehearse the tricky parts, and finally perform the works for the pleasure of the musicians themselves with no formal audience necessarily involved.

I first experienced my mother's soirées in which she gathered skilled choral singers in the large double room in our spacious house in Cambridge. I was encouraged to sit in. She continued the soirées in the Argilla Road community in Ipswich when we moved to my parents' summer house in nearby Essex. Later, Alice and I took part in the famous "sings" at

organizing music—

Henry Drinker's house in Merion, PA, when we were first married and living in nearby Wilmington, DE. Still later we participated in the well-known choral sight-reading gatherings hosted by Klaus Goetze in Cambridge.

Once settled in Lexington, Alice and I picked up the choral soirée tradition. We regularly assembled a chorus of about 30 with an orchestra of six to ten instrumentalists. We first held the soirées in our house, then at the deCordova museum in Lincoln and in the Lexington public library. We enjoyed the conducting services of some prominent musicians who seemed to welcome the experience. When gathering in public places we encouraged audiences to attend, more or less in the style of an "open rehearsal". We worked our way through music such as Bach cantatas, and parts of the oratorios of Handel, Hayden, Purcell, and Vivaldi.

In parallel with the choral gatherings, we had several chamber music soirées. These typically involved getting chamber music-sized orchestras together in our house or at local public facilities. We played standard compositions written for small orchestral groups such as J.S. Bach's Brandenberg Concertos.

A Missed Cue

I was performing one of my favorite choral pieces, J.S. Bach's Christmas Oratorio (BWV 248), in the First Congregational Church in Cambridge. My close colleague, Bob Pyle, was singing in the choir and also scheduled to solo on the French horn in the wonderful chorale which features a famous horn obbligato.

As the horn is used only once in that three-hour piece, Bob had carefully stashed his instrument in a back room of the church so he could sing the early part unencumbered. He sneaked out at the appropriate time to warm up on the horn without being heard by those in the audience. He did not come back. The conductor woefully halted the performance and we sweated it out as we awaited Bob's return. As I had my case of four high trumpets, each of different pitch, with me, I thought I might be able to fill in for Bob even though I might have to play an octave too high. After a somewhat awkward discussion with the conductor within earshot of the mystified audience, we reluctantly agreed to go ahead, with me struggling and unrehearsed, on my substitute instrument. The performance went very well. Later we learned that the sexton had been called home early. He had carefully locked the back room, not knowing that Bob's horn was in there!

Lexington's Messiah Sing

In 1962, Alan Lannom, a Lexington neighbor and conductor of the Boston University chorus and Lexington Masterworks Chorale, started a Lexington tradition of inviting the public to participate in sight-reading Handel's oratorio, Messiah, with invited soloists and a full orchestra (usually around 50 specially invited instrumentalists). This has been held annually ever since. (I have heard that Alice was involved in getting this event going, but I do not recall the details of what she did!)

This "sing" is quite amazing in that Lexington's Town Hall, seating about 780, is filled to capacity for Friday evening and again on Saturday evening, two weeks before Christmas. The whole auditorium is urged to participate, using choral scores rentable as one enters the hall. For about 20 years I played the trumpet in those happy occasions, sweating out the infamous "The Trumpet Shall Sound" duet with the bass soloist many times.

I must confess, corny that it may sound, that the annual Lexington Messiah sing was an unbelievable thrill to me–playing the high trumpet over a roomful of almost 800 singers!

MUSIC BUSINESS VENTURES

WHY HARPSICHORDS?

In the post-WWII era, Boston became a hub for Baroque music, and thus attracted at least six builders of harpsichords to the area. Since I was continually playing this genre of music, I kept running into the inherent difficulties that the harpsichords presented. The two most damaging problems were their tuning instability (sensitivity to temperature and humidity changes) and their innate inability to be loud enough to survive the acoustic demands of many of the performance sites. Accordingly, in my home shop, I did some development work on amplifying the instrument and on using more stable building materials.

Several of my colleagues at the acoustics firm of Bolt Beranek and Newman were intrigued with the effort and gave me substantial help in both aspects of the project. An expert on acoustic and vibration sensors directed me toward some novel pickups to amplify the instruments, while another helped in selecting materials and design concepts for stabilizing tuning.

In trying to improve tuning stability, I built some test instrument frame structures to subject them to extreme temperature fluctuations. I created the test conditions by moving the bulky test models into the local beer and wine store's large refrigerator, much to the entertainment of our nearby liquor dealers!

Through the kindness of one of Alice's aunts who lived in the Chicago area, I was able to try out the instrument for adequate acoustic levels in large performance halls. I set the harpsichord up for Conductor Fritz Reiner on the stage of a Chicago concert hall and he tried it while the hall was empty. He noted the sound, and its quality and level. He encouraged me to continue development since he thought any work to overcome the traditional instrument's fundamental limitations might make harpsichords become useful additions to today's classical music concert scene.

A CLASSIC MISTAKE

One difficult situation arose in trying out a tuning-stabilized and amplified harpsichord in Philadelphia. I cannot recall how exactly I got into this situation, but in the late 1960s I was invited to submit a prototype for evaluation by the Philadelphia Orchestra. I ended up having to "mother" the instrument in its trial.

The orchestra was rehearsing in its usual locale, the so-called "mirror room", upstairs in the Curtis Institute, Philadelphia's major conservatory of music. (Why they rehearse there, I will never know. It seems to me to be the worst possible venue. It is a large, ballroom-like space lined floor to ceiling with glass mirrors which produce overbearing reflective acoustics when such a monstrous orchestra plays there.)

My job was to tune the instrument just before Bill Smith, Eugene Ormandy's Assistant Conductor, played it to accompany Yehudi Menuhin rehearsing the J.S. Bach D-Major Violin Concerto. I had a window of only a few minutes to perform the tuning while the orchestra and its conductor briefly caught their breaths between two rehearsal numbers. I was not permitted silence in the room since it was only a brief break, so I had the correct tools—a contact microphone on the soundboard plugged into an ultra-modern electronic stroboscopic tuning machine which would allow me to tune very accurately, very fast, and under very noisy conditions. Even with all that ideal equipment, I was severely pressed.

When my window of time ran out, the orchestra manager hastily removed me from my tuning position and I sat down next to Menuhin's wife in the back of that miserable room. When Bill Smith played several chords on the instrument to make sure that it was in order, he discovered that, under acute duress, I had selected the wrong frequency on the tuning meter for all the D notes. Most unfortunately, these D's were the tonic "home base" of the concerto that Menuhin was about to play!

Conductor Ormandy hastily restarted the orchestra to rehearse the concerto. Menuhin's wife, sitting beside me, warned that things were about to explode since her husband had a short fuse. Bill Smith, the ultimate "cool cat", did not call time out, but reached for the tuning hammer (the wrench-like hand tool used for adjusting the tuning). While actively accompanying the soloist, he coolly retuned all the D's.

All I could do was to sit still and sweat—which I did—profusely!

THE ORGAN WORLD

My wanderings into pipe organ building and repairing might be labeled as a side adventure. The more I played Baroque trumpet throughout New England, the more I became frustrated with pipe organ problems—their tuning, maintenance, and design as well as their fundamental influence on the functioning of churches and concert halls.

The rebuilt Follen organ console.

One of the most critical organ problems I ran into was at the Follen Community Church in Lexington. The church had been operating on a severely limited budget and yet had an outstanding musical presence in the greater Boston community. This antique Colonial building was noted for its acoustic characteristics and for its stunning octagonal design. Follen was continually sought out as a concert site by the musical community. Its organ, however, was far from adequate to support the church's musical efforts. Accordingly, I organized an effort to rebuild the instrument for the church.

The Follen organ was a packaged instrument common in the small churches of the U.S., built in the 1930s by the Frazee Company of Natick, MA. Technically speaking, it was a pipe organ with a disposition of four ranks, using electro-pneumatic action, played from a "highly borrowing" (or unified) two-manual console, equipped with a 32-note radial pedal board. The console was attached to a 12-foot wide, six-foot deep, 15-foot high swell chamber located at the center/back of the chancel floor of the sanctuary. Because the chancel floor

The Follen organ pipes, finally out in the open for all to see, after we rebuilt the instrument.

was stepped, and several curved rows of choir pews were located on those steps, the console was literally hidden from sight.

This instrument was a classic problem seeking a solution, and the congregation of the church knew it. Looking for an advisor on the subject, we turned to Fritz Noack, a well-regarded organ builder whose shop was then in Georgetown, MA. He did a thoughtful and thorough job of looking around and explaining the various alternatives available to us. Noack was definite that the current instrument should be replaced. He explained a variety of ways to proceed, including installing a rebuilt antique instrument which would be in harmony with the fine antique nature of the building, or, alternatively, building a tasteful small instrument specifically designed for the task. He prophesized that very little of the existing instrument could be reused in any properly upgraded installation. He estimated that even the most modest program would cost at least $50,000.

At that time, the Follen Church's entire annual operating budget totaled only $50,000 per year. We already knew we were facing considerable capital expenditures for building repairs and expansion of the facility to accommodate the rapidly growing size of the congregation. An organ budget of this magnitude seemed far beyond what we could undertake.

We sought further counsel. This time, if I remember correctly, we turned to Barbara Owen, an established organ consultant living in or near Newburyport, Mass. Once she understood the overall picture, she suggested a builder with demonstrated ability to deal with situations such as ours–Gene Kelley, a part-time builder living in North Andover.

Kelley and an organist, Gary McDonald, took a very careful look. After long and searching talks with me, they suggested that I could probably build a proper instrument with help from volunteer church members. Kelley would be willing to oversee and act as an adviser on the project. He also had a large stock of used parts, including critical pipes, stashed away in a warehouse in Haverhill, that would be available at modest prices. He felt that the total cost to the church would be in

WANTED: NIMBLE-FINGERED VOLUNTEERS

Being an electro-pneumatic action instrument, there was an unbelievably complex maze of wiring to go in the new console of the organ. As could only have taken place in our good old Follen Church, congregation members responded to our call for volunteers with an unusual idea. The church had an active knitting club, and this highly dexterous group gladly volunteered to do the complicated job of wiring and soldering approximately 1,000 wires! I laid out the task for them, and delivered the bits and pieces to the group's organizer. She then supervised the work. Success!

Somehow the instrument came together into playable shape and lasted for five or ten years, requiring a certain amount of loving care from me and some help from members of the congregation. I used to check it out early each Sunday morning, and tune it before each concert or important musical event.

Much to my relief, with thanks for some real work on the part of a later organist, Follen's instrument was finally replaced with a proper new organ, which is the sort of instrument which really should be in that elegant space. It is a rebuilt organ from the mid-19th century which probably would have cost us in excess of $75,000 back in the days of our alternative building effort.

the range of $10,000 to $20,000 as long as I, plus members of the congregation, did the actual construction work ourselves. So we jumped in.

The first job was to clear out the existing instrument. It was summertime, so the church was not holding services. Son Nick and I went to the church, making sure that nobody was around. We carefully removed all the organ pipes by stacking the rugged large wooden ones in the rear of the sanctuary, carefully coddling the delicate smaller pipes in carrying trays. We then tied a rope to the top of the organ case and ceremoniously pulled it over onto the floor of the chancel, producing a large cloud of choking dust. To our surprise, this exposed the fact that there had not been any real structure holding up the chancel floor–the choir had been perilously perched on a grossly inadequate structure for more than a century!

Gene Kelley designed an instrument with ranks of pipes to be blown by the existing wind chests, and added one more rank to sit on a new wind chest that could be easily built in my Instrument Guild shop. The whole pipe array was then packaged into a single organ body unit about 10-feet wide, five feet high, and four feet deep. We mounted the body unit on casters so that it could be rolled around and put anywhere on the chancel floor.

We packaged up a new blower and its attendant accordion-like, pressure-regulated air accumulator, quieted it with a lot of BB&N's acoustic insulation, and put it within the body unit. Kelley then specified a two-manual console which could use the existing keyboards plus the existing 32-note pedal board, all housed in a new case, that could be moved around since it was connected to the remotely located pipe body unit by a group of five to ten long telephone cables. This gave us all the flexibility we needed to accommodate a variety of events in the chancel area, including Sunday services, concerts, and slide shows.

Kelley was striving to produce sounds that could be used for music from the Baroque era up through the music of the turn-of-the century French classical masters. To do this, he had reduced the wind pressure, revoiced some of pipes from the old instrument, added a lot of pipes from his extensive collection in storage in Haverhill, and dispatched me down to western Maryland to pick up some classy new reed-style pipe work.

A SIDE TRIP INTO THE BUILDING AND REPAIRING OF PIPE ORGANS

As a partial "payment" to Gene Kelley who had helped us so much during the construction of the interim Follen organ, I started volunteering my services to him in several of his interesting organ rebuilding projects. I had a pickup truck and moving equipment which he badly needed. After a while, it became sort of a sport for me as the increasingly intriguing projects became more challenging. I ended up participating in perhaps five or six of Kelley's projects all over New England over about a five-year period.

ORGAN IN LEXINGTON'S FIRST PARISH CHURCH

The First Parish Church in Lexington had an iconic antique organ built in the mid-1880s which needed continual loving care. When I was working at Arthur D. Little in 1960, my boss asked me to stand in for him during an organ committee meeting at the church. As happens, I found myself irrevocably involved with the "care and feeding" of that instrument from then on!

ORGAN CONTROVERSIES

During the 20th century the organ, as a musical instrument, went through a number of controversies. Its expense was continually in question, the technology of its mechanism was under continual development, its musical importance was undergoing considerable change, and its general role as "King of Instruments" was under constant re-evaluation. The situation was fascinating as well as challenging, and I found myself hooked, trying to comprehend what was going on.

In the late 1930s, a sort of counter-culture emerged in which a small number of pipe organ builders and prominent organists looked back at older organ construction techniques, organ specifications, designs, and tonal qualities of the pipework. They began to produce instruments which seemed to give much of the older established organ literature a renewed life which was especially attractive to discerning listeners. These instruments were generically labeled "tracker-action" instruments—a backward-looking label reflecting the ancient mechanical (as opposed to the more recent electrical or pneumatic) connection from the keyboard to the pipes.

I got thoroughly caught up in this arcane controversy in the process of working on the instruments. We kept coming up with repair, rebuild, or specification situations where the controversy arose. I must admit, however, that exposure to organ technology has made me listen in a different way than I used to, and to come to worship the Handel organ concertos played on a tracker action instrument as among the most wonderful sounds in music.

I also worked with some of the emerging electronic/electric instruments, as well as restoration of some features in antique instruments to improve modern instrument playability while producing historic timbres. I dealt with some of the bureaucratic limitations imposed on the acquisition and use of the instruments by hierarchical religious denominations. I volunteered in efforts to save valuable pipework when historically successful antique instruments were being torn down. This organ work was a rich experience.

Further dissertation on the resulting controversies is not really called for here in this memoir, but I have watched the situation closely throughout my life and participated in several unusual aspects of what was going on. I witnessed a Catholic Church dictum excluding trackers. I ran into repeated snobbism regarding pipe organs as compared to electric/electronic organs. I became disgusted with the "mine's bigger" or show-off aspect of organs of any stripe.

MY POSITIF ORGAN

While playing trumpet, singing in choruses, and doing organ repairs in the Baroque music scene, it became increasingly apparent to me that there was a need for a tastefully voiced small pipe organ. It needed to be readily transportable, and thus available to fill in when a performance site either had no organ or, more likely, when there were problems with the organ already there. I constructed a one-manual, single-rank, three-stop instrument which I could carry around in my pickup truck.

That little instrument became really useful. It traveled several times to Lexington's First Parish Church where the elegant organ already there had been set at the antique tuning pitch of 430 Hertz, which was lower than today's standard "A" of 440 Hertz. Orchestral instruments playing with that antique organ would be out of tune.

Similarly, the positif was used in choral concerts several times in the Wellesley College chapel, which already had two organs. One was a show-piece modern reproduction of an antique instrument, tuned to a much lower pitch than now used. The second, a very large modern instrument, was in such poor repair that it was not reliable.

We also used the positif for our soirées at our house in Lexington as well as in the Lexington Town Hall when doing the annual Messiah sings, and occasionally at local schools which did not already have organs.

JANE LANGTON AND "DIVINE INSPIRATION"

One amusing incident relating to organs involved Jane Langton, the author of a series of mystery stories for which the Boston area was usually the site. I had known Jane for a long time, since she had married a classmate of mine from Michigan. I had also worked for her father while at I was at DuPont.

One day, Jane phoned to ask, "Caleb, how can I arrange to murder a man using an organ?" Now here was a unique request!

I took Jane to Lexington's First Parish Church where I demonstrated that if a person was working on the valve mechanisms underneath the organ pipes (a frequent upkeep job) and the organ air blower was turned on, the person could be squeezed to death by the accordion-like bellows of the air pressure regulator. I then took her up to the Episcopal Cathedral in Nashua, NH, and walked her into the air pressure buffer chamber/room located under the pipes which is tightly sealed to prohibit air leaks. This is a soundproofed hidden space where some poor victim could be attacked and murdered without anybody elsewhere in the church hearing that anything was wrong.

Jane did, indeed, write a fascinating mystery novel, using the organ as a killer. She decided, however, not to use the methods that I had demonstrated. Instead, she chose an even more imaginative solution. In the book the killing is accomplished by an organ which topples over when the wooden pilings under the church rot out due to encroaching groundwater. (Groundwater encroachment had indeed happened to Boston's Trinity Church in Copley Square when the John Hancock tower office building was being constructed nearby.)

The amusing title of her book, "Divine Inspiration" refers to a detail in her plot in which the person who rebuilt the damaged organ adds an extra non-functioning dummy organ stop draw-knob to the console. It is labeled "Divine Inspiration" so that the organist could pull it out to salve his frustration if he got into trouble playing the instrument!

THE ATTRACTION OF HANDBELLS

HANDBELL-RINGING SOIRÉES

Handbells, of course, have been a part of my life since my pre-teen years, and ringing handbells was a logical activity to do in the soirée mode. Alice and I also hosted perhaps five or six offbeat handbell sessions. We limited participants to really experienced musicians, many of whom had staunchly avoided bell ringing previously as perhaps "below their standard of musicianship".

This kind of music-making solved several problems. We found we could attract really competent, otherwise busy musicians who could not commit to regular rehearsal schedules. The lack of an audience eliminated the threat of embarrassment that attends many as they first try to ring bells, as skilled musicianship does not automatically promote proficiency at handbell ringing.

The bells have been used for decades by our young family, the greater family, and by friends and music colleagues. Playing at a family reunion, from left to right, back row: Susie Allen, Hilda Warner, Mary Gorham with daughter Charlotte, Molly Warner. Front row: Alice, Lib Allen.

We recognized that the intense or continual handbell ringing can wear pretty thin on many people (as we have seen not only in our own family, but in several other groups as well). All in all, I chose not to start a true standing/organized handbell choir. This *ad hoc* approach seemed preferable.

Our handbell sessions were rather fun since we did bell "reductions" that I had worked hard to notate. We played interesting works not usually done by bells, such as the splendid Randall Thompson "Alleluia".

HANDBELLS NOW

Having learned that we could easily pull together a bell choir on an "as-needed" basis, we offered to ring for memorial services in several churches in the Lexington area. Surprisingly, the people that volunteered to participate included several of the local church organists, choral conductors, and professional musicians who would not normally have come together under other conditions. For the participants, it turned out to be a satisfying effort. We did this on and off for about ten years.

Today, in later life, I am working on bringing handbell ringing to the elder population. For several years, I have led a handbell ringing group at my retirement community. This great group of fellow residents and I have played at various events, including several memorial services. They have helped me shape new ideas on accommodating the physical challenges of aging to make the bellringing experience an enjoyable one for all.

For greater detail and a few examples of handbell music adapted for my elder friends, see the end of this chapter.

MUSIC AND SOUND TECHNOLOGY

OTHER USES OF TECHNICAL AND MUSICAL SKILLS

Several times each year for about 50 years, I played Baroque style trumpet in a variety of church services, including weddings, memorial services, and high holiday services. I participated as a trumpet player in choral concerts and recitals in Massachusetts, New Hampshire, Connecticut, New York State, Pennsylvania, and Maryland. I can only guess that I played in probably something over 150 performances in that half century.

Realizing my limitations, I wanted to remain labeled as an amateur as a matter of principle, so typically I was not paid. In order to play "union-only" performances I had to join the Boston Musicians' Union, but I turned any money I received back as a donation to whatever organization was sponsoring the performance.

Technically, I have been intimately involved in designing, building, improving, and operating public address systems for use in music since the 1950s. At various times, I did meaningful work in projects involving acoustics and in building audio devices. I have also done quite a lot of arranging of music over the years for various combinations of instruments in various genres, including marching band, dance band, symphonic band, and handbells. Unfortunately, I have a scanty record of composing except for a bit in the areas of marching band and big dance bands.

The routines of harpsichord and organ tuning taught me much about the physics of music, enabling me to perform piano tuning, which I have turned to good advantage. At one point, for about five years, I raised over a thousand dollars a year for the Follen Church by tuning local pianos.

The skill of piano tuning has also been useful since I can help out when an ill-tuned instrument is threatening the assembled musicians as they attempt to perform. (It is amazing how many times this situation has arisen.) I like to taunt my musical colleagues by telling them the skilled tuner's well-kept secret—that the best tuner is someone who can systematically *dis*-tune the apparently out-of-tune musical instrument to make it sound better. (This is inexplicably called "stretching"!)

These days, I continue to arrange music and have become fascinated with digital music notation. My burgeoning interest has been supported by my nephew and friend, Peter Ecklund, who works in the field. I have taught myself to use digital notation on my home computer and have found it particularly useful in the rather specialized type of handbell ringing that we have done here at Carleton-Willard.

MUSIC UPS AND DOWNS

ESPECIALLY MEMORABLE MUSIC EXPERIENCES

Several performances stick out in my mind as especially memorable. In the mid-1960s we were blessed with the presence of Douglas Cheek, a terminally ill Harvard undergraduate student who became a special family member. He did a lot for and with our family for five solid years, summer and winter. He really played the role of a third parent to our children.

When Douglas finally died at the age of 25, I had the difficult job of going to his home in Virginia to represent our family at his hometown memorial service. It was a difficult and heartbreaking situation for me.

I hustled back to Lexington right after the service and drove from the airport directly to Lexington's Town Hall, skidding in just in time to play the trumpet in the annual Messiah Sing. I was deeply afraid that I might not be able to make it through the stirring last twenty minutes of Handel's masterpiece which contains the Halleluiah Chorus, the "Trumpet Shall Sound", and that trumpeter's lip-killing "Amen". For some reason, it went beautifully and I was relieved and truly happy about it. The incident was capped by a remark the next day from our church choir director. "What the devil lifted you up so high last night?"

One of the most moving musical occasions occurred as we played handbells at the memorial service for Alice's beloved brother, Ted Sizer. The service was held at Harvard's Memorial Church on November 21, 2009. The church was filled, and a broad variety of music–choral singing, solo singing, and solo instrumental music, in addition to handbell ringing–was all provided by Sizer family members. Happily, we were able to accommodate family of all ages and musical skill levels in our handbell choir for this important family memorial service.

THE ULTIMATE LOW AND THE ULTIMATE HIGH

Probably the lowest point in my trumpet playing occurred in April of 1952 when we were living in Wilmington, DE. I was feeling my way into what became my "niche" field in high trumpet playing of the Baroque oratorios. Rather naively, I accepted an invitation to play the Bach Magnificat at nearby Haverford College. The timing of the performance, however, could not have been worse. As it turned out, Alice went into labor, and I had to break away from her to go and perform. Shortly thereafter, she gave birth to our first-borne child, Langdon, back in Wilmington, about 25 miles away from the concert site. I frankly am hazy about the details, but I definitely messed up the performance!

The highest point was a performance of the Bach Mass in B Minor in the early 1960s. I was invited to play first chair in the performance by the Lexington Choral Society in the Auditorium of the Lexington High School. Allen Lannom was conducting. The iconic Eunice Alberts was among the soloists. The orchestra members were all professional players–except me, of course–in a standing group which played in most of the suburban choral concerts around the Boston area. (I think they may have used the name "Cambridge Symphony".) This was the occasion for which I joined the Musician's Union in order to be permitted to play.

Exactly one month before the dress rehearsal, I became bed-ridden and quarantined with Hepatitis C. My doctors told me I would be confined, and should stay quiet for 30 days but luckily I got permission from them to practice the trumpet daily. And that is exactly what I did. It was probably the most intensive practice that I ever managed to do. Out of desperation, I thought back to my days at Exeter while working under that methodical "repairman" trumpet teacher who told me that if I ever faced a difficult trumpet playing assignment I should grow a mustache which would strengthen my embouchure. So I added mustache growing to my daily tasks while cooped up trying to beat the Hepatitis.

I had the great luxury of having an excellent second chair who I felt to be a much more skillful player than I was, but was inexperienced at playing this genre of music. He was technically very good and intellectually geared up to learn from the situation. He was a recent graduate of one of the Boston conservatories and shortly after our concert became first chair in one of the New England city symphonies. We worked out a rather complicated lead-swapping routine, whereby I was given a rest just as we approached the high-register sections. There is no way that I can adequately describe the outright thrill of playing the trumpet in that particular piece of music. Let us just leave it at that. Happily, the performance went very well and justified the intense effort that I had put into preparing for it.

CONNECTIONS TO THE MUSICAL INSTRUMENT INDUSTRY

Looking back, I now realize that I have had a rather fascinating look at the musical instrument industry. I got to know quite a bit about two of the giants in the industry: Steinway and Baldwin. I visited the Steinway plant on Long Island regarding possible designs of soundboards for the modernized harpsichords under development by the Cannon Guild. I visited the Baldwin headquarters when it was still in Cincinnati, in the process of selling the Cannon Guild to Baldwin.

I became entangled with the woodwind industry when Friederich von Huene was a client during the Instrument Guild era, and I worked on recorder production problems at the Von Huene shop. Friederich kindly passed me on to Powell Flutes when Powell wanted to diversify into building instruments other than flutes. Friederich also passed me on to Haynes Flute Company where I also worked on modernizing production processes.

I am still not exactly sure how it happened, but I ended up with percussion instrument maker Vic Firth as a very interesting client. I also became active in the pipe organ industry and had a "near-miss" experience with the brass industry in dealing with Vincent Bach. I regularly went to the International Music Products Association trade shows and I also participated in the Boston Early Music Festival concerts.

I consider myself to be fortunate to have been involved with so many aspects of our very extraordinary music industry.

MUSIC: THOSE ROADS NOT TAKEN

TEMPTATION AT THE END OF WW II

Just as WWII ended, my ship was in the Brooklyn Navy Yard preparing to go to the Pacific Theatre. I considered how I might pursue music, once released from my Navy duty. I looked around the New York City area for interesting musical opportunities. I had become really interested in group singing in the big band genre, such as The Modernaires, The Four Freshmen, and The Singers Unlimited. They fascinated me. By then, I had accumulated quite a lot of experience in arranging and performing in group singing with both the Navy and Army bands while on duty in Europe.

Fred Waring was auditioning in his NYC studios for singers for his extensive radio shows. I was tempted to audition, and I even found out how and when auditions were taking place. However, I finally came to my senses and reluctantly decided that was not a wise move. This was a haunting decision, and I have many times wondered what would have happened if I had followed my temptation to audition.

THAT DISAPPOINTING NEAR MISS: THE VINCENT S. BACH, CO.

Turning down the offer to buy the Vincent Bach musical instrument firm was one of the more frustrating situations of my professional life. I am aware that I probably could not have pulled it off successfully, especially in light of my subsequent performance in business management, but it remains one more of those difficult choices that seemed to challenge me all too frequently.

THE ROLE OF MUSIC IN MY LIFE

I firmly believe that any major lifetime activity should provide accomplishment, opportunity to look backward to gain from experience, progress toward the future, and a reasonable amount of enjoyable thrill. Music has done each one of those things for me.

Much of my classical music activity involved the Baroque period, taking me well back into significant times in music history where I found much to learn and to enjoy. My experience in the popular music field was strongly influenced by the privilege of playing in the big band genre, much of it based on the music of the 1930s-50s, essentially at the start of today's popular music. My venturing into computer-aided notation, my exposure to the digital handling of sound, and my attempts at modernizing instrument design and construction all gave me an opportunity to progress forward. Playing the trumpet is unbelievably thrilling, while I found close-harmony group singing similarly satisfying.

My extensive, continuing activity and accomplishment in music was, and continues to be, an important and worthwhile part of my life.

Playing the high trumpet at a church rehearsal.

Above: Playing the recorder with accompaniment by one of
my harpsichords at the Follen Church in Lexington.
Right: The recorder was my second instrument.
This one was made by Von Huene.
Below: As a boy at school, in the Exeter Marching Band.
I am in the second to top row, second from the right.

Navy Dance Band. I am in the back row, third from right, holding my trumpet. This group was used for all occasions on board when music was needed: memorial services, shore side dances, military parades, church services, and more.

The Wilmington, Delaware dance band. I am in the second row, far right.

THE USE OF HANDBELLS IN AN ELDERLY COMMUNITY

With the comparatively recent (1902) introduction in this country and with their increasing use, handbells offer an opportunity to assuage a musical hunger which is ever-present in a community of elders such as we have at Carleton-Willard Village, the retirement community in which I live. When I introduced handbell ringing to our residents, we stumbled into intriguing challenges, and together we overcame them with some innovative solutions.

There are many ardent music listeners who are interested in playing handbells. Some have the musical

Bell rack.

skills to read and perform music, while others are challenged by the notation, exact timing, or rhythm that bell ringing requires. This mix of levels of skill is addressed as I have done in the past by introducing another instrument, such as a flute or recorder, over the bells as a soloist, played by a more experienced musician.

To assist in reading and understanding the written music, I color-code notation on the player's page (red when the bell in the player's right hand is to be played, blue when the left is to be played), and various other colors for additional bells that must be picked up off the table or put down as needed. Over the years, I have found this method of color-coding has worked effectively with individuals of all abilities.

In addition, I have tried something new. Using computer software, I experimented with the idea of re-arranging various well-known pieces of music into an extraordinarily simple format, using only quarter notes, and in only 4/4 time. This may look "sinful" to some upon glancing at the music, but works quite well when used as accompaniment to a good soloist.

Again, we have enabled elder bellringers to participate, and to succeed with satisfaction. The handbell player is left with the enjoyment of participating in music, without the curse of overly difficult performance demands.

The sharp wrist motion necessary to ring a handbell demands physical capabilities of a joint often challenged by aging. Furthermore, if we are using an adequate range of bells, some of the lower-pitched bells will be large and thus too heavy for an elder player to handle.

We developed special racks to hold the handbells off the bell-choir table, with the bell mouths pointed toward the players, so they can be played using a mallet. This setup unburdens a players' wrist and accommodates heavy or overly large bells. A physically challenged player can participate, even if limited to being seated or in a wheelchair.

Handbell ringing by an elder population of varying musical abilities and physical challenges can be done successfully and to the satisfaction of both the bellringers and their audience.

THE HARMONIC CHANGE RING: THE STORY

I wrote this Harmonic Change Ring in 1962 when our family acquired its first set of bells. The piece is so easy to play that we have used it for many years to introduce people to handbell ringing. It creates an unusual atmosphere which has been useful on many occasions, including memorial services and celebratory situations, most effectively in echoing church sanctuaries.

It is based on "St. Paul's Steeple," a familiar nursery song with a tune and in the style typically associated with church tower bells ringing in celebration. The tune starts out with a simple downwards musical scale followed by a set of mathematical sequences called "changes." Following the style of change ringing developed in the 17th century, no attempt is made to produce a conventional melody or harmony or introduce the complication of rhythmic variation.

In this composition, I have used simple change ringing techniques and developed them from the beginning up to Measure 28. (See measure numbers marked at the start of each line, or "brace," on the sheets of music.) The result is a sort of "tease" in the 17th century style of tower bell ringing.

I then venture into more modern forms of harmonic construction. Tower bells, which are huge, very heavy, and relatively slow to sound, are played one at a time. Moreover, they are only roughly tuned in any conventional sense, with overtones which "swear" at each other if two or more bells are played simultaneously. Handbells are agile in the speed with which they can be played, with elegant timbre and fine tuning, so harmonic combinations are pleasing to the ear. This allowed me to branch out from Measure 28 onward in 9-measure groups, using modern "close" harmonic progressions such as those characterizing American dance band music since the 1920s. The successive styles in this piece are:

Measures	Style	When/How Used
1-28	Traditional change ringing	Tower bells, principally in Britain
28-37	Dixieland	New Orleans in the 1920s
37-46	Commercial dance bands	Early 1930s
46-55	Commercial dance bands	Late 1930s into the 1940s
55-64	Glenn Miller	Early in the Big Band era
64-73	Stan Kenton	Middle of the Big Band era
73-82	Woody Herman	Late in the Big Band era
82-87	Coda	Conventional way to wrap up

The bottom line of music on the page—a three-octave descending scale—is not to be played. It provides a convenient way to indicate which player plays which bell.

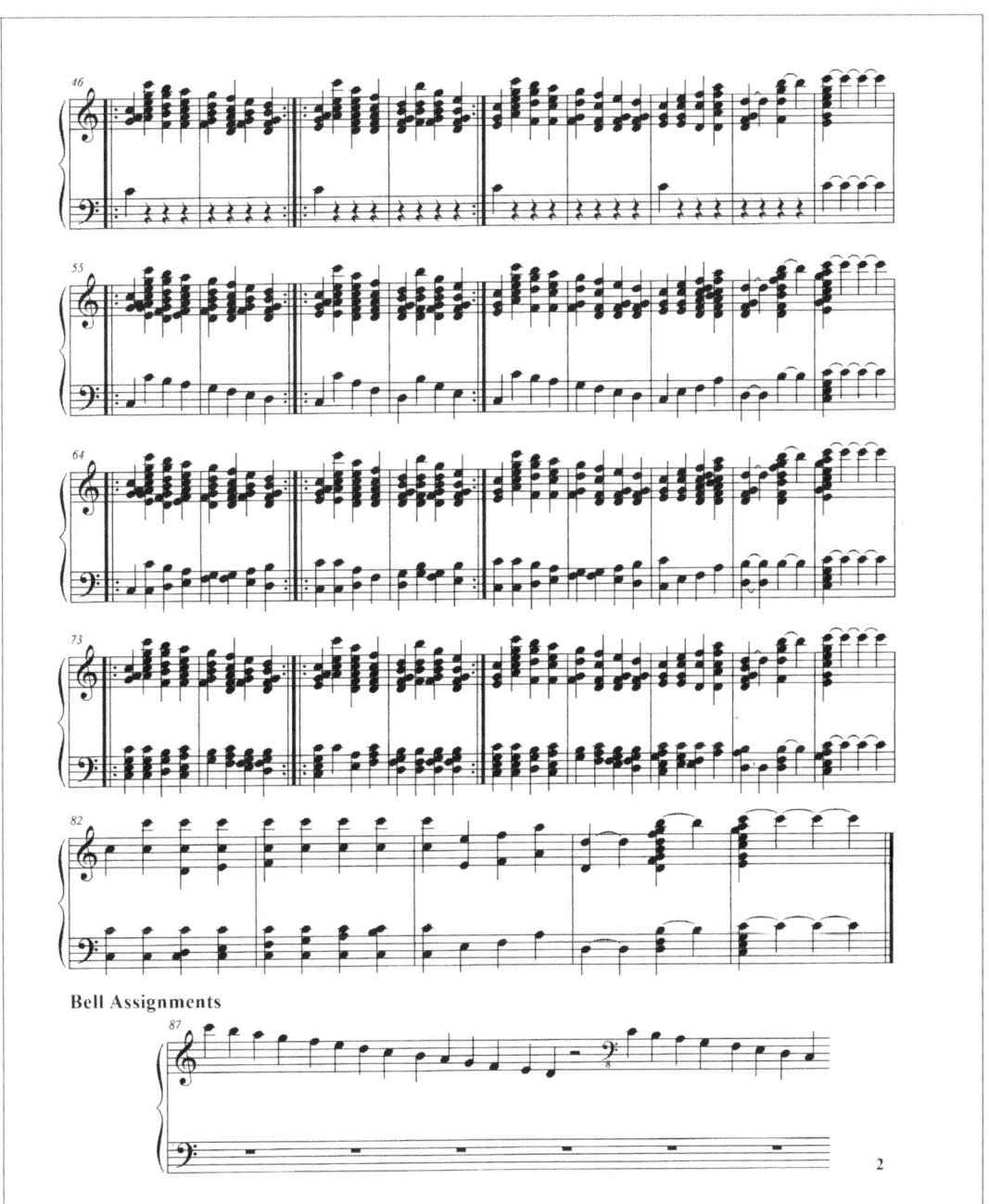

Bell Assignments

Simplified part for one player, making it easy to read and play. There are eleven different parts, one for each player, for this piece, for a total of 22 bells, two bells per person, three octaves.

This piece is sung in many different Christian churches, and is shown here as originally attributed to its composer, John Stainer. I have marked the notes in the music for the player whose bell assignment is shown at the bottom of the piece.

Jesu Joy of Man's Desiring was written by J.S. Bach for an obbligato instrument, choir, and organ or orchestra. My arrangement, here, allows a handbell choir, even an inexperienced one, to play the choir part as well as to back up the obbligato instrument.

Bell Assigment:

B5 C6

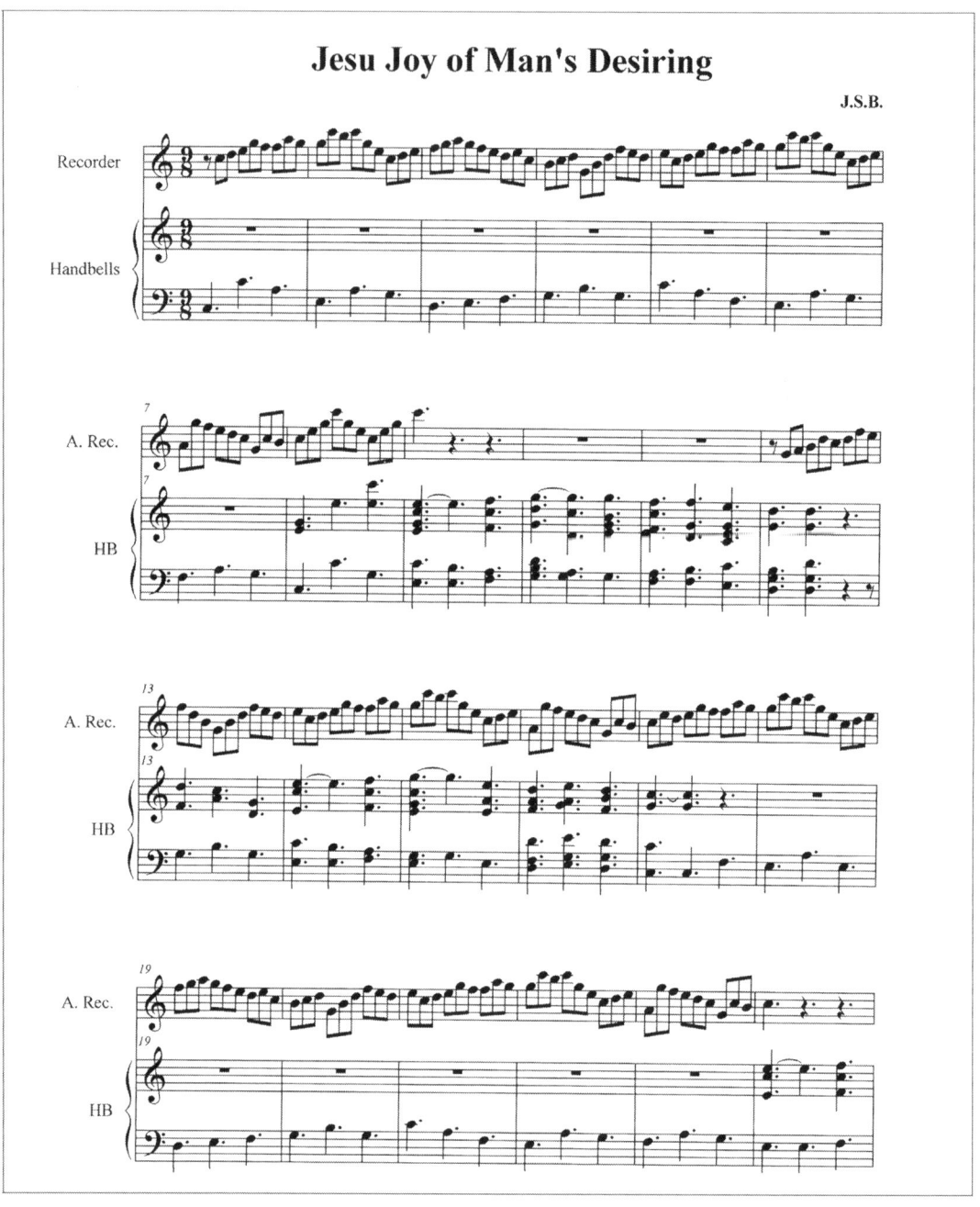

3

This beautiful piece was one of Alice's favorites and was sung at her memorial service, a request she wrote many years before when she penned her final wishes and gave them to daughter Anne. I have often suggested that it be used in place of the Seven Fold Amen, as the words are so appropriate for the end of a church or a memorial service.

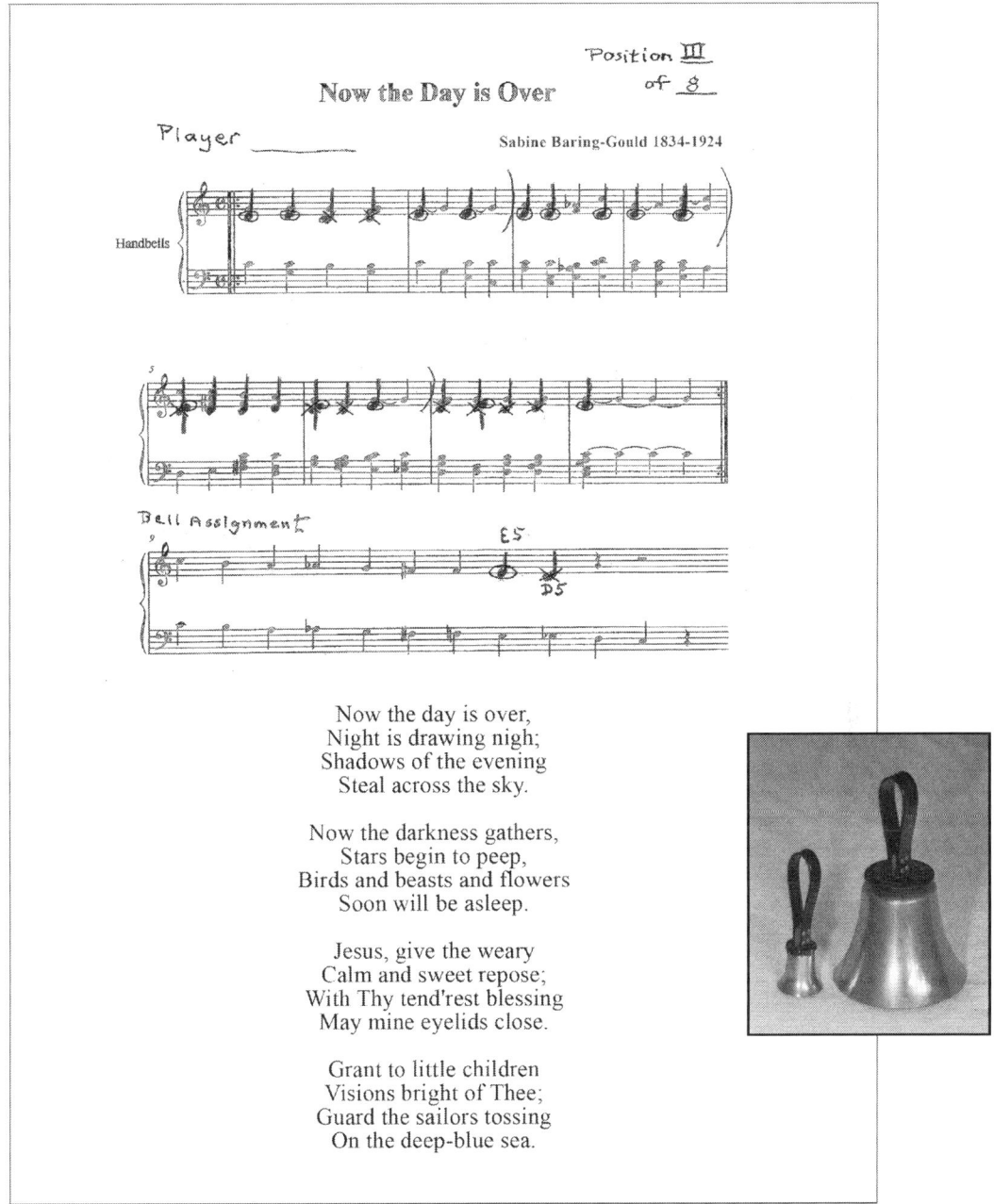

Now the day is over,
Night is drawing nigh;
Shadows of the evening
Steal across the sky.

Now the darkness gathers,
Stars begin to peep,
Birds and beasts and flowers
Soon will be asleep.

Jesus, give the weary
Calm and sweet repose;
With Thy tend'rest blessing
May mine eyelids close.

Grant to little children
Visions bright of Thee;
Guard the sailors tossing
On the deep-blue sea.

Alice and me at Carleton-Willard Village, our continuing care facility, in Bedford, MA.

16

JUST THE TWO OF US...THEN ALONE, ONCE MORE

LORRAINE AND MARGOT

In her later years, Lorraine moved to a continuing care facility in Chatham, PA, near her home. Her children, Laura and Rob, grew to become active adults, and both had families of their own. Laura died in January 2010 at the age of 63. Lorraine died, after a long life, well-lived, on August 23rd, 1997, shortly after her 86th birthday. Her service was at the lovely Quaker Meeting house where she had attended for many years. Our family found it peaceful and especially nice.

My sisters, Lorraine Bulkley and Margot Warner.

Margot lived in her small house in Essex for a good number of years. Dementia set in, and, as her health worsened, she was moved to a facility in Woburn. She died there several years later on August 11, 1999, at the age of 81.

ALICE'S FAMILY

After several years of declining health, Alice's father passed away in 1967. In 1975, after sister Mary's death, John Ecklund married Constance Lyons. Alice's mother Caroline sold the two houses in Bethany and spent her final years in Bridgeport, CT in one of the first continuing care facilities in the country. She died in 1985. One by one, all my brothers-in-law–Alex, Sturgis, John, Yorke,

Ted—have died, as has each of Alice's remaining sisters. Cally passed away in 2007, and Hilda died in March, 2012. Lib, who was living in fragile health near her hometown in Connecticut, passed away in October 2012.

Alice's family (Mid-1970s).
Back row: Alexander Smith Cochran, Yorke Allen, Jr., John Ecklund, me.
Second row: Elizabeth ("Lib") Sizer Allen, Theodore ("Ted")
Ryland Sizer, Sturgis Warner, Hilda Sizer Warner.
Front row: Constance ("Connie") Lyons Ecklund, Alice Sizer Warner,
Caroline Foster Sizer, Nancy Faust Sizer, Caroline ("Cally") Sizer Cochran.

THE LAWN CLUB LEAVES

As the years went by, our kids grew, moved out, and continued on to create their own careers and families. Alice and I found ourselves living together, just the two of us, once more.

We, too, had grown and changed, and we were very different from the young couple that started out their marriage in 1950. Once the kids were out of college, there was a period of years when Alice and I actively pursued our careers during the day, and were together each evening to reflect on daily activities, family and community. As the years went by, Alice struggled through several hip operations, as well as other medical problems.

We looked at our future, and made some decisions. We decided to stay in our house. We planned that, in the future, if we needed the services of a continuing care facility, we'd move to a new one close by in Lexington. We made a full inventory of our possessions in proactive anticipation of the distribution of various belongings to family members. We also lengthened our annual vacations in Southwest Harbor, Maine, where I could sail and motor in our boats around the wonderful coast, Alice could write, and we could take pleasure in the company of each other and the friends we had made in that area during more than a decade of vacations there.

Eventually, I began to notice some significant changes in Alice. These changes were almost imperceptible in the beginning, but became clearer to me little by little each year. She became less and less active in her work, not generating the teaching jobs she had contracted easily over the years. She did continue to write, but struggled with some of its new challenges. I voiced my concern to our kids, who, as they were not living with us day by day, understandably saw her problems less than I did.

In the early months of 1999, I convinced Alice to go to the doctor to see what was wrong. The doctor's results: everything was "fine". He showed Alice's MRI results to Wendy and me. I was not convinced.

We enjoyed another glorious summer, with an extended vacation in Southwest Harbor. It was that August that Margot died, and we started home to put her affairs in order.

OUR LATER YEARS

ALICE'S ACTIVE LIFE COMES TO A HALT

While returning to Lexington, at the end of that 1999 vacation, Alice's active life came to a tragic halt. We can only put the facts together as best we can. Alice was driving our Ford Explorer station wagon, towing our C-Dory motor boat on a trailer. About a half hour from home, a driver in front of her slowed down quickly to see a helicopter landing on the intersecting highway to pick up an accident victim whose Ford Explorer SUV had rolled over.

Alice swerved to avoid the car in front of her, and her whole rig rolled over, boat and all. I was driving our pickup truck/camper some distance ahead, and out of sight. I did not see the accident, but several exits later, I noticed she was not following me. Concerned, I turned around. By the time I arrived at the accident scene, she, too, had been lifted out by helicopter. The police on the scene told me she had a bad head injury.

Two women had rolled their Ford Explorer SUVs on intersecting highways within minutes of each other. Both had been lifted out by helicopter. One was on the way to a hospital, the police knew, in New Hampshire. The other was being flown to Boston. There was some confusion at this point, and I was sent in the wrong direction.

Anne started the drive up from her job in the Waltham area as soon as I called her on her very first brand-new cell phone. Wendy, in Pennsylvania, who had been notified by Anne, called around to locate their mother and soon let us know that we were going in the wrong direction, that Alice was on her way to Boston's Brigham & Women's Hospital. Anne and I both turned around and headed home to drop the truck off at the house and travel to Boston together. As we traveled, Wendy talked to the

ALICE S. and CALEB WARNER
546 Concord Avenue
Lexington, MA 02421-8036

<u>ALICE SIZER WARNER (joined by husband Caleb)</u>

WISH TO GIVE PROFOUND, COLLECTIVE THANKS TO - -
- <u>Five Fields</u> (our neighborhood)
- <u>Follen Community Church</u> (where Alice attends)
- <u>Hancock UCC Church</u> (where Caleb attends)
- <u>Our immediate family</u> (both near and far)
- <u>Our larger family</u> (however far-flung)
- <u>Associates</u> (professional and otherwise)
- <u>Schoolmates</u> (from university and school days)
- <u>Old friends,</u> (some not seen for a long time)
- <u>Stalwarts</u> (of our town, Lexington)
- - and perhaps <u>Uncategorizable Others</u>

FOR SHOWING CONCERN FOR ALICE, AFTER HER RECENT ACCIDENT, BY WAY OF- -
- <u>Visits</u> (to hospital, rehabilitation center and house)
- <u>Flowers</u> (even some not requiring watering, and some for outdoors)
- <u>Food</u> (including whole sumptuous meals)
- <u>Letters</u> (complete with photos)
- <u>Cards</u> (especially welcome)
- <u>Books</u> (including the first two Harry Potters!)
- <u>E-Mails</u> (always a blessing)
- <u>Telephone calls</u> (from near and far)
- <u>Vital Assistance</u> (in unscrambling the household)
- <u>Company</u> (while re-learning walking)
- - but most importantly, <u>General Good Cheer</u>

- - TO THE ALMOST UNBELIEVABLE EXTENT OF ALMOST 300 INSTANCES !

AS A RESULT - -
- <u>Alice continues to make progress daily</u>
- <u>We both are overjoyed to have her home at last !</u>

Dear Nancy and Charlie,
Many thanks for that delicious meal and pleasant visit. Thank you also for your concern for Alice. We are lucky to live in this community of good and loyal people.
— Best to you both ---- Caleb

Tel:(781)862-9278   Fax:(781)863-8678   Mobile:(617)633-5982 75450.250@compuserve.com

We were blessed with an enormous response from our friends and community after Alice's accident. Our thank you note could not adequately begin to reflect the help we received from friends and family alike.

Emergency Room doctors and someone held the phone up to Alice's ear so she could hear Wendy's voice. Alice was conscious, and severely head-injured. She had her first surgery that night.

To this day, I feel remorse and regret. Alice and I had discussed who would drive which vehicle on that fateful trip. The Explorer was a more comfortable car for Alice than the pickup truck, and she wanted to drive it. We had little concern about her towing the boat. This was the way we had driven up to Maine, and it was the arrangement which Alice had said she had preferred on previous trips.

This was a fateful choice, and it was my fault. I was wrong and I blame myself for this: I had already witnessed evidence of Alice's early onset of some sort of brain difficulty well before the accident, even though her doctors hadn't. *I should never have let her get behind the wheel in the first place.*

Ever since, I have carried this haunting responsibility for her accident. Her active life came to an abrupt and horrible halt. She was 69 years old.

ALICE'S RECOVERY

Alice had multiple surgeries on her brain and head. Her long hospital stay was followed by about two additional months of rehabilitation at the Woburn, MA, rehabilitation center. She was then sent home to Lexington where she made further, but only partial, recovery. It was clear that she would forever be left with brain damage.

Our family has always said that Alice "knows how to heal" due to many surgeries she had had throughout her life. She understood that healing takes patience and determination, and Alice had them both. She could not fully recover, and her head injury resulted in a more rapid decline into dementia than if she had not been head-injured at all. She gamely fought her health difficulties, facing a less-than-active life, and drew respect from all of us for her brave efforts.

RETIREMENT FROM SELF-EMPLOYMENT

Over many years, I had found real fulfillment in my Instrument Guild self-employment. By the time of Alice's accident, the business had become increasingly diversified, and demonstrated a record of producing an annual take-home income able to support our family needs at our planned, modest level. With Alice requiring some care from me, and with my Instrument Guild business at a convenient place to taper off, I effectively went into retirement. I maintained a continuing but small professional practice by keeping the Instrument Guild alive but not aggressively seeking new work. I did, however, clean up several loose ends.

CONTINUING CARE

Back in the 1970s, through our efforts within our local South Lexington Civic Association, I had been involved in helping get "Brookhaven At Lexington" going as Lexington's first continuing care retirement facility. Alice and I had put down a deposit and entered our names on the waiting list in about 1990. By the spring of 2000, in view of Alice's and my health, age and general capability, Alice and I, supported by our family, agreed that we should move into Brookhaven.

At the time we needed to move, we were at the top of the list of those aspiring to enter Brookhaven. Most unhappily, however, we were told that Brookhaven did not accept people with Alice's health problems. They also voiced concern about my own peripheral neuropathy, a new diagnosis for me. We were both turned down.

We considered several other retirement communities, including some that were quite remotely located. We visited some locally, and I was intrigued to note that Alice even suggested that Ann Arbor, Michigan, be considered. I was happy to see that the University of Michigan had really won her over.

Carleton-Willard Village in Bedford, MA was comfortingly located near our beloved Lexington, and it became our final choice when we learned that there was actually a place available for us. The only negative aspect was that the space was available only because other aspirants had felt that it was too expensive. By that time, however, we were so desperate that we swallowed hard and allowed ourselves to spend the money and, thankfully, we moved in.

We found true respite in Carleton-Willard Village. Alice contentedly engaged in a lot of walking, reading and even some writing, finishing a final version of her manuscript of "Bethany" and selecting the photos she wanted to include. The living conditions were such that family could visit, participate in her care, and provide comfort and support, which she eagerly looked forward to and genuinely welcomed.

ALICE'S FINAL MOVE

We lived in the comfort of our large townhouse quarters in Andover Court at Carleton-Willard for about two years as Alice's dementia became increasingly severe. I struggled a great deal as a caretaker, and I wish that I had done better by her. By 2002, she was unable to talk, and was more and more confused as she valiantly tried to carry out her daily activities.

Carleton-Willard was in the process of building an Alzheimer's care facility, and a few months after it opened, Alice's condition had disabled her enough that she was moved in to it. Ultimately, although she exhibited both fear and confusion when she made the move, we were all surprised at how quickly she adjusted. I think she was relieved to feel both safe and happy there.

Our children were very supportive of Alice during that difficult time. She was given competent and loving professional care, with family nearby, and often in attendance. Anne, who lived in nearby Belmont, was closely involved with us on a daily basis. Alice and I were both deeply grateful for her help.

I moved to a smaller, more modestly-priced townhouse in Carleton-Willard's Essex Court. This maintained my independent-living status while being near enough for me to see Alice several times each day. This met our separate needs perfectly and proved to be an outstanding living arrangement and stimulating neighborhood for me. I pursued a highly active retired life for about four years, while serving on several Bedford town committees and even doing some professional development work.

AN UNEXPECTED TRIP TO FINLAND

One day daughter Anne burst in unexpectedly waving an airline ticket. It was about time, she declared, for me to take a trip to Finland! She was well aware of my lifelong fascination with that country. She was also aware that it had been hard for me to deal with Alice's move and my new living situation.

I had always wanted to see Finland. I was lucky to have had professional reasons to work in Europe, the British Isles, Asia, and South America, and had of course stayed in almost all the Scandinavian countries, but somehow I had not been to Finland. Long ago I made a personal vow never to travel overseas as a mere "sightseer". This excursion to Finland would be my exception!

The trip was terrific! I stayed in a modest downtown hotel in Helsinki, but was essentially a guest of Maria Heinonen who lived a streetcar's ride away. I had the great pleasure of a day in the suburbs celebrating a family birthday with almost the whole Heinonen tribe. I was more than happy to explore every detail of the fascinating Helsinki waterfront and nearby ferry-connected islands. That place has everything a maritime addict would want—and then some.

A FASCINATION WITH FINLAND

If the truth be known, Finland, its people and its languages, has been an important presence to me throughout my life. When I was a teenager, my parents provided a home for a distinguished couple from Finland, then working at Harvard. Later, the wife became responsible for a program that provided safe refuge for Finnish children sent away from Finland during the "Winter Wars" with the Soviet Union at the beginning of WWII. The couple's presence as guests in our house was a pleasant experience for me.

Years later, when I was interning in Sweden, I got to know some Finnish refugee students, and I enjoyed becoming closely involved. I even played on their nighttime hockey team in the Olympic stadium across the street from where I was living in Stockholm.

Later came the arrival into our Five Fields neighborhood of the Heinonens, a Finnish couple with several children. The husband, Olli, was working at a research laboratory on world health problems, attached to both Harvard and Boston University. He was a leading authority on ethnic factors impacting national health. His wife, Maria, was a member of one of Finland's leading families. Each of their kids became enthusiastic and contributing "members of the gang" in our neighborhood.

Later, daughter Anne lived in Finland for a little under a year before attending college.

For many decades my friendship and admiration for Finland and its people has been growing.

THE END OF ALICE'S LIFE

Alice lived in the Alzheimer's unit for several years, receiving competent and loving care from staff and family alike. She slowly worsened, but was always more cognizant of her surroundings than was apparent to those who did not know her well. For this we were always grateful, as each family member was able to make continual connections with her.

One Sunday, when Alice was unable to speak at all, Wendy sat next to her during a small church service held down the hall from Alice's room. As the minister started the Lord's Prayer, Wendy was astonished to hear her mother pipe up next to her, and recite the prayer in a clear and calm voice, almost verbatim. We were told that this is not uncommon. What is learned early in life is often the very last to be forgotten. Another day, Alice turned in response to a woman who spoke German, Alice's first language, and attempted to respond. Alice had learned German from the Sizer family's much loved Anne-Liese Wellershaus when Alice was a toddler. Alice could also still hold a tune, and, to our surprise, sing the words of a song more than once after she had lost her ability to talk.

Alice.

Alice died peacefully at the age of 76 with Anne and Wendy at her side on May 19, 2006 at Carleton-Willard. Her life was first briefly memorialized at one of the monthly services regularly held at Carleton-Willard Village. The full memorial service was held at Follen Community Church in Lexington on June 4, 2006. Reverend John Gibbons of the First Parish in Bedford, MA officiated. Langdon and Wendy put together the program for the service. Anne spoke, and Nick and a fellow musician played music in Alice's honor. Langdon and Wendy gathered the children in front of the church, and told a story from Alice's childhood. The service was attended by perhaps 150 family members, neighbors and friends. The service ended with everyone singing Dona Nobis Pacem. This well-known round is particularly endearing because of its "Give Us Peace" message, and because it is sung worldwide. It has a special place in the hearts of our family, which has sung it since our children were quite young. Anne, Wendy, and I sang it to Alice in her final hours. Family and friends at Alice's memorial service sang together for her one last time. It was a beautiful service.

One of Alice's classmates reported in the Radcliffe College Quarterly as follows: "Follen Church in Lexington was crowded with people who cared about her and about whom she cared… Walking in, we heard a tasteful jazz version of 'Over the Rainbow' played by her son, Nick, and a friend. There was lots of music, a special time for the children, and many touching recollections… The service reflected her enthusiasm and her positive way of living."

Alice's ashes are with daughter Anne awaiting the time when my own become available. At such time, we've asked that our ashes be strewn together on the outgoing tide along the New England coast.

LIFE WITHOUT ALICE

ON MY OWN

In the time surrounding Alice's death, my own health worsened considerably. I first became aware of my Parkinson's Disease with a sudden onset of severe hand tremor early in May of 2006. The tremor lasted several days, and then went away. Then I developed hazardous balance, and I turned to the use of a walker. Soon after, I was hospitalized, and then spent time in and out of the nursing center

Dona Nobis Pacem

(Translation: Give Us Peace)

Traditional

at Carleton-Willard, as ill health and confusion took over. As a result, I was somewhat reluctantly transferred from the Independent Living level of care to the Assisted Living "Llewsac Lodge" wing. I now have a single room with attached bathroom. Llewsac provides me with around-the-clock nursing availability, health monitoring, and convenient (but unfortunately fattening!) meals three times a day.

A TIME TO REFLECT

At what point does a man stop learning from his actions, from his mistakes? I've learned a great deal about myself in the years without Alice. I wish, needless to say, that I could have garnered some of these lessons when I was much younger as a son, a husband, a father, and an entrepreneur.

As a son, I wish I had known my father differently, and I wish he had known me differently as well. I now thoroughly respect and admire his work. I did not come to appreciate it for a good many years, as his work instead reflected his absence in both my and my siblings' lives.

Although I certainly felt closer to Mother, I had no real sense of her bold accomplishments as a woman in the era in which she lived. She worked hard to introduce me to the world in a way that might nurture healthy interests and a future career. She stuck by me.

In reflection, I have only now come to realize the true effect on me of the procession of notable people at my parents' dinner table. It was certainly thoughtful of my parents to ensure that my siblings and I interacted with this parade of distinguished people as they passed through our doors. I am sure that my parents hoped that it would be an inspiring experience for us as young people. However, for me, just the opposite happened. The situation bred a rather different–almost damaging–attitude in me. From a young age, I found being around such important people produced feelings of inferiority. As I grew up, I came to regret the fact that it would be nearly impossible to live up to their standards.

As a husband, was I good enough for Alice? Did I weigh down her expectations of the future? Did I do right by her? Of course, my answers to these questions are two-fold–a resounding "Yes" *and* a resounding "No" to each question. No marriage is perfect, and anyone in a lifelong relationship knows that what matters most is that we both did our best. The rest is between us. We loved each other very much.

As a father, I'm not sure I knew how to do what needed to be done. Every parent must struggle with the inevitable conflict of values and traditions originating in the far past versus a new generation's ideals and plans for the future. It's not easy. It was a rough ride, and, without Alice, it would have been an impossible one. Our kids grew up to be great adults, thank goodness, and their own values seem to be well grounded. I am proud to be the father of such a strong and gifted group.

As an entrepreneur, I think I was ultimately able to turn some of my childhood feelings of inadequacy into accomplishment. I was always seeking something in my work, and I certainly didn't find what I was looking for in the employ of others. I wanted my work to make a difference, to make a mark, and to shore up the "good" of this world, rather than the "ugly". I also needed to support my family.

Once unshackled from the rules of behavior expected of an employee, I was finally able to turn my feelings of inadequacy around. I gradually learned how to relate to people of great skill and/ or fame. With no attempts made to compete, I simply learned about the areas of limitation that *surrounded* their skills, and sought to offer the Instrument Guild's services to resolve them. This worked quite well for me.

I was therefore positioned to generate some incredibly interesting work for some fascinating people. For a nationally acclaimed brain surgeon, I made pieces to replace areas of bone in an infant's skull. For superstar rock drummers, I designed rugged drum brushes that generated great sound yet could be simply stored and protected in their own handles. I did a lot of work that, in the long run, was varied, fascinating and great fun.

I must admit, however, that the analysis of this never really came into focus until recently when old age has forced me to think about my own young life and its struggles!

TODAY, TOMORROW

I have remained in the Llewsac Lodge facility at Carleton-Willard up to the date of drafting this life story. Langdon lives in Columbia, South Carolina. For a new job, Anne moved to Bethany, Connecticut (Alice's hometown!), and then to neighboring Woodbridge. Wendy now lives in Massachusetts and helps me with errands, doctor appointments, and, of course, writing this book. Nick lives happily in Burlington, Vermont.

I am still growing, changing, and learning. Parkinson's Disease affects my abilities to sing or play music. I have formed a handbell choir here and have learned a great deal about how to teach handbells to an elderly population. I have found an extraordinary amount of musical activity on the Internet. The availability of classical music archives and the ever-expanding notation software provide me with fascinating new types of musical challenges and pleasure. I have also enjoyed doing some live recording and editing with newly updated audio equipment.

I find myself called on several times each day to perform minor, low-level civic services within Carleton-Willard, such as helping to get equipment going properly for neighbors who are facing decreasing ability to handle their TVs, radios, computers, and other modern devices. I have participated in various Residents Association committees.

To be frank, however, all of us here at Carleton-Willard find it frustrating and somewhat depressing to deal with the cognitive decrepitude that is inevitably attacking every one of us. There are, however, a great many fascinating people here. I have enjoyed getting to know them and learning more about their work and families.

❧

I am going to be 90 years old on September 12, 2012. This account has taken over four and a half years for Wendy and me to write. The memories I've noted here are somewhat blurred with time and I worry that they may not be perfectly accurate. Please know I have done my very best.

I am writing this book for Alice, to honor her life and to thank her for helping me live mine.

I write it for my four children, who have grown to be valuable and loving adults, and who have families of their own.

I write this book for my grandchildren, who know me only as an old man, not as a youth with a world at war facing him and shaping his future.

I write this for my great-grandchildren who don't know me well, but know I'm theirs.

I write this for all those who have helped me in my life, who may not know how grateful I am for their interest and encouragement.

I write this book to reach out to you, the generations of family members that I will never meet, but who may wonder what it was like for one man to live in the fascinating, ever-changing 20th century. I hope that you will find fulfillment.

In my years as a father and husband, seeking a way for my abilities, interests, and style of working to support my family, it was clear that I did not easily fit into any typical mold. I struggled, and when I did, I often looked up at the wall of my study, where I had taped a hand-written slip of paper:

> Grant me to find the task
> For which my talents fit me
> With steady strength to strive
> That I may well acquit me;
> And when my work is done
> That something may remain
> For men to use, that I
> Shall not have lived in vain.

Cantata BWV 45/7 by J.S. Bach
"Oh Gott, du Frommer Gott" (second stanza)
English text as translated by Henry S. Drinker, Sr.

May all your lives be as blessed as mine has been.

Caleb Warner

Caleb Warner   June 1928

POSTSCRIPT

TABLE OF CONTENTS

TO MANY PEOPLE, MANY THANKS

TO MANY PEOPLE, MANY THANKS

It is often said, "It takes a village to raise a child."
Writing my life story has enabled me to examine my own "villagers",
and to honor this extraordinary, diverse group of people.

My "villagers" were the many people, from the humble to the legendary,
whose ideals and accomplishments have been a positive influence on my life and family.
My memory is fast-failing, and I am embarrassed to realize that I cannot resurrect the exact names
of some of the people that meant so much to me in the too-distant past.
Their presence, however, is still important to mention.

FATHER'S FAMILY

Uncle Roger Sherman Warner was a strong role model in my life. He initiated the idea that working with my hands and participating in civic affairs were important life goals. He served *in loco parentis* as a father figure and a mentor.

Aunt Molly Hooper Warner, Uncle Roger's wife, will forever be special to me, both as mother-figure and an aunt. Her ability to relate to young people put her in high regard to many, and we often turned to her to discuss our lives. She ruled well but with kindness, and we learned standards of behavior from her.

Roger Warner, Jr. ("Rodge"), my cousin and brother of Sturgis, climbed to career heights in development of amphibious warfare techniques and hardware while working with Lord Mountbatten and Stanley Rosenfeld, then up to a high level in the Manhattan Project, and eventually in the Atomic Energy Commission. I watched his career with interest, and he in turn, really steered my own career.

Sturgis Warner, as both a cousin, and a brother-in-law, was like the older brother I never had. We were very close, and I often turned to him for his sage advice and support as I matured from a young boy to a man. Most importantly, Sturge led me toward my ultimate marriage to his sister-in-law, Alice Foster Sizer.

Jean Wagnière, his wife Margaret ("Peggy"), and their family have been important to me, as well as to my own nuclear family, for four generations. To the Wagnières, I wish to offer my thanks for their continued enthusiasm in forging these strong family relations.

MOTHER'S FAMILY

Laura d'Orèmieulx Roosevelt, my maternal grandmother, was widowed quite young. She was a New York City "fixture." I thank her for introducing me to the city, and giving me a wonderful place to stay while I explored New York. Most importantly, it was my grandmother who gave me a window into the broader Roosevelt family, and offered me real kinship, starting in my teenage years.

Uncle Nicholas Roosevelt taught me what the Theodore Roosevelt family mystique was all about. I also thank him for the awareness that he gave the world in the area of environmental matters.

Uncle Oliver and Aunt Verdrey Roosevelt gave me an especially formative summer in my early teens. It was during that happy summer, full of sailing and companionship, that I came to know with their two sons, West and Wolcott.

Wolcott Roosevelt provided me my first opportunity to play Baroque music seriously. This was a type of music that I would enjoy for the rest of my life.

Ethel Derby, a daughter of Theodore Roosevelt, and her husband, **Richard Derby, MD,** were a joy for me to visit at their home in Oyster Bay, Long Island. Cousin Dick, beyond his distinguished medical career, was a specialist in the design of military draft laws and their application to the proscription of civilians into military service, a matter that he led, nationally, during both World Wars I and II. They were very good to me. For some reason, I just connected very well with them.

Edith Derby (married name Williams), was the eldest of Dick and Ethel Derby's three daughters. Although we did not really know her well, she kindly hosted our son Langdon in the Seattle region at one point.

Sarah Alden Derby (married name Gannett) was the middle in age of the three Derby sisters. On the same day our son Nick received an MA at University of Vermont, Sarah and her husband Bob Gannett were also given honorary degrees by the university: she, for her many years of volunteer service straightening out land rights for the Appalachian Trail, and Bob, for his long-time service as speaker of the House of Representatives of Vermont.

Judith Derby (married name Ames), the youngest of the Derby sisters, and a favorite cousin of mine, married my Exeter schoolmate Del Ames. Del became an important client during my Instrument Guild days when I built some laboratory gear for his use at Massachusetts General Hospital. I believe that Del was the son of one of my father's roommates at Harvard.

Other Members of the Theodore Roosevelt Clan influenced my life in many positive ways. **James Roosevelt Sr.** lent me his Herreshoff S-boat, my favorite among all class sailboats. **Jim (James Jr.)** later worked with me in Intercollegiate Yacht Racing Association regattas. **Phillipa** and her husband did much to alleviate the sensitive schism that had developed between the Franklin D. and the Theodore Roosevelt branches. I am very glad for what they did. Over the years, I struggled with the some of the daunting expectations I faced as a family member of the Theodore Roosevelt clan. Overall, however, the family offered me a considerable kinship, and I now appreciate the friendly support from those members which I have been lucky enough to know.

SHADY HILL SCHOOL

Shady Hill School Faculty set exceptionally high standards that, in turn, helped me set my own throughout the rest of my life. **Katherine Taylor**, Headmistress, was my first exposure to authority outside my family and set a very high standard in my eyes. She was a very understanding individual. Grade teachers **Miss Thorpe, Mr. Smith,** and **Mrs. Hinton,** aided by their apprentices, did well to produce a true learning experience. **Miss Putnam** (Science) and **Miss Edgett** (Math) introduced subjects that proved to be most important in my future profession. I would like to thank **Mrs. Funkhouser** (Music), **Mrs. Stout** (Art), **Mr. Martin** (Shop) as well as several of my athletic coaches. I found it very challenging to try to meet the requirements of daily school activities and did not distinguish myself. Even so, it was a great privilege to start my education in this very special, pioneering grade school.

WHILE LIVING IN CAMBRIDGE

Mrs. John Mahler, my family's resident cook, offered me the exceedingly comforting feeling of fond, parental backup throughout my early years. I knew that I could count on her. I later welcomed my indoctrination into Catholicism by Mrs. Mahler as I came to serve as an assistant chaplain during WWII, when such knowledge proved to be especially important. Her positive influence is still with me as I struggle with religious matters in later life.

Jim Conant provided much-needed friendship and enthusiasm during the challenging times of choosing Michigan as our college choice when we were together at Exeter. I have a tremendous admiration for how he conducted himself while at Ann Arbor and later his remarkable war record in submarines. I sadly welcomed an opportunity to praise his memory at his memorial service following his premature death in the early 1960s.

Bob Storer was a friend, cousin, and great connection with what was happening in the Boston, Cambridge, and Harvard scenes. Prominent in Boston's insurance industry, Bob knew his way around the business community over many years. As a long-time Cambridge resident, he was a good source of what was happening locally.

Ben Olken, founder and owner of The Bicycle Exchange in Cambridge, gave me my first job at age 14, and then proceeded to teach me what it *meant* to have a true paying job and work for a living. I also learned to appreciate the workings of a good merchant, as Ben truly was.

PREP SCHOOL

Exeter's School Dean provided me further experience with an authoritarian structure, and a good one it was. He performed the unbelievably difficult job of administrating an all-boys' prep school. He did it commendably by convincing me that he, beyond all else, was fair, just, and believably correct, while instilling in me the fear of God!

Mr. Darcy Curwen, a highly regarded mentor of students at Phillips Exeter Academy, backed me up when I chose to apply to University of Michigan rather than ivy league colleges, even though he normally was an ardent booster of ivy league institutions to others in the school. I owe him a lot for that important support. He then kindly monitored my progress throughout my college years.

My Science Instructor taught physics in a way that gave me both useful tools and methods I used later as I pursued my engineering career. I now realize that perhaps I should have followed his strong lead and pursued further study in physics as I passed through higher education levels.

One **English Instructor** taught me a great deal about the grammar and structure of the English language. Not being a strong literary type, I found this to be a challenge, but his teachings later proved to be inordinately useful as I pursued my professional career and participated in civic duties.

Arthur Landers, Director of Music, gave me considerable experience in instrumental playing and choral singing in an eclectic variety of styles. This was my first opportunity to get into serious music, which later grew to be such an important part of the rest of my life.

Larry Erdman, my roommate for two prep school years, remained my closest friend for the decades thereafter until his untimely death in the 1980s. Larry and I found common interests in choir, chorus, marching band, symphony orchestra, and, especially, the dance band. As a saxophone player, he was a considerably more accomplished instrumentalist than I. As our friendship and our families evolved, I got to know and admire **Larry's wife Marion** and their vibrant kids. I was lucky to visit Marion after Larry's death since she lived in Charlotte, NC, near where son Langdon currently lives. Larry was the person of my own age that I would have most wanted to be like.

MY TEEN SUMMERS

Margaret Shurcliff showed me the significance of developing artisan's skills, which later became my lifelong interest. We can also thank her for introducing handbell ringing to the U.S., bringing much pleasure to ringers and audiences alike. Above all, I admired her for participating in various civil rights movements, including the women's right to vote and a proactive stand against ethnic bias in the famed Sacco and Vanzetti case.

The skilled boatbuilder, alongside of whom I apprenticed in the high-production wooden boat shop during my teenage summers, taught me a great deal not only about woodworking techniques but also what it meant to do piece-work and also how to get along in a working community. This was a valuable, useful, and maturing education for me.

COLLEGE YEARS

Professor of Naval Architecture, Henry Adams, patiently taught us the important basics of the design of vessels, and was a father figure to many of us studying in that department. He also stood as a symbol of what the institution of the University of Michigan really was and still is.

My Designated College Advisor, a senior materials engineering professor, claimed that he was tasked to assure that Marine Engineering Department at Michigan was doing right by me. I appreciated that he chose to be in a position beside me, rather than over me, an encouraging approach for me as an incoming freshmen. This also bode well for my upcoming relations with the faculty overall.

My Principal Professor in Mechanical Engineering broadened my engineering education significantly. His orientation toward practical application helped me extensively later on in my own professional practice.

The Director of the University of Michigan Band, William Revelli, was renowned nationally. For those of us under his direction, he was an amazing symbol of the best of the John Phillip Sousa tradition. He was demanding and enormously competent, and all of us who played under him were inspired to do our darnedest. Many revered him for his standards of excellence, which, in turn, helped me set my own standards for later brass playing.

Thor Johnson, Conductor of the University of Michigan Chorus, although only in his early 30s, was clearly at the start of a great career in the national music scene. I thank him for a great experience in singing. I enjoyed myself and learned a lot participating in a wide variety of his choral activities. He was later to become a nationally acclaimed conductor of the Cincinnati Symphony.

George Faxon, Church Choir Director/Organist, Episcopal Cathedral in Ann Arbor, taught me a lot as a member of his chorus. Although the usual practice of the Anglican Church was to pay the choir, I turned down payment. In turn, George quietly gave me some useful personal vocal coaching. As an organist, he was also exceptional. George was an inspiration to me, and later to many as head of the organ department at the New England Conservatory of Music and organist at Boston's Trinity Church.

My Naval Architecture/Marine Engineering classmates were my primary college "gang" of 30-40 students. We did almost all activities together, intellectually and socially. This group was my major support, and it made college life easier all around.

My fellow cadets in the Naval Reserve Officers Training Corps were my secondary "gang" during my college days, with an overlap of friends between these two groups. For obvious reasons we all became considerably closer during WWII. Many of us continued to be close once the war was over. I give my thanks to them for their friendship. For those of them who lost their lives during the war, I give a heartfelt thank you for serving our country.

The Master Shipfitter at the Bath Iron Works I worked with over one summer showed me how to combine very physically demanding, complicated manual labor, requiring real skill, while simultaneously successfully acting as a boss and manager of a team. I learned that his was a brand of leadership that would be worth emulating.

The Outside Engineer at the Bath Iron Works was truly a "villager" to me. I learned all about a vessel's machinery under his guidance, and it was by far the best internship experience I could have had as a marine engineering student. He taught me valuable lessons for my upcoming war service and even for my later career as a practicing engineer.

NAVY SERVICE

The USS Melville's Executive Officer (the one who relieved the first Executive Officer) managed to meld the ship's widely differing group of officers together, making life not only tenable aboard our ship, but truly productive.

My Assistant Chief Repair Officer and boss aboard ship symbolized the old-Navy style, which helped me set my own high standards in performing my duties. I welcomed his support.

John Duncan Bulkeley, the skipper of the destroyer on which I served as WWII ended, was a much-decorated national hero and it was an honor to serve under him.

AFTER THE WAR

Dr. Leonard Carmichael, President of Tufts University, showed me that there was a good and sensitive man at the helm. He leveled with me when discussing how I might proceed.

Prof. Walter Farnham, Senior Mechanical Engineering Professor, my immediate boss at Tufts, was just what was needed in those overcrowded days when we were trying to accommodate the swelling flow of career-hungry GI Bill of Rights students returning from WWII. He guided me as his neophyte colleague through those very demanding days.

INTERNATIONAL 14 SAILING TEAM

My close friends, Dick and Janet Besse, both world-class racing sailors with outstanding records, were an important part of the International 14 sailing dinghy scene, and we became loyal friends. It was a luxury to crew for them on the highly demanding racing circuit, and it guaranteed me a place among the team of world-class competitive sailors. Later, Dick was an usher in our wedding.

INTERNSHIP IN SWEDEN

Fru Adel Heilborn, Director, Sweden-America Foundation in Stockholm, provided us, as Americans, the opportunity to become active, aware, and involved in significant elements of Swedish life and to understand and appreciate the lifestyle, the institutions and the traditions of the country.

Christer Von Essen was my connection to the Swedish world of young engineers of the type that I aspired to be in the USA. He showed me much in the Swedish engineering field and he kindly helped me learn and understand the differences and similarities of Swedish and American culture and tradition. I am indebted to him.

President of the DeLaval Co. He took a real interest in my internship and saw to it that I was involved in many aspects of the firm's activities. He also kindly arranged to support me financially so that I was able to do many things beyond the scope of my internship.

DeLaval's brilliant Russian Development Engineer, with a long record of development in his native country, gave me my first experience in a pioneering project in the mechanical engineering field.

DeLaval's Field Service Engineer took me on field trips to assist him, which provided particularly valuable and interesting experience.

DUPONT

Dr. Larry Dodge was the most capable boss I ever had. He had the difficult job of running a planning group for the management of a very significant division of the DuPont Company. Larry provided the work experience that gave me, as a young engineer, some of the understanding and the working tools that became valuable throughout the rest of my career.

My six Planning Group Colleagues and I analyzed and constructively criticized each others' work so that a true consensus could be passed on to top management. We became a close team – the first time I experienced this in a professional working group. This showed me the value of organized collective group thinking, later enabling me to formulate the "Guild" concept for my own business.

ARTHUR D. LITTLE

Alan "Jack" Latham was Vice President of Engineering, under whom I served: I came to revere Jack's leadership ability and admire his exceptionally broad technical knowledge. Later on, when I started the Instrument Guild, I was lucky to have him as one of my first clients. I worked for him on and off for about 20 years and regard him as probably the most significant individual in my professional life. He was the unusual combination of both an outstanding doer and inspirational leader.

Austin W. "Bud" Fisher helped me through the maze of getting ADL's new small business service underway. This experience, and his wisdom, were especially valuable later on as I formed my own practice.

BOLT BERANEK & NEWMAN (BB&N)

Dick Bolt, Co-Founder of BB&N, an icon in the field of acoustics, drew my admiration in his work in national political and scientific affairs, including the American Association for the

Advancement of Science. I was happy to sell him our wonderful land in Lincoln where he then built his home of many years. He did just what Alice and I hoped would be done with that property.

Ira Dyer, Vice President of BB&N, was probably one of the brightest men I have ever met. He set exceptionally high technical and performance standards and urged me into doing a lot of useful learning.

Chuck Malme, one of BB&N's leading project managers, led several of that company's programs that particularly interested and intrigued me. He was especially helpful in technical matters, due to his experience and academic training. We also shared interests in marine matters.

Bill G. "Bilgie" Watters was behind several innovations for which BB&N is noted in architectural acoustics, seismic surveying, and sophisticated acoustic engineering. I had the great privilege of serving on a few of his project teams and seeing successful technical innovation at work.

EDGERTON GERMESHAUSEN AND GREER, INC. (EG&G)

Harold "Doc" Edgerton, one of the founders of EG&G, was a world-renowned pioneer in flash photography and a mentor to many as a professor at Massachusetts Institute of Technology. He served as an example of what constructive innovation is all about and I welcomed working in his shadow.

CANNON GUILD, INC.

I thank **Jim Cannon,** the founder and financial backer of the Cannon Guild, for his truly imaginative and venturesome bent in conjuring up the idea of the Guild. He was willing to take the chance to back it financially, even though in the end it proved not to be sustainable. I am enormously thankful for the experience and for his patience and understanding.

Eric Herz's knowledge of state-of-the-art instrument building was just what we needed in the Cannon Guild. He alerted us to problems we needed to address to make our harpsichords more usable and acceptable. I appreciated his involvement in our venture.

Frank Adams was the epitome of a production artisan. He helped us get instrument building underway using his various manual skills. That team, plus several more in the Guild, gave me tremendous support as we struggled to get it up and going. I am indebted to them for their loyal efforts.

THE INSTRUMENT GUILD PERIOD

I owe **Pat Peppicelli** a lot of thanks for dragging me, kicking and screaming, into the computer-aided-design world. My operation grew in annual billings, thanks significantly to Pat's capability. The relationship between Pat and me continued almost flawlessly through many years of my professional life.

Byron Blanchard, Electronic Engineer, was a godsend in supplying much-needed knowledge to the projects that we tackled. Of course, this was a vital part of almost every development project in the fast-emerging high-tech industry.

George Feick, Inorganic/Organic Chemist and Chemical Process Engineer, was an infinitely wise soul. His breadth of knowledge on technical matters was unusually extensive, and clients respected the maturity of judgment in his problem-solving capabilities. His presence benefited us significantly in dealing with the top management of our client firms.

Bob Pyle, Information Technologist, Physicist and Musician was able to help Instrument Guild clients with his vital information technology know-how. He also was involved in musical instrument acoustics, so we had lots of personal interests in common.

Ed Lavelle, one of my important vendors, educated me in the fast-emerging field of numerically controlled machining. He good-naturedly helped me appreciate the value of the increasingly important application of information technology.

Chuck Dietrich, Industrial and Automotive Safety Engineer, provided the diversity that I badly needed to make a go of it in the Instrument Guild. He got us into the industrial safety and legal support fields, and had useful experience in developing an engineering practice similar to the Instrument Guild.

INSTRUMENT GUILD CLIENTS

Henry Kloss, High Fidelity Sound and Projection TV Pioneer, was my business's largest and longest client. Henry made my practice viable for about 10 years, and for this I am more than thankful. I respected him for his fixation about maintaining manufacturing in this country in an era where it was increasingly going overseas. Henry became a major inspiration for me because he was doing great service to the music field. He also was an example of an innovator, the likes of which I had never seen. I am indebted to him for providing me with good challenges while making sure that I was rewarded for my efforts.

Arthur C. "Proff" Ruge, MIT Professor, Inventor of the Strain Gauge, played a special role in getting me going in my own business as my first client outside of the BB&N work that had followed me in my transition. He was an infinitely wise person and a staunch protagonist of the high tech startup movement sweeping the Boston area. As my first client he was a valuable asset and a knowing and sympathetic coach.

The Von Huene Family, well-known as leading makers of blockflutes, gave me the good fortune to witness an extraordinary example of a family, each with complementary skills and abilities, that was able to team up to form a highly productive and innovative business niche and venture. I am fortunate to have been given a window into their extraordinary lives.

SPECIAL FAMILY FRIENDS

Nancy Morris has held a special place in our family for many decades. She found her way to us at age 16, and has been a special friend with each of us as well as with our whole nuclear family group ever since. As soon as Anne notified her siblings about Alice's accident, Nancy was the first person she called. Nancy is an extremely talented and understanding person and Wendy and I would like to extend our thanks for her unending and patient work as editor of this book, which has been done surrounding the illness and passing of her husband, Bob.

Douglas Cheek, with us for only a short five years, became a "family member" in the truest sense. We were blessed with his presence during a critically busy period for both Alice and me. With the kids developing fast, Douglas quietly stepped in to fill the role of a much-needed third parent before his sudden death. We miss him to this day.

Michael Tackie currently continues to be very good to me, calling me regularly from the Pittsburgh area where he now lives. We have long and very rewarding discussions about everything including sailboats, information technology, what's happening in his industry, all things political, and our kids' activities. He is a profound individual and it is a privilege know him.

Judy Monteux, though living in California, kindly continues to contact me. Judy took on the task of first organizing, keeping the financial records, billing and accounting for the home-based businesses that both Alice and I each built. I owe Judy a lot for having kept us on track and educating us on how to conduct the financial aspects of a small business.

Paul Hopkins has been known to our family since he was a youth. I am grateful to him for his help when I first upgraded our modest house, and then later in my increasing professional activities in my home-based workshop, as he was skilled in shop practices and in applied electronics.

Jim Niccolson was a keyboard player introduced to us by friend and colleague, Eric Herz. He has been a family friend all these years, and our adult kids all have felt a connection with him throughout their lives. At Alice's memorial service, Jim reflected on his friendship with her and with our family.

FIVE FIELDS

Perhaps the most significant part of Alice and my adult lives was strongly grounded in the way of life that the **Five Fields Neighbors** embraced as "our community". We owe thanks both to the community as a whole, and to its prescient founders, The Architects Collaborative (TAC). In the 47 years we lived in Five Fields, there were many, many people who made a positive difference in our family members' lives. I would like to thank them all, and especially a few individuals, as follows: **Arthur and Gladys Katz's** four children, Jamie, Mara, Johanna, and Harry, matched the age of our children. We found much in common with them. **Alice and Jock (our children's pediatrician) Robey** and their kids Sarah, Carol, and Steve also matched the age of our children and similarly played pivotal roles in our neighborhood relationships. **Olli and Maria Heinonen and family**, long-term visitors to Five Fields and Lexington from Finland, became lifelong friends to Alice and me.

CARLETON-WILLARD VILLAGE AND ITS RESIDENTS

We were extremely lucky to find this continuing care community for our retirement years. **Carleton-Willard Village** provided excellent continuing care for Alice during her final years, and has offered me both the care that I need and a healthy environment and a community of interesting residents. I think I can speak for Alice now, and say that we have appreciated the support and concern by the institution and its residents.

ALICE'S FAMILY, THE SIZERS

Theodore and Caroline Foster Sizer, Alice's Parents, were tremendously encouraging to our family. I feel exceedingly lucky to have been their son-in-law, and I am most thankful for their loyal support over the years. As to the **Sizer Family** overall, I was concerned about whether I could meet the standards that seemed to have been set. Happily, I found the family to be markedly welcoming. I think we felt doubly supported, due to the marriage of Alice's sister, Hilda, and my first cousin, Sturgis Warner.

Alice's generation of the Sizers included **Caroline ("Cally") and Alex Cochran, Hilda and Sturgis Warner, Elizabeth (Lib) and Yorke Allen, Mary and John Ecklund, John's second wife, Connie Ecklund,** and of course Alice's younger brother, **Theodore (Ted)** and his **wife Nancy Faust Sizer.** From this group came a rousing 27 children! Those kids and ours have seen each other as often as the families could arrange it over the years, including during the well-attended family reunions. **Ted,** Alice's brother, shared a genuine kinship with her while growing up and I was sincerely honored to have him as my best man in our wedding. **Sturge,** who was a member of *both* of our families, of course, was a lifelong friend to me. **Connie** lives near daughter Anne in Connecticut and is often a welcomed visitor in her home. **Hilda Warner** continued an active relationship with both with me and with my adult children, until her passing at the end of the writing of this book. **Nancy Sizer** has also has an active relationship with me, as well as with my adult children, and has lunched with me on a monthly basis for a number of years.

Alice and I gratefully felt the help and kinship from the Sizers throughout our marriage and it has continued for me after Alice's passing. I feel exceedingly lucky to have been an in-law and it is a great luxury to realize that the feeling of family that pervades my generation continues on to the next. The Sizers have all been very kind to us and we are all better for knowing them.

Molly Warner was the first child born to my cousin Sturge and Alice's older sister Hilda, and as such, she occupied a place of honor to the four of us. She was old enough to be a flower girl when Alice and I were married, and from there grew up to become a friend to us as well as a cousin, and has visited us often over the many years. In July 2000, Anne presented Alice and me with an enormous box. Molly jumped out: the perfect gift for our 50th wedding anniversary!

Peter Ecklund (Alice's nephew) is an ardent professional trumpet player, well-known as a specialist in 1920s jazz, and active in the information technology aspects of music. Peter has been a real source of help in matters concerning brass instrument playing and in today's music, as well as current aspects of its information technology. We also share the curse of Parkinson's disease, and he has been kind enough to discuss in detail some of the situations mutually facing us as PD sufferers.

MY PARENTS AND SISTERS

I have much to thank my parents for. They created a solid situation in which to bring up a child. I was safe, comfortable, and surrounded by caring people. I had good schooling. They kindly did not saddle me with career expectations surrounding family traditions, i.e.: lawyer, doctor, teacher, or following in my parents' fields of work. I am also grateful to my parents' forebears for passing down funds to provide good educational opportunities for myself and even for our children.

To my **Mother,** I owe her much for being a strong supporter of the many things I was striving to do, and I am indebted to her for setting such high standards. I was proud of her accomplishments as a leader in the field of music.

To my **Father,** I give thanks for his insistence on my being intellectually curious and thorough. He also encouraged me as I sought handiwork and artisan skills, so important to me in later life. I, of course, was proud of his outstanding professional accomplishments.

My sister **Lorraine,** and her husband, **Bob** Bulkley, were both friends and staunch supporters for me and I am everlastingly grateful for all they did. Bob's death was difficult for all of us. In retrospect, it brought us considerably closer to their son **Rob,** who we were happy to see slip into our nuclear family as if he had always been there. Sadly, we did not become as much involved with **Laura,** and she, too, passed away unexpectedly last year. Her passing, in turn, however, brought me closer to her son, **Andrew,** with whom we now enjoy an occasional contact.

Margot, the younger of my two sisters, is to be admired. If she had been born in a later era, her life would have been quite different and certainly less challenged; she was spirited, and fought her way through the adversity of being partially physically disabled at birth in an era when physical disabilities were considered a "weakness". She unselfishly cared for our parents and then our French cousin as they grew older, and for this I thank her many times over.

OUR CHILDREN, THE LAWN CLUB

Langdon, Anne, Wendy and Nick have been a source of pride, satisfaction and wonderment to both Alice and me. They have educated *us* as much as we attempted to educate *them* over the years! Now, when I see what an amazing group of people the LAWN Club has become, I know we are fortunate, and I am in awe.

In **Langdon,** I have considerable pride in his chosen field of applied environmental science, an area that is obviously increasingly important in today's world. His role as a teacher for his local school system is invaluable and his work is affecting many future young lives. I want to thank him for helping to monitor this stage of my life, even though from afar. Langdon's ability to quickly assess situations has helped us all. Happily for me, Lang and I share a love of all things maritime.

In **Anne,** I find pride in her achievements in her chosen profession in the crucial field of law, for the time and energy she gave in performing high-level civic duties in her home town, and in her chosen sport of rowing, culminating in her 1976 Olympic Bronze Medal. I will always be especially grateful to her for her difficult, helpful, and caring role during Alice's final illness, when I also was quite sick. She undertook this with an enormous amount of love and dedication. As a family, each of us are fortunate to have Anne assume many of the tasks of dealing tastefully and skillfully with family financial, legal, and procedural matters.

In **Wendy**, I find pride in her civically important career in the local and statewide community service sector in the area of strengthening the capacities of organizations serving children and families. Her work in literacy, child hunger, and with communities on building successful grantsmanship has had an impact on an enormous number of Pennsylvanians. I want to thank her for her tireless, kindly efforts in masterminding this task of making a record of my life. I find in her the strength to pull us together when we need it, and to really "turn to" and help us out in critical times. Our whole family is grateful to her for her help in smoothing out challenging family situations.

In **Nick**, I find real pride in his role as a Project Manager in Community and Economic Development, working on environmentally sensitive projects in his home city of Burlington, VT. Nick is well suited for his profession: knowledgeable on critical environmental needs while uniquely able to juggle the interesting personalities surrounding every project. I want to thank him for having let me be his hockey dad. I had a ball and an education as he played out his role as a true sports nut. I share with him many things musical–Hey Nick, at least one of us actually managed to become a professional musician!

Each of our children has had children of their own, and at the time of this writing, we have seven grandchildren, and seven great-grandchildren. That is an untold joy for an aging great-grandfather!

All in all, I have become shamelessly thankful, grateful, and proud of each of our kids and their families.

OUR FAMILY

FAMILY CHRISTMAS CARDS

Christmas cards were an annual tradition, although we found that sometimes life "got in our way" and we couldn't manage to send them out. Some cards were dated for the year of the Christmas we celebrated, and some were dated for the forthcoming new year. The cards marked the changes in all of our lives, and serve now as a record of the growth of our family and children.

LANGDON

ANNE

Caleb & Alice Warner

MERRY CHRISTMAS
& HAPPY 1959.

WENDY

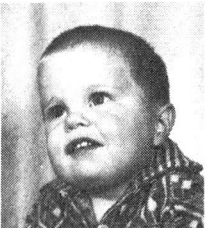
NICKY

546 CONCORD AVE., LEXINGTON, MASS.

MERRY
CHRISTMAS
AND A
HAPPY
1960

NICKY

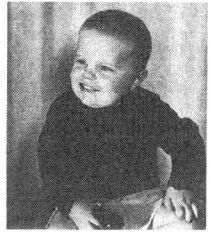

LANGDON

WENDY
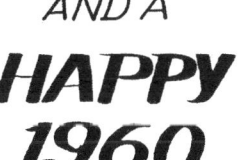

ANNE

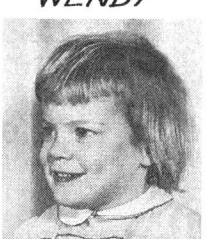

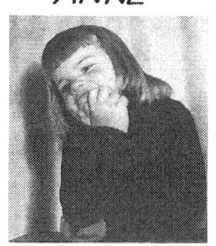

CALEB & ALICE WARNER.   546 CONCORD AVE., LEXINGTON, MASS.

LANGDON   ANNE   WENDY   NICKY

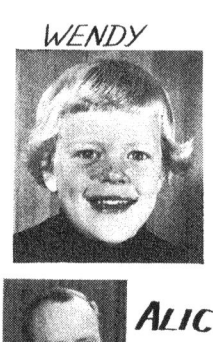

MERRY CHRISTMAS AND A **HAPPY 1962**

ALICE & CALEB WARNER

546 CONCORD AVE., LEXINGTON, MASS.

A NEW WING   "CROUTON" RE-MODELLING   MAGNION, INC., A NEW COMPANY BUILDS ELECTROMAGNETS   READING, WRITING, P.T.A., etc.   PHOEBE   HIGH TRUMPET   HARPSICHORD BUILDING, HOBBY & BUSINESS

VERY MERRY CHRISTMAS and a **HAPPY 1964**

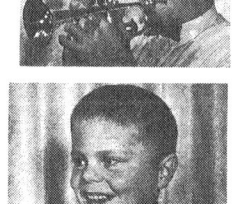

LANGDON   ANNE   WENDY   NICKY

"CROUTON"   PHOEBE   FAVORITE PASTIMES   ASSORTED PETS   "SPIRITA"   INSTRUMENT DEVEL'T.

CALEB & ALICE WARNER   546 CONCORD AVE. LEXINGTON, MASS.

THE LAWN CLUB GROWS UP

Langdon, Wendy, Anne and Nick, date unknown.

At an early Sizer family reunion. From the left: Cliff Taubes, Jakob Lindstrom with Nathaniel Warner in front of him, "Wendy" A. Warner Lindstrom, Becky Lindstrom, Anne Taubes Warner holding Hannibal Taubes, Alice Warner with Ali Taubes in front of her, Langdon Warner, Susan Cutter, Nick Warner, Megan Warner, and me. Missing: Eric Lindstrom.

LANGDON SIZER WARNER

Born: April 20, 1952

Schools:
> Green Acres Day School, Waltham, MA, Nursery School and Kindergarten
> Franklin School, Lexington, MA, Grades 1-3
> Fenn School, Concord, MA, Grades 4-8
> Belmont Hill School, Belmont, MA, Grade 9
> Palfrey Street School, Watertown, MA, Grades 10-12
> Southampton College, Long Island University, BS in Environmental Science
> University of Rhode Island, Masters Degree in Marine Affairs
> Rutgers University, PhD in Geography

Profession: Environmental Scientist/ Secondary School Teacher

Married: December 31, 1982, New Brunswick, NJ, to Susan Lynn Cutter, University Professor

Current Residence: Columbia, South Carolina

Children:
> Nathanial Duque Cutter Warner, b. December 21, 1986, Bogota, Colombia
> Megan Liliana Cutter Warner, b. March 17, 1988, Bogota, Colombia

Photos:
> Top: Nathanial and Langdon; Nathanial and Megan
> Second: Megan; Langdon, Nathanial, Megan and Susan
> Third: Nathanial; Susan and Megan; young Langdon with the family dog

ANNE ELIZABETH TAUBES WARNER

Birth name: Anne Elizabeth Warner
Married name: Anne Elizabeth Taubes Warner

Born: August 24, 1954

Schools:
> Green Acres Day School, Waltham, MA, Nursery School and Kindergarten
> Franklin School, Lexington, MA, Grades 1-2
> Hancock School, Lexington, MA, Grades 3-4
> Belmont Day School, Belmont, MA, Grades 5-6
> Shady Hill School, Cambridge, MA, Grades 7-9
> Cambridge School of Weston, Weston, MA, Grades 10-12
> Year in Finland, studying Marxist Leninist theory and working at the Marimekko Factory
> Yale University, New Haven, CT, BA in Russian Studies
> Harvard Law School, JD

Profession: Attorney

Married: August 21, 1983, Lexington, MA to Clifford Taubes, University Professor. Divorced.

Partner: Daniel Leonard Paul

Current Residence: Woodbridge, CT

Children:
> Alice ("Ali") Lorraine Taubes, b. September 9, 1986
> Hannibal Caleb Taubes, b. November 27, 1989

Photos:
> Top: Hannibal and Ali; Dan
> Second: Ali; Anne; Ali
> Third: Hannibal; young Anne
> Fourth: Hannibal, Cliff, Ali; Hannibal

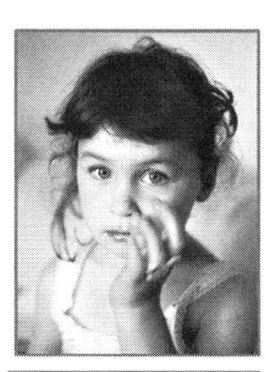

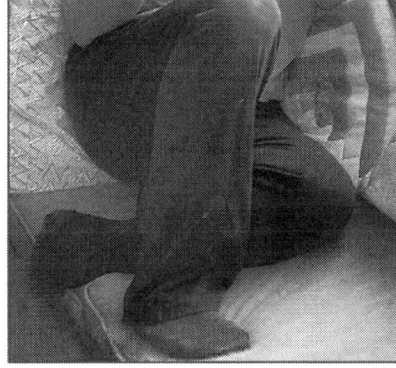
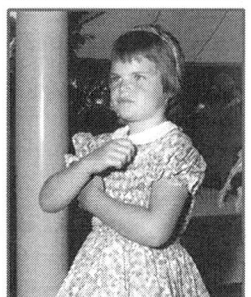

ALICE WENDY WARNER
Birth Name: Alice Foster Warner ("Wendy")
Married name: Alice Warner Lindstrom, changed in 1997 to Alice Wendy Warner

Born: November 3, 1955

Schools:

        Green Acres Day School, Waltham, MA, Nursery School and Kindergarten
        Franklin School, Lexington, MA, Grade 1
        Belmont Day School, Belmont, MA, Grade 1(repeat)-6
        Shady Hill School, Cambridge, MA, Grade 7-9
        Lexington High School, Lexington, MA, Grade 10-11 (graduated)
        Middlesex Community College, Bedford, MA, Associates Degree in Liberal Arts

Profession: Schools and Community Services, non-profit and statewide sectors

Married: January 3, 1976, Lexington, MA, to Eric Kershaw Lindstrom, Paramedic. Divorced.

Current Residence: Lexington, MA

Children:

        Rebecca ("Becky") Selma Lindstrom (m. name: Rebecca Selma Schreiber), b. January 25, 1977
                Married: July 18, 1998, Newport, PA, to Cory James Schreiber, Computer Services
                Children:
                        Elijah Jack Schreiber, b. July 7, 2002
                        Zechariah ("Zach") Cory Schreiber, b. August 28, 2004
                        Simon David Schreiber, b. January 2, 2010
        Eric Jakob ("Jake") Lindstrom, b. June 28, 1978
                Married: October 27, 2001, Somerset, PA to Julie Ann McCabe, Special Education Teacher
                Children:
                        Brooke Madison Lindstrom, b. October 10, 2005
                        Jonah Eric Lindstrom, b. April 5, 2007
                        Aiden John Lindstrom, b. June 21, 2010
                        Emelia Patricia Lindstrom b. November 16, 2011

Photos:

        Top: Becky; Cory; Julie and Jake
        Second: Elijah; Wendy; Brooke
        Third: Zach, Simon, Aiden, Jonah
        Fourth: Eric, young Wendy, Emelia, Bailey

CALEB NICHOLAS WARNER

Born: September 12, 1957

Schools:
>	Green Acres Day School, Waltham, MA, Nursery School and Kindergarten
>	Belmont Day School, Belmont, MA, Grades 1-4
>	Shady Hill School, Cambridge, MA, Grades 5-8 (skipped 6th)
>	Lexington High School, Lexington, MA, Grades 9-12
>	University of Massachusetts, Amherst, MA, 2 years
>	University of Vermont, Burlington, VT, BS in Education
>	University of Vermont, Burlington, VT, Masters Degree in Public Administration

Profession: Project Manager, Community and Economic Development, City of Burlington, VT; and Musician

Married: December 13, 2002, Burlington, VT, to Holly Marie Morehouse, Executive Director of the Vermont Center for Afterschool Excellence

Current Residence: Burlington, VT

Children:
>	Caleb Warner Morehouse, b. February 13, 2001

Photos:
>	Top: Caleb and Nick; Holly and Caleb; Caleb
>	Second: Caleb; Holly and Caleb; Nick
>	Third: Young cousins Roger Allen, Tod Sizer, and Nick; Caleb and Nick; Alice and Caleb

MY PARENTS AND ANCESTORS

Lorraine d'Orèmieulx Roosevelt

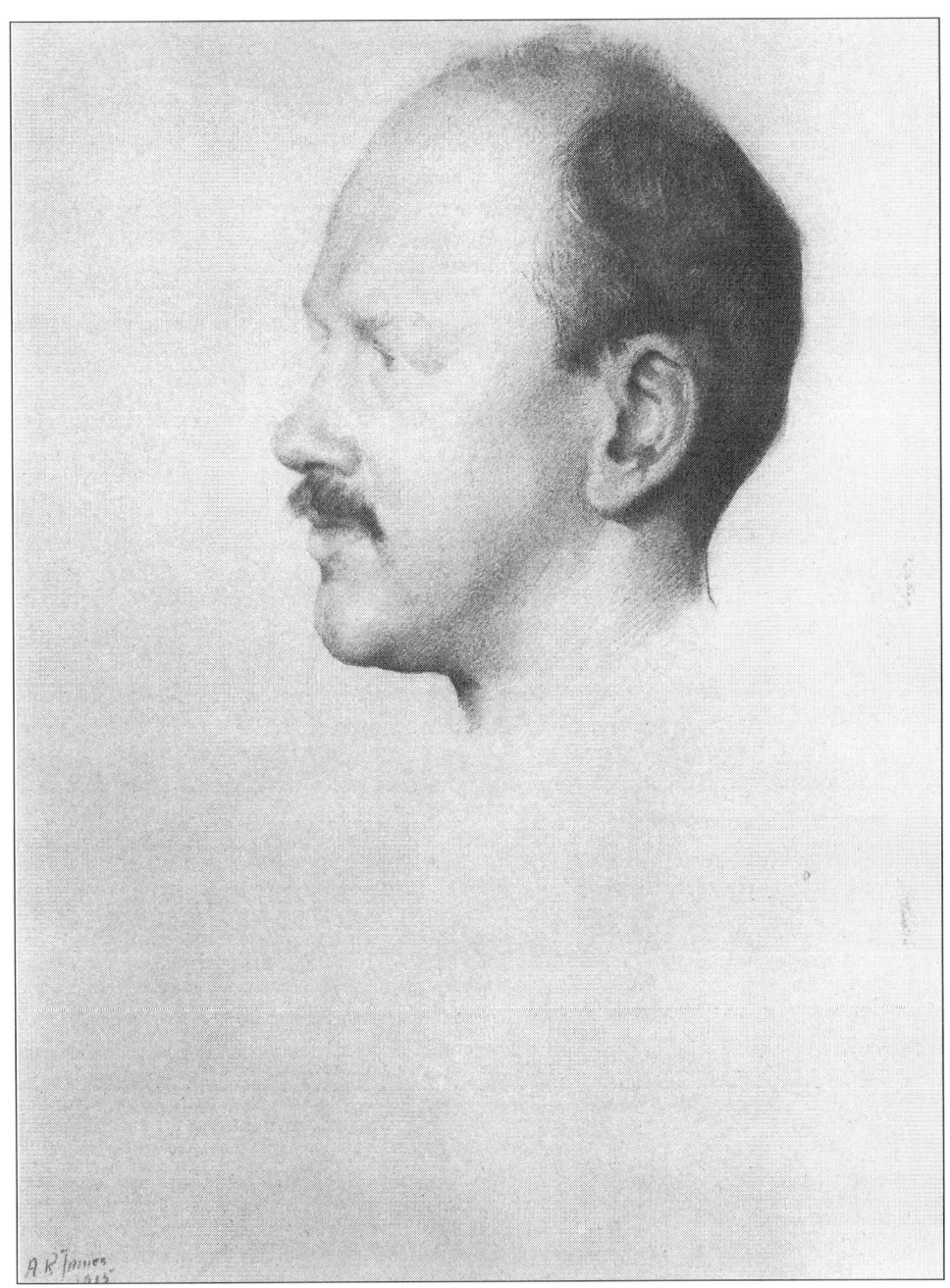

Langdon Warner

BACH CANTATA CLUB AND THE PASSION ACCORDING TO ST. JOHN

My mother, Lorraine d'O. Warner, (see below, "Mrs. Langdon Warner") was the conductor of the Bach Cantata Club. A woman conductor was a rarity in 1935 and it was an honor indeed when she was invited to prepare the Club for the Boston Symphony Orchestra's first performance of The Passion According to St. John, under the direction of Serge Koussevitzky. This program page is from the BSO Archives, reprinted for historical interest, and included in a current-day program for a recent BSO performance.

FIFTY-FOURTH SEASON, NINETEEN HUNDRED THIRTY-FOUR AND THIRTY-FIVE

Twenty-second Programme

FRIDAY AFTERNOON, APRIL 19, *at* 2:30 *o'clock*

SATURDAY EVENING, APRIL 20, *at* 8:15 *o'clock*

Bach-Handel Festival

BACH . . . . . . THE PASSION according to St. John

Evangelist and solo tenor	DAN GRIDLEY
Jesus and solo bass	KEITH FALKNER
Maid and solo soprano	OLGA AVERINO
Solo contralto	MARIE MURRAY
Peter and Pilate	ROYAL DADMUN

Harpsichord, PUTNAM ALDRICH   *Viola da gamba,* ALFRED ZIGHERA
Viole d'amore, JEAN LEFRANC, ALBERT BERNARD   *Organ,* ALBERT W. SNOW

BACH CANTATA CLUB, *Mrs.* LANGDON WARNER, *Conductor*

[*First performances at these concerts*]

Because of the nature of the music, it is requested that there be no applause; also that any who may be unable to stay until the close, leave during the intermission (the afternoon performance will end at approximately 4:15; the evening performance, at 10 o'clock)

[1025]

Program page from the first Boston Symphony performances of Bach's "St. John" Passion, on April 19 and 20, 1935, under the direction of Serge Koussevitzky (BSO Archives)

40

TWO CITIES: KYOTO AND NARA, JAPAN

This article was printed in the *Boston Globe* in the summer of 1955. It reflects my father's involvement in the prevention of bombing by the Allies of the Kyoto and Nara areas of Japan in WWII, thus preserving ancient artwork and cultures.

A Visit to Japan . . . *With Willard de Lue*   Summer of 1955, Boston Globe

How Bostonian Saved Two Cities From Bombs

Langdon Warner's Appeals to President Roosevelt, Stimson And McCloy Got Cultural Centers of Nara and Kyoto Removed From Target List Over Air Gen Arnold's Protests

DE LUE

HORYUJI TEMPLE, near Nara—On a wooded knoll, close to this oldest Buddhist temple in Japan, are memorials honoring a Cambridge man, Langdon Warner, who is credited with having saved the cultural treasures of Nara and Kyoto from probable destruction during World War II. When other Japanese cities were being blasted, no bombs fell here. Warner, curator of Oriental Art at Harvard's Fogg Museum until shortly before his death in 1955, knew Nara and Kyoto well; knew the ancient pagodas of Kofukuji temple, and the works of art that they hold; knew the Great Buddha of Nara, erected in 752 A.D., probably the world's largest bronze figure.

And he knew, above all, this Horyuji, which lies about eight miles from the city—its structures thought to be the oldest wooden buildings known to man. Some go back to 607 A.D. The works of art they embody or contain represent the genius of that remote age, when, through the earliest implantations of Buddhism, the arts of China and Korea were finding fertile soil among the primitive cultures of Japan.

Must these places be bombed? Warner wondered. Was Kyoto and its irreplaceable treasures also to be bombed? Neither city, he felt, was of any military significance.

Langdon Warner never talked much about what he did, but his associates know that, at Washington, he reached everyone he could with his plea that Nara and Kyoto were not logical targets, and should be spared.

Presumably President Roosevelt acted. Someone certainly did, for one day (and this is the story I get here) Secretary of War Stimson called in Assistant Secretary John McCloy.

Stimson was in a relaxed mood.

'It's an Order, General'

"Jack," said he, "would you think I was a sentimental fool if I thought that some places in Japan that are on our list for possible bombing just aren't so important?

I was in Kyoto in the late '20's, and I feel that it can't be playing any important role in the Japanese war effort. And Nara, too."

Stimson had been in this area twice.

McCloy also must have known something of Kyoto

and Nara—Kyoto surely, for he is an Amherst man, and probably was familiar with Amherst's connection with Doshisha University.

McCloy reputedly said that he couldn't see anything foolishly sentimental about what Stimson had in mind.

"I want you to see Hap Arnold tomorrow," said Stimson, "and tell him to take Nara and Kyoto off the list."

"General," said McCloy, "I came over here from the Secretary of War, and he says to take Nara and Kyoto off the list. I'm here to tell you to take them off."

(In Kyoto, as the war drew to a close, some people said the city had escaped bombing because Mary Denton was living there. That veteran missionary of the American Board at Boston, a Midwesterner of New England stock, had insisted on staying on at Doshisha when others were evacuated. So people said:

("The Americans wouldn't bomb Kyoto when Mary is here," and one of her neighbors used to bow toward her home every morning. Another of the rumors was that Vice President Truman had once been a teacher at Doshisha.)

Soon after Langdon Warner's death the Japanese government awarded him one of its highest decorations; and three years late a memorial was dedicated here at Horyuji. The venerable abbot himself participated in the ceremonies.

Mrs. Warner was represented by Kojiro Tomita, curator of Oriental art at the Boston Museum, where as a young man he had worked under Warner. Mr. Tomita planted a small cedar tree beside the temple's tribute.

Deer Roam the Park

To see Nara and the Warner memorials, Mamoru Utsumi and I came from Kyoto by the 11:06 electric train, the cars jammed, for the day is Sunday, and Nara is a popular place for outings.

In an hour we step into the middle of the city, where a short uphill walk in company with hundreds, takes us up to Nara Park. Now there are 900 deer roaming the park and adjacent shrine and temple grounds—deer with "meek eyes imploring food," my guide-book says.

But today they implore nothing. They are filled to capacity. Not even the special little cakes we buy from a vendor interest them.

Near us is the 165-foot five-story pagoda of Kofukuji Temple, the second highest in Japan. It is a beautiful thing, though brown and weathered.

Largest Wooden Building

I think of the early Bostonians who had come here —Edward Sylvester Morse, Dr. William Sturgis Bigelow and Ernest Fenollosa. All were associated with the Boston Museum of Fine Arts.

Fenollosa, one of Tomita's predecessors as curator of oriental art, spent weeks here in what he remembered as "those sweet days of the early eighties."

A gong sounds twice in the temple enclosure, where I suppose there are still the "cool sanded courts crossed irregularly with granite steps and banked with . . . compositions of ancient shrub and mossy stone and trickling stream," which Fenollosa knew . . . and Warner after him.

We hurry on towards the Great South Gate. It is 800 years old, and, like the pagoda we had just left, has a worn and storm-beaten look to it. Yet I can see traces of its former red paint.

Two villainous-looking Guardians of Buddhism are in the gate's deep niches, but we hurry past them with a glance; and having entered another portal, look across a broad court to the enormous Hall of the Great Buddha.

It is perhaps the largest wooden building in the world, 188 by 166 feet on the ground, and 150 high. Those are the temple's own figures, though others I have seen shrink the building a little.

The Hall and the Great Buddha have had many troubles since the huge bronze figure was first set up here 1200 years ago, on a day when Nara was still the national capital, and the Emperor, pledging allegiance to the Buddah, gave origin to a soon-established belief in the divine origin of the imperial house.

First an earthquake damaged hall and statue. Then a leader of the powerful Taira clan burned the building in 1190 and left the Buddha's head a mass of formless metal. Another quake de-

stroyed the . . . been . . . again—but the repaired Buddha, 54 feet high, still sits here on a bronze lotus-flower in imperturbable repose.

Other figures are near him, and still more behind him in the hall, where a hole has been cut through one of the building's 60 wooden pillars, each nearly 4½ feet in diameter. We watch as children are pushed and pulled through the hole, so that they may be assured a place in Buddha's heaven.

In Memory of Warner

With the aid of a map, which a priest had marked for us, we make our way to the Warner memorial. It is on a gentle hill-slope on which a country road runs, just outside the temple's west wall.

Stone steps rise to the low platform or terrace, on which are two sets of monuments. That at the right is dedicated to a venerated temple historian.

At the left end of the terrace an upright tablet is enscribed, "In Memory of Langdon Warner." A Japanese inscription is below it, and beside it is a lantern-like monument. Close to the platform is the tree Mr. Tomita planted . . . now a little seedy-looking, I thought.

From this secluded spot there is a view over trees to the roofs of a little village, and to the green fields beyond them in a valley into which bombs never fell.

In Memory of Warner

In tomorrow's Monday Globe, de Lue tells of the Boston men who cemented ties with Kyoto long before this century.

LANGDON WARNER, one-time curator of Oriental art at Harvard's Fogg Museum.

Writer De Lue Visits Bostonian's Memorial

The granite shaft to left of lantern is inscribed "In Memory of Langdon N. Warner," below which is an inscription in Japanese characters. The memorial is located near the Horyuji Temple.

WARNER FAMILY TREE

Descendants of Roger Sherman, signer of the Declaration of Independence and Revolutionary War general. Simplified and written by Alice for a child's school project

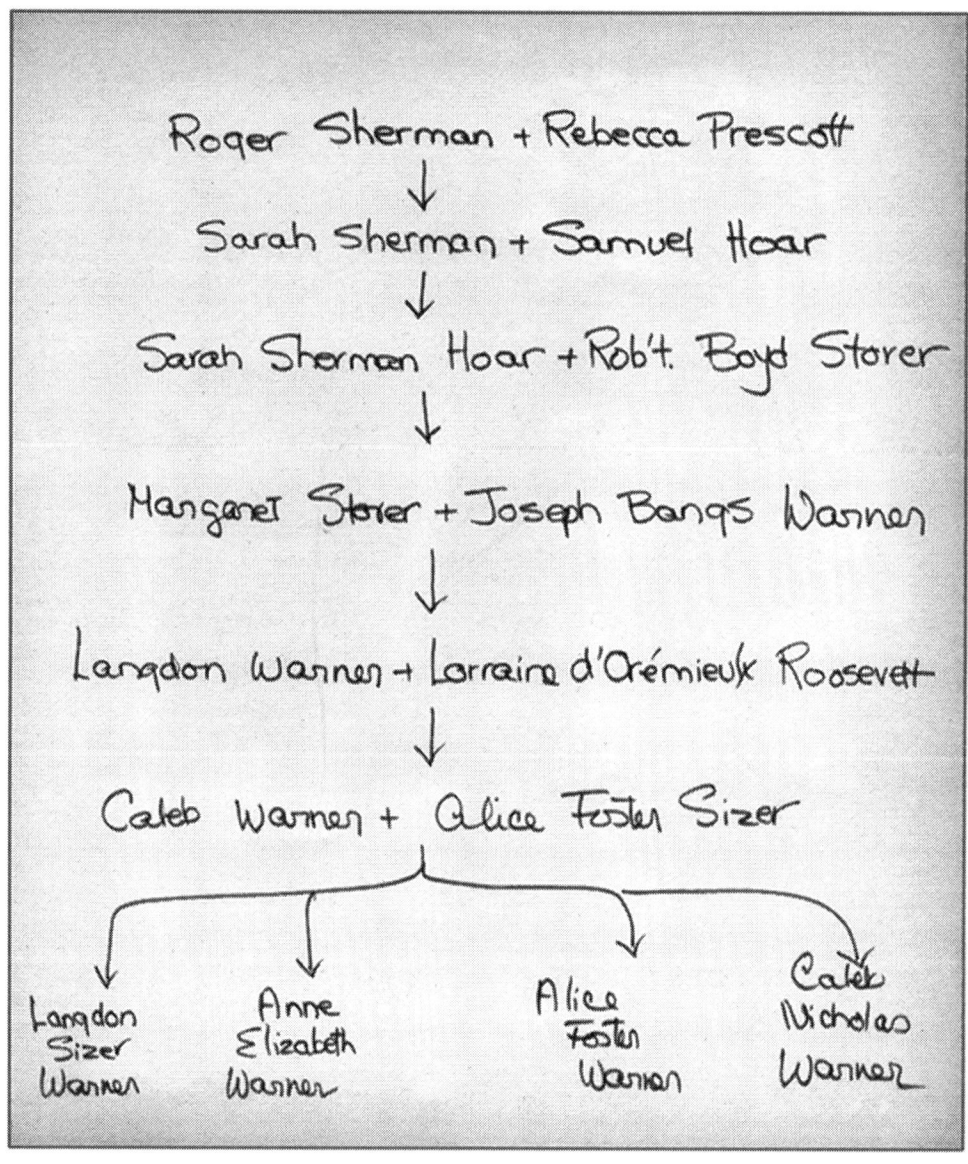

FAMILY GENEALOGICAL COLLECTIONS

ROOSEVELT FAMILY

My mother's family's genealogy has been thoroughly researched. It is available online through various Roosevelt genealogical websites.

WARNER FAMILY

My cousin/brother-in-law Sturgis Warner researched and recorded my father's Warner family genealogy in considerable depth. This information is now housed with his daughter, Molly Warner, and some with his son, Roger Warner.

Mary (Molly) Hooper Warner
9320 40th Avenue NE
Seattle WA 98115
206-523-5192

Roger Warner
171 Argilla Road
Ipswich MA 01938

SIZER FAMILY

Alice's father's Sizer genealogy, and her mother's Foster genealogy can be found with her nephew, Derry Allen.

Frederick (Derry) W. Allen
3807 48th St., NW
Washington, DC 20016
derryallen@aol.com
202-244-5991

Her mother's Foster family tree is inside the back cover of the memoirs of Alice's aunt, "The Memoirs of Hilda Chase Foster" by Anne (Nancy) Morris. Every descendant of Hilda's parents who was born before 1982 received a copy.

Anne (Nancy) Morris
P.O. Box 296
Etna, NH 03750
anne.morris@valley.net
603-643-0172

19313629R00211

Made in the USA
Charleston, SC
17 May 2013